Accounting for Management Decisions

Accounting for Management Decisions

THIRD EDITION

John Arnold

*Director of the Manchester Business School and
KPMG Professor of Accounting and Financial Management*

Stuart Turley

*KPMG Professor of Accounting,
Department of Accounting and Finance, University of Manchester*

 Prentice Hall

FINANCIAL TIMES

An imprint of **Pearson Education**

London • New York • Toronto • Sydney • Tokyo • Singapore
Hong Kong • Cape Town • Madrid • Paris • Amsterdam • Munich • Milan

Pearson Education Limited
Edinburgh Gate
Harlow
Essex CM20 2JE
England

and Associated Companies throughout the world

Visit us on the World Wide Web at:
http://www.pearsoned.co.uk

Typeset in 10/12pt Times
by Mathematical Composition Setters Ltd., Salisbury, UK

Printed and bound in Great Britain by
TJ International Ltd., Padstow, Cornwall

Library of Congress Cataloging-in-Publication Data

Arnold, John, 1944–
    Accounting for management decisions / John Arnold, Stuart Turley.
    — 3rd ed.
        p.   cm.
    Includes bibliographical references and index.
    ISBN 0-13-308818-9
    1. Managerial accounting.   2. Decision-making.   I. Turley,
Stuart.   II. Title.
HF5657.4.A76   1996
658.15'11—dc20   95-35467
                                                                      CIP

British Library Cataloguing in Publication Data

A catalogue record for this book is available from the British Library

ISBN 0-13-308818-9

10 9 8 6
07 06 05 04

Contents

Preface

It is some thirteen years since the first edition of this book was published and six since the second edition. The period since the first edition was published has seen an increasing recognition that conventional management accounting systems too often fail to inform management decisions as helpfully as they might do, with the consequent danger that the conventional systems are ignored. New management accounting systems have been developed to reflect new manufacturing and management procedures.

Aims and objectives

In this current edition we have attempted to reflect the changes which have taken place and to continue to provide an introduction to accounting for management decisions which is based on solid conceptual foundations and which illustrates the concepts by applying them to realistic problems. The book is directed at students who are approaching management accounting for the first time and to managers who are interested in recent developments in the management accounting literature. After reading it, the student should be able to identify and develop accounting procedures which provide managers with information which is useful to them in making decisions.

Structure

As a result of changes in the environment, and in the light of an extensive market survey we have made several major changes to the current edition. The most significant is to develop a new part on cost information which provides an improved link between the basic framework and applications, and which includes a new chapter on cost recording and product costing. Other material has been updated and revised to reflect developments since the second edition. The basic structure and style appear to continue to be well received and, in consequence, we have tried not to interfere with them unnecessarily.

   The first part of the book provides a basic (conceptual) framework. In Chapter 1 we explore the nature of accounting and the objectives of organisations. In Chapter 2 we discuss the meaning and importance of the components of our definition of accounting – communication, measurement and decision making. Chapter 3 is concerned with the meaning and measurement of wealth, the maximisation of which provides a focal point for the decision-making process. Chapter 4 explores the treatment of risk and uncertainty, and in Chapter 5 we explain and illustrate the fundamental principles for the measurement of relevant costs and benefits.

Part 2 comprises two chapters devoted to the analysis of the behaviour of cost flows and the management information system for recording and processing cost information.

The conceptual framework in Part 1 and the explanation of the behaviour of cost flows in Part 2 are then applied to a number of areas of management decisions in Part 3. Individual chapters consider how accounting information can contribute to decisions in a number of specific areas of management, including the level of output, pricing, other operational areas, the allocation of scarce resources, long-term decisions on investments and the acquisition of capital assets, the use of budgets and variance analysis in the planning and control of operations, and the measurement of divisional performance.

Teaching and learning features

We have endeavoured to expand the teaching and learning features of the book. Each chapter now begins with a note of aims and objectives and concludes with a summary. The worked examples, discussion topics and exercises are retained from previous editions, but solutions are now provided at the end of the text for some of the exercises. The bibliographical references previously included at the end of each chapter have been consolidated into a single annotated bibliography. A new expanded Teacher's Manual includes teaching notes, OHP masters, illustrative cases, solutions to the exercises not given in the text, and practical group assignments.

Acknowledgements

We remain indebted to all those who helped with the first two editions. Andy Goss and his colleagues at Prentice Hall International have ensured that we (eventually) produced the third edition. They also organised the market survey which provided much valuable input to the current edition. We are grateful to all those who took the trouble to respond. We acknowledge especially the contribution which Tony Hope made to the first two editions and which is still reflected very much in the pages which follow.

John Arnold
Stuart Turley

PART 1

Basic framework

Concepts and principles governing financial analysis for business decisions

PART 2

Cost information

PART 3

Applications

CHAPTER 1
The role of management accounting

CHAPTER 2
Accounting and decision making

CHAPTER 3
Wealth and wealth maximisation in decision making

CHAPTER 4
Risk and uncertainty in decision making

CHAPTER 5
Costs and benefits for decisions

loaned funds to an organisation. Most organisations publish periodic financial statements which provide external groups with information about the results of past activities, but also generate information for use internally, indicating expectations for the future, in order to assist management in planning activities and allocating resources for forthcoming periods. Table 1.1 lists some of the main points of contrast between financial and management accounting.

The dichotomy between management and financial accounting is, in many ways, both unfortunate and misleading. It implies that there is little, if any, overlap between the information required by managers and that required by others. This is clearly not the case. A shareholder in ICI will probably be as interested as its managers in the future financial prospects of the company. However, it is also the case that shareholders in the company may be interested in information at a level of aggregation different from that required by managers of its factories. Shareholders hope to predict the company's overall future performance as a measure both of the dividends they will receive and of the future value of their shares. Managers will be more concerned with the prospects for their factories because these will affect the decisions they will take concerning the purchase of raw materials, the hiring of labour, the pricing and output levels of products, and so on. A single information recording system may be used to capture the basic data for both financial and management accounting reports, but the data may be processed differently to meet the different reporting objectives. For example, in a manufacturing company

Table 1.1 Financial and management accounting compared

	Financial accounting	Management accounting
Main users	External groups	Internal management
Primary information	Reports on past performance and current position	Forecasts of the future as well as monitoring information on current and past actual performance
Principal measurement	Financial	Financial and non-financial qualitative and quantitative
Level of aggregation	Whole organisation	Disaggregated, e.g. plant, product or customer information
Frequency	Annual	Monthly or more frequent depending on organisation
Regulation	Law and accounting standards, comprising Generally Accepted Accounting Practice	Little formal regulation; management discretion over the information system
Criteria	Truth and fairness; stewardship; comparability with other organisations	Relevance for specific management decisions and control of operations

The role of management accounting

☐ To explain the nature of accounting as both an academic and a practical discipline.

☐ To explain the differences between management accounting and financial accounting, and the nature of the relationship between them.

☐ To outline the role of management in organisations.

☐ To explore the role of accounting as an aid to management.

☐ To describe the information managers need for decision making and explain the part accounting plays in that information.

This is a book about accounting. Specifically it is a book about one area of accounting, often called *management accounting* or *managerial accounting*, which is concerned with the provision of information to those responsible for managing businesses and other economic organisations to help them in making decisions about the future of the organisation and in controlling the implementation of the decisions they make. In this chapter we try to answer some questions which someone embarking on a study of management accounting might naturally ask. Questions such as: What is accounting? What is management accounting and what is its role relative to other branches of accounting? What sorts of decisions do managers have to take and how might accounting information help them?

1.1 What is accounting?

Only in the last few decades has accounting become firmly established as an academic discipline, taught in universities and other educational establishments throughout the world.[1] Accounting traditionally belongs within departments of commerce, or business studies, or within faculties of social science or social studies, along with such other 'applied' subjects as economics, politics, sociology and, sometimes, law. It is not traditionally taught along with medicine or geography or French or Latin or physics. The academic location of the subject as a social science may offer some clues as to the context, or environment, to which accounting belongs.

Most social sciences are concerned primarily with particular aspects of a person's role in society (hence the use of the adjective 'social'). For example, we might view the discipline of *economics* as being concerned with the efficient allocation of society's scarce resources; *law* as being concerned with the framework necessary to regulate individual and corporate behaviour within society; *politics* as being concerned with the political systems under which we live; and *sociology* as being concerned with the interpretation and analysis of individual and group behaviour. There are, as might be expected, some strong links between these various subjects, and these links are frequently recognised in the teaching and content of social science courses – thus some sociology is often taught in politics courses, some economics is taught in law courses, and so on.

So where does accounting fit into this broad spectrum of social science? What is its role, if any, in people's relationship with their environment? We can perhaps begin to envisage a possible role for accounting when we call to mind the notion of commercial activity. In all forms of society, individuals and groups make economic decisions which entail the exchange of property at agreed prices. In order to agree prices, it is necessary to have a unit of measurement or medium of exchange, which is common to all members of the society, and is thus widely understood. In modern societies, this medium of exchange is almost always defined in terms of money – money is used to assign prices or values to property.

Because of its widespread application, the use of a common unit of measurement forms a fundamental role in economic, legal, political and sociological analysis – that is, because of the continuous need to value and measure objects, all social sciences require quantitative information. This is where accounting comes in. Accounting responds to the need for quantitative and, in particular, financial information. Under this view, accounting is essentially an interdisciplinary subject – it draws on and responds to the other social sciences. Consequently the scope and boundaries of accounting change as society changes and new demands for information emerge. In much the same way, the scope of other social sciences broadens or contracts depending upon society's need for the type of analysis they provide. For example, law, economics and sociology are not static disciplines. They respond to, and indeed help to shape, the needs of society.

The above analysis suggests that a definition of accounting depends upon what is asked of it at any point in time by various groups in society. However, in order to define the scope of a book on one aspect of accounting, we must adopt a more practical philosophy – one which enables us at least to choose some working definitions that we can use as a framework for our future discussions. There are many possible working definitions of accounting. The one that best captures our view of accounting and which we shall in consequence adopt is that formulated by

the American Accounting Association (AAA) in 1966.[2] This definition views accounting as

> the process of identifying, measuring, and communicating economic information to permit informed judgements and decisions by users of the information.

In other words, accounting is a language – the language of economic activity. Like all languages it has its own vocabulary, methods of expression, terminology and conventions – and, because of these, its own difficulties of interpretation and understanding. It is a language which pervades, in some measure, everybody's life, and hence it is a language with which everyone should have some familiarity.

A closer inspection of the terms used in the AAA's definition of accounting reveals some interesting features. To understand accounting, we must understand the nature (and practice) of *measurement* and *communication*, the attributes of (economic) *information*, the theories and practices of *decision making*, and we must try to identify the *users* of accounting information. Each of these features poses its own particular problems, and one purpose of this text is to explore these problems.

We particularly like this definition because it accords with the philosophy of accounting followed in this book, which is essentially a philosophy of *providing information to aid good decision making*. However, we should stress that good decision making does not rely solely on accounting information. Rather, accounting information should be seen as a part of the much larger total information set available to decision makers.

1.2 Management accounting and financial accounting

The definition of accounting in the previous section views accounting as a system for providing (primarily financial) information to those who have to make decisions and control the implementation of those decisions. However, the information to be provided by the accounting system depends upon who is making the decision and for what purpose. For example, the sort of information required by the chief executive of a large multinational firm such as ICI or Ford may be very different from the sort of information required by a member of a village cricket club. The former may, for example, require information about the range of products the company is producing and selling; information concerning the quantity, price, cost, competitive position and profitability of each product. The latter may require information about the annual subscription the club will charge its members, the cost of social functions, and so on.

In accounting, a distinction is often made between what is termed 'management accounting' and what is termed 'financial accounting'. (This latter is a rather misleading title as all accounting is, in some respects, financial.) Management accounting is concerned with the provision of information to managers who make decisions about the ways in which an organisation's resources should be allocated. By contrast, financial accounting is concerned with the provision of information to users other than managers: for example, shareholders, customers and those who have considerations concerning goods produced for resale could require information about:

- the detailed costs of past manufacture, for valuing stock in the financial statements;
- analysis of current production quantities and quality, for management control of manufacturing processes;
- expectations about future market conditions to estimate price and revenue attainable when the goods are sold.

The information that is relevant and the measurements that are appropriate will depend on the purpose of the accounting reports and the use that is to be made of them. Understanding the role of management accounting requires an appreciation of what is involved in management and the types of decision that management is faced with.

1.3 Structure of the book

This book is concerned primarily with the provision of accounting information for management decisions. But there are several fundamental notions that are common to all types of accounting information system. To a large extent, these notions are embodied in our adopted definition of accounting, which is not restricted to any one group of users or type of organisation. We discuss these notions in this and the remaining chapters of Part 1 under the general heading of 'Basic framework'. Such a framework applies not only to information for management decisions, but also, with very little modification, to the provision of accounting information to other groups of users.

In the remainder of this chapter we investigate further the objectives of organisations and the environments in which they operate. In Chapter 2 we discuss the meaning and importance of a number of the components of our definition of accounting; in particular we examine the nature of information-communication systems, problems of measurement, and theories of individual and group decision making. Chapter 3 is concerned with the meaning, importance and measurement of wealth. Wealth is a vital component of any decision-making process as it provides a focal point for the process; the maximisation of wealth, properly defined, provides an objective for decision models and decision makers. The discussion in Chapter 4 of risk and uncertainty in decision making reflects the fact that all decisions relate to alternative future courses of action and that the future is always uncertain. Hence all decisions involve a consideration of the problems posed by the existence of risk and uncertainty. Finally, as part of the basic framework, in Chapter 5 we explain and illustrate the fundamental principles for measuring relevant costs and benefits for decision purposes.

Good decision making depends on understanding the way in which the organisation's cash flows will be affected by decisions taken. Part 2 of the book comprises two chapters devoted to the analysis of the behaviour of cost flows and the management information system for recording and processing of cost information. This is an area which overlaps with some aspects of financial accounting. An understanding of the cost implications of actions is important for management decisions, but the system by which costs are 'accounted for' also affects the way in which results are reported in periodic financial statements. We look at the behaviour and estimation of costs in Chapter 6 and cost-recording systems in Chapter 7.

The framework chapters in Part 1 provide a conceptual foundation and a set of principles for decision making which, together with the understanding of the behaviour of cost flows from Part 2, are then applied to a number of areas of management decisions in the third part of the book. Individual chapters consider how accounting information can contribute to decisions in a number of specific areas of management, including the level of output (Chapter 8), pricing (Chapter 9), other operational factors (Chapter 10), the allocation of limited resources (Chapters 11 and 12), long-term decisions on investment and the acquisition of capital assets (Chapters 13 and 14), and the use of budgets and variance analysis in the planning and control of operations (Chapters 15–17).

1.4 The objectives and environments of organisations

Our concern is with the role and design of (management) accounting systems within organisations. An essential first step is to explore the nature of organisations and the procedures which are used to control their progress and development. We should stress at the outset that accounting is but one part of a highly complex decision-making and control process in most organisations. An appreciation of its context and limitations is an important prerequisite to the exploitation of its strengths.

What is an organisation?

The answer to this question is not at all obvious! Take, for example, the case of Marks and Spencer plc (although what we will say applies equally to many other organisations, whether in the public or private sector of the economy and whether or not they are profit oriented). When we talk of Marks and Spencer what do we have in mind – its stores and fittings, administrative buildings, stock of merchandise, fleet of vehicles, and so on? Although these are part of the picture, there is almost certainly more. What about the company's reputation and role as an employer, a purchaser of goods, a borrower, a supplier of goods and – more recently – of financial services, and as an investment vehicle for individual and institutional shareholders? All these aspects of the company's activities depend on people and on the nature of their relationships with each other under the umbrella provided by the activities of Marks and Spencer.

This perception suggests that an organisation might be viewed as a group of participants, each of whom makes efforts (*contributions*) on behalf of the organisation and in return receives rewards (*inducements*). The basic criterion for any individual continuing to participate in the organisation is that his or her rewards (inducements) should exceed his or her efforts (contributions). This view of an organisation as an inducement–contribution process is shown in Figure 1.1.

We might illustrate the meaning of some of the boxes in Figure 1.1 by reference to Marks and Spencer. Managers, for example, make contributions to the organisation which are generally non-financial. They contribute mental and physical effort, creativity and other skills. In return they receive both financial and non-financial rewards. The financial rewards will usually include salary payments and bonuses. Non-financial rewards might involve the pleasure that comes from job satisfaction, status and power. Customers contribute financial revenues when they purchase goods from the company. They may also contribute loyalty by preferring to shop at Marks and Spencer even when similar goods are available at a similar or lower price elsewhere. In return, they enjoy the satisfaction which comes from wearing or using the goods which have been purchased.

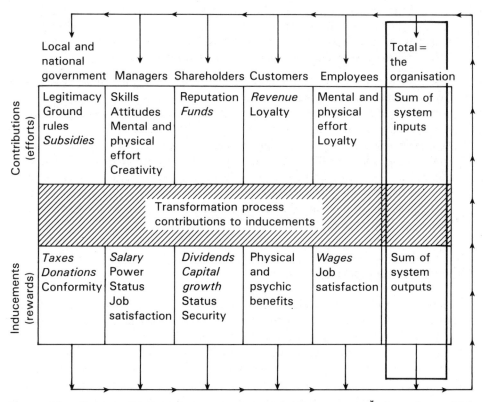

Figure 1.1 Organisation as inducement–contribution process* (based on A.M. Tinker and E.A. Lowe, 'A rationale for corporate social reporting', *Journal of Business Finance and Accounting*, Spring 1980).

*Financial items are in *italics*.

The shaded area in the middle of Figure 1.1 represents the *transformation* process, where the contributions from the various participants (the *system inputs*) are combined together to provide the *system outputs* which are then used to 'pay' rewards to the various groups of participants.

Several interesting conclusions emerge from analysing the nature of an organisation in this way:

1. All contributions (inputs) are combined and 'transformed' to provide the total inducements (outputs) to be distributed to participants. A contribution change by one group may affect the inducements which can be offered to another. For example, the withdrawal of subsidies by local or national government may affect the wages or other employment prospects of employees.

2. The allocation of total inducements between participants must be such that each participant (or possibly each group of participants) receives inducements which are at least equal to the contributions provided.

3. Contributions and inducements may be either financial or non-financial.

4. The efforts which participants are willing to make will be influenced by the rewards they expect. However, their expectations will be conditioned in part by what has actually happened in the past. Thus, the inducements of one period will influence, to some extent, the contributions of the next period.

5. The managers of organisations have a dual role. First, they must satisfy their own expectations and ensure that their rewards are at least as great as their contributions. Second, they must keep all the other participant groups happy in order to maintain the viability of the organisation. Their ability to achieve the first objective will depend in part on their success in achieving the second! Maintaining the viability of the organisation will involve managers in identifying the minimum inducements required by each participant, in ensuring that sufficient total inducements are available to meet the needs of each participant and in ensuring that all participants do receive inducements greater than their contributions.

The task of management

The dual role of management, explained above, is more easily described than accomplished. An organisation is not a self-contained, isolated entity – it has to operate in an environment which constrains its behaviour.

First, the 'technology' available in the environment affects the ability of the organisation to transform total contributions into total inducements. New equipment and machinery will affect its production process. New marketing and selling techniques will affect the way in which and the success with which it markets and sells its products. New computer developments will affect its administrative procedures. These and other changes in available 'technology' complicate the task of management.

The role of management accounting

This is a book about accounting. Specifically it is a book about one area of accounting, often called *management accounting* or *managerial accounting*, which is concerned with the provision of information to those responsible for managing businesses and other economic organisations to help them in making decisions about the future of the organisation and in controlling the implementation of the decisions they make. In this chapter we try to answer some questions which someone embarking on a study of management accounting might naturally ask. Questions such as: What is accounting? What is management accounting and what is its role relative to other branches of accounting? What sorts of decisions do managers have to take and how might accounting information help them?

1.1 What is accounting?

Only in the last few decades has accounting become firmly established as an academic discipline, taught in universities and other educational establishments throughout the world.[1] Accounting traditionally belongs within departments of commerce, or business studies, or within faculties of social science or social studies, along with such other 'applied' subjects as economics, politics, sociology and, sometimes, law. It is not traditionally taught along with medicine or geography or French or Latin or physics. The academic location of the subject as a social science may offer some clues as to the context, or environment, to which accounting belongs.

Most social sciences are concerned primarily with particular aspects of a person's role in society (hence the use of the adjective 'social'). For example, we might view the discipline of *economics* as being concerned with the efficient allocation of society's scarce resources; *law* as being concerned with the framework necessary to regulate individual and corporate behaviour within society; *politics* as being concerned with the political systems under which we live; and *sociology* as being concerned with the interpretation and analysis of individual and group behaviour. There are, as might be expected, some strong links between these various subjects, and these links are frequently recognised in the teaching and content of social science courses – thus some sociology is often taught in politics courses, some economics is taught in law courses, and so on.

So where does accounting fit into this broad spectrum of social science? What is its role, if any, in people's relationship with their environment? We can perhaps begin to envisage a possible role for accounting when we call to mind the notion of commercial activity. In all forms of society, individuals and groups make economic decisions which entail the exchange of property at agreed prices. In order to agree prices, it is necessary to have a unit of measurement or medium of exchange, which is common to all members of the society, and is thus widely understood. In modern societies, this medium of exchange is almost always defined in terms of money – money is used to assign prices or values to property.

Because of its widespread application, the use of a common unit of measurement forms a fundamental role in economic, legal, political and sociological analysis – that is, because of the continuous need to value and measure objects, all social sciences require quantitative information. This is where accounting comes in. Accounting responds to the need for quantitative and, in particular, financial information. Under this view, accounting is essentially an interdisciplinary subject – it draws on and responds to the other social sciences. Consequently the scope and boundaries of accounting change as society changes and new demands for information emerge. In much the same way, the scope of other social sciences broadens or contracts depending upon society's need for the type of analysis they provide. For example, law, economics and sociology are not static disciplines. They respond to, and indeed help to shape, the needs of society.

The above analysis suggests that a definition of accounting depends upon what is asked of it at any point in time by various groups in society. However, in order to define the scope of a book on one aspect of accounting, we must adopt a more practical philosophy – one which enables us at least to choose some working definitions that we can use as a framework for our future discussions. There are many possible working definitions of accounting. The one that best captures our view of accounting and which we shall in consequence adopt is that formulated by the American Accounting Association (AAA) in 1966.[2] This definition views accounting as

> the process of identifying, measuring, and communicating economic information to permit informed judgements and decisions by users of the information.

In other words, accounting is a language – the language of economic activity. Like all languages it has its own vocabulary, methods of expression, terminology and conventions – and, because of these, its own difficulties of interpretation and understanding. It is a language which pervades, in some measure, everybody's life, and hence it is a language with which everyone should have some familiarity.

A closer inspection of the terms used in the AAA's definition of accounting reveals some interesting features. To understand accounting, we must understand the nature (and practice) of *measurement* and *communication*, the attributes of (economic) *information*, the theories and practices of *decision making*, and we must try to identify the *users* of accounting information. Each of these features poses its own particular problems, and one purpose of this text is to explore these problems.

We particularly like this definition because it accords with the philosophy of accounting followed in this book, which is essentially a philosophy of *providing information to aid good decision making*. However, we should stress that good decision making does not rely solely on accounting information. Rather, accounting information should be seen as a part of the much larger total information set available to decision makers.

1.2 Management accounting and financial accounting

The definition of accounting in the previous section views accounting as a system for providing (primarily financial) information to those who have to make decisions and control the implementation of those decisions. However, the information to be provided by the accounting system depends upon who is making the decision and for what purpose. For example, the sort of information required by the chief executive of a large multinational firm such as ICI or Ford may be very different from the sort of information required by a member of a village cricket club. The former may, for example, require information about the range of products the company is producing and selling; information concerning the quantity, price, cost, competitive position and profitability of each product. The latter may require information about the annual subscription the club will charge its members, the cost of social functions, and so on.

In accounting, a distinction is often made between what is termed 'management accounting' and what is termed 'financial accounting'. (This latter is a rather misleading title as all accounting is, in some respects, financial.) Management accounting is concerned with the provision of information to managers who make decisions about the ways in which an organisation's resources should be allocated. By contrast, financial accounting is concerned with the provision of information to users other than managers: for example, shareholders, customers and those who have loaned funds to an organisation. Most organisations publish periodic financial statements which provide external groups with information about the results of past activities, but also generate information for use internally, indicating expectations for the future, in order to assist management in planning activities and allocating resources for forthcoming periods. Table 1.1 lists some of the main points of contrast between financial and management accounting.

The dichotomy between management and financial accounting is, in many ways, both unfortunate and misleading. It implies that there is little, if any, overlap between the information required by managers and that required by others. This is clearly not the case. A shareholder in ICI will probably be as interested as its managers in the future financial prospects of the company. However, it is also the case that shareholders in the company may be interested in information at a level of aggregation different from that required by managers of its factories. Shareholders hope to predict the company's overall future performance as a measure both of the dividends they will receive and of the future value of their shares. Managers will be more concerned with the prospects for their factories because these will affect the decisions they will take concerning the purchase of raw materials, the hiring of labour, the pricing and output levels of products, and so on. A single information recording system may be used to capture the basic data for both financial and management accounting reports, but the data may be processed differently to meet the different reporting objectives. For example, in a manufacturing company

Table 1.1 Financial and management accounting compared

	Financial accounting	Management accounting
Main users	External groups	Internal management
Primary information	Reports on past performance and current position	Forecasts of the future as well as monitoring information on current and past actual performance
Principal measurement	Financial	Financial and non-financial qualitative and quantitative
Level of aggregation	Whole organisation	Disaggregated, e.g. plant, product or customer information
Frequency	Annual	Monthly or more frequent depending on organisation
Regulation	Law and accounting standards, comprising Generally Accepted Accounting Practice	Little formal regulation; management discretion over the information system
Criteria	Truth and fairness; stewardship; comparability with other organisations	Relevance for specific management decisions and control of operations

considerations concerning goods produced for resale could require information about:

- the detailed costs of past manufacture, for valuing stock in the financial statements;

- analysis of current production quantities and quality, for management control of manufacturing processes;

- expectations about future market conditions to estimate price and revenue attainable when the goods are sold.

The information that is relevant and the measurements that are appropriate will depend on the purpose of the accounting reports and the use that is to be made of them. Understanding the role of management accounting requires an appreciation of what is involved in management and the types of decision that management is faced with.

$\boxed{1.3}$ Structure of the book

This book is concerned primarily with the provision of accounting information for management decisions. But there are several fundamental notions that are common to all types of accounting information system. To a large extent, these notions are embodied in our adopted definition of accounting, which is not restricted to any one group of users or type of organisation. We discuss these notions in this and the remaining chapters of Part 1 under the general heading of 'Basic framework'. Such a framework applies not only to information for management decisions, but also, with very little modification, to the provision of accounting information to other groups of users.

In the remainder of this chapter we investigate further the objectives of organisations and the environments in which they operate. In Chapter 2 we discuss the meaning and importance of a number of the components of our definition of accounting; in particular we examine the nature of information-communication systems, problems of measurement, and theories of individual and group decision making. Chapter 3 is concerned with the meaning, importance and measurement of wealth. Wealth is a vital component of any decision-making process as it provides a focal point for the process; the maximisation of wealth, properly defined, provides an objective for decision models and decision makers. The discussion in Chapter 4 of risk and uncertainty in decision making reflects the fact that all decisions relate to alternative future courses of action and that the future is always uncertain. Hence all decisions involve a consideration of the problems posed by the existence of risk and uncertainty. Finally, as part of the basic framework, in Chapter 5 we explain and illustrate the fundamental principles for measuring relevant costs and benefits for decision purposes.

Good decision making depends on understanding the way in which the organisation's cash flows will be affected by decisions taken. Part 2 of the book comprises two chapters devoted to the analysis of the behaviour of cost flows and the management information system for recording and processing of cost information. This is an area which overlaps with some aspects of financial accounting. An understanding of the cost implications of actions is important for management decisions, but the system by which costs are 'accounted for' also affects the way in which results are reported in periodic financial statements. We look at the behaviour and estimation of costs in Chapter 6 and cost-recording systems in Chapter 7.

The framework chapters in Part 1 provide a conceptual foundation and a set of principles for decision making which, together with the understanding of the behaviour of cost flows from Part 2, are then applied to a number of areas of management decisions in the third part of the book. Individual chapters consider how accounting information can contribute to decisions in a number of specific areas of management, including the level of output (Chapter 8), pricing (Chapter 9), other operational factors (Chapter 10), the allocation of limited resources (Chapters 11 and 12), long-term decisions on investment and the acquisition of capital assets (Chapters 13 and 14), and the use of budgets and variance analysis in the planning and control of operations (Chapters 15–17).

1.4 The objectives and environments of organisations

Our concern is with the role and design of (management) accounting systems within organisations. An essential first step is to explore the nature of organisations and the procedures which are used to control their progress and development. We should stress at the outset that accounting is but one part of a highly complex decision-making and control process in most organisations. An appreciation of its context and limitations is an important prerequisite to the exploitation of its strengths.

What is an organisation?

The answer to this question is not at all obvious! Take, for example, the case of Marks and Spencer plc (although what we will say applies equally to many other organisations, whether in the public or private sector of the economy and whether or not they are profit oriented). When we talk of Marks and Spencer what do we have in mind – its stores and fittings, administrative buildings, stock of merchandise, fleet of vehicles, and so on? Although these are part of the picture, there is almost certainly more. What about the company's reputation and role as an employer, a purchaser of goods, a borrower, a supplier of goods and – more recently – of financial services, and as an investment vehicle for individual and institutional shareholders? All these aspects of the company's activities depend on people and on the nature of their relationships with each other under the umbrella provided by the activities of Marks and Spencer.

This perception suggests that an organisation might be viewed as a group of participants, each of whom makes efforts (*contributions*) on behalf of the organisation and in return receives rewards (*inducements*). The basic criterion for any individual continuing to participate in the organisation is that his or her rewards (inducements) should exceed his or her efforts (contributions). This view of an organisation as an inducement–contribution process is shown in Figure 1.1.

We might illustrate the meaning of some of the boxes in Figure 1.1 by reference to Marks and Spencer. Managers, for example, make contributions to the organisation which are generally non-financial. They contribute mental and physical effort, creativity and other skills. In return they receive both financial and non-financial rewards. The financial rewards will usually include salary payments and bonuses. Non-financial rewards might involve the pleasure that comes from job satisfaction, status and power. Customers contribute financial revenues when they purchase goods from the company. They may also contribute loyalty by preferring to shop at Marks and Spencer even when similar goods are available at a similar or lower price elsewhere. In return, they enjoy the satisfaction which comes from wearing or using the goods which have been purchased.

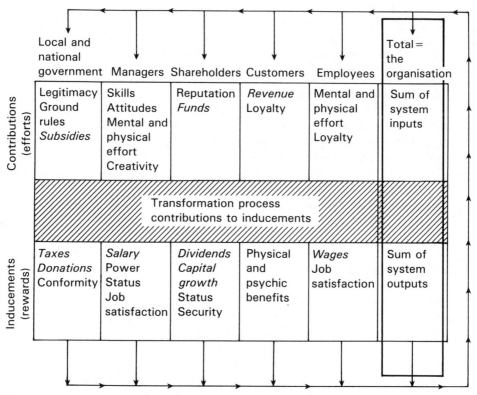

Figure 1.1 Organisation as inducement–contribution process* (based on A.M. Tinker and E.A. Lowe, 'A rationale for corporate social reporting', *Journal of Business Finance and Accounting*, Spring 1980).

*Financial items are in *italics*.

The shaded area in the middle of Figure 1.1 represents the *transformation process*, where the contributions from the various participants (the *system inputs*) are combined together to provide the *system outputs* which are then used to 'pay' rewards to the various groups of participants.

Several interesting conclusions emerge from analysing the nature of an organisation in this way:

1. All contributions (inputs) are combined and 'transformed' to provide the total inducements (outputs) to be distributed to participants. A contribution change by one group may affect the inducements which can be offered to another. For example, the withdrawal of subsidies by local or national government may affect the wages or other employment prospects of employees.

2. The allocation of total inducements between participants must be such that each participant (or possibly each group of participants) receives inducements which are at least equal to the contributions provided.

3. Contributions and inducements may be either financial or non-financial.

4. The efforts which participants are willing to make will be influenced by the rewards they expect. However, their expectations will be conditioned in part by what has actually happened in the past. Thus, the inducements of one period will influence, to some extent, the contributions of the next period.

5. The managers of organisations have a dual role. First, they must satisfy their own expectations and ensure that their rewards are at least as great as their contributions. Second, they must keep all the other participant groups happy in order to maintain the viability of the organisation. Their ability to achieve the first objective will depend in part on their success in achieving the second! Maintaining the viability of the organisation will involve managers in identifying the minimum inducements required by each participant, in ensuring that sufficient total inducements are available to meet the needs of each participant and in ensuring that all participants do receive inducements greater than their contributions.

The task of management

The dual role of management, explained above, is more easily described than accomplished. An organisation is not a self-contained, isolated entity – it has to operate in an environment which constrains its behaviour.

First, the 'technology' available in the environment affects the ability of the organisation to transform total contributions into total inducements. New equipment and machinery will affect its production process. New marketing and selling techniques will affect the way in which and the success with which it markets and sells its products. New computer developments will affect its administrative procedures. These and other changes in available 'technology' complicate the task of management.

Second, the environment provides alternative opportunities for participants and hence influences the minimum inducements they require from the organisation. For example, the environment provides alternative employment opportunities for employees, alternative investment opportunities for shareholders, alternative sources of supply for customers, and so on.

In both of the above respects, the environment is likely to be dynamic – available alternative technologies and opportunities will be in a continual state of flux. The task facing management may be represented as in Figure 1.2. The organisation operates in, and is affected by, a part (or subset) of the general environment which we might call the *substantial environment*. Figure 1.2 illustrates management's task if there are four participant groups – government, employees, shareholders and customers – *and* if, within each group, the contributions made and the inducements required by each participant are homogeneous. (In practice there will be more groups and the interests of participants within each will not be

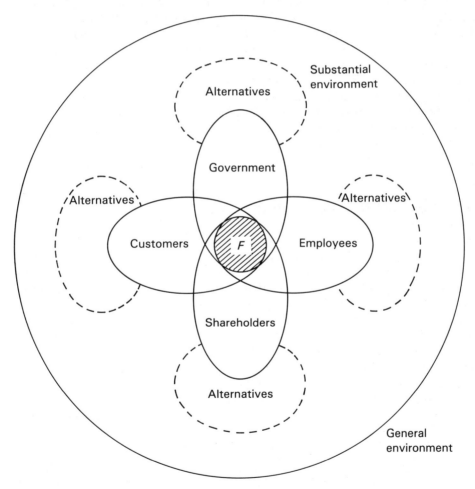

Figure 1.2 Structure of the organisation's environment.

homogeneous.) Hence the area (or set) described as 'shareholders' defines all points in the environment at which the inducements offered to shareholders are greater than the contributions they make. Any point outside that set will be unsatisfactory and will cause shareholders to withdraw their participation in the organisation. What is acceptable to the shareholders will be influenced by the alternative investment and other opportunities available to them.

Similar sets are defined for the other participant groups. The shaded area, F, is the *feasible set*, the only area within which all participants are satisfied. It is the task of management to make sure that the organisation is located in F – and to keep it there! This task is complicated by a number of factors. Because of their available alternative opportunities, each participant group may be pulling in a different direction from each other group. (Remember that, strictly speaking, each participant within a group may be represented by a different set or region.) Furthermore the environment itself will be changing continuously – what was feasible last week may not be so today – for example, a new competitor may enter the organisation's market, a new employer may offer alternative employment opportunities, and so on. The feasible set is unstable and is influenced by a variety of factors, some of which are *controllable* by managers (for example, the prices the organisation charges for its services or products and the number of staff it employs) and others of which are largely *uncontrollable* (for example, the general economic climate, the prices charged by competitors and government legislation).

It should be apparent from the discussion in this section that the task of controlling an organisation (i.e. of sustaining its viability) is an imposing one. In the next section we outline broadly the role which accounting has to play as part of the process of organisational control.

1.5 The role of accounting

As we have seen, management's task is to make decisions which are likely to ensure the continued viability of the organisation and to control the implementation of those decisions. Where does (management) accounting fit in? It is a part (and only a part) of the total information available to management. It is vital to recognise the partial role of accounting. For example, in considering the desirability of producing a new product, management will consider the costs of making and selling it and the revenues it is likely to produce. This is information which the accounting system should provide. However, management will also consider other aspects of the decision with which the accounting system may not be able to help, such as the technical problems of manufacturing the product, the availability of employees with the necessary production and marketing skills, the nature of the market within which the product will be sold, the extent to which the product fits within the company's existing range, etc. Accounting is only one part of a complicated set of informational and organisational structures. The role of accounting is to provide relevant financial information within those structures. It will rarely provide sufficient information by itself to permit an informed decision to be taken or to control the implementation of organisational plans.

Although it is only one part of the total set of information management will need, our definition suggests that accounting can contribute to the management process in a number of ways. It has a role in *identifying* and *measuring* information: that is, in determining what factors associated with a decision are recognised and how they are quantified. As we will see in later chapters, the appropriate approach to these issues may depend on the particular decision being evaluated and the alternatives open to the organisation. Much of accounting, and much of this book, is concerned with techniques and procedures, but our definition also describes accounting as a *process*. Practical techniques are implemented in a human process, and accounting will be influenced by and will itself influence the human context in which it is located, which for our purposes is that of management decision making.

Accounting also has a *communication* role in decision making. This role can have both positive and negative effects. The positive side is that accounting can help to provide a common language whereby managers can understand the effects of choices being considered. The danger with accounting information is that because it attempts to measure the financial consequences of actions (which are of interest to most participants), because it often looks objective and accurate (but rarely is, as we shall see later), and because it is usually more readily available in quite large quantities than are other sources of information, it is accorded undue importance. An organisation whose managers attempt to make and control decisions entirely on the basis of accounting information is unlikely to remain viable for long.

Nevertheless, this is a book about accounting and about the way in which accounting can assist management in decision making and control. In consequence, our main emphasis will be on the explanation and development of management accounting methods rather than on the broader questions of organisational control. The reader should, of course, remain alert to the need at all stages to consider the non-accounting implications of management actions.

1.6 Information for managerial decision making

Within the context described and explained in the previous sections, in later chapters we apply the concepts developed in Part 1 to particular decisions facing the managers of organisations. Figure 1.3 presents a simplified, general framework for managerial planning, decision making and control. At this stage we shall examine briefly the individual steps of the framework. Part 3 looks in detail at (sequential) issues raised when the framework is applied to particular situations.

It is important to recognise the role of the feedback mechanism within the general framework. Feedback loops stress interdependences between the various steps of the framework (i.e. the outcome of any one particular step provides information which may influence the formulation of prior steps). As inter-dependences exist, in some measure, between *all* steps of the framework, feedback is present throughout the entire planning and control system. For illustrative purposes, we have chosen two feedback loops, one linking steps 5 and 1, the other linking steps 7 and 5. The first loop stresses the need to review regularly the goals of the organisation, in the light of the expected outcomes of individual courses of

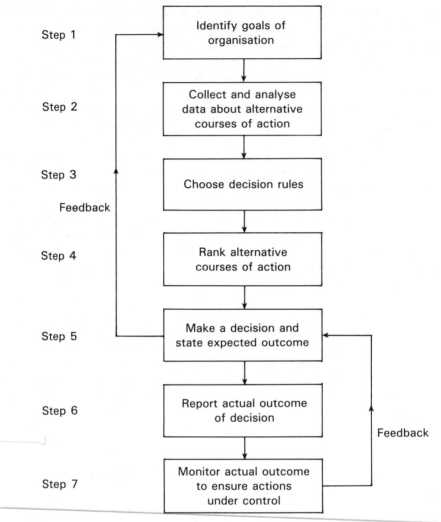

Figure 1.3   Framework for managerial planning, decision making and control.

action; the second loop stresses how the control process helps to formulate the planning cycle for the following period (i.e. the differences between expected and actual figures for any period are useful inputs to the prediction of expected outcomes for succeeding periods).

Step 1 – identification of goals

Planning may be defined as the choice of organisational objectives and the means of their attainment. Thus good planning entails a procedure for determining the direction in which the resources of the organisation should be pointed. Formal planning is of particular importance in a large organisation composed of different divisions or sections. Without a knowledge of the objectives of the whole organisation, individual sections may take decisions that are not in the best interests of the whole.

Choice of appropriate organisational goals is one of the most difficult parts of the planning process. It is often blandly stated, as though it were a self-evident truth, that in a capitalist or 'mixed' economy the most appropriate goal for business activity is the making of the maximum possible profit. Profit maximisation or, more precisely, maximisation of the owners' wealth, represents the business objective which is usually assumed in traditional economic theory: indeed it forms the basis of much microeconomic analysis. It is often rephrased vaguely as 'maximisation of long-run growth' or 'maximisation of long-run survival prospects' or even 'maximisation of market share'. All of these possible goals focus in large measure on the maximisation of the owners' wealth, to the exclusion of the interests of other groups. As we have already seen, these goals fail to represent the reality of business planning in organisations with many different participants, each with their own goals.

When constraints of a societal nature (e.g. the employment of disabled workers, the provision of adequate social and recreational facilities) or, indeed, of a legal nature (e.g. the regulation of prices of particular goods, the restriction of monopolies) are superimposed on other disparate goals, we can see readily that the encapsulation of the whole process in terms of 'maximising profit' may in fact be an unrealistic representation of business practice. Yet management must attempt to point the organisation towards some particular goal(s). Without a guiding aim, business decision making would operate in a vacuum; there would be no benchmark against which to assess the desirability of any course of action.

The primary objective of business planning to be adopted in this and succeeding chapters is the maximisation of the present value of the organisation's future cash flows, as we shall explain in Chapter 3. This objective is chosen for a variety of reasons. First, it is quantifiable and thus provides a ready guide for future actions; second, it avoids the imprecision of profit calculations which are based in large measure on the use of often arbitrary accounting conventions; third, it deals directly with one important means (cash) available to individuals to acquire things which give them satisfaction; and last, it leaves open the question of how the cash is to be distributed among the members of the coalition of interested groups (i.e. it concentrates on maximising the size of the 'cake' available rather than on how the cake is to be distributed).

Step 2 – collection and analysis of data about alternative courses of action

Management must take a wide range of decisions of varying impact on the firm's (cash) resources. Some decisions will commit the firm's resources for a lengthy period of time and involve major changes in the firm's productive capacity. We might label these *long-term* decisions. Others will be of a more *short-term* nature.[3] Indeed, we would expect different levels of management to be associated with the different types of decision; for instance, if the building of a large new factory were being contemplated, or if the firm were thinking of setting up operations in a new country, we would expect senior managers to be involved in these long-term decisions, where the level of risk involved is usually high, and the decision less easily reversible once resources have been committed. On a more short-term basis, lower-level managers may concern themselves with such operating decisions as these:

1. How many units should be produced of a particular product?

2. How should the selling price of a product be fixed?

3. How many workers should be employed on a particular production process?

Whatever the nature of, and the time period involved in, a particular decision, management must attempt to analyse the costs and benefits to the organisation which are likely to arise. This is seldom easy to do. The difficulties should not be underestimated. It may seem intuitively to be quite easy to attach particular 'labels' to the more easily quantified aspects of any decision, but in many situations it is those very aspects which are difficult to quantify precisely which may determine the ultimate success or failure of the particular decision. To illustrate this difficulty, let us borrow an analogy from the world of sport. On five or six occasions each summer, an English cricket team is selected to play against the touring sides. On the basis of the examination of purely quantifiable factors, the deliberations should not take very long; it would simply be necessary to scan the appropriate batting and bowling averages to select the top English performers. Similarly the wicketkeeper with the greatest number of dismissals would be selected. But in fact, the deliberations are not resolved speedily. They last for many hours, and it is by no means obvious at the end of the day that up-to-date statistics form the sole basis for selection of the team. Factors such as leadership quality and the ability to work well with others, though difficult to quantify, may be of equal importance in the ultimate choice. The analogy with managerial decision making should be apparent. Managers will, of course, use the basic quantifiable numbers, the costs and revenues, as the prime inputs to the decision process; but equally they must try to account for the less easily quantified factors inherent in the particular courses of action – factors such as the future economic environment, the strength of competition the firm will face and the uncertainty associated with estimated costs and benefits (discussed in Chapter 4), which may contribute greatly to the ultimate success of any course of action.

Steps 3 and 4 – choice of decision rules and ranking of alternative courses of action

In order to make effective decisions, managers need to understand two fundamental requirements:

- the appropriate *basis* for decision making;

- the *types of data* to use in decision making and, by implication, the types of data not to use.

Decisions involve choices, and decision making entails making choices between alternative, competing courses of action. If no alternative courses of action exist, no decisions need to be made. In effect, the nature of a decision is of the kind 'What difference would it make if we chose to do X instead of not doing X?' More specifically, when we ask this question, we are asking for an assessment of the impact of either doing or not doing X on the organisation's cash resources.

In practice there may be many possible courses of action available to decision makers, each having different potential cash consequences. Furthermore, the alternatives available will change continually over time. The question then becomes 'How is management to choose from among these many possible alternatives so as to maximise the present value of the expected future cash flows?' If alternatives exist, there must be differences between them, and a first step in decision making is to analyse these differences. We might term this analysis *differential* or *incremental* analysis. Differential analysis involves an assessment of the advantages and disadvantages that might arise from the choice of alternative actions, and as it is necessary to express these advantages and disadvantages in a quantifiable form, we attach cash costs and benefits to them. The option showing the greatest net cash benefit to the firm represents, under the principle of differential analysis, the preferred alternative. (Because of the impact of non-cash factors, it may not always be the alternative which is actually accepted.)

These themes are developed in Chapters 5 and 6, where we consider in detail some general rules for determining the costs and benefits attaching to managerial decisions, and in Chapters 10 and 13 where we examine some specific types of short- and long-term decision.

Steps 5, 6 and 7 – decision making and control

Having evaluated alternative courses of action in the light of the organisation's goals, the managers are now in a position to decide which action to take. The final steps in the framework cover the control of the implementation of the decision. A forecast (Step 5) is made of the likely outcome of the decision, usually expressed in the form of a *budget*. The budget is prepared on the basis of the differential costs and revenues associated with the particular course of action which has been adopted, and may incorporate probabilities or ranges of estimates. The difficulties of predicting costs and revenues are examined in Chapter 6. They relate both to the ranking of alternative courses of action and to the preparation of budgets reflecting the decisions taken. The budgets for all decisions undertaken by management are then gathered together into a single unified statement of the organisation's expectations for future periods. This statement is known as the *master budget*. It is a formalised document serving as a written intention of management's plans and is usually drawn up for a period of one year, although it may cover a shorter period (as in an organisation manufacturing and selling fashion goods) or a longer one (as in an organisation building oil tankers). We discuss budgeting in Chapters 15 and 16.

To increase the chances of meeting the budget targets (and therefore reaching the desired goals), and to generate information for subsequent planning, actual performance must be regularly monitored (Steps 6 and 7). The monitoring of performance is known as the firm's *control process*. This process is helped by the use of regular control reports which relate the costs and revenues actually incurred to those expected; they provide *feedback* to help management to decide if any corrective action is required.

The regularity of issue of control reports is an important subject. Management will wish to know as speedily as possible if there is a need for corrective action, and therefore the earlier it receives the information, the swifter will be the cure. The regularity of reporting depends primarily upon the position of the manager: for example, top management may see shopfloor production reports only at quarterly intervals, whereas factory supervisors, who are much closer to actual operations, may require daily reports of levels and costs of production. We discuss control systems in Chapters 17 and 18.

1.7 Management accounting in different types of organisation

Many of the applications that are discussed in later chapters are based on manufacturing business settings, but the principles that underlie the approach to management accounting described are relevant to all types of organisation – service as well as manufacturing and those in the non-profit sector as well as commercial enterprises.

The nature of the business setting will affect the type of management information system needed. For example, in a retailing organisation goods are simply purchased for resale and there will be no need for the kind of accounting information on processing or production that would be required in a manufacturing firm. For supermarkets such as Sainsbury and Tesco, the majority of goods are purchased ready for sale and cost measurement will be related solely to purchase; but for operations such as an in-house bakery a system for accounting for the additional costs of conversion processes will also be needed. In service firms, information will be collected on the activities which comprise the service, but the completion of the service and delivery to the customer are normally coincident and therefore there will be no stock of finished services ready for sale. Stocks of service cannot be accumulated. For example, a hotel may provide laundry and room service, and will need accounting information to control the processes associated with these services for a particular customer, but it will not be able to store these services for future customers. Manufacturing organisations will need information systems which recognise the complexity of the production processes undertaken and also the existence of opening and closing stocks of part-processed and completed products.

In non-profit organisations the focus of the information may be different again. A charity may have a need for information on the revenue consequences of

Accounting and decision making

AIMS AND OBJECTIVES

☐ To explain what is meant by information and to distinguish between valuable and valueless information.

☐ To explore the meaning of communication and explain its importance in accounting.

☐ To introduce some of the problems created by the need to find a stable unit of measurement for accounting.

☐ To explain the practical constraints on both individual and group decision making.

In Chapter 1 we defined accounting as 'the process of identifying, measuring, and communicating economic information to permit informed judgements and decisions by users of the information',[1] and we stated that subsequent chapters would examine each of the major issues thrown up by our definition. The aim of this chapter is to introduce briefly the important concepts underlying the definition so as to understand better the problems of accounting as discussed in Part 3. In particular we discuss the nature of *information*, and some procedures for its *communication*; we also consider the meaning and importance of *measurement*; and finally, we focus attention on a general description of *decision-making procedures*, with specific reference to some differences between individual and group decision making. Our discussion will deal with these concepts both in a general way, and also in the context of their application to accounting.

2.1 The meaning of information

Information is a fashionable word. It is often said that we live in the 'information age' and that future development will be determined by the 'information superhighway'. One of the most important changes in our environment during the last 25 years has been the development of information technology, in the form of advances in both computer hardware and software. The widespread use of the computer, and in particular the development and introduction of inexpensive and powerful personal computers, has made the gathering and dissemination of information a relatively easy task. We receive information from a variety of different sources – from 'indirect' sources such as television, radio, books, newspapers and computer print-outs, and from more 'direct' sources such as conversation. But what is information? How can we distinguish between information and non-information? How do we know when we are 'informed'?

We need here to draw a distinction between data and information. The two words do not mean the same thing, though they are often used synonymously. The *Oxford English Dictionary* defines data, the plural of datum, as 'facts of any kind'. We cannot define information in such a broad way. Information has a more particular meaning. It is a subset of data. An item of data is usually classed as information only if it changes the expectations of the person receiving it, or, more specifically, if it changes the probabilities which the receiver attaches to future events or outcomes. For example, suppose that a traveller is told that the 8.12 a.m. train from Manchester to London will leave at 8.12 a.m., and that, before receiving this message, the traveller fully expected the train to leave on time. This statement possesses no information content, as it does not change the traveller's expectations about the train's departure time. If, however, the traveller is told that the 8.12 a.m. train will leave at 9.00 a.m., this is information, as it changes prior expectations of the departure time.

A further distinction is important for decision making. Not all information is valuable. If our traveller is about to embark on a train journey from Manchester to Glasgow, information about a change in the departure time of the Manchester–London train is of no value. Although it changes expectations of the departure time of the London train, and is hence 'information', *it does not cause the traveller to change his or her planned course of action.* If, on the other hand, the traveller is intending to catch the 8.12 a.m. train to London, a message that the train's departure time has been delayed may be valuable information as it may result in a change in the planned course of action: for example, the traveller may now choose to visit a public library in the intervening 48 minutes!

The distinction between valuable and valueless information is of crucial importance for accounting; accounting should be concerned primarily with the provision of valuable information, otherwise it will be a rather sterile area for study and research. In view of its importance, let us consider a further example of the distinction. Suppose an accounting student is told that last year's accounting examination included a question on the history of accounting. This statement has some information content, unless, of course, the student already knew last year's questions. But the information may be of little value unless the student believes that the examiner's choice of questions for this year's paper will be influenced by the questions in last year's examination. However, suppose the student is told that this year's examination paper will include a question on the history of accounting. If this statement is from a reliable source, it presumably has information content and, almost certainly, is of value to the student. Why is this? Because it will change what the student does; he or she will now spend more (scarce) time in revising the subject matter of accounting history and less on other topics, in the expectation of being able to answer at least one question reasonably well. The value of the information derives from the fact that it enables the student to allocate a scarce resource, time, more efficiently than before.

2.2 The value of information

Let us explore further this idea of the value of information. If the value of a piece of information is dependent upon its impact on future decisions, it follows that the value is personal to the decision taker, the user of the information. In assessing the value of information, we must consider who is going to use the information, and for what purpose. We shall return to these issues later in this section.

The provision of information is not, generally speaking, free. Information has a cost, and one kind of information may be more costly to provide than another. Thus cost is an important factor in the choice of alternative sources of information. Someone who wishes to inform a friend in the USA that his wife has recently given birth may prefer to send a fax message, rather than make a telephone call, because the cost of sending a fax is likely to be cheaper.

We can formalise these practical cost considerations in the following way. Suppose we make a particular decision which we regard as optimal on the basis of existing information. Then suppose we are given an extra piece of information, which causes us to revise our previous view of the optimal decision. The difference between the net benefits (or 'value') we expect from the revised decision and the net benefits we would now expect from the original decision represents the 'value' of the extra information. Information is valuable only if the decision maker's best action with the information is different from his or her best action without the information. This 'value' of the extra information is usually termed its *gross value*, and the difference between the gross value and the cost of providing the information is called the *net value* of the information. We can use the notion of the net value of information to aid two kinds of (important) decisions which involve the production of information:

1. Decisions as to whether a piece of information is worth producing. Production is worthwhile if the net value of the information is positive.

2. Decisions concerning the choice of alternative information production methods. The method with the highest positive net value should be chosen.

Suppose that a land speculator has the opportunity to buy land for possible resale as a development site. The cost of the land is £500,000. Its resale value depends upon whether the speculator will be able to obtain planning permission for development. If planning permission is obtained, the resale value of the land will be £800,000; without planning permission it will be worth only £300,000. The speculator believes that there is a 50:50 chance of obtaining planning permission.

The 'expected' value of the land (i.e. the weighted average of its possible values) is 50% of £800,000 plus 50% of £300,000, which equals £550,000. In Chapter 4 we discuss the nature of expected values and their role in decision making. At this stage we assume that the speculator's decision will be based on the expected value of the land. As the expected value of £550,000 is greater than the cost of £500,000, the speculator will purchase the land. The expected surplus is £50,000, comprising a 50% chance of a gain of £300,000 (if planning permission is obtained) and a 50% chance of a loss of £200,000 (if planning permission is refused).

Suppose now that the speculator is able to buy for £80,000 information about whether or not planning permission will be granted, and suppose, for simplicity, that the information is certain to be correct. What is the value of the information? If the information says that planning permission will be granted, the resale value of the land will be £800,000 and the speculator will buy it and realise a gain of £300,000. If the information says that planning permission will not be granted, the speculator will not buy the land (as to do so would result in a loss) and will realise neither gain nor loss. As each message is equally likely in this case, the expected value of the possible outcomes (ignoring the cost of the information) is 50% of £300,000 plus 50% of zero, which equals £150,000.[2]

We may now calculate the gross and net value of the information. The *gross value* is the expected value of the speculator's best action *with* the information (£150,000) minus the value of his or her best action *without* the information (£50,000), i.e. £100,000. The *net value* of the information is its gross value (£100,000) minus the cost of obtaining it (£80,000), which equals £20,000. In other words, the information is worth purchasing as the expected surplus is increased from £50,000, without the information, to £70,000 with it.

2.3 Information and accounting

These ideas of information value and cost may well be of general interest and importance, but what is their relevance to accounting? Recall our definition of accounting which we set down at the start of the chapter. This definition suggests that accounting is concerned with the provision of information to aid decisions: that is, with the provision of valuable information. 'Valuable' information in an accounting sense is that which relates to the decisions taken by users of such information. And these decisions are likely to vary from user to user. Many groups might be interested in information produced by a large industrial organisation such as BP or ICI. In order to illustrate the nature of the information provision problem facing such organisations, consider the following groups of users and some of the possible decisions for which each group requires information:

User group	Example of decision for which information is required
Shareholders	Buy, sell or hold shares
Lenders/creditors	Increase, reduce or keep constant levels of credit and loans
Employees	Submit claim for wage increase; change employment
Government	Raise taxation; examine the impact of the firm on the environment
Customers	Buy the firm's products
Managers	Determine the level at which to conduct operations
General public	Assess the economic and 'social' impact of the firm

It is clear that these different users may not always require the same information. For example, information on the number of prosecutions suffered by a firm for failure to meet safety requirements may affect decisions of employees, but it is likely to be of less interest to customers. Differing user information needs present a major difficulty for the accountant or other provider of information, who may have to attempt to satisfy them in a single report (or at least in a small number of reports).

Whatever the possible conflicting needs of users of accounting information, it remains necessary to devise suitable channels for communicating information from the reporting entity to those who are interested in its performance and prospects. It is to this issue that we now turn.

2.4 The meaning of communication

The process of communication is at the heart of the accounting information system. To make good decisions it is necessary that those who possess valuable information should be able to communicate this information successfully to those who do not have it. Thus there is a need for accountants to study the process of communication. Most communication systems comprise at least five elements, which we denote as stages A to E in Figure 2.1.[3]

The intention of the system is that the message sent by the sender (stage A) should influence in an appropriate manner the actions of the receiver (stage E). This will occur only if the substance of the message which reaches the receiver is the same as that intended by the sender. Because the message must go through intermediary stages B, C and D, there may be problems of 'noise' (i.e. distortion) within the system which prevent the intention of the sender from being satisfied. Explanation of these intermediary stages may reveal the nature of such problems.

Suppose that the accountant of a limited company is preparing annual information concerning one of the company's divisions for circulation to managers.

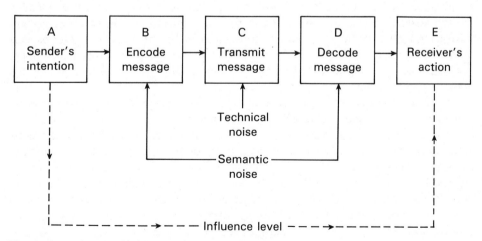

Figure 2.1   A model of the communication process.

Thus the sender of the message (stage A) is the company's accountant, and the receiver (stage E) is its managers. In order to present the message in a comprehensible language, the accountant uses a form of code (stage B). For effective communication to take place, the nature of this code must be understood and agreed by the receiver. The specialised notation which attaches to the accountant's balance sheet and income statement represents a form of code. For example, words like depreciation, profit, current asset, and indeed balance sheet and income statement themselves, are code words which are intended to convey specific meanings.

Having encoded the message, the sender must ensure that it is transmitted properly to the receiver (stage C). For example, accounting reports may be transmitted in the form of printed words or numbers, by computer, or verbally by telephone or in 'face-to-face' conversation.

Distortions to the intended message (*system noise*) may occur either at the encoding/decoding stage, when they are termed *semantic noise*, or at the transmission stage, when they are termed *technical noise*. Broadly speaking, semantic noise occurs when the receiver attaches a different meaning to a message from that intended by the sender, and technical noise stems from distortions arising from the technical or mechanical functioning of the communication equipment. We now consider some examples of technical and semantic noise.

In the context of telephone systems (the dialling of wrong numbers) or computer systems (flaws in the computer program), technical noise can be a major problem. In accounting systems, this kind of 'mechanical' noise may be slight, and involve such relatively minor problems as correct typing, printing and circulation of balance sheets and income statements. However, there is a further aspect of technical noise that may be more significant for accounting. This relates to the physical *capacity* of the receiver to process all the information being transmitted. This is a common problem in many communication systems. Too much information given in any one message may lead to 'information overload', with the result that the most important aspects of the message are lost, buried in a mass of other information, and the ultimate action of the receiver is different from that intended by the sender. It is for this reason that accountants reporting management information often include a separate short summary of the most important aspects of an organisation's or a division's results in a prominent position in their reports. For example, profit, sales and return on assets employed may be highlighted separately in the report.

Semantic noise arises at the encoding or decoding stage if there is confusion in meaning between sender and receiver in relation to the terms used in the message. In particular, semantic noise arises where different meanings are attached to the same word, or series of words. Semantic noise is common in all forms of communication, not least in conversation. How many times, on doing something for which we are criticised, do we answer 'Oh, I didn't know that was what you meant!'? The extent of semantic noise can be very great, especially when international communication takes place. For example, the word 'estate' might mean any of the following to an English speaker: a manor house and grounds, an amount left on death, a housing development, an industrial site, or a type of motor car. Thus a message from a manager to a subordinate to 'buy an estate' might result in the purchase of a large motor car rather than the intended purchase of an industrial site!

Semantic noise presents major problems in accounting. If the sender and receiver of accounting messages cannot concur at the semantic level (the level of meaning), influential and effective communication is impossible. Suppose, for example, that the accountant tells a company's managers that machinery is shown in the balance sheet at £50,000. What meaning should the managers attach to this message? Does it mean that a similar machine would now cost £50,000 (its replacement cost)? Does it mean that the company would receive £50,000 if it sold the machine now (its resale value)? Does it mean that the original cost of the machine less a provision for 'wear and tear' is £50,000 (its written-down historical cost)? Each of these alternative meanings might be used in accounting reports. Each involves a different accounting *measurement*: that is, at the root of the problem of semantic noise in accounting lies the issue of measurement, which we now consider.

2.5 The issue of measurement

The *Oxford English Dictionary* defines the verb 'to measure' as:

> ascertain extent or quantity of (thing) by comparison with fixed unit or with object of known size.

Two important facets of measurement emerge from the definition. First, measurement is *relative* – it is related to something else whose size is known. Second, measurement is *numerical* – it involves putting numbers on things. Measurement is fundamental to all aspects of society, primitive and modern.

To illustrate the use and importance of measurement in a somewhat different society from our own, consider the case of Robinson Crusoe. In particular consider his situation before the appearance of Man Friday. Robinson Crusoe, stranded on his desert island, is faced with a dilemma. He has to eat, and he has two immediate choices in terms of the provision of his food. He can either spend his time fishing with his bare hands, by which method he can catch two fish per day indefinitely, or he can devote one week to the making of a fishing rod which will allow him to catch three fish per day. During the week set aside for the making of the fishing rod he can catch only one fish per day, which is barely enough to live on. Robinson Crusoe has no means of storing fish – he has no freezer!

He is faced with a fundamental investment decision (not different in kind from that facing a large company deciding whether to buy a new machine or to recruit more labour). Either he can have more fish during the following week (two per day), and the same amount later, or he can have fewer fish for the first week (one per day), but the expectation of three per day thereafter. His choice is between more present consumption and more future consumption. The answer to Robinson Crusoe's dilemma depends largely upon an estimate of the costs and benefits associated with each alternative. In order to choose, Robinson Crusoe must *compare* the alternatives. To compare the alternatives he must use some unit of measurement.

Because money is non-existent in his society, he cannot measure in *financial* terms. He may decide to use *fish* as his basis of measurement. We might say that Robinson Crusoe's fishing rod would be 'worth' one extra fish per day for the indefinite future, and that its cost would be one fish per day for the week, which would have to be sacrificed immediately. Robinson Crusoe's decision about whether to make the rod will depend upon his relative preferences for early rather than later consumption of fish.

Accountants do not, of course, usually measure in terms of fish, but they do measure in terms of the medium of exchange demanded by the society in which they operate. Just as fish might be used as an appropriate medium of exchange in Robinson Crusoe's unique society, so modern society demands that money is used as a medium of exchange to compare alternatives. Money is used by accountants to measure costs, values, benefits, profits, and so on. British accountants measure in pounds sterling, French accountants in francs, and Russian accountants in roubles. When organisations trade in many different countries, and thus pay for and are paid for goods and services in different currencies, special problems arise when it becomes necessary to translate these foreign currencies into the currencies of the 'home' countries. And yet if the organisation desires to express the results of its world-wide transactions in one common measuring unit, it must ensure that these translations are carried out.

The use of money involves other problems which are not necessarily of an international nature. The greatest problem concerns its stability as a unit of measurement. Stability is an important attribute of all measuring units, whether of distance, weight, liquidity or money. It is essential for architects and builders to know that their measurement of a metre or of a ton is a 'correct' measure. If not, a bridge may collapse or a house fall down. If architects were unsure as to whether their measurement of a metre was correct, they could take their metre rules to the planetarium in Paris and measure them against a metre length of platinum. Accountants do not have such safeguards. Their unit of measurement cannot be viewed independently of what it can buy. A pound sterling (or a franc or a rouble) is only as stable as the prices of the goods it can buy. Thus if prices rise (as happens during a period of inflation) or drop (as during a period of deflation), the purchasing power of the unit of measurement becomes unstable. Because of this instability, it becomes difficult for the accountant to compare assets, liabilities and profits arising in one period with assets, liabilities and profits arising in any other period. Thus adjustments to the accountant's unit of measurement have been advocated as a way of overcoming this basic problem.

But which adjustments? How should the accountant deal with changes in the measuring unit? Should it be adjusted for changes in the general rate of inflation? Or should it be adjusted to reflect only those price changes that are specific to the reporting organisation's assets and liabilities? This is really the essence of the accountant's measurement problem. There is no agreed 'best' basis for measurement in accounting. We shall return to this issue in later chapters.

Thus far we have discussed the need for *stability* of the measuring unit. Other attributes are also of importance. The measuring unit should be *understandable* to users. It should be *cost-effective*: that is, the benefits from adopting it should be greater than the costs of so doing. It should be *precise*. (But illusory precision should be guarded against. The story of the shepherd and his accountant is salutary. When asked by a shepherd to 'measure' the number of sheep the shepherd owned, the accountant took a swift look and replied immediately '2,007'. 'How did you count them so quickly?' asked the shepherd. 'Well,' said the accountant, 'there are 7 by the river and about 2,000 in the far field'!)

Most important of all, the measurement should be *relevant*. As we have seen when discussing the meaning of information, the object of measurement depends upon the decision to be taken by the user of the information. Thus the basis of measurement should also be relevant to the decision.

In the coming chapters we will consider alternative measurement bases available to the accountant and discuss the extent to which they possess the attributes of measurement bases outlined in this section.

2.6 Theories of decision making

We have now examined briefly the information, communication and measurement issues arising from our adopted definition of accounting. It remains for us to look at the final concept in the definition – the concept of decision making. We will first consider a very general model for decision making and then look at its possible application to decisions taken by individuals and by groups. Throughout we shall stress the contribution of accounting to the model. We differentiate between individual and group decision making because the latter is more complex, primarily as a result of conflicts between individuals in a group and the consequent need for compromise.

Figure 2.2 presents an example of a general model for decision making. A model is a simplified approximation or simulation of real world conditions, constructed from assumed or observed relationships. Accounting models may take the form of verbal expressions, geometric diagrams or, most frequently, mathematical expressions. All of these forms of models may be expressed in computer language, a characteristic of particular importance in the modern world. The model in Figure 2.2 is similar to the first five steps of Figure 1.3 (p. 14). Figure 1.3 related particularly to management accounting, whereas Figure 2.2 relates to decision making in general. A model is an abstraction of the real world which, to be of any use, must relate ultimately to how people or things behave: in other words, it must have some descriptive validity. The six stages of our general decision model are as follows.

Stage 1 involves the establishment of the decision maker's objectives or goals; in order to use the model as a route map, the decision maker must know the intended destination. Objectives are expressed in terms of some desired level of performance (e.g. the decision maker may wish to be earning £40,000 per annum by the age of 30). Stage 2 entails a regular review of expected performance. If expected performance is up to or beyond the desired level, the decision maker may either increase the level of aspirations (e.g. raise the desired level of earnings to £50,000 per annum by the age of 30), or continue on the present course to attain the original target. If expected performance is less than desired (i.e. it is unsatisfactory), the

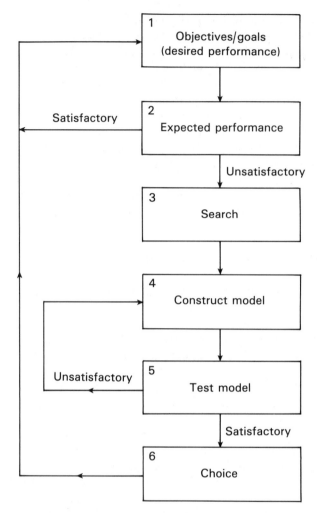

Figure 2.2 A general model for decision making.

decision maker should move to stage 3, and search for alternative courses of action (e.g. alternative employment) which might offer a better chance of reaching the goal. This search for alternative courses of action involves the need to acquire information concerning future opportunities and future environments. *It is the most difficult stage in the whole process.*

In order to aid choice from among the alternative courses of action which have been sought (and found), the decision maker constructs a model (stage 4). This model will predict the effects of the various alternatives on the measures represented in the stated objectives under the various environments that might exist. For example, the model might predict the chance of the decision maker earning £50,000 per annum by the age of 30 in different employments and under different possible environmental circumstances.

Before the model is used to select the opportunity, or combination of opportunities, that seems to satisfy best the decision maker's objectives, it should be critically tested to discover whether it is appropriate for the particular decision maker and whether it predicts efficiently when applied to the decision maker's affairs. The testing of models in the social sciences is very difficult, precisely because such models deal with human behaviour, which is notoriously difficult to predict. If the testing of the model appears satisfactory, the decision maker will be in a position to use the model to choose the course of action which best satisfies the objectives (stage 6). Information about decision alternatives and future environments is fed into the model, and the combination of opportunities is selected which the model reveals to be in best accord with the decision maker's objectives.

The arrowed lines in Figure 2.2, which link various stages of the process, are of particular importance. These are known as 'feedback loops' and they signify that the entire process is continuous and dynamic. In other words, the decision maker should continually review actual performance, expected performance, objectives, available alternatives and the state of the immediate operating environment. A change in any one of these may signal the need for further decisions.

Where does accounting fit into this general model? Accounting is concerned directly with stages 2, 4 and 6 – where quantitative information is required about performance currently expected and about future alternative courses of action. It is, however, important to understand equally well the other stages in order to appreciate the contribution of accounting information to the whole decision-making process.

The following two chapters are concerned essentially with concepts which are fundamental to the general decision model in Figure 2.2. Chapter 3 looks at wealth and wealth maximisation as one possible objective of decision makers, and Chapter 4 deals with risk and uncertainty as a necessary component of all decision making.

2.7 Individual decision making

The basic notion implied by the general decision model in Figure 2.2 is that an individual decision maker will consider *all* possible alternative actions and choose the one which best satisfies the objectives. Phrased in the jargon of economics, the model assumes that individuals will choose rationally from among all alternatives so as to maximise their own (i.e. subjective) expected utility or satisfaction. The model is thus sometimes referred to as the *subjective expected utility* (SEU) model. The SEU model emphasises the ultimate choice or outcome rather than the process of choosing. Its importance rests on the influence it has exerted on much of the thinking in management science. The model depends for its validity upon four key assumptions about the decision maker's process:

1. Information is available about all possible alternatives.

2. The decision maker has sufficient mental capacity to evaluate all alternatives, including the capacity to make the necessary forecasts about future outcomes.

3. The decision maker will behave consistently in choosing between alternatives (e.g. if alternative A is preferred to alternative B, and alternative B is preferred to alternative C, then alternative A should be preferred to alternative C).

4. The decision maker will always seek to maximise utility or satisfaction.

These are very demanding assumptions. How adequately do they reflect the real situation of decision making? The main problem with the SEU model is its failure to recognise that an individual's rationality may be constrained or 'bounded' by, among other things, environment and education, and particularly by limited mental capacity. Thus the notion of *bounded rationality* is often thought to be a more appropriate description of individual decision making.

Bounded rationality implies that individuals have limited mental capacities for making complex choices and therefore adopt simplified decision models which are characterised by:

- satisficing, rather than maximising, behaviour;

- a restricted search for alternatives;

- a tendency to 'block out' alternatives which require substantial changes to the existing position;

- the use of 'filters' to reduce the possibility of information overload. (The filter should, however, ensure that as far as possible 'good' information is not discarded along with 'bad' information.)

As an example of the application of the concepts of bounded rationality, consider the case of an individual who owns and runs a small greengrocery. According to our general decision model, the greengrocer ought *strictly* to be evaluating continuously the possibility of taking over Marks and Spencer or Sainsbury, or of expanding activities to Australia, the United States, and so on. Such diversifications are not impossible, although they may be highly unlikely. Most individuals who run small greengroceries are likely to devote their time to different, and more immediate, problems: which vegetables to purchase, where to find the money to pay next month's rent, and when to replace the delivery van.

There are messages for accountants in the notion of bounded rationality. If accounting is to provide useful information for decision making, as our definition states, it should recognise the constraints under which the users of information actually operate, and provide information accordingly. In particular, accountants should attempt to avoid information overload (which might result, for example, from the generation of piles of computer print-out), by filtering out and discarding what they consider to be non-relevant information; they should present information in an easily understandable form; and they should be aware of the users' objectives so as to present information in a way that is easily related to such objectives. These are difficult targets for accountants. The provision of relevant information that relates to decision makers' objectives implies that the accountant knows who uses accounting information and why and how they use it. It is by no means obvious that such knowledge currently exists.

2.8 Group decision making

The provision of information to groups of users poses further problems for the accountant. A group may be viewed as a coalition or collection of individuals (e.g. a trade union, a board of directors or a students' union). If all individuals within the same group have similar objectives and similar power in decision making, conflicts may not arise in the running of the group, and in this case the general decision model of Figure 2.2 may be applicable to group decision making in much the same way as to individual decision making.

If, as is more likely, conflicts between objectives exist within the group, problems arise over and above those encountered in individual decision making. For example, suppose that two doctors combine in partnership and agree to share profits equally. Prior to the setting up of the partnership, Doctor A has divided the week between work and golf on the basis of four days' work and three days' golf, whereas Doctor B has worked for six days and played golf on one day. The solution to the work/leisure problem will ultimately be a compromise, but the outcome of the compromise is likely to reflect the relative bargaining power of the two partners. The outcome may be an agreed five days' work and two days' leisure, or it may be four or six days' work if one partner can impose his or her will on the other and bring about a change in the other's personal preferences. The conflict might also be resolved by a change in the profit-sharing ratio. Imagine this 'conflict situation' transposed to a large industrial organisation whose decision makers (users of accounting information) include such groups as managers, trade unions, shareholders, creditors and customers. If these groups have conflicting objectives, both for themselves and for the organisation, then both decisions and the information needed to make decisions will involve trade-offs which reflect the power of the particular groups.

Finally, we should note that group decision making involves the delegation of decision taking. This in turn may lead to the possibility of suboptimisation within the organisation, meaning that different groups (or individuals) take decisions which maximise their own satisfaction in a way which conflicts with the objectives of the organisation. For example, suppose that a firm makes two products, muesli and honey, and that the objective of the firm is to maximise total cash available from the production and sale of its two products. It may happen that the muesli division undertakes an extensive advertising campaign as a result of which sales of muesli expand and the division's cash surplus increases. However, many of the new consumers of muesli previously ate toast and honey for breakfast and, in consequence of their new-found taste for muesli, their demand for honey declines. The result is that sales of the firm's honey fall and the cash surplus of the honey division decreases, possibly by a larger amount than the increase in the cash surplus of the muesli division. Hence, the muesli division, by maximising its cash surpluses, has caused a decrease in the cash surplus of the firm as a whole. It is one role of accounting information, as we explain in Chapter 18, to resolve this kind of suboptimisation problem.

CHAPTER SUMMARY

In this chapter we have looked at three important concepts for understanding the contribution of accounting to managerial decisions – information, communication and decision making.

We have seen that data are information only if they change the expectations of the person receiving them, and that information has value only if it changes the decision maker's planned course of action. The value of information is the difference between the values of the courses of action the decision maker would take with and without that information.

If information is to influence decisions then it must be communicated to the decision maker. The process of communication can be distorted by *noise*, and the principal source of noise in accounting information is measurement. For accounting measures to be useful for decisions, they should be based on a stable measurement unit, be understandable, cost-effective and precise; but the most important attribute for information is relevance to the decision to be taken.

Models of decision making tend to assume a process of rational choice, whereby the decision maker sets his or her goals, identifies and evaluates alternative courses of action, and selects the alternative that is most consistent with the goals set. In practice, however, much decision making is not completely rational in the sense assumed in such models. Individual decision making is subject to the constraints of bounded rationality, and group decision making will be affected by factors such as conflict between individuals and delegation.

REVIEW QUESTIONS

1. Discuss the differences between 'valuable' and 'valueless' information. Give examples from your own personal experience to illustrate the differences.

2. The problem of 'information overload' is common to many communication systems. Explain the nature of the problem and discuss some possible ways of overcoming it.

3. Why might different users of accounting statements require different information? Can you envisage situations in which different users might require the same information?

4. Discuss the importance of measurement in accounting. Which characteristics of the measuring unit are essential for accounting purposes? Do these characteristics still apply when measurements are used for non-accounting purposes?

5. Is 'rationality' a quality which most of us apply to our decision making? If not, why not? Give examples from your own experience.

Notes

1. American Accounting Association, *A Statement of Basic Accounting Theory*, American Accounting Association, 1966, p. 1.
2. 50% of £300,000 is the probability that the information will confirm that planning permission will be granted; 50% of zero is the probability that the information will indicate that such permission will *not* be granted.
3. The model in Figure 2.1 is an adaptation of the communication model first suggested by C. E. Shannon and W. Weaver in *The Mathematical Theory of Communication*, University of Illinois Press, 1964.

```
┌─────────────┐
│  CHAPTER 3  │
└─────────────┘
```

Wealth and wealth maximisation in decision making

AIMS AND OBJECTIVES

☐ To explain the meaning of wealth and wealth maximisation and their importance in decision making.

☐ To discuss the importance of the time value of money.

☐ To explain the role of discounted present values in the measurement of wealth.

☐ To discuss the importance and treatment of non-financial items in decision making.

In Chapter 2 we discussed a general model for decision making and control. We now turn to the problem of applying the decision model and to a consideration of its implications for accounting. The first stage of the model of the decision process presented in Figure 2.2 was establishing the decision maker's objective. If accounting is to contribute to management decision making then knowledge of the organisation's objective or goal should influence the type of information collected and the choice of criteria used for making recommendations on decisions. In this chapter we look at an objective which is commonly assumed in financial appraisal – wealth maximisation. We consider the meaning of 'wealth' and why it is important in decision making. We also discuss the need to take account of the time value of money and the role of discounted present values in the measurement of wealth. We conclude this chapter with a discussion of the importance and treatment of non-financial data in decision making. In an appendix to the chapter we explain the use and relevance of compound interest tables.

3.1 The meaning and importance of wealth and wealth maximisation

In general, all individuals are concerned with planning their lives in order to achieve the pattern of 'consumption' over time which gives them the most satisfaction. We use 'consumption' here, and indeed throughout the book, in its normal economic sense: that is, to include all goods, services and other 'experiences' that provide satisfaction to the recipient. The above statement of individuals' objectives is self-evident – in order to apply it to a decision-making process we must identify and measure those elements of an individual's life which provide satisfaction, and develop a means of comparing the relative importance of the various elements. It is perhaps helpful to start with a simplified version of the general decision model introduced in the previous chapter. The main steps in the model are as follows:

1. Set objectives.

2. Enumerate available alternatives.

3. Choose alternatives that best satisfy objectives.

The role of accounting is to provide information that clarifies the available alternatives and helps to quantify their effects on objectives. Thus, in order to do their job properly, accountants should be aware of the existence and consequences of available courses of action, and of the objectives of the individual, or group of individuals, for whom they are providing accounting information.

In the previous chapter we considered various groups of users of accounting reports, and the sort of decisions for which they might require information. In order to illustrate the diverse nature of the information that may be needed by just one individual to achieve the preferred pattern of consumption over time, we consider the case of a college student making plans for the coming year. For simplicity, we restrict the time horizon to one year. The information required by the student depends upon his or her objectives and on the entities which will affect his or her life during the coming year. Some possible entities, and the sort of information that might be required from them, are shown in Table 3.1. The list is by no means exhaustive, and will vary from student to student. However, it serves to demonstrate that every individual is likely to require a variety of information from a large number of different sources.

Table 3.1 also draws attention to two further points. The first is that, as we are considering only a one-year decision horizon, the information required relates to the coming year. For example, the student is interested in returns from investments (if any!) and grant income next year, the prices of books, food, clothes, social activities, etc. next year, train and bus timetables for next year, and so on. Published (accounting) information about an entity generally relates to past periods (e.g. as regards returns on investment) or to the present (e.g. with commodity prices). Thus it is often necessary for an individual decision maker to make predictions from information available about the past and the present. This is one of the fundamental problems involved in using and evaluating accounting information, and one to which we shall return.

The second point highlighted by Table 3.1 is that the information required is not exclusively financial. For example, in order to plan for the coming year, the student requires course details from the college, train and bus timetables, concert

Table 3.1 Information a student might require for decision making

Entities affecting student	Information required
Government	Levels of grant and loans available
Local authority	Levels of grant available
College	Scholarships available
Parents	Financial support available
Companies, etc. in which student has invested/ may invest	Returns on investment
Bank	Overdraft and loan facilities available
College	Course details
	Tuition fees
	Costs of residence, meals, etc.
Electricity and gas companies	Lighting and heating costs
Oil companies	Petrol prices
Telephone company	Telephone charges
Post Office	Postage charges
Local bookshop	Prices of academic books
Supermarkets	Food prices
Department stores	Clothes prices
Railway and bus corporations	Train and bus fares
	Train and bus timetables
Local hostelries	Drink prices
	Types of drink available
Local sports stadia	Admission prices
	Fixture lists
Local theatres and concert halls	Programme of future events
	Admission prices

programmes, and so on. We consider the importance of non-financial information further at the end of this chapter. Although non-financial factors have an impact on an individual's decisions, it is often the case that the goods and services of which consumption consists are available only in return for the payment of a cash price. Consequently, while acknowledging the importance of non-financial factors, we shall initially consider the concept of wealth in terms of expected costs and benefits expressed in cash terms.

Individuals are faced with three basic financial decisions:

1. The *investment* decision. How much of the individual's resources should be committed to investment: that is, sacrificed immediately in return for the expectation of increased resources being available at some time in the future? Which particular opportunities should be undertaken with the amounts available for investment?

2. The *financing* decision. How much finance should individuals raise to enable them to undertake their investment and consumption policies? From what sources should this finance be obtained?

3. The *consumption* decision. How much of the individual's resources should be spent on immediate consumption? On what should the resources be spent?

The same three decisions also face firms of all sizes, except that the consumption decision becomes a distribution decision: how much should be distributed to the firm's owners by way of dividend or otherwise? The three decisions are interdependent. The amount committed to investment will depend upon the return available on investment opportunities and also on the cost and availability of finance and the individual's personal consumption preferences. The financing decision will depend upon the cost of finance and upon available investment opportunities and desired patterns of consumption. The consumption decision will depend upon consumption preferences and on available investment and financing opportunities.

Let us consider again the case of a college student. Suppose the student expects to receive in the coming year a local authority grant of £1,800 plus an amount to cover college course fees, a parental gift of £2,600, a student loan of £1,200 and a college scholarship of £400. These amounts, totalling £6,000, represent part of the finance available to be spent. Suppose also that the student estimates costs of £4,800 during the year for essential residence, food, travel, clothes and books. This sum represents part of the amount that will be spent on consumption. Thus after paying essential costs, the student expects to have a cash surplus of £1,200. He or she must decide how much of it to spend on consumption: that is, on goods, services and so on that will not provide benefits in future years, and how much to invest. For example, the student may decide to spend £1,000 during the year on social activities, tickets for concerts and clothes (i.e. on additional consumption) and to invest £200 in a bank deposit account providing an amount of £200 plus interest in *future* years.

In deciding how much to consume and how much to invest, the student will have to weigh the benefits from immediate consumption against the benefits from investment which provides funds for future consumption. This is partly a matter of personal preference and will be influenced by many factors, including the pleasure derived from early rather than delayed consumption, the returns available on investment, and the funds the student expects to have available from other sources in future years. The decisions in respect of the coming year are, in fact, more complicated than we have so far implied. Many students may decide to increase current consumption or investment by borrowing additional funds, for example from the bank or from their parents. This is part of their financing decision.

What sort of information is necessary for decision makers to decide which set of alternatives (investment, financing and consumption) provides most satisfaction or, in other words, which set of alternatives maximises their wealth? It is apparent from the above discussion that, when we talk of wealth as a measure of the current value of future satisfaction, we do not mean only the cash resources and other possessions of an individual at the present time. Consider an example. Who is the better off – an accounting student with little immediate cash and the prospect of very high earnings in the future, or an unskilled worker with some immediate cash resources and little prospect of ever earning much more than basic living expenses? If we consider only the current cash resources of the student and the unskilled worker, we ignore the future cash and other prospects of both, which undoubtedly contribute to the satisfaction they will obtain throughout their respective lives. Thus in order to measure wealth we need to consider both current resources and future prospects.

The importance of such a measure of wealth, which incorporates present position and future prospects, is that it may be used as a criterion in evaluating alternative courses of action – a course of action which increases wealth is worthwhile, one which decreases wealth is not. The measurement of wealth in this sense is not easy, however, even if we restrict our consideration to the cash consequences of alternatives. The basic problem is that we cannot simply add cash expected at different times in the future in order to obtain a measure of present wealth. Few of us would be indifferent between the receipt of £1,000 now and the (certain) receipt of £1,000 five years from now. Such differences between the desirability of £1 at different times in the future give rise to the concept of the time value of money, to which we now turn.

3.2 The time value of money

In the previous section we suggested that £1 now is worth more than £1 at some time in the future. Why is this so? The time value of money is the result of the existence of investment, lending and borrowing opportunities, of the preference that many individuals have for immediate rather than future consumption, and of expected inflation. These factors mean that those who wish to have cash for consumption sooner rather than later incur a cost (pay a price) in so doing, and that those who are willing to defer having cash available for consumption enjoy a benefit (receive a price). The prices paid or received are normally expressed in terms of interest rates which represent the costs or benefits of transferring money from one period to another, in much the same way as costs or benefits arise when other resources are acquired or disposed of.

In practice, a spectrum of interest rates exists at any time in the capital market (i.e. the market in which funds are borrowed and loaned). Rates of interest vary from borrower to borrower and from lender to lender, depending upon the amounts involved, the status of the individual or entity concerned, and so on. In order to simplify our discussion of the role of interest rates in the measurement of wealth, we make two rather unrealistic assumptions at this stage. (Some of the implications of relaxing these assumptions are discussed in Chapter 13.) First, we assume that there are perfect markets for borrowing and lending funds: that is, perfect capital markets. Three conditions must be satisfied if this assumption is to hold:

1. No lenders or borrowers are large enough for their transactions to affect the ruling market price for funds (the interest rate).

2. All traders in the market have equal and costless access to information about the ruling price and all other relevant information.

3. There are no transactions costs involved in using the market and no taxes that would alter economic decisions.

Second, we assume that the future is known with certainty. If these two assumptions hold, there will be a unique market rate of interest, which we shall call i, at which all users of the capital market are able to borrow or lend as much as they wish. Under the conditions assumed, competitive forces are likely to eliminate opportunities to lend or borrow at any interest rate other than i. The assumption of a unique market rate of interest leads to a useful simplification in the measurement of wealth: cash flows which arise at different points in time may be compared without the ambiguities which might arise if a number of different possible interest rates existed.

Given the unique market rate of interest, i, an individual presently in possession of £C could lend it to yield £$C(1 + i)$ after one year, i.e. the return of capital, £C, plus interest £$C \times i$. (In these expressions and all relevant subsequent ones in this chapter, i should be interpreted as the rate of interest expressed as a decimal of 1. Thus, for example, an interest rate of 6% would be written as 0.06 and one of 20% as 0.20.) If capital and interest are lent for a further year, the total returns at the end of the second year will be £$C(1 + i)(1 + i)$, which equals £$C(1 + i)^2$. In general, if an amount £C is invested for n years at an annual compound rate of interest, i, the amount to which it will have accumulated after n years will be £$C(1 + i)^n$. (The word 'compound' indicates that, once the interest for a period has been earned, that interest itself earns interest during subsequent periods. Nowadays this practice is virtually universal in lending and borrowing.) This process is known as *compounding*, and enables us to re-express present values in terms of equivalent future values. A rational individual should be indifferent between £$C(1 + i)^n$ after n years and £C immediately, because possession of the latter could be converted to the former by lending at the market rate of interest.

For the purposes of measuring present wealth, we are interested not so much in re-expressing present values in terms of equivalent future values as in the opposite process of re-expressing expected future cash flows in terms of equivalent present values. This process is known as *discounting*, and provides us with a common basis for measuring wealth, in terms of (discounted) present values.

Suppose an individual expects to receive £C after one year. What is the present value (PV) of the expected receipt? Let us think of PV as the immediate amount the investor would have to lend in order to accumulate £C after one year. Then:

$$PV(1 + i) = £C, \text{ and}$$

$$PV = \frac{£C}{(1 + i)} \qquad \text{(sometimes written as } £C(1 + i)^{-1})$$

By similar reasoning, it may be shown that the present value of £C receivable or payable after two years is £$C/(1 + i)^2$ and, in the general case, that the present value of £C receivable or payable after n years is £$C/(1 + i)^n$. A rational investor should be indifferent between any expected future amount and its present value. For example, in the general case, an individual expecting to receive £C after n years could convert it to £$C/(1 + i)^n$ immediately by borrowing, and an individual with £$C/(1 + i)^n$ could convert it to £C after n years by lending.

The equivalence between an expected cash receipt or payment and its discounted present value enables us to measure the impact of a future cash flow on an individual's or firm's present wealth. It also provides us with a means of calculating the total wealth of an individual or firm, provided we can estimate the amount and timing of all relevant future cash flows; the process is to estimate the future cash flows, discount them to present values and sum the present values. Although we have assumed the existence of a unique interest rate for discounting purposes, the procedure described is often valid in an environment where multiple interest rates exist. Of course, such environments create the additional problem of selecting a discount rate or rates which reflect the individual's or firm's particular borrowing and lending opportunities and the risk associated with expected cash flows. We discuss these problems briefly later, for example in the next chapter, although a detailed consideration of them is beyond the scope of an introductory text.

Let us suppose, as an illustration, that an individual expects to receive net cash inflows (i.e. cash receipts from salary, investment, etc. less essential living expenses) of £3,000 immediately, £5,000 after one year, £7,000 after two years, £8,000 after three years and zero per annum (p.a.) thereafter. In this context, essential living expenses may be regarded as equivalent to the operating expenses of a business. They may be thought of roughly as the expenses of maintaining an 'acceptable' living standard and, in consequence, may vary depending upon the individual's place of work and residence. The relevant interest rate, i, is 10% (0.10) p.a. Assuming that the individual expects no other cash flows and has no other resources, what is his or her present wealth? Following the process described above, we may calculate the individual's wealth as the discounted present value (PV) of the expected net cash inflows:

$$PV = 3,000 + \frac{5,000}{(1+i)} + \frac{7,000}{(1+i)^2} + \frac{8,000}{(1+i)^3}$$

$$PV = 3,000 + \frac{5,000}{(1.1)} + \frac{7,000}{(1.1)^2} + \frac{8,000}{(1.1)^3} = £19,341$$

The individual's present wealth is £19,341.

This concept of wealth is extremely important in decision making; it provides a cornerstone for the decisions of individuals and firms who wish to measure the impact of alternative courses of action on their wealth. In the next section we consider the role of wealth in the evaluation of alternative courses of action.

3.3 The role of present values

So far in this chapter we have discussed the role and importance of wealth measurement primarily as it relates to individuals. It is important to recognise that the discounted present value concept discussed is equally applicable to other economic units, for example businesses or machines. When we apply the concept to such other economic units, we do not generally talk about their wealth, but rather about their value and, in particular, about their 'economic value'.

Take the case of a firm which expects to receive, and distribute to its owners, net cash inflows (i.e. cash receipts from sales, etc. less operating costs) of £50,000 after one year, £65,000 after two years and £100,000 after three years, and nothing thereafter. The relevant interest rate, i, is 15% (0.15) p.a. What is the present economic value (EV) of the firm? Calculating the discounted present value of expected net cash inflows and summing gives:

$$EV = \frac{50,000}{(1+i)} + \frac{65,000}{(1+i)^2} + \frac{100,000}{(1+i)^3}$$

$$EV = \frac{50,000}{(1.15)} + \frac{65,000}{(1.15)^2} + \frac{100,000}{(1.15)^3} = £158,379$$

The present economic value of the firm is £158,379.

Let us now consider the role of discounted present values in evaluating new opportunities. Suppose that the firm in the above illustration is offered the opportunity of investing in a new project. The investment cost would be £10,000, payable after one year, and the project would produce additional net cash inflows of £8,000 after two years and £9,000 after three years. If the firm's owners wish to increase their wealth, the new opportunity should be accepted if it increases the firm's present economic value. The new value (EV$'$) would be:

$$EV' = \frac{(50,000 - 10,000)}{(1.15)} + \frac{(65,000 + 8,000)}{(1.15)^2} + \frac{(100,000 + 9,000)}{(1.15)^3} = £161,650$$

The new project appears worthwhile – its acceptance would increase the present economic value of the firm by £3,271 (£161,650 – £158,379). This increase in the discounted present value of the firm's future cash flows is called the *net present value* (NPV) of the project, and may be calculated more directly by discounting the cash flows of the new opportunity:

$$NPV = \frac{-10,000}{(1.15)} + \frac{8,000}{(1.15)^2} + \frac{9,000}{(1.15)^3} = £3,271$$

A positive net present value implies that acceptance of the project being considered will increase the firm's value (by the amount of the net present value). A negative net present value implies a decrease in the firm's value, and a zero net present value implies no change in the firm's value. Thus net present value provides a useful decision rule for firms whose owners wish to increase the firm's economic value: new investment opportunities should be accepted if their net present values are positive and rejected if they are negative. The firm should be indifferent between acceptance and rejection of projects with zero net present values. This is a most important decision rule which is developed further in Chapter 13.

The meaning and interpretation of net present value may be further clarified in simple cases by regarding it as an additional amount which could be made available for immediate distribution (or consumption) if the opportunity were accepted. In the case of the illustration above, suppose that the firm decides to accept the project and distribute its net present value immediately. As the firm has no cash on hand, it decides to borrow the amount required (£3,271) from its bank at 15% p.a. interest, the rate of interest assumed to be relevant. It also decides to borrow the amount needed to invest in the project, in order not to disturb existing distributions to its owners. Table 3.2 shows the firm's loan account with the bank. The investment opportunity provides just sufficient cash to repay the two loans with interest. In other words, the interest adjustment incorporated in the discounting process takes exact account of the actual money interest cost involved.

For interested readers we now provide a symbolic representation of the measures used so far in this chapter for calculating economic value (wealth) and net present value. Economic value, or wealth, may be described by the expression:

$$EV_0 = \frac{C_1}{(1+i)} + \frac{C_2}{(1+i)^2} + \frac{C_3}{(1+i)^3} + \cdots + \frac{C_n}{(1+i)^n}$$

where: EV_0 is the economic value at time 0 (i.e. the present time),
C_1 is the net cash inflow expected at time 1 (i.e. after one year),
C_2 is the net cash inflow expected at time 2, and so on,
n is the last time at which a cash flow is expected to arise,
i is the appropriate interest rate.

Table 3.2 Firm's loan account with the bank

	£
Immediately: Borrow project NPV for distribution to owners	3,271
After one year: Interest at 15%	491
Borrow for investment in project	10,000
Loan outstanding at the end of one year	13,762
After two years: Interest at 15%	2,064
	15,826
Use first cash inflow from project to repay part of loan	8,000
Loan outstanding at the end of two years	7,826
After three years: Interest at 15%	1,174
	9,000
Use second cash inflow from project to repay balance of loan	9,000
Loan outstanding at the end of three years	0

This expression may be more conveniently written:[1]

$$EV_0 = \Sigma_{j=1}^n \frac{C_j}{(1 + i)^j}$$

The net present value (NPV) of a project may be described by:

$$NPV = \Sigma_{j=0}^n \frac{F_j}{(1 + i)^j}$$

where: F_j is the net cash inflow expected at time j,[2]

n is the last time at which a cash flow is expected from the project,

i is the appropriate interest rate.

3.4 The importance of non-financial data

So far in this chapter we have concentrated on the application of financial data to the measurement of wealth. We now turn to a brief consideration of the importance of non-financial data. Although accounting reports are traditionally concerned with financial data, the wealth of those who use the reports, and in consequence their decisions, may also be influenced by factors which are generally not expressed in money terms: that is, by non-financial factors. Indeed for some decisions, particularly in the public sector, concerned for example with health and education services, non-financial factors may be much more important than financial ones. We discuss first some decisions which may be affected by non-financial factors, and then consider the extent to which accountants might help in the provision of information about such factors.

In Chapter 2 we considered a variety of users of accounting reports. Such users may use non-financial as well as financial information in their decision processes. Investors in quoted companies, for example, make decisions about buying, holding and selling shares and about the extent to which they should intervene in the management of companies in which they hold shares. In addition to financial factors, non-financial information may be of interest to them. Their decisions may be influenced by the prestige of a company and by the investors' political and moral beliefs (for example, some investors may not wish to hold shares in tobacco companies). They will require information about such aspects of the company, and about the extent to which their actions as shareholders might affect the company's behaviour.

The employees of an organisation may also require non-financial information in making decisions about whether to stay with their present employers or change jobs, and in negotiating wage and salary claims. Like shareholders, they may be conscious of the prestige differences between organisations (some journalists, for example, may prefer to work for a national rather than a local newspaper) and about their different political and moral behaviour. They may also be interested in conditions of work (health and safety regulations, the length of the working week, holiday entitlements, and so on) and in job satisfaction (most university teachers, for example, probably regard this as a major attraction of their employment).

Government is also likely to require non-financial information from organisations. For example, if it wishes to formulate legislation designed to protect the environment, government will require information from public and private sector organisations about the extent of pollution and other factors harmful to the environment, caused by the organisation's activities. A company's potential customers will be interested, among other things, in the quality of the company's products. A student, in deciding which courses to take, will require information about staff–student ratios and the quality of staff in different departments, and about the interest level of different courses.

The need for non-financial information is not restricted to those outside the organisation – management too may make use of such information. In recent years there has been an increasing emphasis on non-financial measures as part of the management information system. These measures have been used to help communicate objectives throughout the organisation, to motivate staff and to give additional dimensions to performance measurement. For example, measures such as the number of credit notes issued, the volume of goods returned, and the number of times orders are not fulfilled or delivery deadlines are missed are all non-financial measures related to ideas of how well the organisation is serving customer needs. Similar measures may be used in service organisations. For example, a travel agent might measure the average time before a customer is served or a telephone caller is answered. These forms of non-financial measurement are sometimes referred to as *key performance indicators* and have become increasingly prevalent in the management of businesses of all kinds during the last ten years.

The above examples illustrate the sort of non-financial information that might be required about organisations' operations by different groups. It is apparent that such information will often have a significant impact on the eventual decision. The questions we now need to ask are: Should accountants attempt to provide this sort of information? Are they in a position to provide it?

As we noted earlier, the role of the accountant is traditionally restricted to the provision of financial information. However, if decisions are to be taken in the light of the maximum possible relevant information, someone ought to be providing information about non-financial factors, and accountants would seem to have as strong a claim to this role as any other group. (Whether accountants would welcome this additional burden is another question!) As accountants are already responsible for providing a substantial part of the information required for decisions – that is, the financial part – there would seem to be some sense in their providing at least some of the remaining information.

Accountants also appear to be in a good position to provide non-financial information. In some cases it may be possible and helpful to assign financial values to items which, at first sight, appear non-financial. For example, various studies evaluating the worth of constructing the Victoria Line on the London Underground system included attempts to put financial values on the time that would be saved by commuters and others if the line was built.[3] Even if financial values cannot be imputed, it will often be possible for wealth measurement and decision making to adopt a different unit of measurement: for example, the number of students to each member of staff in a college department, the number of hours in a working week at a particular organisation, or the quantity of chemicals introduced into a river by a particular production process. If accountants are to assume some responsibility for the provision of non-financial information, their eventual aim should probably be to use financial measurements wherever reasonable and feasible, and to quantify other factors using the most appropriate available unit of measurement. In this way, those responsible for making decisions will have available to them the maximum possible amount of quantitative data. They must then use their own judgement to weigh financial and non-financial factors in arriving at a final decision.

In the remainder of this book we recognise the traditional role of the accountant as being primarily a provider of financial information. Nevertheless, where non-financial items arise in subsequent examples and discussions, we attempt to suggest ways in which they might be handled.

CHAPTER SUMMARY

A knowledge of the decision maker's objectives is important if accounting is to fulfil a role in providing relevant information about alternative courses of action that the decision maker is considering. Accounting information should help relate actions to objectives by quantifying the effect of different alternatives on the realisation of objectives. In the context of economic decision making it is common to assume an objective of *wealth maximisation*, and in this chapter we have looked at the implications of this objective for accounting information. Under this approach alternatives that are wealth enhancing are considered worthwhile.

Two important aspects of the information that will be relevant for decision making are, first, that it will involve prediction and consideration of future flows (to measure wealth it is necessary to look at both current resources and future flows) and, second, that non-financial information may be relevant as well as financial.

In evaluating future flows of resources, the cash outflows and inflows associated with a course of action, account must be taken of *the time value of money* – the fact that the effect of a cash flow on wealth depends on its timing. *Discounting* gives a procedure for allowing for the time value of money and expressing future flows in terms of their present value. Opportunities that have a positive *net present value* should be accepted as wealth enhancing, and those with a negative net present value rejected.

A wide variety of information will be relevant to any decision. As well as data for a financial appraisal, this will include much information that is non-financial. The use of non-financial indicators as part of the management information system has increased significantly in recent years. Accounting is concerned primarily with the provision of financial information to support decisions (the subject of this book), but accountants may also be involved in collecting and processing non-financial information.

Use of compound interest tables

Earlier in this chapter we introduced the ideas of compounding and discounting, particularly for purposes of calculating economic values and net present values. Such compound interest methods are now widely used in accounting and will be referred to again in the remainder of this book. In practice, the calculations involved may be quite complex and for this reason they are often undertaken by use of a computer. Where a more simple calculator is used, special tables, known as compound interest tables, are available to facilitate the calculations. The purpose of this appendix is to explain and illustrate the use of compound interest tables, and to deal with a number of other problems frequently encountered when discounting or compounding calculations are undertaken.

A full set of compound interest tables is provided at the end of the book (pp. 418–29). Each table is based on a different interest rate. For simplicity, we will use only one interest rate, 8%, in this appendix. Each table consists of seven columns. The first column (headed n) relates to the number of years involved in the calculation to be performed. The remaining six columns give either compounded or discounted values, under various circumstances, for a basic unit of £1 or £1 per annum (or for basic units of 1 dollar, 1 franc, 1 yen, 1 mark, etc.). We now provide an explanation of each of these six columns. Throughout the appendix i means the annual compound interest rate and n means the relevant time period.

The meaning of each column in compound interest tables

$(1 + i)^n$

In words, each figure in this column represents the amount to which £1 invested now at a compound rate of interest i will accumulate *after n years*. We use annual periods for ease of exposition. Periods of other lengths may be used, provided that the interest rate is expressed as a rate per the appropriate period. This is the column to be used to compound the value of a single sum.

Illustration: An individual invests £100 in a bank deposit account at a compound interest rate of 8% p.a. To what amount will the £100 have grown by the end of seven years?

Terminal value $= 100(1 + i)^7 = 100(1.08)^7$

From the table, $(1 + i)^n = 1.7138$ for $n = 7$ and $i = 8\%$.

Terminal value $= 100(1.7138) = £171.38$

Now suppose that the £100 is invested in a bank deposit account at a compound interest rate of 3% per *quarter*. To what amount will the £100 have grown by the end of three years (i.e. by the end of 12 quarters)?

Terminal value $= 100(1 + i)^{12} = 100(1.03)^{12}$

From the table, $(1 + i)^n = 1.4258$ for $n = 12$ and $i = 3\%$.

Terminal value $= 100(1.4258) = £142.58$

$V_{\overline{n}|}$ (pronounced 'V angle n')
In words, each figure in this column represents the value *now* (the present value) of £1 expected in n years' time, at a compound rate of interest i. Each value given is the reciprocal of the equivalent figure in the $(1 + i)^n$ column, i.e. each figure is calculated from the expression $1/(1 + i)^n$. This column should be used to discount the value of a single sum.

    Illustration: An individual expects to receive £700 after five years. What is the present value of the expected receipt, assuming an annual compound interest rate of 8%?

$$\text{Present value} = \frac{700}{(1 + i)^5} = \frac{700}{(1.08)^5}$$

From the table, $1/(1 + i)^n = V_{\overline{n}|}\,i = 0.680583$ for $n = 5$ and $i = 8\%$.

Present value $= 700(0.680583) = £476.41$

In other words, £476.41 now should grow to £700 after five years. We may check this answer by using the previous column:

$476.41\ (1.08)^5 = 476.41\ (1.4693) = £700$

$S_{\overline{n}|}$ (pronounced 'S angle n')
In words, each figure in this column represents the value *at the end of n years* of £1 p.a. payable or receivable for n years. The first payment or receipt arises at the *end* of year 1 and the last one at the end of year n. A series of annual receipts or payments of identical amount is known as an annuity. Thus this column is used to find the future or terminal value of an annuity. Each value given is based on the expression:

$$S_{\overline{n}|} = \left(\frac{(1 + i)^n - 1}{i} \right)$$

This expression is the summation of the geometric progression:

$$1 + (1 + i) + (1 + i)^2 + \cdots + (1 + i)^{n-1}$$

where the first term (1) is the terminal value of the last receipt or payment (of £1), the second term $(1 + i)$ is the terminal value of the penultimate receipt or payment (of £1) and so on.

Illustration: An individual intends to invest £50 in a bank deposit account at the end of each of the next seven years. What amount will be accumulated in the deposit account at the end of year 7, assuming an annual compound rate of interest of 8%?

$$\text{Terminal value} = 50(1 + i)^6 + 50(1 + i)^5 + \cdots + 50(1 + i) + 50$$
$$= 50[(1 + i)^6 + (1 + i)^5 + \cdots + (1 + i) + 1]$$

From the table,

$$[1 + (1 + i) + \cdots + (1 + i)^{n-2} + (1 + i)^{n-1}]$$
$$= S_{\overline{n|}}i = 8.9228 \text{ for } n = 7 \text{ and } i = 8\%$$
$$\text{Terminal value} = 50(8.9228) = £446.14$$

$S_{\overline{n|}}^{-1}$ (pronounced '*S* angle *n* minus 1')
In words, each figure in this column represents the annual sum that it is necessary to invest at the end of each of the next *n* years in order to accumulate £1 *at the end of year n*. Each value given is the reciprocal of the equivalent figure in the $S_{\overline{n|}}$ column, i.e. each figure is calculated from the expression $1/S_{\overline{n|}}$. This column should be used to convert a single future sum into an annuity.

Illustration: An individual wishes to accumulate £5,000 in four years from now in order to purchase a motor car. How much is it necessary to invest at the end of each of the next four years, assuming an annual compound rate of interest of 8%?

If we call the annual amount to be invested *a*, then:

$$5,000 = a(1 + i)^3 + a(1 + i)^2 + a(1 + i) + a$$
$$5,000 = a[(1 + i)^3 + (1 + i)^2 + (1 + i) + 1]$$
$$a \quad = 5,000\left[\frac{1}{(1 + i)^3 + (1 + i)^2 + (1 + i) + 1}\right]$$
$$= 5,000\left[\frac{1}{S_{\overline{n|}}i}\right]$$

From the table, $1/S_{\overline{n|}}i = S_{\overline{n|}}^{-1}i = 0.221921$ for $n = 4$ and $i = 8\%$.

$$\text{Annual amount} = 5,000(0.221921) = £1,109.60$$

Obviously, the same answer could be obtained by dividing the required terminal amount by the relevant factor in the $S_{\overline{n|}}$ column:

$$\text{Annual amount} = \frac{5,000}{S_{\overline{n|}}8\%} = \frac{5,000}{4.5061} = £1,109.60$$

The sort of calculation involved in this illustration is usually called a 'sinking fund' calculation.

$A_{\overline{n}|}$ (pronounced 'A angle n')

In words, each figure in this column represents the value *now* (the present value) of £1 p.a., payable or receivable for n years. The first payment or receipt arises at the *end* of year 1 and the last one at the end of year n. This column is used to find the present value of an annuity. Each value given is based on the expression

$$A_{\overline{n}|} = \left(\frac{1 - \dfrac{1}{(1+i)^n}}{i} \right)$$

This expression is the summation of the geometric progression:

$$\frac{1}{(1+i)} + \frac{1}{(1+i)^2} + \cdots + \frac{1}{(1+i)^n}$$

where the first term is the present value of the first receipt or payment, and so on.

Illustration: An individual expects to receive £50 at the end of each of the next seven years. What is the present value of the expected receipts, assuming an annual compound interest rate of 8%?

$$\text{Present value} = \frac{50}{(1+i)} + \frac{50}{(1+i)^2} + \cdots + \frac{50}{(1+i)^7}$$

$$= 50 \left[\frac{1}{(1+i)} + \frac{1}{(1+i)^2} + \cdots + \frac{1}{(1+i)^7} \right]$$

From the table,

$$\left[\frac{1}{(1+i)} + \frac{1}{(1+i)^2} + \cdots + \frac{1}{(1+i)^n} \right] = A_{\overline{n}|}i = 5.2064$$

for $n = 7$ and $i = 8\%$.

Present value $= 50(5.2064) = £260.32$

In the above illustration we used the same basic annuity data as in the $S_{\overline{n}|}$ illustration. Both $A_{\overline{n}|}$ and $S_{\overline{n}|}$ columns sum annuity values to a single amount – the former at the start of the annuity period and the latter at the end. The relationship between the figures in the two columns is as follows:[4]

$$A_{\overline{n}|} = S_{\overline{n}|} \times V_{\overline{n}|}$$

Using the annuity in the above illustrations:

$260.32 = 446.14 \times V_{\overline{7}|}8\% = 446.14 \times 0.583490$

$A_{\overline{n}|}^{-1}$ (pronounced 'A angle n minus 1')

In words, each figure in this column represents the annual sum that it is necessary to pay at the end of each of the next n years in order to repay *an immediate loan of £1*. Each value given is the reciprocal of the equivalent figure in the $A_{\overline{n}|}$ column, i.e. each figure is calculated from the expression $1/A_{\overline{n}|}$. This column is used to convert a single immediate sum into an annuity.

Illustration: An individual borrows £16,000 from a building society to be repaid, with compound interest at 8%, by equal annual instalments over the next 20 years. What is the amount of the annual payment that will have to be made at the end of each of the next 20 years?

If we call the annual amount to be paid a, then:

$$16,000 = \frac{a}{(1+i)} + \frac{a}{(1+i)^2} + \cdots + \frac{a}{(1+i)^{20}}$$

$$16,000 = a\left[\frac{1}{(1+i)} + \frac{1}{(1+i)^2} + \cdots + \frac{1}{(1+i)^{20}}\right]$$

$$a = 16,000\left[\frac{1}{\dfrac{1}{(1+i)} + \dfrac{1}{(1+i)^2} + \cdots + \dfrac{1}{(1+i)^{20}}}\right]$$

$$= 16,000\left[\frac{1}{A_{\overline{20}|}i}\right]$$

From the table, $1/A_{\overline{n}|}i = A_{\overline{n}|}^{-1}i = 0.101852$ for $n = 20$ and $i = 8\%$.

Annual amount $= 16,000(0.101852) = £1,629.63$

The same answer could be obtained by dividing the amount borrowed by the relevant factor in the $A_{\overline{n}|}$ column:

$$\text{Annual amount} = \frac{16,000}{A_{\overline{20}|}\,8\%} = \frac{16,000}{9.8181} = £1,629.63$$

Perpetuities

We saw in the previous section that the present value of an annuity may generally be calculated using the $A_{\overline{n}|}$ column of the compound interest tables. We now consider a particular type of annuity, known as a perpetuity, for which this treatment is inappropriate. A perpetuity is an annuity which is expected to last indefinitely: for example, undated government stocks on which a fixed amount of interest is paid each year, but on which the capital is unlikely ever to be repaid. The figures in the compound interest tables are all based on finite time periods, and in consequence are unsuitable for streams of receipts and payments which are expected to last indefinitely. Fortunately, a very simple formula is available for calculating the present value of a perpetuity. Let us consider again the expression for calculating the present value of an annuity of £1 p.a., described above:

$$A_{\overline{n}|} = \left(\frac{1 - \dfrac{1}{(1+i)^n}}{i} \right)$$

As the value of n increases, i.e. as the life of the annuity lengthens, the value of the term $1/(1+i)^n$ in the above expression becomes smaller. As n tends towards infinity (i.e. as the annuity tends to become a perpetuity), the value of $1/(1+i)^n$ tends towards zero and the value of the whole expression tends towards $1/i$. Thus:

$$\text{Present value of perpetuity of £1 per annum} = \frac{1}{i}$$

It follows that the present value of any perpetuity is given by the annual receipt or payment divided by the relevant rate of interest. So the present value of a perpetuity of £100, at an annual compound rate of interest of 8% is:

$$\text{Present value} = \frac{100}{0.08} = £1,250$$

Looked at another way, £1,250 invested at 8% p.a. will produce a return of £100 each and every year.

Deferred and advanced annuities and perpetuities

The tables and formulae discussed so far for calculating the present values of annuities and perpetuities are based on the assumption that the first annual receipt or payment is due after one year (i.e. at time 1). In other words, the formulae give the lump sum value of the annuity one year before the first receipt or payment is due. Adjustments are necessary if the annuity being considered does not comply with this pattern: that is, if its starting date is deferred or advanced.

Consider first the case where the first receipt or payment is deferred. For example, suppose that an individual expects to receive five annual amounts of £100, the first receipt being after two years (i.e. at time 2). What is the present value (at time 0) of the annuity, assuming an annual compound interest rate of 8%? If we simply apply the five-year $A_{\overline{n}|}$ factor from the 8% table to the annuity, we get the value one year before the first receipt, i.e. at time 1. We require the value at time 0.

The necessary adjustment may be achieved in one of two ways. The first is to discount the calculated time 1 value to time 0, using the $V_{\overline{n}|}$ factor for one year:

$$\begin{aligned} \text{Present value} &= 100 \times A_{\overline{5}|}\, 8\% \times V_{\overline{1}|}\, 8\% \\ &= 100(3.9927)(0.925926) = \pounds369.70 \end{aligned}$$

The second is to take the annuity factor for the period from the present to the time of the last annual receipt (time 6 here), subtract from it the annuity factor for the period of deferral (one year here), and multiply the difference by the annual amount:

$$\begin{aligned} \text{Present value} &= 100 \times (A_{\overline{6}|}\, 8\% - A_{\overline{1}|}\, 8\%) \\ &= 100(4.6229 - 0.9259) = \pounds369.70 \end{aligned}$$

Consider now the case where the first annual receipt or payment is advanced. For example, suppose that an individual expects to receive five annual amounts of £100, and that the first receipt is due immediately. What is the present value of the annuity, assuming an annual compound rate of interest of 8%? It is necessary now to split the annuity into two parts; the immediate first instalment (due at time 0) and the remaining instalments (due at times 1, 2, 3 and 4) which comply with the pattern assumed in the annuity formula:

$$\begin{aligned} \text{Present value} &= 100 + 100 \times A_{\overline{4}|}\, 8\% \\ &= 100 + 100(3.3121) = \pounds431.21 \end{aligned}$$

Further comments

We conclude this appendix with two further comments which may be of use to the student with little previous experience of compound interest methods. The first is that, of the six columns described earlier, two ($V_{\overline{n}|}$ and $A_{\overline{n}|}$) are used much more frequently in accounting than are the remaining four. The mastery of these two columns in particular will greatly facilitate the understanding of a number of subsequent sections of this book.

The second comment is that a mechanical application of the factors in the tables to uncertain estimates will often result in an answer which appears extremely precise. Suppose that a new project costs £100 and is expected to produce one net cash inflow of roughly £200 at the end of seven years. We may calculate the net present value of the project, assuming an interest rate of 8%, as:

$$\begin{aligned} \text{NPV} &= -100 + 200 \times V_{\overline{7}|}\, 8\% \\ &= -100 + 200(0.583490) = +\pounds16.698 \end{aligned}$$

The precision implied by the net present value is illusory, given the approximate nature of the net cash inflow estimate. It may be sensible to round the answer to the nearest £1, £5 or £10 if the decision maker is not to be confused. We consider in the next chapter some more refined methods of dealing with risk and uncertainty!

REVIEW QUESTIONS

1. What is 'wealth' and why is it important in the decision-making process? Describe the factors that you might consider in attempting to measure your own wealth.

2. Outline the three basic financial decisions which face most entities and illustrate the interdependences between the decisions.

3. Explain what is meant by the 'time value of money' and discuss its importance in the measurement of wealth.

4. Define the 'economic value' of an enterprise and the 'net present value' of a project and explain the relationship between the two.

5. Discuss, giving examples, the importance of non-financial data to the measurement of wealth and consider the extent to which accountants should be responsible for the provision of non-financial information.

EXERCISES

3.1 Mr Bizet expects to receive net cash inflows (i.e. cash receipts from salary, investment and pension less essential living expenses) of £20,000 immediately, £80,000 after one year, £30,000 at the end of each of the subsequent twenty years and zero thereafter. He assesses his relevant discount rate at 15% p.a. He expects no cash flows other than those described above and has no other resources.

Estimate Mr Bizet's present wealth. (Solution at end of text.)

3.2 Dvorak plc expects to make the following cash distributions (dividend payments) to its owners:

Time	Dividend payment (£000)
After 1 year	500
After 2 years	550
After 3 years	600
At the end of *each* subsequent year, continuing indefinitely	700

The directors of Dvorak plc estimate that the return required by the company's owners is 20% p.a.

(a) Estimate the value of Dvorak plc to its owners, based on expected future dividend payments.

(b) Discuss any other factors which might influence the value of Dvorak plc to its owners. (Solution at end of text.)

3.3   Byrd Ltd has recently undertaken a feasibility study at a cost of £20,000 to assess the desirability of adding a new product, the blake, to its existing range. The new product would have a life of five years and the feasibility study suggests that 10,000 units could be sold annually at a price of £3 each.

   The production manager of Byrd Ltd estimates that variable cost per unit would be £1.50 during each year of the product's life. He also argues that the blake would have to bear its 'fair share of fixed costs' and suggests an allocated cost of £1 per blake. The total fixed costs of Byrd Ltd (excluding depreciation on the special machine required) would be the same whether or not blakes were manufactured.

   Manufacture of blakes would require the purchase of a special machine for £50,000, payable immediately. The machine has an expected economic life of five years, at the end of which it could be sold for scrap for £2,000. Byrd Ltd can lend and borrow money at a compound interest rate of 10% p.a. Assume that all cash inflows and outflows will arise at the end of the year to which they relate, with the exception of the initial cost of the machine.

   (a) Prepare calculations showing whether Byrd Ltd should manufacture blakes.

   (b) Justify the appraisal method you have used in (a), and note any reservations you have about your advice.

3.4   *Compound interest problems*
   Assume a relevant interest rate of 10% in each of the following problems. Show your workings.

   (a) Mr Baldovinetti wishes to purchase a 20-year annuity. He has available a sum of £10,000 to spend on the annuity. What annual amount should he expect to receive?

   (b) An investment is expected to produce annual cash returns of £3,000 indefinitely. The first receipt is expected to arise in one year's time. What is the present value (PV) of the investment?

   (c) How would your answer to (b) differ if the first receipt was expected immediately?

   (d) How would your answer to (b) differ if the first receipt was expected after two years?

   (e) Klee Ltd has the opportunity to invest in a project which will produce only one cash return: £7,000 after six years. What is the maximum amount Klee Ltd should be willing to pay immediately to undertake the investment?

   (f) Berg Ltd has just purchased a new machine for £50,000. The machine is expected to last for four years. The company wishes to set aside and invest a constant annual amount at the end of each of the next four years which, together with accumulated interest, will provide for replacement of the machine at the end of its life. The cost of a replacement machine in four years is expected to be £75,000. How much should the company set aside each year?

(g) How would your answer to (f) differ if the annual amount was to be set aside and invested at the beginning of each of the next four years?

(h) Mrs Ives buys a car on hire-purchase. She pays a cash deposit of £1,000 and agrees to pay the balance by four annual instalments of £800. The first instalment is due one year after the purchase date. What is the 'cash price' of the car (i.e. the price if Mrs Ives paid in full at the time of purchase)?

(i) Mr Arne decides to provide for his retirement (18 years from now) by investing £500 at the end of each of the next 18 years. What lump sum will he have available on retirement?

3.5   It is 31 March 19X1 and Papageno is presently employed looking after the birds in the local zoo for which he was paid £20,000 for the 12 months to 31 March 19X1. His employers have assured him that his post with the zoo is safe for the next five years and that his salary will be increased to keep pace with general inflation levels. However, Papageno feels that he may be able to improve his position if he buys a pet-shop business which has just come up for sale. The pet-shop owner has provided the following details for the year ended 31 March 19X1.

Pet sales	£60,000	(expected to increase at 8% p.a.)
Feed and other costs	£12,000	(expected to increase at 13% p.a.)
Site rent	£4,000	(fixed for the next five years and payable at the start of each year)

The pet-shop owner is asking £200,000 for his business and has estimated that if the business is managed in a proper fashion then Papageno should be able to sell it 'for a minimum of £280,000 in five years' time'.

Papageno is only interested in looking five years into the future and conducts his affairs in such a way that it is a reasonable approximation to assume that all his cash flows (with the exception of site rent) arise at the end of each year. The bank manager has offered to lend Papageno £200,000 at a fixed rate of interest of 12% for the next five years. The bank manager has also told Papageno that his best estimate of the rate of general inflation for the next five years is 10%.

(a) Prepare calculations to show whether Papageno should buy the pet-shop business.

(b) Explain to Papageno any reservations you have about the calculations performed in part (a).

(c) Discuss what other factors should be considered by Papageno.

Notes

1. The Greek letter Σ (sigma) is convenient mathematical shorthand, meaning the sum of all values in a particular series. By introducing lower and upper limits (written below and above Σ), we may define the summation of a particular series between certain limits. So:

$$\sum_{i=1}^{i=n} x_i \left(\text{or} \sum_{i=1}^{n} x_i \right) = x_1 + x_2 + x_3 + \cdots + x_n$$

2. Usually, the first cash flow (at least) associated with a project will be negative, i.e. the investment cost. The introduction of negative signs before some of the F_j values does not affect the validity or application of the NPV expression.

3. See, for example, C. D. Foster and M. E. Beesley, 'The Victoria Line: social benefit and finances', *Journal of the Royal Statistical Society*, Series A, **128**(1), 1965; and 'Estimating the social benefit of constructing an underground railway in London', *Journal of the Royal Statistical Society*, Series A, **126**(1), 1963.

4. This relationship may be easily proved, using the definitions of $A_{\overline{n}|}$, $S_{\overline{n}|}$ and $V_{\overline{n}|}$ given earlier:

$$\left(\frac{1 - \dfrac{1}{(1+i)^n}}{i} \right) = \left(\frac{(1+i)^n - 1}{i} \right) \times \frac{1}{(1+i)^n}$$

Multiplying each side by $(1+i)^n$ gives

$$\left(\frac{1(1+i)^n - \dfrac{(1+i)^n}{(1+i)^n}}{i} \right) = \left(\frac{(1+i)^n - 1}{i} \right)$$

Risk and uncertainty in decision making

AIMS AND OBJECTIVES
- ☐ To explain the importance of risk in decision making.
- ☐ To discuss the role of probabilities and expected values in the evaluation of risk.
- ☐ To explain and illustrate the concept of portfolio analysis.
- ☐ To introduce other approaches to the treatment of risk and uncertainty.

A main feature of the approach to accounting adopted in this book is the emphasis on deriving accounting information *which is useful for decision making*. This emphasis applies to all types of accounting information – whether for use by managers within the organisation, or for external use by shareholders, government and other interested parties.

Information for decision making invariably possesses both quantitative and qualitative characteristics. Decisions are rarely taken on the basis of numbers alone. Intuition, experience and judgement often constitute a major element of the decision process. But there is one facet of decision making which is always present, irrespective of the nature of the decision. Every decision entails making a *prediction*.

Decisions are characterised by their orientation to the future. Past events in themselves are virtually never relevant to current decisions, as they cannot be affected by any decision which is taken (although, as we discuss later, they may play an important role in the prediction of relevant future events). But prediction is a notoriously difficult task. We are never able to predict the future with certainty – it would indeed be a dull world if we could. Thus we might say that the very essence of decision making, in our personal lives as in business situations, lies in the making of predictions which try to accommodate the many uncertainties that the future holds.

We note at this stage that a distinction is often drawn between risk and uncertainty. Risk is defined as a situation in which there are several possible outcomes and there is material statistical evidence relating to them. Risks are normally capable of being insured. Uncertainty is said to exist where there are again several possible outcomes, but where there is little previous statistical evidence to guide the decision maker in predicting them. Most business decisions fall into this category. The distinction between risk and uncertainty in decision making seems to be of little practical assistance and henceforth the terms will be used interchangeably.

4.1 'Probably' statements

When speaking of future intentions or outcomes we frequently use the word 'probably'. We use it to qualify the chosen verb, because we cannot know precisely what will happen in the future. For example, looking at next weekend's football fixtures, we might say that 'Oldham Athletic will probably lose on Saturday'. We cannot be absolutely sure about this, but as we see that they are playing Liverpool then we believe there is a good chance that we are right.

Predictions, or 'probably' statements, do not in themselves mean a great deal. The mere making of a prediction does not imply the making of a decision. If, however, we choose, on the basis of a prediction, to take a decision which involves us in a subsequent course of action, then the prediction itself assumes importance. For example, if we say that 'As it will probably rain tomorrow (prediction), we will go to the cinema in the afternoon (decision)', we are, in effect, saying that it is the probability of rain which determines the cinema visit. In summary, although we can make a prediction without making a decision, we cannot make a decision without making a prediction.

4.2 Predictions and probabilities

Our discussion of predictions has not so far involved us in any refined attempt at quantifying the likelihood of a particular event occurring. Our examples have involved intuitive guesses (perhaps based on past experience of similar situations) which express our opinion that there is a good chance that a particular outcome will occur. In many situations, however, decisions may be based on a more mathematically ordered prediction of future outcomes. For example, we might say that 'As there is a 90% chance that Oldham Athletic will lose to Liverpool, we will not go to the game'. The percentage figure expresses our personal degree of confidence in the outcome of our prediction.

In mathematical terms a probability of outcome is usually represented by a decimal number on a scale from 0, which denotes a nil likelihood of occurrence, to 1, which signifies absolute certainty – a definite occurrence. For example, a 70% chance of rain tomorrow is expressed as a probability of 0.7.

Probabilities are based on mathematical laws which depend for their validity upon the existence of a large number of situations. (This observation will assume more importance as we develop our explanation of probabilities in a business situation.) The application of probability theory is intended to give decision makers two important pieces of information. First, it provides a notion of the *range* of possible outcomes of the decision, and second, it offers information on the *likelihood* and *size* of deviations of actual outcomes from the expected outcome. Probabilities are used to calculate not the *specific* value or outcome of any particular decision, but rather the *expected* value or outcome. The terms 'expected value' and 'expected outcome' will be used widely in our subsequent discussion of business decisions, so we should be quite clear as to their meaning. In a statistical sense, the word 'expected' refers to the 'average' or 'mean' outcome of a decision. Strictly speaking the expected value of a decision represents the *long-run average outcome, expected if a particular course of action is undertaken many times.* For example, the assertion that there is an equal probability of a tossed coin landing 'heads' or 'tails' really means that, if the coin is tossed a large number of times, it will come down heads about half of the time, and tails about half of the time.

4.3 Business decisions and expected values

The attachment of probabilities to expected outcomes is of fundamental importance in business life. Business decision makers do not live in a deterministic (certain) world. They live, as we all do, in a world of uncertainty – a world of probabilities. For example, a business manager contemplating the purchase of a large expensive machine which is intended to increase a firm's productive capacity will try to predict (among other things) the additional yearly cash flows which will accrue to the firm because of the decision to buy the machine. These cash flows will be uncertain, both in their timing and in their amount, and the manager may use probabilities to determine their expected values. The expected (present) value of these uncertain future cash flows may well influence the purchase decision. Alternatively, the manager may be contemplating an addition to the firm's existing range of products. In this case he may use probabilities to estimate the level of market share he can expect on the basis of alternative pricing policies. Equally, shareholders might wish to estimate the likely level of dividends receivable from their shareholdings. The use of probabilities may help in this estimation.

Expected values can be derived in a variety of ways which use different levels of intuition, experience and formal mathematical analysis. Indeed most derivations of probabilities use *all* of these qualitative and quantitative factors, although the proportions of each may vary depending on the particular decision. Probabilities will normally be determined in the light of past experience. For example, shareholders may choose to invest in a particular company on the basis that its ability to earn profits and pay dividends in the future will reflect its proven ability to earn profits and pay dividends in the past. Managers who are considering whether to undertake a new investment may base their predictions of the likely net benefits from the investment on the results of similar investments undertaken previously. The degree of formality employed in any decision will usually be determined on a cost–benefit basis: that is, the extra costs involved in pursuing a more rigorous approach to the determination of expected values should be viewed not in isolation, but rather in relation to the benefits obtained from the extra information provided by the more rigorous analysis.

In the remainder of this chapter we look in more detail at possible approaches to incorporating uncertainty into decision making, with particular emphasis on two methods: expected value analysis and portfolio analysis.

Expected values: illustration 1

Suppose that a company, Ninian plc, is considering whether to undertake a new contract, of similar size and characteristics to a contract which has been undertaken 100 times previously. The results of the previous contracts, expressed in terms of the present value of the cash surplus (or deficit) are as follows:

Result cash surplus/ (deficit) (£) (1)	Number of times the result has occurred (2)	Probability of occurrence (3)
(20,000)	8	0.08
(5,000)	22	0.22
3,000	40	0.40
7,000	18	0.18
10,000	12	0.12
	$\Sigma = 100$	$\Sigma = 1.00$

Column 1 reveals that there have been five different outcomes from the previous 100 contracts, varying from a deficit of £20,000 to a surplus of £10,000. Column 1 thus gives information on the *range* of outcomes which have occurred in previous situations. Column 2 of the table shows the *frequency* with which the five outcomes have occurred. The total of column 2 (expressed by the Greek symbol Σ) must equal the number of observed outcomes – in this case 100. Column 3 translates the absolute numbers from column 2 into probabilities, expressed as decimals, on the assumption that past outcomes are a good basis for predicting future results. Each figure in column 3 is equal to the figure on the same row of column 2 divided by the total number of outcomes (100). Thus the probability of a deficit of £20,000 is 8 divided by 100, which equals 0.08. The total of column 3 must sum to 1, as the sum of the probabilities of occurrence must always equal unity. If the total is less than 1, all possible outcomes are not included. If it is greater than 1, one or more of the probabilities assigned to individual outcomes is incorrect.

We are now in a position to calculate the expected value of the new project. The expected value is represented by the sum of each possible outcome multiplied by the probability of its occurrence. Thus we have an expected value of:

$$-20,000(0.08) - 5,000(0.22) + 3,000(0.40) + 7,000(0.18) + 10,000(0.12)$$
$$= -1,600 - 1,100 + 1,200 + 1,260 + 1,200$$
$$= +£960$$

On the basis of the numbers produced by application of the expected value technique, it appears that Ninian plc should undertake the new investment. *On past experience* the average expected value of the new project is a cash surplus of £960. Is this an adequate analysis of the uncertainty associated with the project? Before we answer this question, let us consider a more complex business decision.

Expected values: illustration 2

Suppose Ninian plc is now considering the purchase of a new machine for £3,500. The directors feel very confident that they can sell the goods produced by the machine so as to yield a yearly cash surplus of £1,000. There is, however, some uncertainty as to the machine's working life. A recently published trade association survey shows that members of the association have between them owned 250 of these machines, and have found the lives of the machine to vary as follows:

Number of years of machine life	Number of machines having given life
3	20
4	50
5	100
6	70
7	10
	$\Sigma = 250$

In order to decide whether to purchase the machine, Ninian plc might proceed as follows. First, calculate the present value of the cash surplus or deficit arising if the machine lasts 3, 4, 5, 6 or 7 years. The present value of the cash surplus or deficit is represented by the difference between the *discounted* annual cash flows of £1,000 and the cost of the machine, which is £3,500.[1] If we assume a discount rate of 10%, the net present value for each different machine life is as follows:

Machine life	Net present value (£)
3	(1,013)
4	(330)
5	291
6	855
7	1,368

As the machine life lengthens from 3 to 7 years, and Ninian plc receives a greater number of yearly cash flows, the net present value of the machine changes from −£1,013 (i.e. a situation which does not warrant purchase) to +£1,368 (i.e. a situation which favours purchase).

Table 4.1 Calculation of the expected net present value of purchasing a machine

Machine's life in years (1)	Net present value (2)	Number of machines having given life (3)	Probability of occurrence (4)	Expected net present value (£) (5)
3	(1,013)	20	$\frac{20}{250} = 0.08$	(81)
4	(330)	50	$\frac{50}{250} = 0.20$	(66)
5	291	100	$\frac{100}{250} = 0.40$	116
6	855	70	$\frac{70}{250} = 0.28$	239
7	1,368	10	$\frac{10}{250} = 0.04$	55
		$\Sigma = 250$	$\Sigma = 1.00$	263

In order to calculate the expected value of these different net present values, we need to perform two further calculations. First, each individual net present value is multiplied by its probability of occurrence; and second, the totals derived are added together. Table 4.1 shows both sets of calculations.

Column 5 of Table 4.1 shows the expected net present value of purchasing the machine. The individual values appearing within column 5 are calculated by multiplying the net present values in column 2 by the probability of their occurrence, as shown in column 4. On the basis of the expected value calculation, supported by 250 previous observations, it appears that Ninian plc should go ahead with the purchase of the machine as it yields a positive expected net present value of £263.

4.4 Decision trees and joint probabilities

In each of the illustrations of expected value calculations in the previous section, Ninian plc was facing a single source of uncertainty – the present value of the returns from the contract in the first example, and the length of life of the machine in the second. In practice there may be more than one source of uncertainty which must be simultaneously taken into account when making a decision, and the interaction of different sources of uncertainty can greatly increase the number of possible outcomes. The expected value criterion can still be used to evaluate opportunities, but it must be based on the joint probabilities of the different sources of uncertainty associated with each outcome. *Decision trees* provide a useful means of representing a decision problem in a way that illustrates the interaction of different variables and choices leading to the range of possible outcomes. We can demonstrate the use of both decision trees and joint probabilities with a further example.

Let us suppose that Ninian plc is contemplating a third opportunity, launching a new product. If the product is introduced, the value of the returns obtained will depend on two uncertain factors: (1) the state of the economy, which will determine market demand, and (2) the actions of competitors in introducing similar products. Figure 4.1 represents this problem in the form of a decision tree.

The left-hand point of the tree and the two branches emerging from it represent the decision whether or not to launch the product. If the product is not introduced, clearly the present value of returns will be zero. If introduction goes ahead, the return will depend first on the state of the economy. For simplicity we will assume three states: high growth and high demand, low growth and moderate demand, and no growth and low demand. Each of these possibilities creates a separate branch in the next stage of the decision tree diagram. Within each economic condition, there is a further source of uncertainty concerning competitors' actions. Each branch for the state of the economy is therefore followed by two further branches for the introduction and absence of competing products. The right-hand side of the decision tree is the set of possible outcomes taking together the interaction of the different sources of uncertainty. In this case a decision to launch the product leads to six possible outcomes, showing the combinations of three possible economic conditions with two possible competitive positions.

To apply expected value analysis, we must calculate the probability associated with each outcome. The probabilities for the individual branches can be included as shown in the diagram. Thus, there is a 30% chance of a high-growth economy, a 50% chance of low growth and a 20% chance of no growth. The probability of each independent outcome is the joint probability of the branches forming the pathway leading to that outcome, which is found by multiplying together the probabilities on that pathway. In the case of Ninian plc's new product, the probability that there will be high growth in the economy and that there will be no competing product, an outcome which would give a present value of £15,000, is:

0.3 (probability of high growth) × 0.3 (probability of no competing product) = 0.09

The value of the outcome associated with each branch can then be multiplied by the associated probability in order to complete the expected value calculation. For Ninian plc, Figure 4.1 shows that the expected present value associated with introducing the new product is £7,785, which when compared with the value of zero without the introduction, obviously suggests that the company should go ahead with the product launch. Note that, as with all expected value exercises, the total of the probabilities of the independent outcomes must equal 1, that is, 100%.

It is not always necessary to construct a decision tree in order to carry out analysis involving joint probabilities of different sources of uncertainty, but this technique does provide a useful graphical way of representing decision problems and their possible outcomes, and of keeping track of the many interactions between different variables that can occur.

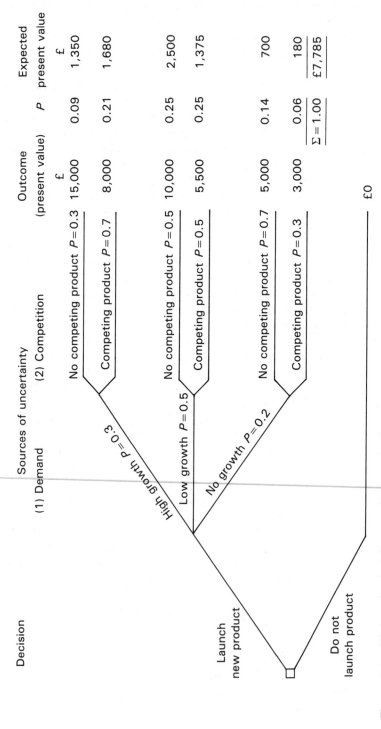

Figure 4.1 Ninian plc: decision tree for launch of new product.

4.5 Some problems with the expected value criterion

Let us now return to the question we asked previously. Is the expected value method a sufficient treatment of the problem of uncertainty? In other words, should an enterprise always accept projects with positive expected values and reject those with negative expected values? To answer these questions we need to understand what lies behind the expected value approach. The approach is based upon the application of probabilities, however derived, to a specific situation, in order to produce a 'long-run average' solution. It does not accommodate the decision taker's risk preferences. It does not indicate whether the decision taker is prepared to take the chance of incurring the various possible outcomes which contribute to the 'average' solution.

Let us digress to reinforce this point. Suppose that Mr X and Mr Y are considering whether to play a coin-tossing game. They agree that the rules of the game will be as follows. The coin will be tossed only once. If it turns up 'heads', Mr X gives Mr Y £10,000, whereas if the coin turns up 'tails', Mr Y gives Mr X £10,000. The expected value of Mr X's cash flows, assuming an unbiased coin, are:

Event	Outcome (£)	Probability	Expected outcome (£)
Heads	−10,000	0.5	−5,000
Tails	+10,000	0.5	+5,000
		Expected value	0

Mr X's expected value (i.e. his expected gain or loss) on this gamble is zero, but that will not be the actual outcome. In fact, he might gain or lose £10,000. The crucial question is whether (as the expected value criterion suggests) Mr X would be indifferent to playing the game or not, knowing that although he could win £10,000, he could also lose the same amount. In this situation the expected value would be an appropriate basis for choice only if the two gamblers were neutral to risk – if they were prepared to take the chance of winning or losing £10,000 with equal probability. Note that if the two players agree to play the game not just once but a number of times, the chance of a zero average outcome will become progressively more likely the more times the coin is tossed. This is the basis of probability theory to which we referred earlier. The principle is known as the *law of large numbers*. Hence probability is strictly defined as the long-run relative frequency of a particular event. It may be used to provide a calculation of expected outcome or expected value: that is, the long-run average outcome or value expected if a particular course of action is undertaken many times.

With these ideas in mind, let us return to the first two of our earlier examples. In the first, concerning the undertaking of a new contract, the application of the expected value method suggested acceptance of the project on the basis of a positive expected value of £960. Note that this 'average' figure has never actually been achieved. The most likely (or *modal*) result is in fact a surplus of £3,000. When we explore in more detail what underlies the expected value of £960 we see that, on the basis of the previous 100 observations, there is an 8% probability that the project will incur a loss of £20,000 and a 22% probability that the project will lose £5,000: that is, there is a 30% chance that a deficit will occur. The broad question then becomes: is the management of Ninian plc willing to run the 30% risk of a loss in return for a 70% chance of generating a cash surplus? It may be, for example, that a loss of £20,000 or even £5,000 would be so significant in terms of the firm's size and current position that its occurrence would force the firm out of business. Many managers would be unwilling to run the risk of such an outcome, even though it was more likely that the project would generate a surplus.

In the second example, concerning the purchase of a new machine, there is an 8% chance of showing a negative net present value of £1,013 and a 20% chance of a negative net present value of £330, depending upon whether the new machine lasts for three or four years. These results are based on a sample of 250 similar observations. The number of observations used as the basis for attaching probabilities may affect the confidence we have in the expected value results; the more observations we take, the more confident we are likely to be in the results. In this case Ninian plc must determine whether the 28% chance of incurring some loss is compensated by the 72% chance of earning surpluses. In this example, the amounts involved are small. A deficit of £1,013 or £330 is unlikely to bankrupt the firm, and the management may decide that the high probability of some surplus makes purchase of the machine worthwhile.

The crucial factor which will eventually determine the decision in each of the above cases is the decision maker's attitude to risk. This is the critical variable which is excluded from the expected value calculations, and yet it is the variable that may weigh most heavily in any decision. The level of risk which any of us will be willing to bear in our own decisions cannot be simply plucked out of the air. It depends upon many different aspects of our personal situations including our individual nature – whether we are risk takers or risk avoiders – and on the resources we possess (i.e. on the amount of money we can afford to lose). We cannot evaluate levels of risk independently of available resources. The same is true for management decision making: the level of acceptable risk depends upon many factors, including the nature of the particular decision, the amount of funds available to management, the return demanded by and the risk acceptable to providers of funds, and the attitudes to risk possessed by managers – the actual decision makers.

The practical limitations of the expected value technique should now be clearer. Because it ignores the risk attitudes of the decision maker(s) it is appropriate as a basis for choice only in limited situations. We might characterise these situations as follows:

1. The decision involves an opportunity which can be undertaken many times under independent conditions: that is, the outcome of each opportunity is independent of the outcomes of all others. (These conditions form the basis of insurance transactions.)

2. The decision involves amounts that are small in relation to the total size of an organisation.

3. Decision makers are neutral to risk.

In the likely event that none of these characteristics holds, a more sophisticated method has to be found to incorporate risk and uncertainty into decision making. One such approach, which has received wide support in both theory and practice, is the method of *portfolio analysis.*

4.6 Portfolio analysis: introduction

Among the criticisms we might level at the expected value method is its ignorance of the possible relationship between the outcome of any one decision and the outcomes of other decisions taken by the same individual. This is a serious shortcoming. Few firms put all their (financial) eggs in one basket; rather they try to minimise the level of risk by spreading it around a variety of projects. This spreading of risk is known as *diversification*, and diversification lies at the heart of portfolio analysis.

Portfolio analysis is the study of the interrelationships between the different financial elements which in total make up a portfolio (for example, a portfolio of shares or of projects). Basically it is a term to describe a commonsense activity in which most of us engage. If we were given a particular endowment of resources, and a degree of choice as to how we used the endowment, most of us would try to spread our risks in such a way that if one decision proved to be a loser then others would turn out to be winners. For example, an individual with available funds to invest might consider a variety of possible uses for them, such as the purchase of 'risky' shares, 'safe' shares and government stocks, deposits in building societies and banks, and a regular gamble on the football pools or the national lottery. It is unlikely that the returns from all these investments will fail simultaneously.

Portfolio analysis helps to explain why, for example, it is more likely that a substantial and risky project, promising either an excellent or a disastrous pay-off, will be more acceptable to a large organisation than to a small one. The consequences of a few failures out of a wide portfolio of projects are likely to be less catastrophic than the failure of an organisation's single project.

The principles underlying the portfolio approach also help to explain why so many large companies engage in such diversified and divergent activities. Some of the very large UK-based multinational companies, such as Unilever and ICI, produce and sell a variety of different products in order to help minimise the levels of risk associated with business life. For example, Unilever sells soap powder and cereals. Perhaps a more immediately recognisable example of this type of business diversification is the huge increase that has taken place in the sale of food and drink as a proportion of the total activities of Marks and Spencer. Marks and Spencer can no longer be thought of simply as a company which sells clothes through its retail stores. It may also be pointed out that there has been an equally impressive increase in the contribution to Marks and Spencer's total profits which has been provided by its sales of food and drink. Whatever the economic climate, we must still eat and drink!

An ideal form of diversification and risk minimisation is to place funds in sources which have 'negatively correlated' returns: that is, the returns from some sources are high when the returns from others are low and vice versa. Let us take a simple example to illustrate this point. Suppose an investor decides to place 50% of her funds in the shares of an umbrella manufacturer and 50% in the shares of an ice-cream manufacturer. Also suppose that returns from the investment in the umbrella manufacturer will drop when the weather is fine but that those from investment in the ice-cream manufacturer will rise, and that the situation will be reversed when the weather is bad. The investor is hedging her bets by spreading the risk inherent in the investment. The risk of the portfolio depends not upon the variability of the returns from the shares in the individual companies but rather on the effect on the *total* portfolio returns of the various economic (and climatic) circumstances. Even investments that are susceptible to large variations in their returns may be good (risk) choices for the use of funds provided that they are *negatively correlated* with other investments within the portfolio. It is this notion of negative correlation which is important in minimising the level of risk in any business situation.

We now use a simple example to explain the principles of portfolio analysis. At this stage, we restrict ourselves to a summary of basic concepts. In the next section we explain in greater detail the mechanics of portfolio analysis.

Mr Filbert possesses £1,000 cash and no other assets. He has the opportunity of investing his cash in one of three companies, or in a combination of any two of the three companies. No other investments are available now or in the foreseeable future. Mr Filbert is a risk-averse investor; he wishes to achieve the lowest possible level of risk for a given expected return. An investment in each company produces a single return after one year, but the size of the return depends upon which of three sets of economic circumstances (known as states of the world) prevails. The possible returns from an investment of £1,000 in each company are shown in Table 4.2.

The first step in Mr Filbert's investment decision is to calculate the expected value of investing in each company. The expected value calculations are set out in Table 4.3. The weighted average of the returns expected from an investment of £1,000 is £1,200 in each case. On the basis of the expected value criterion, Mr Filbert would be indifferent between the investments. However, as we noted earlier, the expected value criterion may be an inadequate decision rule. Mr Filbert is interested in minimising the level of risk associated with his investment.

Observation of the figures in Table 4.2 suggests that the returns from company E are less volatile (i.e. vary less depending upon which environment prevails) than are the returns from either of the other companies. For example, returns from company E will be in the range £1,100 to £1,300, compared with £800 to £1,600 for

Table 4.2 Mr Filbert: returns from investment

State of the world	A	B	C
Probability of state of the world	0.4	0.3	0.3
Returns from investment of £1,000 (£)			
Company D	1,200	800	1,600
Company E	1,200	1,100	1,300
Company F	1,200	1,700	700

Table 4.3   Mr Filbert: expected value calculations

State of the world	Return (£)		Probability (£)		Expected value
Company D:					
State A	1,200	×	0.4	=	480
State B	800	×	0.3	=	240
State C	1,600	×	0.3	=	480
			Expected value		1,200
Company E:					
State A	1,200	×	0.4	=	480
State B	1,100	×	0.3	=	330
State C	1,300	×	0.3	=	390
			Expected value		1,200
Company F:					
State A	1,200	×	0.4	=	480
State B	1,700	×	0.3	=	510
State C	700	×	0.3	=	210
			Expected value		1,200

company D and £700 to £1,700 for company F. If Mr Filbert could invest in only one company he would, as a risk-averse investor, choose company E. However, he is not restricted to investment in only one company; he may, if he wishes, spread his cash between two of the companies. Again, observation of the figures in Table 4.2 reveals that the returns of company D and company E are positively correlated; both companies do relatively badly under state B and relatively well under state C. The returns of company D and company F, and of company E and company F are negatively correlated; company F does relatively well under state B whereas companies D and E do relatively badly, and vice versa under state C.

The above observations suggest that investment in companies D and F or in companies E and F offers more scope for reducing the risk of Mr Filbert's portfolio

Table 4.4   Mr Filbert: returns from investment in companies E and F

State of the world	A	B	C
Probability of state of the world	0.4	0.3	0.3
Investment of £833.33 in company E and £166.67 in company F:			
Return from company E (£) (83.333% of returns shown in Table 4.2)	1,000	917	1,083
Return from company F (£) (16.667% of returns shown in Table 4.2)	200	283	117
Total return (£)	1,200	1,200	1,200

than does investment in companies D and E or in one of the three companies alone. In fact, by investing 83.333% of his funds in company E and 16.667% in company F, Mr Filbert may eliminate risk completely. The results of this strategy are shown in Table 4.4, which demonstrates that whichever state of the world obtains, Mr Filbert will receive a return of £1,200. In the next section we explain in more detail the formal analysis which will lead to this result.

4.7 Portfolio analysis: further considerations

As we noted in the previous section, Mr Filbert is a risk-averse investor, interested in minimising the level of risk associated with his investment. He is thus interested in determining the extent to which the return from each company *covaries* with the return from each of the others: that is, to what extent the return from company D covaries with that from company E, company E with company F, and company D with company F. Although the analysis in this section involves some basic statistics, that in itself is no bad thing. Statistical manipulations in many different guises confront us every day of our lives. It is, however, important not to lose sight of the message we are trying to convey, by becoming too immersed in the statistics. The message, which was demonstrated simply in the previous section, is that one (and possibly the best) method of dealing with business risk is to look not at the risks of individual projects and investments in isolation, but rather at how these risks move together or covary with the risk attached to other projects and investments.

The preferred combination of investments for a risk-averse investor will be that combination in which the expected returns offset each other: in other words, that combination which has the highest negative correlation coefficient. Correlation coefficients lie in the range from -1 to $+1$. A correlation coefficient of -1 (perfect negative correlation) means that risk can be diversified away completely: poor returns from one project are offset exactly by good returns from the other. A correlation coefficient of $+1$ (perfect positive correlation) means that no risk diversification is possible: good returns from one project are accompanied by good returns from the other, and bad returns from one by bad returns from the other. All other correlation coefficient values mean that some risk can be diversified away, and the nearer is the value of the correlation coefficient to -1, the greater is the amount of risk that can be eliminated.

The correlation coefficient (r) for any two projects (x and y) is found by dividing the joint risk of the two projects (the covariance) by the product of the individual risks. The most popular measure of individual risk used in statistical analysis is given by the standard deviation (σ). We can express the correlation coefficient for two projects (x and y) as follows:

$$r_{x,y} = \frac{\text{covariance } (x, y)}{\sigma_x \times \sigma_y} \tag{4.1}$$

We have not yet explained how we derive the standard deviation, or why we use it as a measure of individual risk. The standard deviation gives a *monetary* indication to decision makers of how confident they can be in the occurrence of the expected (average) outcome, by providing information about the likely *dispersion* (or range) of outcomes around the expected outcome, and about the size of the possible deviations of the actual outcome from the expected outcome. In statistical terms the standard deviation is the square root of the variance. To derive the standard deviation of a project we thus need first to calculate the variance (or σ^2). We may calculate the variance in four simple stages:

Stage 1   Calculate the deviation of each possible outcome (x_n) from the expected outcome (E_x), i.e. $(x_n - E_x)$.

Stage 2   Square this answer to make all the values positive, i.e. $(x_n - E_x)^2$.

Stage 3   Multiply this term by the probability (P_n) of actually getting the outcome x_n, i.e. $P_n(x_n - E_x)^2$.

Stage 4   Sum the results of stage 3 to give a measure of the variability of the likely outcomes, the variance, i.e. $\sigma^2 = \Sigma P_n(x_n - E_x)^2$.

    The above symbols represent a straightforward set of calculations. Let us return to the figures in our example to illustrate them. To calculate the standard deviations

Table 4.5   Mr Filbert: calculation of the standard deviation of each investment

State of the world	Return x_n	Expected value of return E_x	Deviation $(x_n - E_x)$	Deviation squared $(x_n - E_x)^2$	Probability P_n	Sum $P_n(x_n - E_x)^2$
Company D:						
State A	1,200	1,200	0	0	0.4	0
State B	800	1,200	−400	160,000	0.3	48,000
State C	1,600	1,200	+400	160,000	0.3	48,000
					Variance $(\sigma^2) = \Sigma =$	96,000

Standard deviation = $\sqrt{96,000}$ = £309.84

State of the world	Return x_n	Expected value of return E_x	Deviation $(x_n - E_x)$	Deviation squared $(x_n - E_x)^2$	Probability P_n	Sum $P_n(x_n - E_x)^2$
Company E:						
State A	1,200	1,200	0	0	0.4	0
State B	1,100	1,200	−100	10,000	0.3	3,000
State C	1,300	1,200	+100	10,000	0.3	3,000
					Variance $(\sigma^2) = \Sigma =$	6,000

Standard deviation = $\sqrt{6,000}$ = £77.46

State of the world	Return x_n	Expected value of return E_x	Deviation $(x_n - E_x)$	Deviation squared $(x_n - E_x)^2$	Probability P_n	Sum $P_n(x_n - E_x)^2$
Company F:						
State A	1,200	1,200	0	0	0.4	0
State B	1,700	1,200	+500	250,000	0.3	75,000
State C	700	1,200	−500	250,000	0.3	75,000
					Variance $(\sigma^2) = \Sigma =$	150,000

Standard deviation = $\sqrt{150,000}$ = £387.30

or measures of risk for each of the three investments, we proceed as in Table 4.5. The standard deviation calculations in Table 4.5 show that the return from company E varies less, depending upon which state of the world prevails, than do the returns from investment in company D or company F (i.e. investment in company E produces the same average return and lower variability of return than investment in either of the other companies). Does this mean that Mr Filbert should apply his £1,000 entirely to investment in company E? So far we have calculated separately the variability of the returns from each company. We now need to see if Mr Filbert's level of risk can be reduced by investing in a combination of any two of the companies.

Suppose Mr Filbert invests his total capital equally in the shares of two companies (i.e. £500 is invested in each company). Which two companies should he choose? The three possible combinations, or portfolios, of returns from this strategy are shown in Table 4.6, and the standard deviation of each is shown in Table 4.7. (Each return is one-half of the total return shown in Table 4.2.)

Tables 4.6 and 4.7 show that by investing in a diversified portfolio Mr Filbert can obtain the same return with a lower level of risk than was possible by investing in the shares of one company alone. Each portfolio and each company offer an expected return of £1,200. However, the calculations in Table 4.5 demonstrated that the lowest standard deviation possible from investment in only one company (company E) is £77.46. The figures in Table 4.7 show that this standard deviation

Table 4.6 Mr Filbert: possible combinations of returns

State of the world	A	B	C
Probability of state of the world	0.4	0.3	0.3
	(£)	(£)	(£)
Portfolio 1 – equal investment in company D and company E			
Return from company D	600	400	800
Return from company E	600	550	650
Total return	1,200	950	1,450
Expected value of returns		1,200	
Portfolio 2 – equal investment in company E and company F			
Return from company E	600	550	650
Return from company F	600	850	350
Total return	1,200	1,400	1,000
Expected value of returns		1,200	
Portfolio 3 – equal investment in company D and company F			
Return from company D	600	400	800
Return from company F	600	850	350
Total return	1,200	1,250	1,150
Expected value of returns		1,200	

Table 4.7 Mr Filbert: calculations of the standard deviation of each portfolio

State of the world	Return x_n	Expected value of return E_x	Deviation $(x_n - E_x)$	Deviation squared $(x_n - E_x)^2$	Probability P_n	Sum $P_n(x_n - E_x)^2$
Portfolio 1						
State A	1,200	1,200	0	0	0.4	0
State B	950	1,200	−250	62,500	0.3	18,750
State C	1,450	1,200	+250	62,500	0.3	18,750
					Variance $(\sigma^2) = \Sigma = $	37,500

Standard deviation = $\sqrt{37,500}$ = £193.65

Portfolio 2						
State A	1,200	1,200	0	0	0.4	0
State B	1,400	1,200	+200	40,000	0.3	12,000
State C	1,000	1,200	−200	40,000	0.3	12,000
					Variance $(\sigma^2) = \Sigma = $	24,000

Standard deviation = $\sqrt{24,000}$ = £154.92

Portfolio 3						
State A	1,200	1,200	0	0	0.4	0
State B	1,250	1,200	+50	2,500	0.3	750
State C	1,150	1,200	−50	2,500	0.3	750
					Variance $(\sigma^2) = \Sigma = $	1,500

Standard deviation = $\sqrt{1,500}$ = £38.73

Table 4.8 Mr Filbert: covariance calculations

State of the world	(Deviation $(x_n - E_x)$	× Deviation $(x_n - E_x)$	= Product)	× Probability	= Covariance
Portfolio 1	Company D	Company E			
State A	0	0	0	0.4	0
State B	−400	−100	40,000	0.3	+12,000
State C	+400	+100	40,000	0.3	+12,000
			Covariance (D, E)		+24,000
Portfolio 2	Company E	Company F			
State A	0	0	0	0.4	0
State B	−100	+500	−50,000	0.3	−15,000
State C	+100	−500	−50,000	0.3	−15,000
			Covariance (E, F)		−30,000
Portfolio 3	Company D	Company F			
State A	0	0	0	0.4	0
State B	−400	+500	−200,000	0.3	−60,000
State C	+400	−500	−200,000	0.3	−60,000
			Covariance (D, F)		−120,000

may be reduced to £38.73 by investing equally in a combination of companies D and F: that is, by investment in portfolio 3. The returns from D and F are negatively correlated so that an unusually poor performance by one company is always accompanied by an unusually good one by the other.

We can now return to our statistical formulae to interpret these conclusions more formally. We have previously defined the covariance as being related to the joint risk of two investments. In order to find the degree of joint risk (covariance) it is first necessary to determine the deviation of each investment's outcomes from its expected outcome and to calculate the product of the deviations of each investment under each possible economic state. The answers are then weighted by the probability of each economic state. Table 4.8 shows the calculation of the covariance for each of the three portfolios. The 'deviation' figures for each company's returns are taken from Table 4.5. We now have the figures necessary to determine the correlation coefficients – the degree of co-movement of each combination of projects.

Substituting the covariances from Table 4.8 and the standard deviations from Table 4.5 into the correlation coefficient equation (equation 4.1: $r_{x,y}$ = covariance $(x,y)/\sigma_x \times \sigma_y$), gives the following coefficients:

$$r_{D,E} = \frac{\text{covariance (D, E)}}{\sigma_D \times \sigma_E} = \frac{+24{,}000}{309.84 \times 77.46} = +1$$

$$r_{E,F} = \frac{\text{covariance (E, F)}}{\sigma_E \times \sigma_F} = \frac{-30{,}000}{77.46 \times 387.30} = -1$$

$$r_{D,F} = \frac{\text{covariance (D, F)}}{\sigma_D \times \sigma_F} = \frac{-120{,}000}{309.84 \times 387.30} = -1$$

The combinations of the returns of companies E and F and the returns of companies D and F are perfectly negatively correlated: that is, they offer the opportunity of eliminating risk completely. At first sight, this seems an odd conclusion in view of the figures in Table 4.7, which showed that investment of equal amounts in E and F (portfolio 2) or in D and F (portfolio 3) resulted in portfolios with positive, rather than zero, standard deviations: in other words, neither portfolio eliminates risk. The explanation for this apparent paradox is that, in order to exploit fully the risk reduction properties of investments in two companies, it will almost certainly be necessary to invest unequal amounts in each one. A detailed consideration of the procedure for selecting the appropriate proportions is outside the scope of this chapter. However, we may demonstrate the 'truth' of the correlation coefficient by considering investment in companies E and F. In order to eliminate risk completely, it is necessary to invest 83.333% of available funds (i.e. £833.33) in E and 16.667% of available funds (i.e. £166.67) in F. The results of this strategy were shown in Table 4.4, which demonstrates that, whichever state of the world obtains, Mr Filbert will receive a return of £1,200. In other words, the standard deviation of the portfolio in Table 4.4 is zero.

In contrast to investment in either E and F or D and F, investment in D and E offers no opportunity at all for risk reduction by diversification, as returns from investment in the two companies are perfectly positively correlated. Investment in E alone offers the same return and a lower variability (standard deviation) than does any combination of investment in E and D. In summary, because Mr Filbert is risk-averse, he should invest his funds either in a combination of shares of E and F or in a combination of shares of D and F.

4.8 Management decisions and risk and uncertainty

Although our explanation of portfolio analysis has been phrased in terms of an individual considering investment in three companies, a similar procedure is appropriate for decisions in which managers are faced with a choice of projects. In practice, the procedure is somewhat more complex than our example suggests (as indeed it is for the investor). The manager must consider not only the returns of and correlations between the returns of new projects but also the correlations of the returns of new projects with the existing activities of the organisation. The task is to find a combination of return and risk which is optimal for the participants of the organisation as a whole. This is further complicated by the need to trade off the risk of a project against its expected return. Many investments provide the possibility of greater returns only if a greater level of risk is accepted.

4.9 Other approaches to risk and uncertainty

Before leaving the subject of the techniques that may be used to incorporate some consideration of risk and uncertainty into the decision-making process, we will mention briefly some additional methods.

Sensitivity analysis

One of the most useful approaches not involving a strict application of probability theory is *sensitivity analysis*. This involves calculating the expected pay-off from a project on the basis of most likely outcomes, and subsequently investigating the implications of various deviations of actual outcomes from forecast. The value that a particular variable will take if the profit expected from the project is to be reduced to zero may be ascertained and the difference in value expressed as a percentage of its most likely value. For example, if a project with a net present value of £2,000 involves cash flows associated with the acquisition of materials with a present value of £20,000, then we can calculate that the value of material flows can increase by 10% to £22,000 before the project is no longer worthwhile. This provides an indication of the sensitivity of the project's expected profit to changes in the value of individual variables, and points to those estimates in which a small deviation may be critical for the success or failure of the project. These estimates should be examined most carefully before a decision is made on the project. The advent of microcomputers and spreadsheet packages has made the use of sensitivity analysis rapid and inexpensive. We look in more detail at sensitivity analysis in Chapter 13.

Simulation

It will sometimes be the case that the cost and difficulty of applying a method based on the use of probabilities mean that another method of dealing with uncertainty may be more appropriate. While the decision tree approach outlined earlier can be helpful in conceptualising the way in which outcomes can arise as a result of decisions, in complex situations where there are many different sources of uncertainty, allowing for all their interactions can result in thousands of possible outcomes. An additional approach to complex problems is to build a computer model of a project, incorporating all the factors that are likely to affect its outcome. The values and probabilities associated with the elements in the model can then be varied in order to *simulate* different operating and environmental conditions and estimate the resulting outcome. Simulation has two main advantages. First, it forces management to consider explicitly the relationships between different factors that can affect a project. Second, it allows a large number of possible conditions to be tested and generates a large amount of information about the pattern of returns that can be expected from a project.

CHAPTER SUMMARY

All decision making depends on implicit or explicit views about the future and what will happen as a result of the decision. The future is inevitably uncertain and, consequently, all decision making involves uncertainty and prediction. We have concentrated in this chapter on two methods which explicitly incorporate risk and uncertainty into decision making – the basic expected value method and the more sophisticated portfolio analysis approach. We have chosen to look at expected values because they involve the use of probabilities – that is, quantified estimates of the likelihood of future events occurring – and portfolio analysis because it seems to us to be the most relevant and potentially useful means of dealing with risk and uncertainty in practice.

We will return only in passing to expected value and portfolio analysis calculations in future chapters. That, however, does not mean that the reader should promptly forget what has just been discussed. This chapter is one of the most important in the entire book. In everything that follows – in most of the examples, illustrations, explanations and problems which we shall use – it should be borne in mind that underlying all our words and figures is the existence of uncertainty.

REVIEW QUESTIONS

1. Discuss the distinction between decisions and predictions. Do you accept the assertion in the chapter that every decision entails making a prediction?

2. Discuss some possible methods by which decision makers could attempt to attach probabilities to outcomes. What factors in practice determine the choice of method?

3. Discuss the advantages and disadvantages of the expected value technique for good decision making.

4. Why is it important to incorporate the notion of risk into decision-making procedures? Whose risk should be reflected in decision making?

5. Explain the distinguishing characteristics of portfolio analysis and, in particular, discuss the concepts of variance, covariance and correlation coefficient. Have you ever used this technique in your own decision making? If so, how?

EXERCISES

4.1 The plant manager of Mahler Ltd, confronted with a need to replace a machine, has a choice between machine A and machine B, either of which is satisfactory. Each machine has an estimated life of three years, but machine A will cost £40,000, and machine B £100,000. An analysis of the operating costs associated with each of the machines reveals that the cost per unit with machine A is £10 and with machine B is £5, excluding depreciation. The product's selling price is £30.

The manager feels that the number of units required for each of the next three years may be 2,000, 3,000 or 5,000 units. An annual requirement of 3,000 units is the most probable. The following table shows the probabilities:

Annual requirements (units)	Probability
2,000	0.2
3,000	0.6
5,000	0.2

(a) Calculate the net present value for each of the three activity levels for machines A and B using a discount rate of 6%.

(b) Calculate the expected net present value for each machine. Which machine would you recommend to the manager?

(c) Discuss briefly the limitations of the expected value technique. (Solution at end of text.)

4.2 Watteau Ltd, a novelty toy company, is considering whether to produce a new toy called 'Spyman', modelled on the hero of a currently popular television series. A special machine, having no other use, would be required. It would cost £200,000. The company's cost of capital is 5%. The direct cost of a Spyman is expected to be £10, and whatever the number sold the price will be £20. The demand for the toy is not thought likely to last more than three years. The sales in each year are highly uncertain.

The directors have estimated the various possible levels of demand in each year, and forecast the likelihood of the occurrence of each of these demands as in the table below. Because of the nature of the product, the level of demand achieved in any one year is independent of that obtained in any other year.

Year 1		Year 2		Year 3	
Probability	Sales (units)	Probability	Sales (units)	Probability	Sales (units)
0.2	5,000	0.2	2,500	0.2	1,000
0.2	10,000	0.3	5,000	0.2	2,500
0.4	20,000	0.3	7,500	0.3	5,000
0.1	25,000	0.1	10,000	0.3	7,500
0.1	30,000	0.1	20,000	–	–

The preliminary design studies for the 'Spyman' have already been completed, at a cost of £10,000. If the project is rejected, they could be sold for £25,000.

(a) Calculate the project's expected net present value.

(b) Would you necessarily recommend acceptance if this value were positive?
   Specifically, how would your conclusion be affected if the company was:
   (i) a one-person firm with no other project available, and the £200,000 required to finance the project was the entrepreneur's lifetime savings?
   (ii) a very large company undertaking many similar projects? (Solution at end of text.)

4.3 Pollock Ltd is considering the establishment of a new production centre to manufacture a new product, the fladget. For strategic reasons, the selling price would be set at £50 per unit. However, Pollock is uncertain about the scale of demand at that price. It estimates that two states of demand are equally likely: state A representing relative failure in competing with established products, state B representing relative success in that competition. Once the state has been identified, there remains some uncertainty about the actual level of demand because of uncertainty about general economic conditions:

State A		State B	
Volume per annum (units)	Probability	Volume per annum (units)	Probability
8,000	0.2	12,000	0.2
11,000	0.6	15,000	0.6
15,000	0.2	19,000	0.2

It would be possible to commission a market research survey to discover with virtual certainty whether state A or state B prevails.

The manufacture of flidgets would require the purchase of a machine. Two models are available, one which costs £400,000 and has a capacity of 12,000 units per annum, and one which costs £600,000 and has a capacity of 20,000 units per annum. Both models would have lives of five years and no scrap value at the end of that time. In addition to the costs of a machine, the manufacture of flidgets would involve variable costs of £25 per unit and an increase of £100,000 per annum in the fixed costs of the firm.

The cost of capital of Pollock is 15% p.a. Levels of demand, prices and costs may be assumed to remain constant for the lives of the machines. Sales may be assumed to take place and production costs to be incurred on the last day of each year.

(a) Calculate the expected net present value of purchasing each model of the machine and hence recommend which should be purchased, assuming that no market research is undertaken.

(b) Calculate the maximum sum which Pollock should be willing to pay for the market research survey, assuming that the decision would be based on a calculation of expected net present values. (*Hint*: Re-read section 2.2 of Chapter 2 before answering this part of the question.)

(c) Discuss shortly the limitations of calculations of expected net present values as a basis for investment decisions.

4.4 The following mean returns and standard deviations have been calculated for the three following securities:

	Mean	Standard deviation
Walton	0.07	0.093
Williamson	0.10	0.070
Walter	0.12	0.085

The correlation coefficients between these three securities are:

	Walton	Williamson	Walter
Walton	+1.000	+0.137	+0.476
Williamson		+1.000	+0.422
Walter			+1.000

(a) Compute the expected return and variance of equally weighted portfolios of the following stocks:
   (i)   Walton and Williamson
   (ii) Walton and Walter
   (iii) Williamson and Walter
   Why is the variance for portfolio (ii) greater than that for (i)?

(b) Examine the effect on the variance of an equally weighted portfolio of Williamson and Walter where the standard deviations are as given in the question, but where the correlation coefficient between Williamson and Walter is:
   (i)   +1
   (ii)   0
   (iii) −1
   Comment on the results. If the correlation coefficient is −1, what portfolio weights would lead to a portfolio with zero variance?

(c) Which security or portfolio would a 'risk-neutral' wealth-maximising decision maker prefer?

4.5   Chattox Ltd makes low-quality clothes on a mass production basis. At present there is idle capacity in the plant and an American importer has approached Chattox, requesting it to supply stylish men's shirts at a contract price of £125 per dozen. Management at Chattox is uncertain as to whether the order should be accepted because demand can vary, as shown below, depending on the success of the US advertising campaign.

Demand (dozens)	Probability
3,000	0.3
4,500	0.6
6,000	0.1

The shirts can also vary in quality because of the use of two different types of material, depending on the ultimate customer's preference. The variable cost per dozen can thus be either £100 or £82.50, but the selling price for Chattox remains constant at £125 per dozen. The market research department of the American importer, who supplied the above demand probabilities, has also estimated that 75% of customers will prefer the more expensive material, while the remaining 25% will prefer the cheaper kind. Consumer preference probabilities are independent of sales demand probabilities. It is estimated that the incremental fixed costs, if the order is accepted, will amount to £120,000.

(a) Calculate the incremental profit or loss in the *six* states of the world that can occur.

(b) Compute the probability of the occurrence of each of the six states.

(c) Determine the probability that the project will be profitable.

(d) Calculate the expected value if the order is accepted.

(e) Discuss whether the order should be accepted.

Notes

1. This technique of project appraisal, which involves the discounting of future cash flows, is usually referred to as the 'net present value' method. It was described briefly in Chapter 3 and will be discussed in more detail in Chapter 13.

Costs and benefits for decisions

AIMS AND OBJECTIVES

☐ To distinguish between accept or reject and ranking decisions.

☐ To describe the principles involved in the identification of relevant costs and revenues for decisions.

☐ To illustrate the calculation of relevant costs and revenues by the use of alternative budgets.

☐ To compare the approach recommended with conventional cost accounting.

All decision making involves choice between alternatives. The choice may be simply whether or not to follow a particular course of action, what we shall call *accept or reject* decisions; or it may be that a selection must be made from a number of available courses of action, what we shall call *ranking* decisions. Accept or reject decisions arise when an organisation is considering a particular opportunity, acceptance of which will not affect its ability to accept any other opportunities that are expected to become available. In such a case, a decision may be taken about the worth of the opportunity under consideration without having to compare it with other opportunities. In this chapter we deal with accept or reject decisions in order to establish certain principles about what should be considered relevant information for decision making. These principles will be used in analysis throughout the subsequent sections of this book, and their application to a number of specific types of management decision will be discussed in Chapter 10.

Ranking decisions involve the choice between two or more competing opportunities. The need to rank the opportunities arises because circumstances exist that prevent the organisation from accepting all opportunities that appear to increase the present value of its cash flows. Such circumstances generally involve either a shortage (scarcity) of resources or mutual exclusivity between opportunities. *Scarce resources* are said to exist when a firm has insufficient supplies of one or more of its resources (e.g. labour, materials, factory space) to accept all available opportunities that appear to be favourable. In this situation, the firm must endeavour to apply its scarce resources in the most profitable way. How it might do so is considered in more detail in Chapters 11 and 12. Two or more opportunities are said to be *mutually exclusive* when acceptance of one of them precludes acceptance of the others, for reasons other than scarcity of resources. Mutual exclusivity normally arises when different means of achieving the same or similar ends are being considered: for example, alternative production methods having the same output capacity, or alternative locations for a new factory. In such situations, management must compare outcomes from the different alternatives and choose the most favourable.

5.1 Principles of relevant cost and revenue determination

A central problem facing organisations is how to identify and evaluate the relevant costs and benefits resulting from the various available alternatives. In this section, the principles involved will be explained with particular reference to costs. Similar principles should be applied to benefits, however.

The principles to be applied in determining costs and benefits depend upon the decision maker's objectives. For all decision models, the costs and benefits that are relevant are those which can be affected by the decision. Clearly, if a particular cost or benefit is independent of the decision, it should not be allowed to influence it. Recognition of this fact leads immediately to our first two principles of cost evaluation. The first is that *only future costs are relevant*. Decisions can be taken only about alternatives that affect the future. No one can take decisions that will alter the past, except perhaps to the extent that it might be possible to show the past in a different light. Costs that have been incurred include costs that have already been paid and also costs that are the subject of legally binding contracts, even if payments due under the contract have yet to be made. This latter category are called *committed costs*. Although past costs may be useful aids for predicting future costs (see Chapter 6), they are not of themselves relevant to decisions.

This notion of the irrelevance of past costs to decision making seems intuitively appealing and sensible, but it is a very difficult one for many decision makers to implement. Perhaps this is because it may contradict the workings of human nature. People often have an inbuilt desire to 'recover' their past outlays in particular situations. Human nature is not always rational or forward looking. Many examples come to mind. If we are contemplating the sale of a ticket which we hold to a football match or a concert, for example, it is often difficult to rid ourselves of the notion that we would like to receive at least as much as we originally paid. Yet in decision making we should ignore these past costs and choose the alternative with the greatest incremental effect on future cash flows, regardless of whether it permits the recovery of past outlays.

The second relevant cost principle that follows from recognition of the fact that costs which are independent of a decision should not be allowed to influence it, is that *only those costs which will differ under some or all of the available alternatives are relevant*: that is, only differential (or incremental) costs should be included in the analysis.

For example, take the case of an accountant considering the two alternatives of whether to travel to the office by train on five or six occasions during the coming week. Whether travelling five or six times, it is cheaper to purchase a weekly season ticket than to pay fares daily. The cost of the season ticket is the same whether five or six journeys are made and thus is not relevant to the choice between the two alternatives. It follows that any apportionment of the cost of the season ticket (say on an 'average cost per journey' basis) is also irrelevant to the decision on whether to go to the office on five or six occasions during the week. The cost would be relevant, however, if a third alternative were to be considered: the possibility of not travelling to the office at all in the coming week. In this situation there would be no need to purchase the season ticket, the cost of which should then be considered as differential and relevant to the decision.

We have argued so far that only future differential costs (and revenues) are relevant for decision purposes. There remains one outstanding problem – the choice of a basis for measuring costs and revenues. Like the first two principles, this choice depends upon the decision maker's objectives and upon the decision model. In previous chapters we have argued for a decision objective which involves maximising the present value of future cash flows. Thus the third, and final, principle of relevant cost estimation is that *only cash costs are to be included*, suitably adjusted for differences in their timing if appropriate.

Our choice of cash as a measurement basis is perhaps less obvious than the first two principles of relevant cost determination: for example, it may not be appropriate for all individuals and firms or for the public sector (central government, local authorities, nationalised industries, etc.). If decision alternatives involve costs that are not easily expressed in cash terms (e.g. the possibility of a strike if production methods are changed), an attempt may be made to express such costs as cash flows. If this proves impracticable or inappropriate, the decision maker will have to make a value judgement as to whether net cash benefits are large enough to justify incurring 'non-cash' costs, or vice versa.

The three basic principles discussed above may be summarised as follows: *for making decisions, only differential future cash flows should be considered.* All changes to cash flows resulting from a decision should be taken into account and not just those easily identified with a particular project. So if a decision to be taken in one department of an organisation would cause an increase in cash costs in another department, that increase should be taken into account in assessing the worth of the decision to be taken in the first department, assuming our objective is to maximise the cash flows of the organisation as a whole.

5.2 The role of alternative budgets

Alternative budgets can play an important part in the determination of relevant costs and revenues. Where a number of opportunities have to be ranked, because they are mutually exclusive or because some resources are scarce, it may be helpful to prepare a series of budgets showing the worth of each opportunity. Even where only one opportunity is under consideration, two alternatives are implied: acceptance of the opportunity or rejection. In order to assess the desirability of the opportunity, future incremental cash flows associated with both acceptance and rejection must be considered. One way of doing this would be to prepare (cash flow) budgets for each alternative. In practice it is unusual (and therefore probably confusing to the decision maker) to present two budgets as an aid to making a decision about a single opportunity. In consequence, the figures in the two budgets are normally combined in a single-column cash flow statement. It is crucial to remember, however, that each figure in the statement represents the cash flow if the opportunity is accepted *compared with* the cash flow if it is rejected – the latter is always the implied alternative to acceptance.

In this section, we concentrate on the determination of costs and revenues for inclusion in a single budget to evaluate an opportunity, acceptance of which will not impair a firm's ability to accept other opportunities. The extension of this procedure to ranking decisions is considered in Chapters 11 and 13. An important characteristic of the cash flow budget is that its 'bottom line' (i.e. the 'surplus' if the opportunity is accepted) should be easily interpreted. The simplest form of interpretation is presumably that if the surplus is positive the opportunity should be accepted, and if it is negative the opportunity should be rejected. A (positive) surplus indicates that acceptance of the opportunity would add more to cash resources than would alternative applications of the resources required for acceptance. Such alternative applications of resources already owned include their possible resale. Perhaps the most obvious alternative for resources not yet owned is not to purchase them!

We consider now the general procedures to be followed in determining relevant costs. The procedures are illustrated in the numerical example which follows. The relevant cost of using a particular resource on a project may be found by calculating the difference between cash flows expected if the resource is applied to the project and those if it is not. This is the differential cash flow approach to decision making. In order to calculate the expected cash flow relating to a resource if the opportunity under consideration is rejected, it is necessary to establish the best alternative use to which the resource could be put in the event of rejection. Thus the procedure for calculating the relevant cost of using a resource is in two steps:

1. Estimate cash flows expected if the resource is put to its best alternative use.

2. Compare these cash flows with those expected if the resource is applied to the project under consideration.

If the cash outflow resulting from applying the resource is greater than the cash outflow resulting from the best alternative use, the difference is called a cost. If cash inflows are involved, rather than outflows, a cost arises if the cash inflow expected from the best alternative use is greater than the cash inflow expected from application to the project. A mixture of cash inflows and outflows may be handled using the same principles.

Let us take an example. Nicholson plc manufactures a wide range of fashion products. The directors are considering whether to add a further product, the spur, to the range. A market research survey, recently undertaken at a cost of £5,000, suggests that demand for the spur would last for only one year, during which 50,000 units could be sold at £18 per unit. Production and sale of spurs would take place evenly throughout the year. The following information is available regarding the costs of manufacturing spurs.

Raw materials

Each spur would require three types of raw material: white, hart and lane. Quantities required, current stock levels and costs of each raw material are shown in Table 5.1. White is used regularly by the company and stocks are replaced as they are used. The current stock of harts is the result of overbuying for an earlier contract. The material is not used regularly by Nicholson plc and the best use of any stock that was not used to manufacture spurs would be to sell it. The company does not carry a stock of lanes and the units required would be specially purchased.

Labour

Production of each spur would require 1/16 hour of skilled labour and 1/2 hour of unskilled labour. Wage rates are £12 per hour for skilled labour and £8 per hour for unskilled labour. In addition one supervisor would be required to devote all his working time for one year to supervision of the production of spurs. The supervisor is paid an annual wage of £25,000. Nicholson plc does not currently employ any skilled labour and must recruit specifically for the new product. If spurs are not manufactured, Nicholson plc expects to have available 100,000 surplus unskilled labour hours during the coming year. Because they intend to expand their activities in the future, and because of the high cost of making staff redundant, the directors have decided not to dismiss any unskilled workers in the foreseeable future. The supervisor is due to retire immediately on an annual pension, payable by the company, of £10,000. He has agreed to stay on for a further year if necessary, and to waive his pension for one year in return for a year's wage. Subsequent pension rights would not be affected.

Table 5.1 Raw material information

			'Costs' per metre of raw material		
Raw material	Amount required per spur (m)	Current stock level (m)	Original cost (£)	Current replacement cost (£)	Current resale value (£)
White	1.0	100,000	2.10	2.50	1.80
Hart	2.0	60,000	3.30	2.80	1.10
Lane	0.5	0	–	5.50	5.00

Machinery

Two machines would be required to manufacture spurs, a marchi and a medwin. Some details of each machine are given in Table 5.2. Depreciation has been charged on each machine for each year of its life using the formula: $D = (C - S) \div L$, where D is the annual depreciation charge, C is the original cost of the machine, S is the expected resale value at the end of the machine's useful life, and L is the useful life in years, estimated when the machine was purchased. This is known as the *straight line method*, and is one of a number of depreciation methods commonly used by accountants.

Table 5.3 contains details of various values of the two machines at the start and end of the year during which spurs would be manufactured. Nicholson plc owns a number of marchi machines which are used regularly on various products. Each marchi is replaced as soon as it reaches the end of its useful life. Medwin machines are no longer used, and the one which would be used for spurs is the only one the company now has. If it were not used to produce spurs it would be sold immediately.

Overheads

In addition to machinery costs, Nicholson plc incurs various other production overheads. Some, such as rent and rates, are fixed in total regardless of output levels and of the mix of products manufactured. Others, such as lighting and heating, have

Table 5.2   Details of machinery

	Marchi	Medwin
Original cost (£)	70,000	50,000
Accumulated depreciation (straight line) (£)	30,000	36,000
Written-down value (£)	40,000	14,000
Age (years)	5	6
Expected remaining useful life (years)	5	1
Expected resale value at end of useful life (£)	10,000	8,000

Table 5.3   Values of machines

		Start of year (£)	End of year (£)
Marchi:	Replacement cost	80,000	65,000
	Resale value	60,000	47,000
	Discounted present value*	90,000	73,000
Medwin:	Replacement cost	13,000	9,000
	Resale value	11,000	8,000
	Discounted present value*	0	0

*Discounted present value of expected net receipts from continuing to operate the machine in its present use.

a fixed element and a variable element, the latter depending upon the volume of activity. For costing purposes, fixed overheads (including costs which are fixed in total and the fixed elements of other costs, but excluding depreciation) are allocated by the company to products on the basis of total labour hours required. The allocation for the coming year is £14.00 per labour hour. Variable overhead costs for spurs are estimated at £1.20 per unit produced.

Evaluation

We now consider the relevant cost to Nicholson plc of using each resource required for the production of spurs, applying the procedure outlined earlier: that is, in each case we compare the cash flows associated with manufacture with those associated with non-manufacture. The difference between the two represents the incremental cost (or benefit) of each item. It should be noted that these figures may differ from those obtained by applying conventional cost accounting methods. The two approaches are compared in the next section.

Raw materials

Cash flows are as follows:

	Manufacture (£)	Non-manufacture (£)	= Difference (£)
White	−125,000	0	−125,000
Hart: Sale of surplus	0	+66,000	
Purchase of additional units	−112,000	0	−178,000
Lane	−137,500	0	−137,500
			−440,500

Note: A minus sign signifies a cash outflow and a plus sign a cash inflow.

Fifty thousand metres of white would be required (50,000 spurs each requiring 1 metre). As white is used regularly by the company and stocks are replaced as used, the 50,000 metres required would be replaced for use on other jobs at the current replacement cost of £2.50 per metre, a total cash outflow of £125,000. This cash outflow would not be incurred if spurs were not produced. A hundred thousand metres of hart would be required (50,000 spurs each requiring 2 metres). If spurs were manufactured, Nicholson plc would use the 60,000 metres it has in stock, which have already been paid for, and would buy a further 40,000 metres at £2.80 per metre, a total cash outflow of £112,000. If spurs were not produced, the company would sell its current stock of harts for £1.10 per metre, a total cash inflow of £66,000. Twenty-five thousand metres of lane would be needed (50,000 spurs each requiring 0.5 metres), and these would be specially purchased at £5.50 per metre, a total cash outflow of £137,500. There would be no cash flows associated with lane if spurs were not produced. To summarise, the relevant cost of raw materials is generally given by their current replacement cost, unless the materials are already owned and would not be replaced if used, in which case the relevant cost of using them is their current resale value, or their value if applied to another product if this is greater than the current resale value.

Labour

Cash flows are as follows:

		Manufacture (£)	Non-manufacture (£)	Difference (£)
Skilled:	Wages	−37,500	0	−37,500
Unskilled:	Wages	−200,000	−200,000	0
Supervisor:	Wages	−25,000	0 ⎱	−15,000
	Pension	0	−10,000 ⎰	
				−52,500

Manufacture of spurs would involve 3,125 skilled labour hours (50,000 spurs each requiring 1/16 hour) and 25,000 unskilled labour hours (50,000 spurs each requiring 1/2 hour). The additional wage payments for skilled labour will be £37,500 (3,125 hours × £12 = £37,500). Unskilled labour of £200,000 (25,000 × £8 = £200,000) will be the same whether or not spurs are produced. Thus unskilled labour wages are not relevant costs. The relevant cost of the supervisor is the difference between the wages paid and the pension cost that would be avoided.

Machinery

The likely effect of using a marchi machine is to bring closer the time at which it will have to be replaced. In order to estimate the relevant cost of using the marchi machine we need strictly to estimate all future cash flows associated with marchi machines on the alternative assumptions that spurs are and are not manufactured, and to discount them to present values to give measures of relevant cash flows. In practice, where a machine is used regularly, it may be sufficient to use the fall in its replacement cost value as an approximation to the relevant cost of using it. By following this procedure we are, in effect, implying that the firm is willing to expand its general machine capacity by buying a machine of equivalent age to the one to be used either immediately (if the manufacture proceeds) or at the end of the production period (if it does not). A rigorous analysis of the relevant cost of using fixed assets is beyond the scope of an introductory text.[1] Determination of the cash flows associated with the medwin machine is straightforward: it will be sold either immediately (if spurs are not manufactured) or after one year (if they are), at the prices given in Table 5.3. On the assumption that a second-hand marchi machine will be purchased, the cash flows associated with machinery are:

	Manufacture (£)	– Non-manufacture (£)	= Difference (£)
Marchi: Replacement cost	−80,000	−65,000	−15,000
Medwin: Resale value	+8,000	+11,000	−3,000
			−18,000

Overheads

Cash flows are as follows:

	Manufacture (£)	– Non-manufacture (£)	= Difference (£)
Variable overheads	−60,000	0	−60,000
Fixed overheads	−X	−X	0
			−60,000

Variable costs (i.e. costs which vary with the level of activity) are £1.20 per spur produced, a total cash outflow of £60,000 (50,000 × £1.20) incurred only if manufacture takes place. All other overhead costs are fixed, i.e. the same in total whether or not spurs are produced. Whatever their level (we have assumed £X in total), it will be the same for manufacture and non-manufacture. This illustrates the important rule that, for decision purposes, only costs that will vary as a result of the decision being taken are relevant.

Sales revenue

If we apply to revenue the differential cash flow analysis used for costs, we find, not surprisingly, that relevant revenue equals unit sales price (£18) multiplied by the number of units expected to be sold (50,000):

	Manufacture (£)	– Non-manufacture (£)	= Difference (£)
Sales revenue	+900,000	0	+900,000

For presentation to management, the results of the above analysis (i.e. the figures in the 'Difference' column) may be summarised in a single statement. A possible form of such a statement is given in Table 5.4. Supplementary information should be

Table 5.4 Relevant costs and revenues expected from the manufacture of spurs

		£	£
Raw materials:	White	125,000	
	Hart	178,000	
	Lane	137,500	440,500
Labour:	Skilled	37,500	
	Unskilled	0	
	Supervisor	15,000	52,500
Machinery:	Marchi	15,000	
	Medwin	3,000	18,000
Variable overheads			60,000
			571,000
Sales revenue			900,000
Surplus from manufacture			329,000

provided concerning the basis of calculation of the figures in the statement, along the lines discussed previously in this section, dealing particularly with points of possible contention, such as the cost of using the marchi machine. The surplus figure of £329,000 is the expected increase in the company's cash resources which will arise as a result of manufacturing spurs rather than applying the resources required to their best alternative uses. Thus, on the basis of the figures in Table 5.4, production and sale of spurs is worthwhile.

The figures presented in Table 5.4 may not represent the complete picture, however. As we noted earlier, the direct cash consequences of a decision may not be the only factors of interest to the decision maker. In our example, production of spurs may have implications beyond those we have considered. For example, the new product may complement or compete with existing products; it may entice new customers to the company's whole range of products; it may change the risk associated with the company's overall activities; and so on. These and other similar factors should be quantified and incorporated into the analysis as far as possible. At the very least they should be mentioned in notes appended to the decision budget so that decision makers can use their own value judgements to balance them against the cash items included in the budget.

We have made no attempt in our statement to adjust for differences in timing between cash flows. In practice, where cash flows arise at significantly different times (for example, if all costs are payable at the start of a year and all revenues receivable at the end), it will be necessary to apply an interest adjustment to ensure that distortions created by the timing differences are removed.

One important conclusion to emerge from the analysis in this section is that for no resource was the cost already incurred (i.e. historical cost) the appropriate measure of its relevant cost. This conclusion is unfortunate because accounting records have conventionally been, and to a large extent still are, based on the measurement, recording and matching of historical costs (also called original, past or sunk costs). We now turn to a more detailed consideration of this problem.

5.3 A comparison with conventional cost accounting

The figures in Table 5.4 differ from those we would have obtained by applying conventional cost accounting to the problem of Nicholson plc. Conventional cost accounting often involves the use of *standard costs* for measuring the costs of using resources. Standard costs are discussed in detail in Chapters 7 and 15–17. Each resource is assigned a standard cost which may be based on its historical cost, its current cost (the cost at today's prices) or its expected cost (the cost expected at the time the resource will be used). The use of standard costs has the advantage that it avoids the need to calculate the cost of each resource on each occasion that a new opportunity is being evaluated. On the other hand, it sometimes means that the idiosyncrasies of a particular decision are overlooked. Broadly speaking, the conventional cost accounting approach involves matching the historical, current or expected costs of the resources actually used on a project against its revenues. These costs sometimes include fixed costs which are allocated on one (or more) of a number of bases. Even if current or expected costs are used, the conventional approach may over- or underestimate the worth of particular opportunities. The dangers involved in allocating fixed costs, and effectively treating them as if they are variable, are illustrated more fully in Chapter 18 (pp. 397–400).

Consider the statement in Table 5.5, which includes costs measured according to the historical costs of resources required, and compare the figures with those in

Table 5.5 Conventional accounting 'profitability' of manufacturing spurs

	£	£
Cost of market research survey		5,000
Raw materials:		
White (50,000 metres at £2.10)	105,000	
Hart (60,000 metres at £3.30 +		
40,000 metres at £2.80)	310,000	
Lane (25,000 metres at £5.50)	137,500	552,500
Labour:		
Skilled (3,125 hours at £12.00)	37,500	
Unskilled (25,000 hours at £8.00)	200,000	
Supervisor	25,000	262,500
Depreciation of machinery:		
Marchi ([40,000 − 10,000] ÷ 5)	6,000	
Medwin ([14,000 − 8,000] ÷ 1)	6,000	12,000
Overheads:		
Fixed (28,125 × £14.00)	393,750	
Variable (50,000 × £1.20)	60,000	453,750
		1,285,750
Sales revenue		900,000
Loss from manufacturing spurs		385,750

Table 5.4. The first difference concerns the treatment of historical costs. This application of conventional cost accounting practice involves charging resources to particular projects at their original cost as, for example, with the market research survey, raw material white and the first 60,000 metres of raw material hart. In support of this procedure, it might be argued that if the value of a resource has fallen (or risen) since purchase, the loss (or profit) should be taken into account; but if the value has changed, the consequent loss (or profit) has already occurred regardless of any decision to be made now, and it should not be added to (or subtracted from) the costs of the opportunity under consideration. The crucial question is: which cash flows will be affected by the decision? The answer to this question depends on the currently available alternative uses of the resource, and will be equal to its historical cost only by accident.

The second difference is the treatment of depreciation of assets. The straight-line method of depreciation has already been mentioned. It is widely used in the reporting of financial information, and in common with other conventional methods of depreciation has the characteristic that the annual depreciation charge is based on an allocation of the original cost of the asset less its expected ultimate resale value. The treatment of depreciation is thus an extension of the conventional practice of matching or recovering past costs. For decision purposes we need to know the sacrifice involved in using the asset on the particular project under consideration. There is no obvious reason why this should correspond to the writing off of original cost that typifies the conventional accounting concept of depreciation.

A third area of difference concerns fixed costs. Costs that are fixed regardless of the decision under consideration (for example, unskilled labour wages and fixed overhead costs in the case of Nicholson plc) are not relevant costs of that decision, for they cannot be affected by it. Nevertheless, in conventional accounting practice, fixed costs are often allocated to available opportunities. Later chapters explore cost allocation problems in more detail.

A final main area of difference relates to the impact of a project on a firm's other activities (for example, the deferral of the supervisor's pension in the case of Nicholson plc). Under conventional practice, only the amount paid for the resource is treated as a cost; cash flow changes elsewhere in the organisation are not usually considered even though they are a direct consequence of the decision being taken.

The differences between conventional practice and differential cash flow analysis may lead to startling differences in 'profitability'. In our example a conventional 'loss' of £385,750 is in fact an incremental cash surplus of £329,000. In general, when prices are rising, the application of conventional historical cost accounting results in the understatement of the current relevant cost of using resources such as stock and fixed assets, and a consequent overstatement of profitability. On the other hand, inclusion of allocated fixed costs overstates relevant costs and leads to an understatement of profitability. Such differences may lead to incorrect advice, as in the case of Nicholson plc.

Some of the differences outlined above may be reduced if current or expected costs are used instead of historical costs in conventional cost accounting statements. Two main adjustments are required to historical cost figures for the purpose of determining current costs. The first is to increase the cost of stock used (e.g. of raw materials) from its historical cost to its current cost. The second is to base the depreciation charge for fixed assets (e.g. machines) on the current cost rather than the historical cost of the assets concerned.

The adoption of current costs rather than historical costs would have some effect on the statement in Table 5.5. The precise changes would depend upon which of a number of possible methods for measuring current costs were chosen. The cost of raw materials and depreciation would probably be adjusted to figures very similar to those in the relevant cost statement in Table 5.4. In other respects (inclusion of the cost of the market research survey, unskilled labour wages and fixed overheads, and the omission of the saving on the supervisor's pension), the use of current costs instead of historical costs fails to remove problems created by the application of conventional accounting procedures.

CHAPTER SUMMARY

The approach to the determination of relevant costs and revenues for decisions which we have recommended in this chapter recognises that the cost of using a resource depends upon the alternative uses to which it could be put. We described and illustrated three broad principles: that only future costs and revenues are relevant; that only those costs and revenues which will differ under some or all of the available alternatives are relevant; and that only cash costs and revenues are to be included. In summary, for making decisions, *only differential future cash flows should be considered*. We conclude the chapter by noting that such an interpretation of cost is consistent with the economist's concept of *opportunity cost*, which is normally defined in terms of the value of the best opportunity forgone by not applying a resource to an alternative use. Agreement between definitions of cost used by accountants and economists would have many benefits, particularly where accounting data are being used as input to economic models. Unfortunately, there is still some way to go before such agreement is achieved.

REVIEW QUESTIONS

1. Explain the difference between accept or reject and ranking decisions, and discuss the importance of the distinction.

2. What are the main principles of relevant cost and revenue determination? Illustrate your answer with applications of each principle.

3. 'Past costs are irrelevant to *all* decisions.' Do you agree? Can you think of any decisions in which past costs might play a part? Are committed costs the same as past costs?

4. 'The economist's notion of opportunity cost is a valuable contribution to managerial decision making.' Discuss.

5. Explain the distinction between fixed costs and variable costs, and discuss its importance to the determination of relevant costs for decision making.

EXERCISES

5.1 Memlinc Ltd manufactures scientific instruments. It is considering whether or not to accept a contract to manufacture a batch of oscilloscopes. The contract would last for 52 weeks. The company's cost accountant prepares the following statement on the basis of which it is recommended that the contract should not be accepted.

		£	£
Materials:	A—already in stock (original cost)	18,750	
	B—ordered (original contract price)	22,500	41,250
Labour			87,500
Machinery:	Leased at £1,250 per week	65,000	
	Already owned—depreciation	50,000	115,000
General overheads: 100% on labour			87,500
			331,250
Contract price offered			300,000
Loss on contract			31,250

The cost accountant supplies the following additional information:

1. Material A was purchased two years ago. If sold now it would realise £12,500. Alternatively it could be adapted and used on another job as a substitute for material presently costing £20,000. It would cost £3,750 to make the necessary adaptation. Material B was ordered six months ago. Delivery has been delayed by a strike at the supplier's factory and agreement has been reached between the supplier and Memlinc Ltd that a discount of £5,000 be allowed against the original contract price to compensate for the delay. If material B is not used on the job under consideration, the only alternative is to sell it for £11,250.

2. The accountant's estimate includes £25,000 in respect of a supervisor's wages. Unlike the rest of the labour used on the job, the supervisor will be employed whether or not the contract is accepted. However, if the supervisor does have to work on the job under consideration, the company will have to employ someone else at £375 per week to do the work he or she could otherwise have done.

3. Two machines will be used on the job. One is a machine the company leases for £1,250 per week. This is at present being used in another department, and if it is transferred for use on the job being considered, another machine will have to be leased for £700 per week and additional labour costing £750 per week hired to maintain production in the other department. The second machine was purchased by the company three years ago for £250,000. Its estimated life was then five years and hence depreciation at the rate of £50,000 per annum is being written off. If not used on the job, the machine would be sold now for £62,500; otherwise it will be sold after completion of the contract for an estimated price of £30,000.

4. As in past years, general overheads, which include such items as rent, rates and other administrative expenses, are recovered at the rate of 100% on direct labour. All expenses included under this heading will remain unchanged whether or not the contract is accepted.

5. The storage space necessary if the job is undertaken can be provided only if the construction of a new works canteen is delayed for one year.

(a) If you think it necessary, redraft the cost accountant's statement. Explain any alterations you make.
(b) Advise Memlinc Ltd whether or not to accept the contract. (Solution at end of text.)

5.2 The Van Dyck Motor plc has recently suffered a strike which lasted for two weeks. During that time no cars were produced. The company issued a press statement to the effect that the cost of the strike was £15 million. This figure was arrived at by the managing director, who estimated that production lost was 1,000 cars, each of which could have been sold for £15,000 giving a total loss of turnover of £15,000,000. The company's cost accountant feels that the managing director was overstating the cost of the strike and provides the following statement to support his view.

	£000
Expenses avoided	
Materials (£3,000 per car)	3,000
Production labour (£1,500 per car)	1,500
Depreciation of machinery	5,250
Overheads: 200% on labour	3,000
	12,750
Loss of sales revenue	15,000
Cost of strike	2,250

The following additional information is available:

1. Depreciation of machinery is based on the conventional straight-line method of calculation. The plant manager estimates that the machinery will fall in value by £600,000 each week regardless of the level of production. In addition, it is felt that its value will fall by £450,000 for every 100 cars that are produced.

2. Overhead expenses are recovered at the rate of 200% on production labour. Most of the overhead expenses are unaffected by the level of production (e.g. rent, rates, maintenance, staff wages), but some, such as power and lighting, vary directly with production. The general manager estimates that the latter type of overhead expense, varying directly with the level of production, amounts to £30,000 for every 100 cars produced.

3. During the period of the strike the maintenance staff, whose wages are included in the fixed overhead expense, carried out a major overhaul on one of the company's machines using materials costing £30,000. This overhaul would normally have been performed by an outside contractor at a price, including materials, of £300,000.

4. The sales manager feels that about one-half of the production lost could be made up and sold in the next month by the production labour working overtime. Labour is paid at the rate of time-and-a-half for overtime working.

Prepare a statement clearly showing the cost to the company of the strike. State any assumptions which you make and explain any differences between your figures and those of the cost accountant. (Solution at end of text.)

5.3   Ketchum Ltd is considering the manufacture of certain components, incorporated in its range of final products, which have previously been purchased from outside suppliers. This additional manufacturing operation would cover only the next 12 months, since capacity which is presently unused will then, it is expected, be required to fill rising demand for the final products themselves. The following information has been assembled:

1. 90,000 units of the component would be required over the year.

2. 1 kg of raw material type A is required for each unit of the component. The current cost of such material is £8 per kg, but an alternative material, with a current replacement cost of £9 per kg and a realisable value of £5, could be used. The company has in stock 30,000 kg of the alternative material which would be sold if not used to manufacture the component.

3. 1 kg of raw material type B is required for each unit of the component; 125,000 kg which cost £1 million are currently in stock. If not

used for the manufacture of the components, this material might be transferred to another department where it can be used in place of material currently costing £7.50 per kg. Alternatively, it might be sold for £6.25 per kg.

4. Additional labour will be required at the rate of one half-hour of skilled labour and two hours of unskilled labour per unit. Hourly wage rates are currently £15 for skilled labour and £7.50 for unskilled labour. Further supervisors would be required at a minimum annual cost of £70,000; this would increase by £35,000 for each 15,000 units, or part thereof, of the component manufactured in excess of 60,000 units.

5. A training programme for the skilled labour force, costing £140,000, has already been carried out in anticipation of a decision to manufacture the components. A further expenditure of £70,000 will be required if units to be manufactured exceed 60,000.

6. It is estimated that existing machinery can be used for the manufacture of 45,000 units, with the result that its future scrap value will be reduced by £100,000. (The present value of this reduction is estimated at £60,000.) For every 15,000 units in excess of that production level, a machine must be hired for £30,000.

7. Variable overheads are estimated at £4 per hour of direct labour and the application of the company's normal costing techniques would involve a charge of £6 per direct labour hour in respect of fixed overheads other than depreciation.

8. The cost of one unit of the component from outside suppliers is expected to be £55.

(a) Produce a statement showing the total cost of the 90,000 units if the company chose to manufacture at each of the following levels and purchase the balance from the outside supplier:

30,000 units
45,000 units
60,000 units
75,000 units

(b) Comment on any matters, not quantified in the statement produced in answer to (a), which you feel would be relevant in arriving at a final decision.

5.4 Because of a fall in demand for its products, the production manager of Beltrami Ltd has proposed that over the next six months idle capacity and labour should be used for the manufacture of a component normally purchased from outside suppliers. The following statement is used to support this case:

Cost of manufacturing 200,000 units required	£
Materials:	
Type A, 100,000 kg at actual cost of £2 per kg	200,000
Type B, 5,000 kg at actual cost of £35 per kg	175,000
Type C, 10,000 kg at estimated cost of £15 per kg	150,000
Labour:	
Grade 1, 16,000 hours at £16.25 per hour	260,000
Grade 2, 4,000 hours at £12.50 per hour	50,000
Grade 3, 10,000 hours at £10.00 per hour	100,000
Overheads	
Depreciation of existing machines,	
8,000 hours of machine time at £5 per hour	40,000
Depreciation of additional machines,	
£300,000 at 10% for six months	15,000
Other overheads, 10,000 machine hours at £16 per hour	160,000
Total cost	1,150,000
Cost per unit	5.75

The following information is also available:

1. Type A material is regularly used by the company; large stocks are currently held because of substantial purchases made before a recent price increase to £3 per kg.

2. 3,000 kg of type B material have been in storage since excess stocks were purchased for a special order last year. The company has been looking for an opportunity to recover the cost, since the resale value of the material is only £25 per kg. The cost of purchasing type B material at the present time would be £35 per kg.

3. Grade 1 labour is normally in short supply in the area, so no lay-offs are contemplated, although 16,000 hours of labour of this type will be idle if not employed in the manufacture of the components. If the labour involved is so used, the trade union has insisted on an extra payment of £2.50 per hour in excess of the normal hourly rate of £13.75 because of the unfamiliar work.

4. One hour of either grade 1 or grade 2 labour is needed for every 10 units of production. The production manager suggests that grade 2 labour be employed only to supplement instead of to replace grade 1 labour, despite the lower hourly rate, because of the problems of recruiting a substantial amount of grade 2 labour for the short term.

5. Grade 3 labour can be hired as needed.

6. Production plans for the company's normal activities indicate that 8,000 hours of machine time (sufficient for 160,000 units) will be available during the six-month period. The depreciation charge included is based on the company's usual costing policies; however, it is not anticipated that the use of the machines will have the effect of reducing measurably their scrap value when they are replaced next year on the company's planned move to a new factory.

7. Two additional machines would be required to raise production of the component to the level of 200,000 units. These would be purchased for £300,000 or leased for six months for £20,000 each. If purchased, they would be stored after use in the manufacture of the components, for eventual installation in the new factory next year.

8. The charge for other overheads is based on the company's usual costing system and includes £6 per machine hour for fixed costs and £10 for variable costs. It is not anticipated that the manufacture of the components would involve the incurring of any additional fixed costs, and it is expected that the amount of variable overheads will conform with the company's usual experience.

9. The cost of each component bought from the existing supplier is £6.

(a) Prepare a recommendation supported by appropriate calculations as to what policy should be pursued by the company, on financial grounds alone, assuming that the additional machines referred to in paragraph 7 will be leased and stating any other assumption which you make.

(b) Discuss any factors other than those quantified in your answer to (a) which you feel might be relevant in arriving at the final decision.

Notes

1. Readers who wish to pursue this problem further might refer to W. T. Baxter, *Depreciation*, Sweet & Maxwell, 1971, or to B. V. Carsberg, 'On the linear programming approach to asset valuation', *Journal of Accounting Research*, Autumn 1969.

PART 1

Basic framework

PART 2

Cost information

Understanding the financial flows associated with organisational activity

CHAPTER 6
Cost behaviour and estimation

CHAPTER 7
Cost recording and product costing

PART 3

Applications

Cost behaviour and estimation

AIMS AND OBJECTIVES

☐ To describe different methods of classifying costs.
☐ To describe different patterns of cost behaviour relative to output levels and explain the importance of the differences.
☐ To introduce the notion and importance of cost drivers.
☐ To explain, illustrate and evaluate different methods of predicting costs.
☐ To explain and illustrate the learning curve.

The use of incremental analysis explained in the previous chapter requires the identification of those costs which are relevant to decision making. In particular, incremental analysis demands a knowledge of which costs change, and which costs do not change, as a consequence of a particular decision. Identification of the ways in which the enterprise's costs behave in response to changes in the level of its activities is, therefore, an important first step in helping to estimate the effects of particular decisions on future cash flows. The responses of costs to changes in circumstances (including changes in activity levels) are known collectively as *cost behaviour*. We might be better able to understand the importance of cost behaviour in the following way. As one important objective of a firm's managers is to generate from operations the maximum possible amount of cash, managers must strive to attain the level and pattern of operations which are expected to maximise cash resources. Therefore, information on how costs behave in relation to changes in output levels or in other attributes of operations is vital for optimal planning and decision making.

6.1 Classifying costs

So far we have deliberately avoided attaching labels to particular costs. We have simply stated that a cost is relevant to a decision if it involves an incremental future cash flow to the organisation. In practice, however, it is usual and useful to classify costs in certain basic ways, and to group together related or similar costs. Different cost categories can be recognised on the basis of the source of cost (e.g. materials for processing, labour and bought-in services), and according to the functional nature of the operations with which the costs are associated (e.g. manufacturing, distribution, research and general administration). For decision making and control, however, acknowledging the source and functional nature of costs is less important than understanding the pattern of cost behaviour: that is, the relationship between cost being incurred and the underlying activities conducted within the business. Cost classifications and groupings which reflect differences in cost behaviour can help to identify relevant and irrelevant costs, and are important in methods of analysis such as cost–volume–profit analysis, which we shall consider in more detail in Chapter 8.

The terminology of cost behaviour can sometimes be confusing because the same cost may be described by a number of terms, depending on the basis of the classification. Examples of some of the ways in which costs may be classified for analytical purposes are set out in Table 6.1.

The three classifications in Table 6.1 are each concerned with different aspects of cost. Product or period refers to the treatment of cost expenditure in financial reports; direct or indirect refers to the link between costs and some other aspect of the firm's operations of interest; and variable or fixed refers to the pattern of incidence as operations are changed. For example, within the staff costs incurred by a firm, accounting and data-processing staff would be treated as a period cost while labour employed in manufacturing would be included in product costs; within manufacturing labour, employees working directly on a single product would be regarded as a direct cost of labour, while staff engaged in quality inspection of all products would be an indirect overhead; the total costs associated with inspection could include a fixed element, such as the cost of inspection equipment, and variable costs, such as the amount of time worked by the quality control staff.

Table 6.1 Cost classification terminology

Product Costs associated with making or acquiring particular products for sale.* Product costs may be used as the basis for valuing stock at any point in time.	*Period* Costs not related to products or services provided. Such costs are treated as expenses of the period in which they are incurred.
Direct Costs which can be traced directly to a particular *cost object* that is a separate aspect of operations, such as a product, a department or a region.	*Indirect* Costs which cannot be traced to such objects, but which are general to a range of activities. Also referred to as overhead costs.
Variable Costs that change in proportion to changes in the level of activity.	*Fixed* Costs that remain unchanged across different levels of activity.

* Note that in a service firm, the 'product' could be the provision of a particular service.

Following the principles established in Chapter 5, the most important aspect of cost behaviour is the link between changes in activity and changes in cost incurred. Some relationships are easy to identify – for example, between raw material inputs and products manufactured – but others can only be established through a detailed analysis of the activities and processes which make up the business. Such analysis involves asking why a cost is incurred – what activity or operation is performed which gives rise to the cost. Identifying the activity associated with a cost can then lead to some measure of activity or *cost driver* which can be used when estimating future costs and allocating actual costs incurred. In the next section we look at ways in which costs behave with activity in more detail, with particular reference to how costs respond to changes in output levels. Identifying cost drivers for different activities is discussed in section 6.5.

6.2 Patterns of cost behaviour

Variable costs

A cost is variable if it is expected to vary as a function of some measure of activity, such as the level of output or the level of sales. Raw materials and labour paid on an hourly basis are good examples of costs which vary with the level of output; sales commission is an example of a cost which varies with the level of sales. Accountants often assume that variable costs are linear (i.e. the functional relationship between costs and output is expressed as a straight line, such as the line $0A$ in Figure 6.1). This assumed linear relationship means that the cost per unit of output is presumed to be constant at all levels of output. The relationship can be expressed by the equation:

$$y = bx$$

where y = expected cost, x = expected level of output and b = constant cost per unit. (This relationship is an example of a cost 'model'. Models were first introduced in Chapter 3.)

For instance, if labour is a variable cost, and each unit of output requires two hours of labour at £8 per hour, then 100 units of output should require a total labour cost of £16 × 100 = £1,600 (i.e. y = £1,600 where b = £16 per unit and x = 100 units). Knowing that labour is a variable cost will help the firm to plan for future decisions which involve the use of labour.

However, for reasons discussed in the next section, the simple linear relationship between costs and output may not always hold, and a curvilinear function may be a better representation of actual cost behaviour, as shown in Figure 6.2. For curve $0B$, an extra unit of output causes a *less* than proportional increase in cost (e.g. it takes less than two labour hours to produce an additional unit at high output levels, due perhaps to the workers becoming more efficient); for curve $0C$, an extra unit of output causes a *more* than proportional cost increase (e.g. it costs more to produce an additional unit at high output levels, perhaps because it is necessary to work overtime and hence incur additional costs).

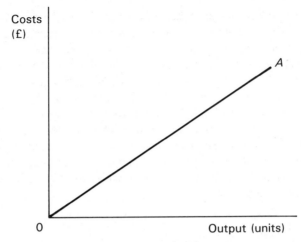

Figure 6.1 Variable cost function.

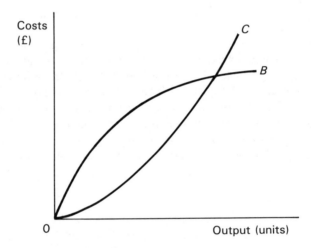

Figure 6.2 Curvilinear cost functions.

If the variable cost function is curvilinear, appropriate cost calculations can become very complicated. For this reason, linear functions are often used as approximations within certain relevant output ranges which the firm has experienced in the past. Figure 6.3 provides an illustration of a linear approximation (the dashed line). The importance of the relevant range is discussed further in section 6.3.

Fixed costs

Fixed costs are those costs which are likely to remain unchanged regardless of the level of activity or the particular decision under consideration. Rent, rates and directors' salaries are examples of costs which are often fixed for a particular

Figure 6.3 The relevant range and linear approximation.

decision. Note that the term 'fixed' relates primarily to short-term decisions. In the long term very few costs are irrevocably fixed. Indeed the long run is frequently defined in economics textbooks as a period over which all costs are avoidable. A graphical description of a linear fixed cost function (*AB*) is shown in Figure 6.4. The function can be expressed by the equation:

$$y = a$$

where y = expected cost and a = constant amount.

It should be clearly understood that the decision variable x (the level of output) does not affect the level of fixed costs (i.e. it does not enter the cost equation). For

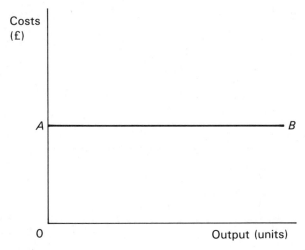

Figure 6.4 Fixed cost function (1).

instance, if a firm expects to pay £5,000 for the rent of a factory during the forthcoming year, then, provided that the level of production does not require the use of another factory, the number of units produced will not affect the amount to be paid for factory rent. It will remain constant at £5,000, and will be independent of the level of output. Such a fixed cost is not relevant for short-run decisions, as explained in the previous chapter.

The presumption in Figure 6.4 is that the item of fixed cost under consideration will remain constant at all output levels, including zero output. It may be more realistic to assume that there are some fixed expenses which are avoidable at zero output, but are constant at all other output levels. (For example, if the firm referred to above decides to produce nothing, it may be able to avoid payment of rent on the factory.) If so, a function similar to that shown in Figure 6.5 may be more representative. In Figure 6.5, the fixed cost line does not begin at point A on the vertical axis, but rather at point A_1, which corresponds to the output level O_1, the point at which the cost is incurred.

Step costs

Step costs result from input factors which cannot be increased in very small amounts. They can be increased only in discrete 'steps'. Strictly speaking, nearly all variable costs fall into this category. Examples of such costs might be certain items of small equipment, secretarial salaries and supervisory labour. For instance, for output levels of 0–1,000 units, the firm may need only one supervisor, for levels of 1,001–2,000 units, two supervisors may be needed, for levels of 2,001–3,000 units, three supervisors may be needed. Thus a pattern develops similar to that shown in Figure 6.6.

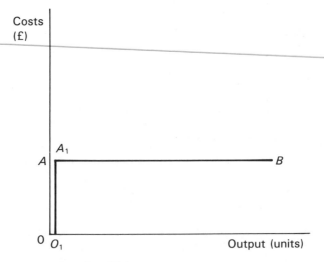

Figure 6.5   Fixed cost function (2).

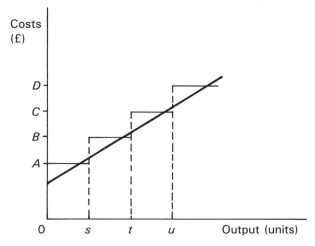

Figure 6.6 Step cost function.

Figure 6.6 shows that the cost item remains constant at an amount of £A for output levels between 0 and s. When output increases beyond s, the cost increases to £B and remains at this amount up to output level t, when it increases to £C, and so on.

Step costs cannot be described by a simple algebraic function and, for simplicity, such costs are often dealt with in one of the following ways:

1. If the steps are sufficiently shallow and frequent, a continuous function of the form $y = bx$ may be used as an approximation, as shown by the straight line in Figure 6.6.

2. If the likely output range lies completely within one step – for example, between s and t, or between t and u – the step cost may be treated as a fixed cost.

3. If neither of the above conditions is satisfied, and step costs cannot be treated as being variable or fixed, more elaborate analysis is needed. The form of this analysis is explained in Chapter 8.

Semi-variable costs

Costs which possess both a fixed and a variable component are called 'semi-variable' or 'mixed' costs. A good example of such a cost is an electricity cost, which includes a basic fixed charge irrespective of use, and a cost element which depends solely upon use; or a telephone cost, which is in the nature of a fixed rental together with an additional charge for each call made. The variable element of a semi-variable cost function may be either linear or curvilinear, as explained earlier. For simplicity, we show the semi-variable function as a linear function as in Figure 6.7.

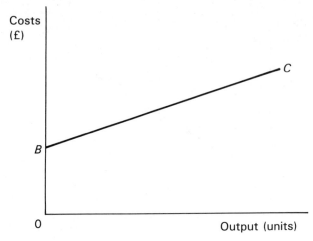

Figure 6.7   Semi-variable cost function.

The line *BC* shows the total cost, which cuts the vertical line at point *B*, representing the constant level of fixed cost. The semi-variable cost function can be expressed by the equation:

$$y = a + bx$$

where y = expected cost, a = constant amount (i.e. the fixed element of the cost), b = variable cost per unit of output and x = level of output.

This, as we shall see, is a very important cost function because it mirrors the organisation's total cost function (i.e. it involves the estimation of both fixed and variable costs). The estimation of the total cost function, which is often fundamental to business planning, is discussed later in this chapter.

The four patterns of cost behaviour described here are not the only patterns which can be observed. Rather, they are guidelines to be used in the determination and construction of the cost functions necessary to analyse and evaluate business decisions. In particular, two points concerning the behaviour of costs should be clearly recognised: the linearity assumption and the use of the relevant range.

6.3 The linearity assumption

Much cost behaviour can be described accurately only by non-linear functions. In practice, linear approximations are often used to simplify the calculations involved in the analysis of cost behaviour. This is not unreasonable as statistical studies have presented evidence which suggests that, within specified output limits, organisations do have cost functions which are approximately linear.[1]

6.4 The relevant range

The assumption of linearity may be unrealistic if taken to extremes. As there are usually upper and lower limits to the levels of an organisation's attainable output, there will equally be upper and lower limits to the firm's cost functions. For each organisation there will be a relevant range of output levels within which it is likely to incur costs. One dimension of this is the range of time periods over which the cost functions are valid (the period during which the nature of demand for the firm's output can be reasonably predicted is usually fairly short). Furthermore, it may be unwise to extrapolate a cost function indiscriminately, to estimate costs for an output level outside the range for which the function was originally calculated – the behaviour of the function may well have changed by then. It is, therefore, imprudent to be categorical about the appropriate classification of certain costs. Very few costs are always variable and fewer still are always fixed. *A cost which is fixed for one decision or one time period may well be variable for a different decision, or in another time period.* Each situation must be assessed individually and treated on its own merits.

6.5 Cost drivers

In the examples used in preceding sections of this chapter, the pattern of cost behaviour has been described mainly in terms of its relationship to the level of output. However, for many areas of cost the pattern of incidence may respond to something other than this aspect of activity. For example, delivery costs may be higher for a large number of small orders than for a small number of large deliveries, even though the total volume of output, or quantity delivered, could be higher under the latter alternative. In this case delivery costs respond to, or are driven by, the number of separate orders.

In both understanding the behaviour of costs in an enterprise and estimating the future cost implications of decisions, what management really needs to know is the way in which a cost item changes in relation to its own *cost driver*. Cost drivers are those measures of activity which have a cause–effect link to the incidence of a cost. It is unlikely that all costs will move in line with a single overall measure of activity. Different activity measures should be recognised as the drivers for different areas of cost because of the potential distortion that can result from estimating all costs with one driver. For some costs, such as raw materials, the level of production may be the most appropriate driver, but for many areas of expenditure other factors will drive costs. For example, the cost associated with equipment maintenance might be driven by the complexity of the products rather than the volume in which they are produced, and the cost of inspection for quality control might be driven by the number of changes and variations in product specification. With many indirect or overhead costs, identifying a direct measure of activity can be difficult and a surrogate measure must be used as the cost driver.

With reference to the figures and equations used earlier in this chapter to illustrate cost patterns, the use of different cost drivers means that a different measure is used for the horizontal axis – that is, a different measure of x – with each area of cost. The consequences of this approach for cost estimation are twofold:

1. The process of estimating future cost consequences of decisions should reflect the complexity of operations by looking at each cost in terms of the specific related driver.

2. Many costs which might be regarded as fixed, or as overheads, when related to production output, because they do not change in proportion to output, can be estimated more accurately by looking at their individual drivers.

Cost driver analysis will be important to a complete understanding of the behaviour of costs in a firm, but its benefits will depend on the specific business situation. In some cases it may be difficult to identify single drivers for specific costs. The benefits of estimation using cost drivers are likely to be greatest in more complex production environments where the number of factors affecting cost will be greater. In relatively simple production environments, the level of aggregation and averaging implicit in using a global estimator such as production output may not detract from the accuracy of the estimates obtained.

Identifying drivers as part of the analysis of costs has been advocated in connection with the ideas of activity-based costing, which uses activity-specific drivers for allocating costs to products. This approach is described more fully in Chapter 7.

6.6 The prediction of costs

For purposes of decision making, managers will wish to know which costs are likely to change with changes in activity (and hence affect the firm's cash outflows) and which costs are likely to remain unchanged (and have no incremental impact on cash resources). In most cases this knowledge is not easy to acquire. Management's knowledge of how a firm's costs actually behave is limited to an analysis of the results of *past* decisions, whereas planning requires estimates of *future* costs. Although costs cannot usually be predicted with absolute accuracy, it may be possible to identify a cost function which can be used to *estimate* the costs which the firm is likely to incur. For example, if it can be shown that costs are related to some independent variable such as machine hours or units of output, it may be possible to estimate the level of future costs associated with different levels of this independent variable by using a relationship based on past cost levels.

The basic idea underlying cost prediction is to estimate the variable and fixed component of different types of cost. Some costs, such as raw materials, will have only a variable element; some, such as rent, rates and insurance, will have only a fixed element, at least in the short term; others, such as telephone and electricity costs, will have both a fixed and a variable element. The most common form of a simple cost function to be used for estimation purposes may be written as:

$$y = a + bx$$

where y is the total cost and is known as the *dependent* variable, because its amount depends upon some other factor. In this case that other factor is denoted by the *independent* variable x, which may be the quantity of output produced, or the number of orders processed, or any other measure of activity which is thought to influence the level of costs (i.e. the cost driver). The parameters, a and b, the total fixed cost and the variable cost per unit of activity respectively, attempt to explain and predict the relationship between the dependent variable y and the independent variable x. For example, suppose that the total cost of using electricity per month is estimated to be £500 plus £0.3 per kilowatt-hour used. Kilowatt-hour is the independent variable. If usage for the following month is expected to be 3,000 kilowatt-hours, the total cost of using electricity will be:

$$y = £500 + £0.3\,(3,000)$$
$$= £1,400$$

It is important to ask whether such a simple cost function can adequately solve the problem at hand. We have already discussed the need to recognise that many different cost drivers will influence total costs incurred. Given this situation, it is obviously unrealistic to assume that total cost is influenced by only one independent, explanatory variable. A more sophisticated multiple cost function is required. The representation of such a function for production costs might be of the form:

$$y = a + bx_1 + cx_2 + dx_3$$

where x_1, the first explanatory variable, might be the labour hours used in production, x_2 the machine hours used, and x_3 the number of production runs. Future cost levels may also be influenced by changes in the prices of inputs and by changes in efficiency. We consider later in the chapter how expected changes in prices and efficiency might be incorporated into an analysis of future cost behaviour.

While recognising the existence of different cost drivers, in order to simplify the analysis and to highlight the important features of alternative *methods* in our discussion of cost estimation procedures, we shall assume the existence of only one explanatory variable in addition to expected price and efficiency changes. This explanatory variable will usually be the level of output.

We must also add that an analysis of past costs, however sophisticated the technique used, is appropriate for managerial decision making only if management is contemplating undertaking similar activities in the future to those previously undertaken. If no similar activities have been undertaken in the past, then there will be an absence of comparable data to be used as a basis for analysis, and so alternative methods of cost estimation will be needed. One method which anticipates how future operations should be carried out is known as the *engineering method*.

6.7 The engineering method of cost estimation

Suppose that a firm is considering the production of a product never previously manufactured as part of its normal business activities. The product could be as physically large and expensive as an oilrig, or as small and cheap as a toothbrush. How might the firm estimate the costs to be incurred by the new product? The firm's managers have no previous experience of this type of production and have no database from which to make projections. One possible method might be to estimate directly the required production inputs needed to yield a certain output. These estimates of production inputs will usually be carried out by the firm's engineers, hence the name given to this method.

The engineers will calculate the raw material inputs based on the estimated material content of the product specification; labour inputs may be based on 'time and motion' studies; and an estimate of the capital equipment needed for production will provide the basis for a calculation of the relevant cost of using such equipment. Expected prices for each input factor can then be used to estimate the direct production costs. It is important to note that material, labour and equipment represent physical factors of production, and if these physical factors are relatively easy to identify with units of output, including the impact of any economies or diseconomies of scale, then cost estimation may be straightforward. However, problems arise immediately when the engineers attempt to calculate costs which are not so easily identifiable with units of output: for example, indirect production costs such as maintenance, insurance and power. Nevertheless, the observation and measurement by expert engineers of relationships between inputs and outputs can lead to very accurate predictions of future costs, and may yield results which benefit the overall planning system of the firm. For example, observation of the efficiency with which the labour force carries out its work on particular contracts may give useful information on how to set appropriate standards for work undertaken elsewhere within the firm by the labour force. In addition, if the new product has been manufactured previously by other firms (e.g. the oilrig or toothbrush mentioned earlier), information may be available about the production cost functions of those firms.

The biggest disadvantage of the engineering approach, which may limit its general use, is its costliness. If the production process is complex, the preparation of a full specification of inputs will require much expert work, entailing a large cost, which will be worthwhile only if the additional net benefits it creates are greater than the costs involved. However, the engineering method, or at least some variation of it, may have to be used if there are no past costs on which to base an analysis.

6.8 Historical cost-based methods of cost estimation

Few firms change the nature of their activities to the extent that cost estimation based on past activities is useless, but before we examine some of the methods used to predict future costs based on past data, a word of explanation is necessary. The use of past costs as aids to decision making does not violate anything we have previously said concerning the irrelevance of past costs as direct inputs to rational decisions. In the particular area of cost prediction it is not the past, historical costs *per se* which are useful for decision making, but rather the probability that they may offer some clues as to the likely levels of future costs, the real decision variables.

Where it is believed that past costs can be useful for information purposes, three preparatory steps should be undertaken to ensure that the greatest possible benefit is gained from using the data: choice of independent variable, selection of time period and examination of accounting data.

Choice of independent variable

The choice of an appropriate independent variable (basis of activity measurement or cost driver) is of vital importance in cost estimation. It may not always be obvious which basis should be used, particularly when the firm produces many different products. For example, in a manufacturing firm the total cost for any item might well vary with the level of output, the number of labour hours worked, the actual wages paid to labour, the number of machine hours used, and so on. The art lies in choosing the activity measure whose variations are most closely associated with fluctuations in the cost item which is being estimated. If more than one measure shows a very high correlation with changes in total cost, then management may well choose the one which entails the least expense in gathering the data. As most important managerial decisions in a manufacturing firm are concerned, in some way, with the level of output produced, it is usual to express costs as a function of output levels. This explains why we use units of output as the measure of activity level throughout the remainder of this chapter.

Selection of time period

The time period covered by past observations should not be chosen arbitrarily. It should be long enough to allow periodic costs to be included, and yet should attempt to allow for fluctuations in activity levels. In particular, the chosen time period should be one in which the firm's production process has remained reasonably constant. For example, if there have been changes in technology or changes in the make-up of the skilled labour force, or, indeed, changes in the prices of input factors, costs and activity levels may not be comparable. Where such environmental changes are significant, it may be unwise to use observations for time periods before the changes took place. This poses a major problem for the cost estimator. On the one hand, he or she would like to include as many observations as possible in order to increase the accuracy of the estimates; on the other hand, the estimator wants to use a time period during which there have been few changes in the production process. Resolution of the problem must always be on an individual basis. Trade-offs between using sufficient observations to impart a high level of statistical significance to the results and including only reasonably up-to-date information are inevitable.

Examination of accounting data

The accounting policies used by the firm may determine the ways in which data are accumulated in the financial records. For instance, the wages paid in one period may be calculated by reference to output in the previous period. Suppose, for example, that the firm's labour costs, the dependent variable y, and the output level, the independent variable x, are derived as follows for three successive weeks of the year:

	y (£)	x (units)
Week 1	20,000	4,500
Week 2	18,000	6,200
Week 3	24,000	7,000

If the firm follows the policy of paying its labour force in the succeeding week for output reached in the previous week, then it would not be a valid basis for estimation to attempt to correlate the £20,000 for wages paid in week 1 with the 4,500 units of output of week 1. The wages paid in week 2 of £18,000 relate to the output of week 1, and those paid in week 3 (£24,000) relate to the output of week 2. Adjustments must be made to correct the inherent bias in the data. The wages figure should also be examined closely to eliminate any possible bias arising from changes in labour rates during the period.

For cost prediction purposes it is necessary to ensure that all costs have been adjusted to current price levels; unadjusted data may produce misleading estimates of future costs. For example, suppose that management is attempting to correlate wages paid to the labour force over a period of five years with output produced during those years in order to predict the level of wages dependent upon output for 19X5. The unadjusted data for the five-year period are as follows:

		Wages paid (£)
Year	19X0	1,000,000
	19X1	1,300,000
	19X2	1,600,000
	19X3	1,800,000
	19X4	2,700,000

Suppose information is given that the labour force was given a wage increase of 20% at the beginning of 19X1 and a further increase of 15% at the beginning of 19X2. In order to ensure that the amounts for wages paid will produce consistent estimates of future costs, it is necessary to adjust those yearly payments which do *not* incorporate the increases of 20% and 15%. Thus the payments for 19X0 and 19X1 should be indexed by a factor reflecting the change in rate. There is no need to change the figures for the final three years, as these already incorporate the increased rates. Adjusted figures for the two years then become:

19X0	£1,000,000(1.2)(1.15)	= £1,380,000
19X1	£1,300,000(1.15)	= £1,495,000

The factors of 1.2 and 1.15 represent the adjustments necessary to reflect increases of 20% and 15%. Note that both factors are applied to the 19X0 payments, as two years' adjustments are necessary to update the 19X0 figures to 19X5 levels.

Having chosen the appropriate independent variable, selected the time period and adjusted for any bias in the accounting data, we now examine some of the possible methods of estimating future costs. First let us pause to remind ourselves exactly what it is we are trying to achieve. Suppose that a firm's production manager has been informed that during the last month the firm produced 1,000 units and incurred total costs (cash outflows) in so doing of £50,000. There is obviously some information contained in this message – the manager now knows both the level of production and the total cost of production. But in planning for the future, more information would be desirable. The manager will be particularly interested in the breakdown of the total cost figure, and will wish to know what proportion of the cash flow of £50,000 is fixed over different levels of production and what proportion is variable. It is this segregation of total costs into fixed and variable elements which the analysis of past costs attempts to achieve.

We might equally state that the analysis of past costs is intended to determine both the intercept (the level of fixed costs, a) and the slope (the variable cost per unit of activity, b) of the total cost function. The graph below presents the familiar cost function to be estimated:

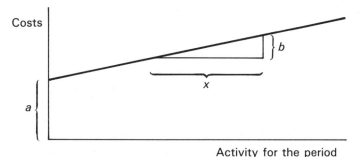

Our estimation of the likely cost relationship is preceded by two actions: derivation of the relevant past data and plotting the data.

We will use the following data for all our illustrations in this chapter. These data show the total manufacturing costs *adjusted to current price levels* and total units of output produced, our chosen activity base, in respect of Goodison plc for the first six months of the year; we wish to predict the cost–volume relationship for July.

	Output (units)	Total manufacturing costs (£)
January	80	10,200
February	90	10,900
March	100	12,100
April	80	10,800
May	120	13,700
June	110	12,500

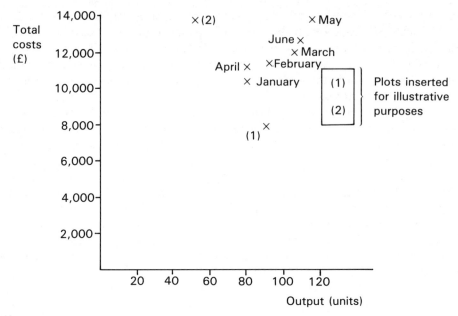

Figure 6.8 Scatter plotting of total manufacturing costs per month.

We can now plot the data as in Figure 6.8. Each cross represents a relationship between costs and output. The pattern revealed by Figure 6.8 shows no very unusual or abnormal relationships (i.e. the plots are reasonably closely clustered and total cost increases with units of output). But if, for example, one or more of the observations fell obviously outside the general relationship, as with plots (1) and (2), it would be necessary to find the reasons for these unusual observations and, if they were considered to be abnormal and unrepresentative, to discard them.

We are now in a position to look closely at three approaches to the estimation of the firm's total cost function; or, expressed differently, we will examine three ways of predicting the level of fixed costs, *a*, and the variable cost per unit, *b*, in the total cost equation. The methods chosen for estimation are not the only ones used by management in predicting costs, but they are probably the most widely used in practice. Note that in practice many managers make use of computer programs that apply these and other more refined methods.

6.9 The 'high–low' or 'range' method

The high–low method is the cheapest and easiest to use of the three methods. It attempts to segregate total past costs by examining only two observations, those representing the highest and lowest costs or, alternatively, the highest and lowest levels of past activity, over the range of observations. The slope of the line which connects these two points is then taken to represent the variable cost per unit of activity for *all* levels of activity. Using the data for Goodison plc, we can use the high-low method as follows:

Total cost function $\qquad\qquad\qquad$ TC $= a + bx$

(1) Highest cost level (May) gives $\qquad$ £13,700 $= a + b$(120 units)
(2) Lowest cost level (January) gives $\quad$ £10,200 $= a + b$(80 units)
(1) minus (2) gives $\qquad\qquad\qquad$ £ 3,500 $= 0 + b$(40 units)

$b = \dfrac{£3,500}{40 \text{ units}} = £87.5$ per unit

Substituting for b in equation (1) gives
£13,700 $= a + £87.5$(120)
£13,700 $= a + £10,500$
$\qquad a = £(13,700 - 10,500) = £3,200$
The estimated total cost function is £3,200 $+ 87.5x$

A graphical representation of the total cost function estimated by the high–low method is given by Figure 6.9. The total cost line does not in fact exactly bisect any of the other four observations (i.e. those for February, March, April or June), but equally, the vertical differences (deviations) between these four plots and the estimated total cost function are quite small. If there were no deviations from the line, we would say that we had very high confidence in the particular method chosen. In the case of Goodison plc, the high–low method appears to offer some promise for

Figure 6.9 Total cost function using high–low method.

cost estimation, but the method does have some important shortcomings. The most critical of these lies in the very name given to the method: because only the highest and the lowest observations are chosen for study, all other observations lying between the two extremes are ignored. Thus the reliability of the estimates generated for *a* and *b* depends upon how typical of the whole range of data the highest and lowest points are. It may well be that it is undesirable to use extreme values simply because they are untypical of the relationship between costs and activity.

6.10 The visual inspection method

The visual inspection method entails plotting all the relevant observations on a scattergraph, and then fitting a line to the data by visual inspection. Figure 6.10 shows a freehand line drawn to fit the data for Goodison plc. The line intercepts the vertical axis at approximately £3,400, the estimated level of fixed costs. Thus the total cost function can be estimated by calculating the total costs at any particular activity level and subtracting £3,400 so as to give the variable cost element of total costs. For example, at a level of 120 units, the total cost freehand line shows £13,800. Therefore total variable costs are £13,800 − £3,400 = £10,400, and the variable cost per unit is £10,400/120 = £86.7. The estimated TC function becomes £3,400 + £86.7x.

Figure 6.10 Scattergraph.

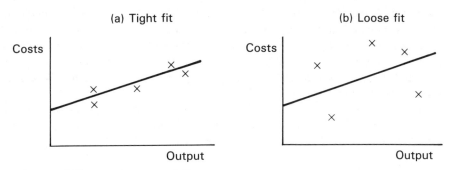

Figure 6.11 Different degrees of fit.

As with the high–low method, visual inspection has its disadvantages. Although it uses all the data, and not merely the two extreme points, it is very subjective. It is unlikely that everybody would construct the same freehand line, and different estimates could easily be derived for the total cost function; but perhaps most important of all, neither the high–low method nor the visual inspection method gives any clue as to how inaccurate the estimates derived from the methods can be. For example, a mistake in drawing the line may result in a substantial error which could directly affect the quality of management planning. In addition, even though the line may be 'well' drawn, it may represent a tight fit for some data sets, and a loose fit for others, as shown in Figure 6.11. Thus there is no indication of how much reliance can be placed on estimates made from the line.

The defects of these comparatively unsophisticated methods can be overcome by the use of the statistical technique known as *linear regression analysis*.

6.11 Linear regression analysis

Linear regression analysis refers to the measurement of the average amount of change in one variable (e.g. manufacturing costs) which is associated with unit increases in the amounts of one or more other variables (e.g. output). It is a method of regressing *y* (the dependent variable) on *x* (the independent variable). It is widely used where computing facilities are available.

Regression analysis has two purposes. First, it fits a line to the observed relationships between costs and volume, which is known as the *line of best fit*, and second, it tells the user how much confidence can be placed in the goodness of the fit of the regression line. Neither of these two purposes is fulfilled by the approaches of the high–low method or the visual inspection graph. This section considers the procedure for determining the line of best fit; how the goodness of fit of the line might be measured is explained in the next section.

Regression analysis fits a line to the data so as to minimise the sum of the squares of the vertical distances from the regression line to the plots of the actual observations: that is, so that the sum of the squares of these deviations is less than the sum of the squared deviations from any other line. Thus it is a method of line fitting which is free from subjectivity. The mathematical technique which gives this assurance is called the *least-squares* method. Squared figures are used because, as a squared number is always positive, values for each observation can be added to arrive at a measure of overall difference. If unsquared figures were used, large positive and negative amounts might cancel out, with the result that misleadingly close relationships might appear.

The least-squares method entails the use of two mathematical equations known as *normal equations* which must be solved simultaneously to derive values for *a* and *b* for inclusion in the total cost function. These equations are of the form:[2]

(1) $\Sigma y = na + b\Sigma x$
(2) $\Sigma xy = a\Sigma x + b\Sigma x^2$

where $n =$ the number of observations; $\Sigma x =$ the sum of the observations of the independent variable (e.g. $x =$ level of output); $\Sigma y =$ the sum of the observations of the dependent variable (e.g. $y =$ total costs); $\Sigma x^2 =$ the sum of the squares of the x observations; $\Sigma xy =$ the sum of the product of each pair of observations; $a =$ total fixed costs; $b =$ variable cost per unit of output.

Before we use the available data to calculate the regression line for Goodison plc, we briefly mention some of the assumptions which underlie linear regression analysis. The use of sophisticated mathematical models can often blind us to the fact that they may be based on simplifying assumptions which, if they do not hold up, can cast doubts on the results of the model. The results of applying regression analysis are only as good as the input data fed into the model.

There are at least three important assumptions underlying linear regression analysis. First, linearity of the relationships between costs and volume is assumed (we return to this aspect later); second, it is assumed that there is a uniform dispersion of actual costs about the regression line; and third, it is assumed that successive cost measurements do not depend on each other. These latter two assumptions relate to technical problems of statistical analysis, which will not be explored further. We now use linear regression analysis to determine the total cost function of Goodison plc.

Substituting the appropriate figures from Table 6.2 into the simultaneous equations gives:

(1) $70,200 = 6a + 580b$
(2) $6,890,000 = 580a + 57,400b$

Multiplying equation (1) by 580, and equation (2) by 6 we have:

(1) $40,716,000 = 3,480a + 336,400b$
(2) $41,340,000 = 3,480a + 344,400b$

Subtracting (1) from (2) gives:

$624,000 = 8,000b$
$b = 78$

Table 6.2 Regression analysis data

Month	Output x	Total manufacturing costs y	xy	x^2	y^2
January	80	10,200	816,000	6,400	104,040,000
February	90	10,900	981,000	8,100	118,810,000
March	100	12,100	1,210,000	10,000	146,410,000
April	80	10,800	864,000	6,400	116,640,000
May	120	13,700	1,644,000	14,400	187,690,000
June	110	12,500	1,375,000	12,100	156,250,000
Totals	$\Sigma x = 580$	$\Sigma y = 70.200$	$\Sigma xy = 6.890.000$	$\Sigma x^2 = 57.400$	$\Sigma y^2 = 829.840.000$

Substituting 78 for b in (1) gives:

$$70,200 = 6a + 45,240$$
$$a = 4,160$$

With these two calculated values of a and b we now write our straight-line equation of

$$y = 4,160 + 78x$$

It is estimated that the manufacturing costs for Goodison plc comprise a fixed element of £4,160 and a (linear) variable element of £78 per unit of output.

6.12 The coefficient of correlation

We have now derived an expression which may be used to predict the future level of total costs for Goodison plc. As yet, however, we do not have any indication as to how accurate the predictions from the regression model are likely to be. The statistic which is normally used to assess the goodness of fit of a regression line is known as the *coefficient of correlation* (first introduced in the discussion of the portfolio approach to risk measurement in Chapter 4). The correlation coefficient can be measured from the following mathematical formula:[3]

$$r = \frac{n(\Sigma xy) - (\Sigma x)(\Sigma y)}{\sqrt{[n(\Sigma x^2) - (\Sigma x)^2]}\sqrt{[n(\Sigma y^2) - (\Sigma y^2)]}}$$

The correlation coefficient squared, r^2 (known as the *coefficient of determination*) is a widely used statistic. It indicates the percentage of the variation in total costs that is accounted for by the changes in the observed values of output levels. It denotes the predictive value of the model. Its value will always lie between 0 and 1. For instance, if all the plotted observations fell on a straight line, then the r^2

statistic would be exactly +1, and we could say that costs and output were perfectly correlated. If, however, the plots appeared in the form of a circle around the regression line, then r^2 would approximate to zero. This would indicate that no single line was better than any other in explaining the cost/output relationship. Thus r^2 gives information as to how confident management can be in the explanatory and predictive power of the model. Figure 6.12 gives some examples of graphical representations of different possible relationships.

The calculations of r^2 for Goodison plc can be determined as follows:

$$r = \frac{6(6,890,000) - 580(70,200)}{\sqrt{[6(57,400) - 580^2]}\sqrt{[6(829,840,000) - 70,200^2]}} = 0.977$$

$$r^2 = 0.954 \ (\text{or } 95.4\%)$$

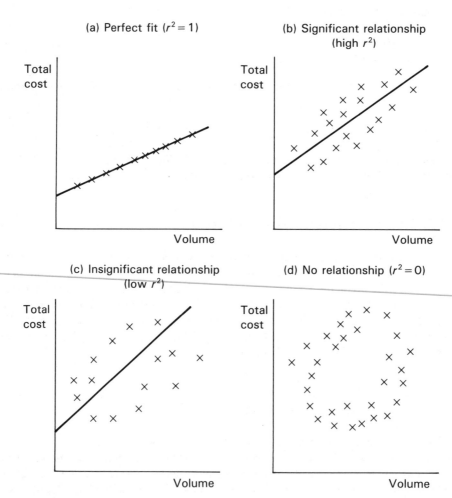

Figure 6.12 Some examples of statistical relationships.

This indicates that 95.4% of the variation in the total manufacturing costs of Goodison plc for the six-month period is accounted for, although not necessarily caused by, changes in the level of output produced during that same period. The remaining 4.6% is explained by random variation and also by the effect of other interacting, but unknown, variables. In the case of Goodison plc, management can be very confident that a single independent variable, the level of output, will provide a reasonable predictor of changes in total manufacturing costs. In a situation where a low r^2 is obtained, consideration should be given to whether a cost function which uses a single independent variable provides an adequate estimate of total costs. It may be necessary to add further explanatory variables to the cost function. For instance, as suggested earlier in this chapter, an appropriate form of the cost function may be:

$$y = a + bx_1 + cx_2 + dx_3 + \cdots + nx_n$$

This form of cost function can be solved by the use of *multiple linear regression* techniques. These measure the changes in the cost for each of the explanatory variables, while keeping the others constant.

6.13 Evaluation of cost estimation methods

We have looked now at three separate methods of cost estimation, and seen how each one has yielded a different total cost function. The cost functions for the three methods, each of which used exactly the same data, are as follows:

Method	Cost function $(a + bx)$
High–low	£3,200 + £87.5x
Visual inspection	£3,400 + £86.7x
Regression analysis	£4,160 + £78.0x

As we move through various stages of sophistication, we can see, in this instance, the counterbalancing effects of the three methods: the fixed element of total costs increases and the variable cost per unit falls. These conclusions would not, of course, necessarily hold true for any firm other than Goodison plc. The importance of the different functions lies in how they are used. Management will wish to use the data to predict future costs, and therefore to plan future operations for the firm. Suppose, for example, management expects to produce 130 units in July. If it uses regression analysis to predict total costs at this level of output, it will expect to incur £4,160 + £78(130) = £14,300; using the high–low method, total costs will be expected to be £3,200 + £87.5(130) = £14,575. The differences in predicted total costs are small, but the differences between the two elements of cost are substantial. We have earlier stressed the relevance of incremental costs in decision making. The high–low method predicts a variable cost for each additional unit produced of £87.5; regression analysis, at a very high level of confidence, predicts a variable cost per unit of £78. If it transpires that Goodison plc's fixed costs are indeed constant over wide ranges of output, so that the incremental costs relevant for decision making correspond to the variable costs, then the planning of costs for decision making may take on very different perspectives, depending upon which cost function is accepted.

6.14 The learning curve

There is one particular respect in which the uncritical use of past data to predict future costs may result in errors in estimation. When a new product is to be manufactured or a new production process started, it is frequently the case that employees will take longer to produce the first units of the product than to produce subsequent units, because there is a learning process involved. As the employees become more familiar with the production process, they produce an increasing number of units in a given period of time. The rate at which their efficiency increases is called the *learning rate* and is usually estimated by a *learning curve*. In estimating future costs, it is important that the management should take account of this learning effect, which will influence not only the labour cost but also the cost of other resources, the use of which varies with labour time, such as power costs. The learning curve is essentially an empirical phenomenon: that is, it has been observed to occur on certain kinds of production process, particularly those which are labour intensive and in which the workforce performs repetitive tasks which they can learn to carry out more efficiently.

Let us consider a simple example to explain the meaning of the learning rate. Suppose that a company has received an order to produce eight oilrigs. It estimates that the first rig will take 200 days to manufacture and that the learning rate, on the basis of past experience, will be 90%. What this means is that, when the cumulative number of units produced doubles, the average time per unit taken to produce *all* units will be 90% of the average time per unit taken to produce the previous (cumulative) units. The calculations of the oil rigs are shown in Table 6.3. The cumulative average time for the first two rigs (180 days per rig) is 90% of the time taken to produce the first rig (200 days). So the total time taken to produce two rigs is 360 days (180 days × 2 rigs) and the marginal time taken to produce the second rig

Table 6.3 Learning curve effect (90% learning rate)

Cumulative units	Cumulative average time per unit (days)	Total time for cumulative units (days)	Marginal time per unit for additional units (days)
1	200	200	200
2	90% × 200 = 180	180 × 2 = 360	360 − 200 = 160
4	90% × 180 = 162	162 × 4 = 648	$\frac{648 - 360}{2}$ = 144
8	90% × 162 = 145.8	145.8 × 8 = 1,166.4	$\frac{1,166.4 - 648}{4}$ = 129.6

is 160 days (360 days – 200 days). Similar calculations are undertaken for each successive doubling of output.[4]

The rather cumbersome nature of the calculations arises because the learning curve is based on real-world observations – the relationships described are empirical. For repetitive, labour-intensive tasks, the learning rate appears to vary between 65% and 90% in the early stages of production. It eventually reaches a steady state in which no further efficiency gains from learning are achieved. Whenever an estimate of the costs of a new production process is being made, the predicted effects of learning, based on past experience, should be included. However, it should be borne in mind that the effects will not continue indefinitely and may not exist at all for some non-repetitive, non-labour-intensive processes.

6.15 The relevant range revisited

We cannot leave the subject of cost estimation without returning to the problem of linearity. In our example of Goodison plc, we examined only output levels in a range from 80 to 120 units, and yet from this limited range of observations we developed a cost function which could be used to predict costs at all output levels. Or could it? Figure 6.13 (which is unrelated to the example of Goodison plc) points out some possible difficulties in making any sweeping generalisations from particular observations.

The middle five plots represent actual observations in the range from 2,500 to 3,000 units of output, the firm's regularly achieved level in any particular period. The straight line represents the total cost function as estimated by regression analysis. It may well explain most of the variations in total cost, but the actual cost function may be of the curvilinear form shown on the graph, and the plots on the

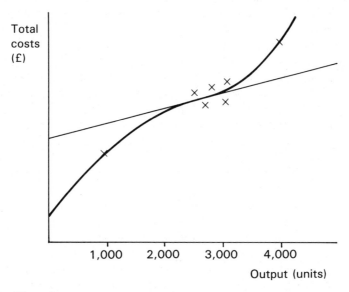

Figure 6.13 The relevant range.

curved line may better estimate levels of total cost at the more extreme ranges of 1,000 units and 4,000 units respectively. If this is so, then management would indeed make large errors in cost prediction if, say, only 1,000 units were produced during any period.

The moral of this exercise is important. Regression analysis may give a high value for the r^2, but this value may only hold for the relevant range of observations; the more extreme are the output levels beyond the observed range, the less will be our confidence in the prediction of future costs.

CHAPTER SUMMARY

In order to be able successfully to undertake the kind of incremental analysis that we have argued is relevant for decision making, it is important to be able to estimate how cost flows will change as a result of particular decisions. In this chapter we have looked at two major aspects of the analysis of costs – identifying the nature and pattern of behaviour of costs, and estimating future flows in order to provide information to support decisions.

Costs can be classified and described in many different ways, but of greatest importance is knowledge of their pattern of variation in response to different aspects of organisational activities, and of which particular aspects of activities different costs are sensitive to. An important idea underlying cost analysis is to identify the extent to which costs will change with changes in operating activity and the extent to which they will remain unchanged: that is, the variable and fixed components of different types of cost. The behaviour pattern of individual costs or aggregate sets of costs can be expressed as cost functions in which costs are seen as dependent on other organisational variables, or cost drivers. Different costs will be affected by different cost drivers.

When predicting costs for a completely new activity, management may rely on 'engineering' specifications of required production inputs. More commonly in practice, however, information from existing and past operations will provide historical data which will be used in estimating future costs. Past data can be analysed, using linear regression or other methods, in order to identify a cost function which can be applied to generate future predictions. Both the use of simple cost functions as a means of describing cost behaviour and the use of past data when producing future estimates have limitations, particularly if there is to be any significant change in operations. Care must be taken to correct for any biases or incompleteness in past data. However, within the relevant range, where there can be expected to be a reasonable correspondence between past and future operating conditions, analysis of the historic behaviour of costs can assist with preparing future estimates.

REVIEW QUESTIONS

1. 'In the long term there are no fixed costs.' Discuss what is meant by this statement.

2. Explain the following concepts used in this chapter:

   Relevant range
   Curvilinear functions
   Cost drivers
   The learning curve
   The engineering method

3. 'Cost classifications such as "variable" and "fixed" are misleading. Only *differential* costs are important for managerial decision making.' Discuss.

4. Discuss some of the factors which should be considered when choosing an appropriate activity base for cost prediction.

5. 'The use of past data for cost estimation necessarily possesses many disadvantages.' Suggest what some of these disadvantages might be and how they might be overcome.

EXERCISES

6.1 The following graphs reflect the pattern of certain overhead cost items in a manufacturing company for a year.

   (a) Identify which graph represents the overhead cost items shown below (a graph may be used more than once):

	Brief description	Details of cost behaviour
(i)	Depreciation of equipment	When charged on straight-line basis
(ii)	Cost of a service	£50 annual charge for subscription: £2 charge for each unit taken, with a maximum total charge of £350 p.a.
(iii)	Royalty	£0.10 per unit produced, with a maximum charge of £5,000 p.a.
(iv)	Supervision cost	When there is one charge hand for every eight workers or less, and one supervisor for every three charge hands, and when each person represents 40 hours of production, thus:

Hours	
Under 320	one charge hand
321–640	two charge hands
641–960	three charge hands,
etc.	plus one supervisor

	Brief description	Details of cost behaviour
(v)	Depreciation of equipment	When charged on a machine-hour rate

J

K

| (vi) | Cost of a service | Flat charge of £400 to cover the first 5,000 units |
| | | |

Per unit
£0.10 for the next 3,000 units
£0.12 for the next 3,000 units
£0.14 for all subsequent units

(vii)   Storage/carriage service   *Per ton*
£15 for the first 20 tons
£30 for the next 20 tons
£45 for the next 20 tons
No extra charge until the service reaches
100 tons; then £45 per ton for all subsequent
tonnage.

(viii) Outside finishing service   *Per unit*
£0.75 for the first 2,000 units
£0.55 for the next 2,000 units
£0.35 for all subsequent units

(b) Give an example of an overhead cost item that could represent those graphs to which you do not refer in your answer to (a).

(c) Draw one graph of a pattern of an overhead item not shown and give an example of an overhead cost item that it would represent. (Solution at end of text.)

6.2   Rothko Ltd produces a single product for distribution to wholesalers. The product has a list selling price of £10 per unit. Variable costs of production are £5 per unit, and fixed costs of production are £50,000 p.a. The distribution of the product results in additional costs of 90p per unit (variable) and £11,500 p.a. (fixed).

(a) Calculate the expected break-even point.

(b) Assuming Rothko Ltd predicts sales of £200,000 for the year, calculate the expected profit (assuming sales and production are equal).

(c) The company does have some idea about the effects on demand of changes in prices, advertising, competitors' actions, etc. Assume that a 5% decrease in price will increase total volume by 15% (in units), that an additional expenditure of £7,500 on advertising will further increase the original volume by 5%, but that the increased production will result in an increase in variable costs of production by 10p per unit in excess of 21,000 units. Maximum practical capacity is 25,000 units. What effect will these changes have on net profit?

(d) As an alternative, Rothko Ltd can also expand its sales by 20% (volume) by offering its wholesalers a rebate of 1% on all the units they purchase, and by incurring advertising expenditure of £20,000. Is this a better alternative than (c)? Support your reasoning with calculations. (Solution at end of text.)

6.3   The following table shows turnover and advertising expenditure for ten similar small manufacturing companies.

Company	Advertising expenditure (£000)	Turnover (£000)
A	2.6	138
B	3.1	163
C	3.5	166
D	3.7	153
E	4.1	177
F	4.4	201
G	4.6	216
H	4.9	208
I	5.3	226
J	5.8	238

(a) Which is the dependent and which is the independent variable?

(b) Calculate a regression equation linking advertising expenditure and turnover by the least-squares method.

(c)   (i) What turnover is expected for nil advertising expenditure?
     (ii) What turnover would £12,000 advertising expenditure be expected to produce?
     (iii) Comment on (c)(i) and (ii).

6.4   A division of Munch Ltd processes a single type of chemical. Processing costs and output for the last 13 accounting periods (of four weeks each) have been as follows:

	Period												
	1	2	3	4	5	6	7	8	9	10	11	12	13
Costs (£):													
Materials	1,260	1,480	1,610	1,740	1,990	1,930	2,160	2,140	2,010	1,780	1,570	1,660	1,590
Direct labour	1,870	2,140	2,160	2,260	2,540	2,340	2,520	2,550	2,400	2,690	2,500	2,560	2,480
Overheads	770	820	810	830	960	900	940	950	940	870	800	820	790
Total costs	3,900	4,440	4,580	4,830	5,490	5,170	5,620	5,640	5,350	5,340	4,870	5,040	4,860
Output (tons)	120	150	160	170	200	170	200	200	180	160	140	150	140

The price of materials was increased by 10% at the end of period 5; a wage increase of 20% was given to all employees classified as 'direct' at the end of period 9. There have been no other increases in processing costs during the past year.

You have been requested to prepare a flexible budget for the coming year.

(a) Describe what calculations you would undertake, using the above information, as a basis for your budget.

(b) Explain how you would establish the reliability of the budgetary estimates derived from the calculations.

(c) Discuss the limitations of your method of calculation.

6.5   At the end of last year Mr Hutton, a manufacturer of wooden furniture, accepted a contract to produce 200 cricket bats. The details of the contract were:

	£
Materials: Wood	2,000
Rubber	800
Labour (400 hours @ £8/hr)	3,200
Variable overheads	1,200
	7,200
Profit	800
Sales value	8,000

Hutton was slightly concerned over how long his staff would take getting used to the new manufacturing methods, and noticed that the first 100 bats took 250 hours to produce and the second 100 only 150 hours. The staff feel that they have not fully adapted to the new product and could do still better. Hutton's estimates for the variable overheads incurred on the contract were £2 per labour hour plus £2 per bat.

Hutton has received three more contracts to supply first 600 bats, secondly 100 bats and finally 300 bats.

Find the marginal cost of each successive contract using:

(a) A tabular approach for the first contract.

(b) For the other contracts the formula:

$$y = ax^{-b}$$

Notes

1. See, for example, J. Johnston, *Statistical Cost Analysis*, McGraw-Hill, 1960 (especially chapters 4 and 5).

2. It is beyond the scope of this text to explain how these simultaneous equations are derived. Interested students should refer to an introductory statistics book. For our purposes we shall accept the mathematical validity of the simultaneous equations.

3. For a detailed explanation of the derivation of this formula, interested students should consult an introductory statistics book.

4. The following formula is available to calculate the cumulative average time per unit:

$$y = ax^{-b}$$

where $y =$ cumulative average time per unit (or batch)
  $a =$ time taken to produce the first unit or batch
  $x =$ number of units (or batches) produced in total

$$-b = \frac{\log \text{ of } r}{\log \text{ of } 2}$$

  $r =$ learning rate.

Cost recording and product costing

Management decision making depends on identifying the relevant cash flows associated with individual decisions, and this can be done most easily if management has a good understanding of how costs and revenues behave over particular activity levels. Decision making should be based upon expectations about the future costs and revenues that will result from actions taken, but management's expectations will be influenced by knowledge of the flows associated with current operations and of the results of past decisions. In this chapter we look at systems for the recording of cost information about actual operations.

Cost accounting systems are intended to answer the question: *what does it cost* to produce a product, provide a service or satisfy a contract? At one time the subject of cost accounting was largely synonymous with that of management accounting, and the maintenance of cost accounting systems remains a significant part of the activities of accountants in business enterprises. The emphasis of this book, however, is on the provision of information to support particular kinds of managerial decisions, and for our purposes an understanding of the general principles underlying the main approaches to the recording of costs is sufficient. The detailed aspects of the treatment of individual cost items and the accounting entries associated with record keeping can be found in other texts more specifically concerned with cost accounting.[1]

We begin this chapter by considering why information on the cost of products (or services) is required. We then outline the structure of the main general approaches used for product cost recording – *job order costing* and *process costing*. Both these approaches involve choices about the basis of cost measurement, concerning the inclusion or exclusion of certain items as part of product cost and how these items are valued. We look at how these issues have been dealt with traditionally in cost accounting and then at the implications for product cost measurement of the analysis of activity-based cost drivers, introduced in the previous chapter. Throughout the chapter we shall refer to the measurement of *product costs*, but the issues and methods discussed apply equally to services and other activities.

7.1 Why product cost information is important

While all decision making depends on expectations about the future consequences that will follow from a decision, recording information about the costs associated with current activities is an important part of a managerial information system for a number of reasons:

1. When producing periodic reports on performance, it is generally necessary to determine which costs should be charged against revenue in calculating the profit or loss of the period, and which should be carried forward as part of the stock valuation. A costing system helps provide information about the cost of products for this purpose. This information is needed for the annual financial statements reported to those outside the organisation, but it will also form part of internal management reports. It is essentially a scorekeeping function of the management accounting system, attributing costs to provide a stock value and a measure of period performance. The way in which costs are recognised will influence reported profits.

2. Unit cost information may be influential in decisions about pricing and the level of activity. Many surveys have shown that product costs are critical to management's approach to pricing in practice. Even in very competitive situations, where prices are effectively set by the market, a knowledge of costs allows concentration on the best mix of products, or assists in approaches such as *target costing*, where emphasis is placed on producing within a certain level of costs which is expected to give an adequate return when products are sold at the price the market will accept. (Decisions about the level of operating activity are discussed further in Chapter 8 and pricing decisions in Chapter 9.)

3. For many practical decision purposes, the best information management will have on which to base expectations about the future is the evidence of past costs. As we pointed out in our discussion of cost estimation in Chapter 6, there

are considerable dangers in using past information to predict the future, as it cannot be assumed that future operating conditions will be the same as those that have applied in the past. Nonetheless, used appropriately, knowledge of current and past performance is obviously important for management planning.

4. Costing systems also give information which can assist with the control and correction of performance. For example, they can help identify areas of operation where management should devote attention in order to improve efficiency. Information on actual results is essential in order to determine whether expectations are being fulfilled or should be adjusted and to begin to understand why actual performance is different from planned. This approach of comparing actual and expected performance is known as *variance analysis* and is discussed in Chapter 17.

Thus, the cost recording and information system can help serve management purposes with respect to scorekeeping, decision making and control. If cost accounting systems are to make this contribution to management functions, then it is important that costs are defined and measured in appropriate ways. Later in the chapter we look at a number of important issues concerning the measurement of costs, but first we will describe the structure of the two main approaches used for accumulating product costs – job order cost systems and process cost systems.

7.2 Job order costing systems

Job order costing is used to provide costs for a separate order, a one-off project or a single batch of production. As the name implies, such systems identify separate jobs for which costs are accumulated. For example, a job could be a single contract for a construction company, a motion picture in a film studio or a specific client for whom the staff of an accounting firm are providing various services. In a less commercial setting, changes in the management of hospitals in recent years have led to systems where an individual patient can be separately identified and allocated costs – for example, for surgery, ward time, nursing care and clinics – to arrive at a total treatment cost.

The primary feature of job costing systems is the identification of a separate job, and this approach is suitable for situations where a business has a limited product range or provides products or services which vary according to individual customers' needs.

Costs are accumulated for the individual job order according to the following steps:

1. Charges for direct costs such as materials and labour or a subcontracted service are recorded for the job. This is usually the actual material cost plus amounts paid to staff, but in situations where there are similarities between jobs, it may be based on predetermined standard cost rates (which we discuss later).

2. Overhead costs are allocated on the basis and to the extent determined by the management (discussed in more detail later).

3. At any point in time, the amount of cost accumulated for a particular job (subject to adjustment for any payments received or write-offs that might be necessary) constitutes the work-in-progress value of the product or service. At the end of the job, the total amount represents the total product cost. Where a batch of production has been treated in this way, the unit cost will equal the total job cost divided by the number of units in the batch.[2]

4. When the job cost is matched with revenues, a profit for the specific job can be calculated.

Figure 7.1 provides a simple example of a job costing record for a motor mechanic's contract to make customised modifications to a customer's car. The cost entries show the accumulation of the costs of direct physical inputs and labour (step 1 above). In this case, most items are recorded at the actual cash cost of acquisition, but paint used in respraying is charged at a pre-set standard rate. Overheads are added to the cost of the job on the basis of a set rate per labour hour worked on the job (step 2). This approach effectively assumes that overheads in this business are a

Adams Custom Cars			Job No.: 9X/3–1
			Contract Price £2,895.00
	Period 1 £	Period 2 £	Total £
Materials and parts			
Materials for engineering custom parts	205.00		205.00
Parts, specially purchased @ cost	575.60		575.60
Parts, ex stores		264.80	264.80
Paints, 15 litres @ standard £8.25		123.75	123.75
	780.60	388.55	1,169.15
Labour			
Engineering 28 hours @ £12/hour	336.00		336.00
Fitting/assembly 10 hours @ £9.5/hour	95.00		95.00
8 hours @ £9.5/hour		76.00	76.00
Paint shop 5 hours @ £7/hour		35.00	35.00
	431.00	111.00	542.00
Overheads			
Labour hours × overhead rate £6.00			
Period 1 – 38 hours	228.00		
Period 2 – 13 hours		78.00	306.00
Total costs	£1,439.60	£577.55	£2,017.15

Figure 7.1 Job order costing record.

function of labour time. At the end of period 1 the work-in-progress value of the contract is £1,439.60 (step 3 above), and at the end of period 2 the total cost of £2,017.15 can be compared to the contract price of £2,895 to reveal a profit of £877.85 (step 4).

The specific presentation format and measurement rules used for a job cost record can vary between different businesses and enterprises, but the basic principle of approach remains the accumulation of costs under a separate job or batch of production. Job costing systems can provide detailed information on cost incidence, which will be necessary in contracts where a price is agreed that is to be based on costs, but which may also be helpful in considering bids for repeat work. Comparison between the detailed cost record and budget or planned amounts can also give information which may be useful for managerial control purposes.

7.3 Process costing systems

Process costing is used where the production involves a steady stream of identical products. Whereas job costing identifies a unit job or batch with which costs can then be associated, here the costing system identifies processes. Costs are accumulated within each process and then attributed to the production that has passed through that process. The total of the unit costs for all the processes that a product has passed through will give the finished cost of production: that is, the product cost.

This kind of approach is suitable for businesses with mass production or a series of successive operations. Examples include petrochemicals, glass bottle manufacture and soft drinks. These products are homogeneous (one can of Coca-Cola is identical to another), the production process is continuous, and the link between the production of individual items and specific customer orders is hard to identify. Rather than assign separate costs to individual jobs, product costs are estimated through the average costs of production processes.

The steps involved in process costing are as follows:

1. Costs are assigned to production processes for a period: for example, the cost of all material inputs and labour time used in a particular process within a week or a month.

2. Allocations of overheads may be included in arriving at the total cost of the process for the period.

3. Production recording must also measure the volume of production that has passed through the process in the period.[3] The total cost of a process is then spread across the total quantity of production, resulting in an average processing cost:

$$\frac{\text{Total costs of process}}{\text{Quantity processed}} = \text{Average unit cost for period}$$

Two points should be noted about this calculation. First, the calculation of unit cost for successive periods might vary, reflecting the cost implications of different levels of production, changes in the cost of inputs, and efficiencies or inefficiencies in production. Some organisations use a 'normal' level of activity as the basis for spreading costs (the denominator in the above equation) to avoid very different product cost calculations resulting from fluctuations in activity between periods.

Second, in some situations, where several products pass through the same process, the number of processing hours may be used as the measure of production activity rather than the actual quantity of product processed, resulting in an average cost per processing hour. Different products will then be assigned costs on the basis of the number of hours' processing they have used during the period.

4. As units of product move from process to process they are assigned the cost resulting from the above calculations for each separate process. At any point in time, work in progress will be valued at the total cost of processes so far completed. The final completed product cost will be the total of the amounts from all the separate processes. This figure will be used for stock valuation and therefore the cost of sales calculation when the stock is sold.

A simple illustrative example of process cost recording is shown in Table 7.1. In this example there are three processes in a chemical plant: mixing, blending and bottling. For ease of illustration we will assume that a single product is being processed and that there was no opening stock of work in progress at the start of the period. The direct costs of ingredients, containers and labour used are charged to the individual processes (step 1 above), and additional overhead allocations are also included (step 2). (The possible bases for the measurement of these items is discussed in the next section.) The total cost of each process is then spread across the volume of product passing through that stage of production (step 3). A litre of the chemical that went through all three stages within the period would have a

Table 7.1 Process costing illustration

	Mixing (£)	Blending (£)	Bottling (£)
Materials:			
Primary ingredients	4,300		
Additives	1,621	1,705	
Containers			375
Labour	5,200	3,200	500
Overheads:			
Power (based on machine time)	1,640	660	290
General (based on labour hours)	1,230	610	105
Total cost	13,991	6,175	1,270
Volume processed (litres)	850	650	500
Average cost per litre	£16.46	£9.50	£2.54

product cost equal to the total of their average costs, i.e. £28.50 (£16.46 + £9.50 + £2.54), while the work in progress cost of the chemical which has been mixed and blended but has still to be bottled would be £25.96 per litre (£16.46 + £9.50), and of that which has only been through mixing, £16.46.

Information about the costs of individual processes can be compared to budget, and variances calculated to assist with evaluating the efficiency of production, the need for control action to adjust operations, the need for any adjustment in product pricing, etc.

7.4 Measuring costs

Product costing is a process of estimation – it is unlikely that the exact product cost can be measured precisely. What is important is that management is given the best estimate that can be produced in a timely and economic manner. The design of a costing system must identify which costs are to be included in product cost, how these are to be measured, and which costs are to be excluded.

Cost estimates may be affected by the application of accounting conventions which result in the exclusion of some costs which it could be argued are part of a product's costs. For example, research and development and advertising expenditures are likely to be treated as period expenses and charged to the income statement of the period in which they are incurred, rather than allocated to products, although it could be argued that those activities are directly supporting the products. Financial reporting standards lay down rules regarding what can be included in product cost for the purposes of stock valuation in the annual financial statements. Only manufacturing costs can be treated as product costs for external reporting, and non-manufacturing costs must be taken as period costs. These rules can in turn become a very strong influence on the way in which costs are recognised in management reporting as well. Although there is no reason in principle why management should not use different conventions and measurements for its own information system, in practice the costs and potential ambiguity associated with maintaining two systems may be difficult to justify.

The manufacturing costs of inputs or activities that are directly related to producing a product, such as direct materials and direct labour, can usually be attributed to that product and included for the purpose of calculating product cost. For example, if it is known that certain staff have been employed entirely on a particular product during the preceding month, then all of that staff time can be treated as part of that product's cost. However, the related *financial* cost will depend on how that time is *valued* within the costing system. For example, if labour hours include a mixture of normal working and overtime, for costing purposes management may price those hours at a single standard rate and account for the extra overtime cost separately, or use actual amounts paid during specific production runs. Difficulties in measuring product cost also arise with indirect costs – items which do not change directly in relation to the level of production, including fixed costs, or which are common costs for a number of products. In these situations some basis must be found for allocating costs to products, or they must be excluded from the measurement of product cost altogether. The design of a costing system must therefore incorporate policies on three measurement issues, each of which is discussed below:

1. Whether or not fixed overheads are to be included in product cost, i.e. the choice between variable and absorption costing.

2. How individual cost inputs are to be valued, i.e. the choice between actual and standard costs.

3. How costs, including overheads, which are indirectly related to individual products or common to more than one product, are to be allocated to form part of product cost.

Variable costing and absorption costing

The difference between variable costing and absorption costing approaches to measuring product costs rests on the treatment of fixed manufacturing overheads.

Under variable costing, fixed manufacturing overheads are excluded from product cost calculations and are charged as expenses in the income statement in the period in which they are incurred. Under absorption costing, these overheads are allocated to products, so that they can be included in stock valuation, and are recognised in the income statement in the period in which the stock is sold. Effectively, absorption costing treats fixed overheads as though they were variable. Absorption costing is also known as a *full cost* method because it is suggested that the inclusion of allocated fixed overheads results in a measure which is closer to the full cost of production. The difference between these methods is illustrated in the example shown in Table 7.2.

The example indicates the fact that the different treatment of overheads under the two approaches will have an effect both on stock valuation and on the measurement of periodic income. The income and the stock valuation figures are higher under the absorption costing column (£852 and £1,032 respectively, compared to £684 and £864 for variable costing) because some of the fixed manufacturing costs are carried forward and will appear as a charge against income when the stock is subsequently sold, whereas under variable costing all the fixed costs (£420) are charged against income immediately. The debate on which approach is more appropriate depends to some extent on views about the purpose of the information on product costs. Variable cost is more consistent with the ideas of relevance introduced in Chapter 5, and is more appropriate for decision-making purposes because it focuses on the incremental change that can be expected from a decision. Absorption costing pays more attention to the importance of fixed costs and to matching full product cost with the related revenue when the product is sold for the calculation of profit. Absorption costing tends to be used more widely in practice, partly because of external reporting requirements. The procedures accepted in financial accounting for measuring cost and stock valuation often lead to similar approaches being adopted within management reporting.

Table 7.2 Absorption cost and variable cost calculations compared

		Absorption costing		Variable costing
Direct materials 400 kg @ £3		£1,200		£1,200
Direct labour 60 hours @ £12		720		720
Variable overheads 60 hours @ £4		240		240
Fixed overheads 60 hours @ £7		420		–
Cost of production		£2,580		£2,160
Volume produced		200		200
Volume sold @ price £20		120		120
Closing stock		80		80
Unit cost of production	(£2,580/200)	£12.90	(£2,160/200)	£10.80
Income statement effect:				
		£		£
Sales value (120 @ £20)		2,400		2,400
Less				
Cost of sales	(120 @ £12.9)	1,548	(120 @ £10.8)	1,296
Manufacturing overheads		–		420
Operating profit		£852		£684
Balance sheet effect:				
Closing stock value	(80 @ £12.9)	£1,032	(80 @ £10.8)	£864

Actual costs and standard costs

A further issue in the way in which product costs are measured is the choice between actual costs and standard costs. Actual costs are those expenditures specifically incurred as the productive process is implemented. Thus if product A uses 200 kg of a material input in a period when 4,000 units are produced, and the expenditure in acquiring that input is £20 per kg, then the cost of product A should include £1 per unit for material (200 kg @ £20 each = £4,000 for 4,000 units).

An alternative to calculating product cost on the basis of actual expenditure is to use predetermined standard amounts. It is possible to use predetermined standard allowances for both the quantities of inputs and their prices. If in the example in the preceding paragraph it had been estimated that each kg of material input would be sufficient to produce 25 units and would cost £18 to purchase, then a standard allowance for materials could have been set at £0.72 per unit (£18/25 units). The costing system would use this figure to estimate product cost for the 4,000 units produced instead of the actual cost of £1.00 per unit. Standard amounts for the different inputs to production, including standard overhead allocations, can be aggregated to give a total standard cost for a product.

With this approach it will be necessary periodically to compare actual results with the costs accounted for by the standard costing system. So in the example above, the amount actually spent of £4,000 would be compared with the amount accounted for by the costing system of £2,880 (4,000 units at 72p each). The procedure for making this kind of comparison and calculating variances is described in Chapter 17.

While intuitively it might seem that using actual expenditure will result in more accurate measurement of product costs, standard costs are often used in practice for a number of reasons:

- to accommodate variations in the level of activity, which could result in very different costs being shown for the same product item if calculations are performed frequently;

- to produce timely information, without the delay that might be caused by waiting for information on actual costs;

- to assist with planning and budgeting by establishing pre-set amounts;

- to provide targets or benchmarks against which actual performance can be evaluated.

One of the main difficulties with standard costing is to determine what the appropriate standard should be. It is implicit that the standard should be based on expectations of future costs, but these are uncertain. If the standard is intended to measure full cost, it will also depend on the way in which fixed and common costs are allocated across production, an issue which we discuss below. The use of standard costing for the purposes of budgeting and control is described in Chapter 17.

Allocations in measuring product costs

While some costs can be attributed directly to products relatively easily, the measurement of product costs, whether using standard or actual costs, can also include allocations of certain costs that do not vary directly with the production of a single product. Cost allocation is a means of spreading expenditure over production. The major problem that arises with this procedure is the difficulty of deciding the basis on which the costs are to be allocated to different products. Most commonly the traditional approach to allocation has involved a two-stage process of allocation, whereby expenditures are first assigned to departments and then allocated from departments to products. The first stage means that costs are initially collected together under headings which may be useful for control purposes, and the second leads to the ultimate estimation of product cost for the purposes of stock valuation and income measurement. This approach is illustrated in Figure 7.2.

For example, Table 7.3 shows how the costs for parts, labour and lubricants associated with servicing and repairing production machinery for Manor Manufacturing plc are first collected together under the departmental heading of Maintenance (stage 1 allocation). The total for this department (£30,000) can be

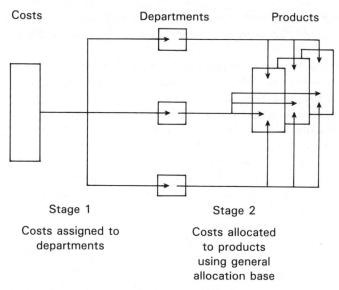

Costs	Departments	Products

Stage 1	Stage 2
Costs assigned to departments	Costs allocated to products using general allocation base

Figure 7.2   Conventional two-stage allocation system.

Table 7.3   Manor Manufacturing plc: Maintenance cost allocation

Stage 1: Allocation to department

Costs incurred	£	Allocated to Maintenance department
Labour: Wages records	19,100	
Parts: Purchased	5,600	Department total
Ex stores	4,600	£30,000
Lubricants: Ex stores	700	

Stage 2: Allocation to products

Product	Machine hours	Output in period	Hours/ unit	Maintenance cost/unit (£)	Total costs allocated (£)
A	3,000	2,000	1.5	7.50 (£5 × 1.5)	15,000
B	1,000	500	2.0	10.00 (£5 × 2)	5,000
C	2,000	2,000	1.0	5.00 (£5 × 1)	10,000
	6,000				30,000

Maintenance
cost per hour = £5.00 (£30,000/6,000)

compared with the budgeted expenditure, which will assist management to form a view of the cost of this aspect of operations, to evaluate performance and possibly take control actions.

In order to include the maintenance costs in the estimates of product costs (stage 2 in Figure 7.2), some basis of allocation must be applied. The most commonly used bases traditionally have been general measures of the overall level of production activity, such as direct labour hours, direct labour cost or machine hours. These approaches assume that the most significant determinant of costs for individual products is the amount of labour input (measured by hours or expenditure) or the amount of processing time, and that other costs can therefore be treated as though they vary with these measures. In our example, Manor Manufacturing plc uses machine hours to allocate maintenance expenditure. As the total cost of maintenance was £30,000 in a month when machinery had been in production for 6,000 hours, then products would be allocated £5 in respect of maintenance for each hour of machine time used. Product A, which used 3,000 machine hours to produce 2,000 units, is allocated £15,000 for maintenance overheads (£5 × 3,000), i.e. £7.50 per unit is included as part of the measurement of product cost (£15,000/2,000 units or £5 × 1.5 hours/unit). Similar allocations for products B and C are shown in Table 7.3.

As noted above, the allocation bases used most commonly in practice have tended to be general measures of the volume of production activity, such as labour and machine time. In some situations a single base has been used for the distribution of all costs that are to be allocated. The use of general volume-related measures of activity may be acceptable in some relatively simple production processes, but, as we have already seen in Chapter 6, the incidence of different costs is likely to be related to different cost drivers, and a proper understanding of the cost structure of an enterprise should incorporate consideration of all these factors. The more complex the production process and the more diverse the types of cost that are being incurred in production, the less likely it is that the averaging implicit in using general measures of volume for allocations will result in accurate estimation of product costs.

7.5 Activity-based costing

In recent years there has been considerable criticism of the traditional approaches to costing, coupled with a search to identify ways of improving the product cost calculation to give measurements which are more suitable for management purposes. The main substance of the criticisms has been as follows:

1. The allocations made using general measures of the volume of production activity as the allocation base are too simplistic and involve too much averaging to give accurate product costs in modern, complex manufacturing environments.

2. Financial accounting conventions lead to some aspects of cost being excluded from the measurement of product cost. Management decisions about products should be based on all costs associated with those products, whether or not financial reporting rules permit their inclusion in stock valuation.

3. Variable costing is an inadequate reaction to the problem of simplistic allocations because it fails to take account of all relevant costs. A proper understanding of the drivers associated with costs can mean that costs previously regarded as fixed or indirect can be more directly linked to products and services provided.

4. The nature of production has changed over recent years. Advances in technology have made manufacturing less labour centred. One consequence of more advanced production technology can be that the proportion of total costs that are direct and variable reduces and the proportion that are indirect (or have traditionally been classified as 'fixed') increases. While simple allocation bases may have been acceptable when only a small proportion of total costs was being allocated, that is no longer the case and a fuller understanding of the behaviour of indirect costs is needed to measure product costs accurately.

These criticisms are severe as they challenge both the recognition and the measurement aspects of product costing: that is, what cost items are included in product cost and how those items are valued. A response to these problems can be found in the ideas of activity-based costing.

Activity-based costing starts from the proposition that costs are incurred by a firm because it performs certain operational activities. For this purpose an 'activity' may be defined as 'any discrete task that an organisation undertakes to make or deliver a product or service'.[4] In the previous chapter we introduced the idea that activities can be analysed to identify those factors, or *cost drivers*, that influence the incidence of cost, and that different activities might have different drivers. Activity-based costing recognises these drivers as the basis for attributing costs to products. Activity-based allocations can be used within a job costing system or a process costing system. This approach challenges the traditional distinction between fixed and variable costs because it asks not whether a cost varies directly in relation to the level of production, but rather: what is it that causes the cost to be incurred and to change? In the medium to long run all costs may be avoidable, and the basis on which they are incurred should be understood. Rather than assuming that the link between costs and volume of production should determine how a cost is treated, cost allocation should begin with the activities which incur costs. Activity-based costing also challenges traditional approaches to costing because it suggests that allocations used to trace costs to products should be based on the cost drivers rather than general volume measures.

To illustrate these points, consider the example of the production of computer games. The manufacture of a game once it is designed may be relatively inexpensive, but the cost of the research and design activities is likely to be very high. A firm engaged in design and manufacture of computer games faces two problems in measuring product costs. First, financial accounting rules may suggest that certain research or design costs should be omitted from product costs for stock valuation, and be charged directly to the income statement in the year in which they are incurred. However, from a management perspective it is surely important that the link between the design activity and individual products is fully understood, in order that proper control can be exercised. Second, if the firm is to include an allocation of design costs in product costs, it cannot be assumed that the amount of cost is linked to the volume of production. A relatively simple game that sells in large quantities cheaply may have involved a great deal less design cost than a complex, novel game selling in small quantities. A system of cost allocation which simply averaged an allocation of design costs across *all* units of production would provide misleading information on product costs for management decisions.

As illustrated in Figure 7.3, activity-based costing as a basis for measuring product costs still involves a two-stage process of allocation, but it differs from that described earlier in two main respects:

1. Costs are collected initially into cost pools associated with individual *activities* rather than aggregated under departmental headings.

2. The second stage allocation of the cost of activities is based on the cost driver for each individual activity, rather than on a general allocation base applied to several cost heads. In this way, much of the averaging implicit in the conventional approaches is avoided.

The difference between the two-stage allocation process under activity-based costing and that applied conventionally in cost accounting can be illustrated by returning to the example of Manor Manufacturing plc. Earlier we described how the costs of the Maintenance department for a period could be allocated to

Figure 7.3 Activity cost-based two-stage allocation system.

products on the basis of a general measure of the level of operation, machine hours. To calculate activity-based product costs, we must first investigate what activities are undertaken by the Maintenance department. For Manor Manufacturing plc we might identify that the maintenance heading covers three main activities: regular servicing of machinery, set-up preparation of machines for production runs, and repairs following breakdowns during production. The need for general servicing could be related to the amount of machine time operated, and machine hours would therefore be the cost driver for servicing costs. However, set-up costs are more likely to be driven by the number of production runs for which set-up is required, and breakdown repairs might be related to differences in the complexity of production causing variation in the pattern of breakdowns between products.

Table 7.4 provides revised estimates of the amounts that should be included in product costs to reflect maintenance activities for Manor Manufacturing plc. Costs are allocated to the separate activities of servicing, set-up and repair (stage 1

Table 7.4 Manor Manufacturing plc: maintenance cost allocation using activity-based measures

Stage 1: Allocation to activities

	Servicing	Production set-up	Breakdown repairs
Labour: Wages records			
Parts: Purchased Ex stores	Allocations to separate activities		
Lubricants: Ex stores			
Total	£6,000	£16,500	£7,500

Stage 2: Allocation to products

Product	Servicing Machine hours	£	Production set-up Production runs	£	Breakdown repairs Break-downs	£	Total cost (£)	Output	Cost/ unit (£)
A	3,000	3,000	2	3,000	–	–	6,000	2,000	3.00
B	1,000	1,000	1	1,500	4	5,000	7,500	500	15.00
C	2,000	2,000	8	12,000	2	2,500	16,500	2,000	8.25
	6,000	£6,000	11	£16,500	6	£7,500	£30,000		
Activity cost/ driver	£1.00 (£6,000/6,000)		£1,500 (£16,500/11)		£1,250 (£7,500/6)				

allocation) and then measures of the cost drivers for these activities are used to allocate activity costs to products (stage 2). When the resulting product costs are compared to those in Table 7.3, it can be seen that the averaging implicit in using a general measure such as machine hours to allocate all costs had produced a very different and potentially distorted view of the costs of products. Under the conventional approach, using a single cost allocation base, product A was allocated £7.50, product B £10.00 and product C £5.00, compared to £3.00, £15.00 and £8.25 respectively using activity-based allocations. Products B and C are both given higher estimates under activity-based costing because of the recognition that higher repair and set-up costs are incurred on these products. For example, product C appears to be produced in relatively small runs (8 runs for total output of 2,000 units) and so takes a much higher share of the set-up costs than B, which has all been produced in a single batch.

As a general framework for approaching the analysis of operations to apply activity-based costing, it is sometimes suggested that production activities can be classified into the following four categories:

1. *Unit level* – where the volume of activity is directly related to the number of units produced.

2. *Batch level* – where the volume of activity is associated with the number of batches rather than the quantity within individual batches.

3. *Product related* – activities that support the production and sale of individual products, and which will therefore increase with diversification in a firm's product range.

4. *Facility related* – the support activities that make production possible, although the costs are not incurred directly as a result of the volume of production, the way it is organised or the product range.

The cost drivers used in cost analysis and, for many items, in allocating costs to products should reflect the nature of these cost classifications. Thus, unit-level activities should be measured by unit-related measures, such as the number of units produced or the number of machine hours' production, batch-level costs should be allocated using batch-related measures, such as the number of production runs, and so on.

7.6 Activity-based management

In the above section we have looked at activity-based costing in relation to the basic subject of this chapter, which is the measurement of product costs. The use of the information generated by an activity-based cost approach for management decision making is known as *activity-based management*. It is sometimes claimed that this approach can enhance management's perspective on the operations and thus lead to better decision making. This enhanced perspective follows from two points. First, activity-based cost analysis should provide better information than the application of the more simplistic fixed/variable cost classification which has traditionally been used in cost accounting. As we have seen in Manor Manufacturing, activity-based analysis can result in more accurate cost measurements. Second, understanding the nature of activities and their cost drivers allows distinction to be drawn between activities that are 'adding value' to products or services – that is, are having some effect that customers value – and those that are not adding value. Management's approach to organisational planning and control can be influenced by this understanding. An activity-based management approach would place emphasis on improving the efficiency of value-adding activities and on eliminating or controlling non-value-adding activities.

The difficulties in pursuing this approach include the cost and complexity of undertaking the required analysis to identify what tasks should be classified as 'activities' for cost recognition, and also identifying the appropriate drivers which can be used as measures of activity. It can also be difficult to promote reliance on activity-based information if the incentive structures and performance measurement schemes relate to other aspects of operations. In addition, designating certain activities as 'non-value-adding' may create resistance within an organisation, particularly if it is perceived that such activities are to be eliminated as far as possible.

Nonetheless, while they are still far from universally accepted, activity analysis and activity-based costing have been among the most significant influences on the development of management accounting in recent years.

7.7 Product cost and relevant cost

Before leaving the subject of product costing, we should emphasise that nothing that has been said about the procedures for accounting for the costs of current operations, or about the methods and practice of allocating costs, should be interpreted as changing the basic rules established in Part 1 regarding what is relevant information for decision making.

In Chapter 5 we analysed decisions in terms of their consequences, and concluded that only differential, future cash flows are relevant for decision making. This rule will be applied in subsequent chapters to discuss the contribution management accounting can make in different types of decision context. A system for accounting for, and providing information about, past and current costs may assist in two ways. First, knowledge of the patterns of behaviour of past costs may be of value in predicting future flows as a basis for decisions. Second, comparison of actual experience with predictions can lead to revisions of expectations for the remainder of the planning period, which might then suggest corrective action (or control decisions) in order to affect future flows. Activity analysis will be of value if it enhances the understanding that management has about the pattern of behaviour and incidence of costs as a basis for developing expectations about the future. It remains the case, however, that decisions should be based on expectations about differential, future cash flows.

CHAPTER SUMMARY

In this chapter we have presented a broad review of systems for recording and measuring product costs. These systems may generate information which can assist management in forming expectations about the future and deciding whether to adjust operations to influence future flows. The chapter has:

- reviewed the reasons why costing systems may be used to record product costs;

- described the main structure of the two main types of costing system that have been used traditionally – job costing and process costing;

- looked at how product costs might be measured, whether full cost or variable cost is measured, whether values are calculated using actual or standard costs, and how allocations are made;

- described the use of activity-based costing for the measurement of product costs and the implications of this method for the classification of costs and for management's approach to cost control.

In most circumstances a costing system will provide only an estimate of true cost, because of the averaging implicit in many calculations and the use of allocations. Activity-based costing can be thought of as a means of achieving more accurate cost allocations. It will be most advantageous in complex environments, where the distortions introduced by averaged allocations are likely to be more significant. The objective of cost analysis and recording remains to provide better information about differential future flows through which decision making can be supported.

REVIEW QUESTIONS

1. What are the reasons for estimating costs for individual products or services?

2. What are the principal differences between the types of organisation in which you would expect to find job order costing systems and those in which you would expect to find process costing systems?

3. Discuss what is meant by a 'standard cost' and evaluate how such a measure might contribute to management control and decision making.

4. Outline the arguments for the use of (a) general measures of production activity and (b) activity-related cost drivers as the bases for allocating overhead costs to products.

5. Compare the two-stage allocation system used under conventional cost accounting with that used in activity-based costing.

EXERCISES

7.1 Royle plc manufactures and lays multipurpose outdoor sports surfaces for sports clubs. The company accounts separately for the manufacturing costs incurred at its production plant and the costs of laying the surfaces on-site at clubs. The manufacture is automated and machine intensive, and overheads are allocated on the basis of production time (at a rate of £10 per production hour). In contrast, the on-site work is very labour intensive and consequently overheads are allocated on the basis of labour hours (at a rate of £7.50 per labour hour).

During May 19X7 Royle worked on the following three contracts, each of which is treated as a separate job for cost recording:

	Manufacture	Laying on-site
Job No. 2XC45		
Labour hours	400	500
Production hours	1,000	–
Cost of labour	£4,000	£4,500
Cost of materials	£21,500	£1,200
Job No. 2FR56		
Labour hours	900	1,100
Production hours	2,250	–
Cost of labour	£9,000	£9,900
Cost of materials	£45,500	£2,600
Job No. 3DR67		
Labour hours	100	300
Production hours	500	–
Cost of labour	£1,000	£2,700
Cost of materials	£7,500	£600

The overhead costs recorded for manufacture and on-site work for the month of May were £41,500 and £12,200 respectively.

(a) Calculate the amounts of overhead to be allocated to each of the three jobs and the resulting total cost for each job.

(b) Compare the total amount of overhead allocated to the jobs with the actual amount of overheads incurred. (Solution at end of text.)

7.2 Worsley plc has recently undertaken an exercise to estimate the level of manufacturing overhead costs relating to its processing plant that will be incurred during 19X7, and to establish the cost drivers for the different areas of overhead cost, as part of an evaluation of whether to change its existing basis of overhead allocation, which relies solely on machine processing hours. The resulting information is shown below:

	Estimated costs (£)	Cost driver	Expected level
Handling materials	30,000	Times machines filled	500
Production set-up	80,000	Set-up hours	2,000
Processing inspection	90,000	Number of inspections	600
Machine maintenance	50,000	Processing hours	20,000
	250,000		

The expected costs and levels of activity are used as the basis for determining the overhead rates used for making allocations to products.

During January, processing included production of the following two products:

	GTD4	XTD7
Cost of material inputs	£16,000	£14,000
Cost of direct labour	£12,000	£9,000
Processing hours	600	480
Labour hours	1,500	1,100
Times machines filled	30	5
Set-up hours	100	20
Inspections	30	10
Volume of units produced	3,000	2,500

(a) Assuming that all overheads are allocated on the basis of machine processing hours, calculate the unit cost of each product.

(b) Assuming that overheads are allocated using their specific cost drivers, calculate the unit cost of each product.

(c) Discuss the results of (a) and (b) for the choice being considered by the management of Worsley plc concerning the future basis of cost allocation. (Solution at end of text.)

7.3 Birch Furniture plc has recently completed an order for 1,200 upholstered chairs for a hotel chain, at a total contract price of £234,000. The chairs were manufactured using standard frames which cost £60.00 per chair, fabric and padding costing £24.00 per chair and metal fittings costing £2.50 per chair. On average each chair was completed in four hours by one employee, and the completed chairs were subject to inspection and testing for half an hour each. Manufacturing employees are paid at a rate of £9.00 per hour and inspectors £11.50 per hour. It is company policy at Birch Furniture to allocate overheads to jobs at a rate of £4.50 per labour hour. In addition, packaging and delivery costs have been assigned to this job totalling £3,600.

(a) Prepare a job cost record for the contract for the 1,200 chairs.

(b) Calculate the cost per chair incurred by Birch Furniture and the profit or loss per chair achieved.

7.4   Platt Products manufactures three products, the production data for which for 19X6 are shown in the table below:

	Product A	Product B	Product C
Material and labour costs assigned directly to products	£40,000	£40,000	£45,000
Machine hours	15,000	5,000	10,000
Production runs	65	190	135
Materials usage (kg)	250,000	150,000	400,000
Labour hours	2,000	1,000	3,000
Volume produced	20,000	10,000	30,000

Manufacturing overheads have been allocated to activity-based cost pools. The amounts recorded for each activity and the level of the related cost driver identified by Platt Products' accountants were as follows:

Activity	Amount	Cost driver	Level
Servicing/maintenance	£139,000	Machine hours	30,000
Production scheduling	£130,000	Production runs	390
Material handling	£320,000	Quantity of material (kg)	800,000

(a) Calculate the unit product cost using the identified cost drivers to allocate overheads to the three products.

(b) 19X6 is the first year that Platt Products has recorded overhead cost using activity-based classifications. Previously labour hours were used to allocate all overheads to products. Calculate the unit product cost for A, B and C using this approach.

(c) Compare the results of estimating product costs using the different methods in (a) and (b), and explain any differences in the estimates for each product.

(d) Discuss the difficulties of identifying suitable cost drivers for overhead costs in practice.

7.5 As part of a major review of its management information, Anson plc has recently introduced an activity-based cost recording system. During the development of the system, the following data were collected for the overhead costs for a department which assembles small electric motors:

Activity	Estimated cost (£)	Driver identified	Estimated driver activity
Ordering components from stores	25,000	Number of orders	500
Power	35,100	Production hours	2,340
Maintenance	21,000	Machine hours	14,000
Supervision	59,670	Assembly labour hours	35,100
Testing and quality control	45,000	Number of components assembled	15,000

Before the introduction of the activity-based costing system, all the overheads in this assembly department were allocated on the basis of machine hours.

(a) Develop a linear equation which describes the pattern of overhead cost incidence suggested by the information in the above table.

(b) Discuss the effect that the change to an activity-based costing system is likely to have on the measurement of product costs by Anson plc, and compare the rationale for the cost drivers suggested above with a general allocation based on machine hours.

Notes

1. See, for example. C. T. Horngren and G. Foster, *Cost Accounting: A managerial emphasis*, 8th edn, Prentice Hall International, 1994, and C. Drury, *Management and Cost Accounting*, 3rd edn, Chapman and Hall, 1992.
2. The valuation of long-term jobs extending beyond the period covered by a single set of financial statements, e.g. major construction contracts, may include an allowance for profit earned as well as cost, under rules established by the accounting standard-setting body in the UK.
3. Often some units will not have completed a particular process at the end of the period. It will then be necessary to estimate the *equivalent full units of production* that constitute the quantity of processing undertaken. In this way, opening and closing work in progress still being processed is allowed for.
4. A. A. Atkinson, R. D. Banker, R. S. Kaplan and S. M. Young, *Management Accounting*, Prentice Hall International, 1995, p. 64.

PART 1
Basic framework

PART 2
Cost information

PART 3
Applications
The use of accounting information for management decision making and control

CHAPTER 8
Cost−volume−profit analysis

CHAPTER 9
Pricing decisions

CHAPTER 10
Relevant information for operating decisions

CHAPTER 11
The effect of scarce resources on short-term decisions

CHAPTER 12
Dual prices and opportunity costs

CHAPTER 13
Long-term decisions: the net present value rule

CHAPTER 14
Long-term decisions: internal rate of return and other methods

CHAPTER 15
The budgeting process

CHAPTER 16
The master budget and the cash budget

CHAPTER 17
Variance analysis and standard costing

CHAPTER 18
Divisional performance

CHAPTER 19
Summary and review

Cost–volume–profit analysis

AIMS AND OBJECTIVES

☐ To describe and illustrate the use of break-even charts in cost–volume–profit analysis.
☐ To explain the importance of the contribution margin.
☐ To discuss the usefulness of flexible budgeting.
☐ To discuss the difficulties involved in applying cost–volume–profit analysis to multiproduct firms.

In previous chapters, we have argued that management decision making requires a good understanding of the way in which costs incurred are affected by changes in the organisation's operations. Information about costs must also be combined with expectations about the behaviour of revenues in order to appreciate the overall financial result associated with a particular pattern or level of activity. Planning and decision making involve a consideration of the combined effect on *both* cost and revenue functions of changes in operations. One way of achieving this is by an examination of the intricate relationship between revenue and costs at different levels of activity, which in turn gives insights into the incremental impact on cash flows of the various choices open to management. The technique used in this examination is usually referred to as *cost–volume–profit (CVP) analysis*.

The use of the term 'profit' here may be slightly misleading, as the analysis does not involve the kind of treatment of costs and revenues that would be applied in calculating profit for reporting in annual financial statements. A more appropriate description of the relationships to be analysed would be 'cost–volume–surplus cash flow'. The principal purpose of this analysis is to improve management's understanding of the relationship between financial flows and the level of operating activity. The technique is thus relevant to not-for-profit organisations as well as profit-seeking enterprises.

8.1 Cost–volume–profit relationships

Cost–volume–profit analysis is based on the following relationship:

Profit = Revenues – Total costs

If we use the term π to denote profit for the period, P to denote the selling price per unit, x to denote the level of output produced and sold during the period, a to denote the level of fixed costs for the period, and b to denote the variable cost per unit produced and sold, we can then derive the expanded CVP equation as follows:

$$\pi = Px - (a + bx)$$

CVP analysis thus assumes that the firm's total costs can be separated into their fixed and variable components. However, as we have seen in Chapter 6, it is seldom immediately obvious which costs are fixed and which are variable, and the pattern of cost incidence might reflect several different cost drivers as activity level changes. Quite sophisticated statistical techniques may be necessary in order to analyse cost behaviour and to segregate costs into appropriate categories for decision-making purposes.

Using the data for Burnden plc given in Table 8.1, we can see how the cost–volume–profit equation might be used to answer certain questions relevant to managerial decision making, such as:

1. What is the output level in units at which Burnden plc breaks even (i.e. makes neither a profit nor a loss, or, put another way, exactly covers its total costs)?

2. How many units must be sold to show a profit of £5,000?

3. What selling price would have to be charged to show a profit of £6,000 on sales of 10,000 units?

Table 8.1 Burnden plc: cost–volume–profit data

Selling price (£)	5
Fixed costs per annum (£)	30,000
Semi-variable costs:	
Fixed element (£)	10,000
Variable element (£ per unit)	1
Variable costs (£ per unit)	2
Relevant range of output (units)	6,000–24,000

1. *Break-even point in units*

$$\pi = Px - (a + bx)$$

Then Burnden plc breaks even at a level of output (x) where:

$$a + bx = Px$$

Substituting in the above we have:

$$40,000 + 3x = 5x$$
$$\therefore \quad x = 20,000 \text{ units}$$

2. *Units to be sold to show a profit of £5,000*
   Substituting in the CVP equation we have:

   $$5,000 = 5x - (40,000 + 3x)$$
   $$2x = 45,000$$
   $$\therefore \quad x = 22,500 \text{ units}$$

3. *Selling price to be charged to show a profit of £6,000 on sales of 10,000 units*
   Substituting in the CVP equation we have:

   $$6,000 = P(10,000) - (40,000 + 3(10,000))$$
   $$6,000 = 10,000P - 70,000$$
   $$10,000P = 76,000$$
   $$\therefore \quad P = £7.60 \text{ (i.e. an increase of £2.60 per unit)}.$$

The above equations are one means of presenting CVP information. An alternative form of presentation, which may serve to clarify the underlying cost and revenue relationship assumed, is the use of graphs. Two graphs in particular are used to portray CVP relationships, the break-even chart and the profit–volume chart.

8.2 The break-even chart

The break-even chart, used frequently by accountants, serves a variety of functions. The initial purpose of the chart may have been simply to inform management of the level of output at which total revenue just covers total cost. Nowadays, in conjunction with the relevant range notion, the chart can be used to give an estimate of profit at different output levels (i.e. the break-even chart can be viewed as representing a series of summarised income statements).

Using the data for Burnden plc taken from Table 8.1, we can construct a break-even chart by summing the various cost categories. The chart is shown in Figure 8.1. There is no 'best' order of aggregating the costs vertically. However, it is most usual to begin with fixed costs, then to add the semi-variable costs and finally to add the variable costs. We shall deal with the problem of step costs later in this chapter. The two most important linear functions in Figure 8.1 are the total revenue function and the total cost function. The construction of the chart should reflect management's

Figure 8.1 Break-even chart.

understanding of the relationship between production, the performance of certain activities and expenditure.

The point (*X*) at which the total revenue line cuts the total cost line is the point where Burnden plc makes neither a profit nor a loss. This is the *break-even point*, which lends its name to the chart. Visual inspection of the graph shows the break-even point to be 20,000 units, the amount arrived at by application of the basic CVP equation.

This break-even output information may be useful to the firm in assessing the probability of making a profit in the coming year. After calculating the break-even point, managers may assess how likely it is that an output of at least 20,000 units will be produced and sold. It will be less useful in guiding the firm to an optimal output decision (what output level will produce the highest profit?). Within the limits imposed by the relevant range, it is apparent from the chart that the maximum output (24,000 units) will produce the highest profit. It also seems that, without the upper limit imposed by the relevant range, any increase in output above 24,000 units will increase profit. In theory, the optimal level is infinity. This conclusion follows from the assumed linearity of the cost and revenue functions, and is one of the weaknesses of the method.

8.3 Break-even analysis and the contribution margin

We can see from the break-even chart in Figure 8.1 that, at output levels below 20,000 units, Burnden plc makes a loss equal to the distance between the total cost line and the sales revenue line; above 20,000 units, Burnden plc makes a profit equal to the distance between the sales revenue line and the total cost line.

Suppose now that Burnden plc sells only 19,999 units, one unit *below* the break-even point. What will be the amount of the loss? Recall that the cost–volume–profit equation is:

$$\pi = Px - (a + bx)$$
$$\therefore \quad \pi = 19,999(5) - (40,000 + 19,999(3))$$
$$\therefore \quad \pi = -£2 \text{ (i.e. a loss of £2)}$$

Now suppose that Burnden plc sells 20,001 units, one unit *above* the break-even point. What will now be the profit for the year? Substituting in the basic CVP equation, we have:

$$\pi = 20,001(5) - (40,000 + 20,001(3))$$
$$\therefore \quad \pi = £2 \text{ (i.e. a profit of £2)}$$

What is the significance of these figures of £2 loss and £2 profit respectively? Is it a coincidence that the answer is £2 in each case? The significance lies in the fact that each additional unit produced and sold is generating an incremental profit of £2, as represented by the difference between the selling price per unit of £5 and the variable cost per unit of £3. This incremental profit is known as the *contribution margin* or *contribution* on each unit sold, and as we shall see throughout later chapters, this is a widely used and important concept in managerial decision making. Its use may be seen more immediately by an examination of the second graphical representation of the data for Burnden plc, the *profit–volume chart*, shown in Figure 8.2.

While the break-even graph is obviously useful for estimating the break-even point, it is less useful as a means of highlighting the profit or loss at different volume levels (i.e. to find profit figures from the break-even chart, it is necessary to determine the difference between two sloping lines). A more convenient method of showing the impact of changes in volume on profit is the profit–volume chart. The horizontal axis of the profit–volume chart denotes the various levels of sales volume; the vertical axis shows the amount of profit or loss for the period. In our example, if Burnden plc sells zero output, the maximum loss it will incur is the fixed costs of £40,000. It cannot lose more than its outlay on fixed costs. With each additional unit sold, a contribution of £2 is being made to total fixed costs, until Burnden plc reaches a sales volume level of 20,000 units (the break-even point), at which point the contribution generated of £40,000 (20,000 x £2) exactly covers the fixed costs. This is the point at which the sloping line cuts the horizontal axis. With each successive unit sold above 20,000 units, Burnden plc generates a surplus of £2.

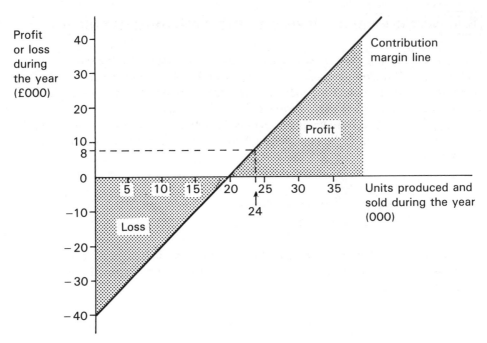

Figure 8.2   The profit–volume chart.

If, for instance, Burnden plc sells 24,000 units (as shown by the broken line on Figure 8.2), it will show a profit of £8,000, represented by the contribution margin of 24,000 units at £2 per unit = £48,000, minus fixed costs of £40,000. This excess of actual sales over the break-even sales level is often referred to as the *margin of safety*. The magnitude of the margin of safety indicates the possible reduction in sales which the firm can withstand before it incurs any loss. Thus the slope of the profit line in the profit–volume graph is always determined by the contribution margin, which in this case is £2 per unit or 40% of selling price.

Many of the problems posed by CVP analysis can be addressed more directly by the application of the concept of the contribution margin. The contribution margin per unit is simply the difference between the selling price per unit P and the variable cost per unit b. Our cost–volume–profit equation is of the form:

$$\pi = Px - (a + bx)$$

Rearranging the terms in the equation to accommodate the notion of contribution, we now have:

$$\pi = (P - b)x - a$$

where profit equals the contribution margin per unit $(P - b)$ multiplied by the number of units sold (x) less the fixed costs for the period (a). This is the relationship which is shown by the profit–volume chart. If we further rearrange the profit equation as follows:

$$\pi + a = (P - b)x$$

we can see the real meaning of contribution margin. The term is not used in isolation; the units sold by the firm make a contribution to *two* items: profit (π) and fixed costs (a). Phrased differently, we might say that before the firm can earn profits it must cover its fixed costs; this it does by selling sufficient units which yield a positive contribution.

Using the idea of contribution margin, we can now answer some possible questions raised by the example of Burnden plc.

1. *What is Burnden plc's break-even point in units?*

   For profit to equal zero: $a = (P - b)x$

   $$x = \frac{a}{(P - b)}$$

   $$\text{Break-even point in units} = \frac{\text{Fixed costs}}{\text{Contribution margin per unit}}$$

   $$= \frac{\pounds 40,000}{\pounds 2}$$

   $$= 20,000 \text{ units}$$

2. *What is Burnden plc's break-even point in sales revenue?*

   For profit to equal zero: $x = \dfrac{a}{(P - b)}$

   Multiplying both sides by P gives: $Px = \dfrac{a}{(P - b)} \times P$

   Break-even point in sales revenue

   $$= \frac{\text{Fixed costs}}{\text{Contribution margin per unit}} \times \text{Sales price}$$

   $$= \frac{\pounds 40,000}{\pounds 2} \times \pounds 5$$

   $$= \pounds 100,000$$

3. *How many units must Burnden plc sell to show a profit of £5,000?*

To cover fixed costs and generate profit: $\pi + a = (P - b)x$

Rearranging for x gives: $x = \dfrac{a + \pi}{(P - b)}$

$\text{Level of sales required} = \dfrac{\text{Fixed costs + Required profit}}{\text{Contribution margin per unit}}$

$$= \frac{£40,000 + £5,000}{£2}$$

$$= 22,500 \text{ units}$$

4. *What is the level of sales revenue which results in a profit of £5,000?*

To determine the units necessary for a given level of profit: $x = \dfrac{a + \pi}{(P - b)}$

Multiplying both sides by P gives: $Px = \dfrac{a + \pi}{(P - b)} \times P$

$\text{Level of sales} = \dfrac{\text{Fixed costs + Required profit}}{\text{Contribution margin per unit}} \times \text{Sales price}$

$$= \frac{£40,000 + £5,000}{£2} \times £5$$

$$= £112,500$$

8.4 Break-even analysis and flexible budgeting

In practice, organisations will probably incur fixed costs in large indivisible lumps (e.g. the purchase of new factories or machines), and the total 'fixed' cost function will be analogous in form to the step variable functions discussed in Chapter 6 (pp. 110–11). Suppose that Burnden plc has a total cost function whose variable element remains £3 per unit. But now assume that the relevant range restriction is relaxed and that the 'fixed' element of total costs increases in lumps at various output levels as follows:

Output range	Total fixed cost (£)
0 – 5,000	10,000
5,001–10,000	15,000
10,001–15,000	20,000
15,001–20,000	25,000
20,001–25,000	35,000
Above 25,000	Increases by £15,000 for each additional 5,000 units

It is not worthwhile producing above 25,000 units, for each additional 5,000 units above that level yield a contribution to fixed costs of £10,000 (£[5 − 3] × 5,000), which is less than the increase in fixed costs of £15,000.

The break-even chart reflecting the revised cost figures is shown in Figure 8.3. It is apparent from this chart that maximum profit is attained at output levels of either 20,000 or 25,000 units. At both these points, the difference between total revenue and total cost is £15,000. As the total cost function is not a smooth curve, there is no simple algebraic formula that will yield either the break-even points or the level of output that maximises profit. The break-even point (or points) is normally determined most easily from a graph. The output level (or levels) leading to maximum profit may also be observed from the chart. Alternatively, we may calculate the profit at various feasible levels of output, choosing the one that yields the highest profit. This is the basis of the procedure known as *flexible budgeting*.

Where step costs are involved, the optimal output level will often lie at one of the points just before a new injection of fixed costs becomes necessary. We may, therefore, decide that we shall obtain a satisfactory approximation to the optimal plan if we prepare flexible budgets for output levels of 5,000, 10,000, 15,000, 20,000 and 25,000 units. The calculations are shown in Table 8.2 and confirm the results obtained by examining the break-even chart. The optimal output levels are 20,000 and 25,000 units. To reinforce the earlier claim that an increase in output above 25,000 units is not worthwhile, consider the profit at, say, 30,000 units; it is £10,000.[1] This is less than the profit expected at 20,000 or 25,000 units, and

Figure 8.3 Break-even chart with step costs.

Table 8.2 Flexible budgets

	Output level (units)				
	5,000	*10,000*	*15,000*	*20,000*	*25,000*
Variable costs (£3 per unit)	15,000	30,000	45,000	60,000	75,000
Step fixed costs	10,000	15,000	20,000	25,000	35,000
Total costs	25,000	45,000	65,000	85,000	110,000
Sales revenue (£5 per unit)	25,000	50,000	75,000	100,000	125,000
Profit	–	5,000	10,000	15,000	15,000

consequently is an inferior output level in terms of the firm's assumed objective of maximising cash resources.

Both graphical analysis and flexible budgets lead us to the same answer. Which is superior? The flexible budgeting approach boasts a numerical precision that graphical analysis may not always be able to match. On the other hand, a break-even chart illustrates graphically the relationship between cost and profit for all output levels. It may be a simpler means of conveying the often complicated nature of this relationship to management. In addition, the break-even chart shows the range of output levels at which profits are expected to be made. In our example, the firm expects to make a profit at all output levels between 7,500 and 25,000 units. Had we extended the graph to cover higher volumes, we should have seen that output levels between 25,000 and 30,000 units and between 32,500 and 35,000 units were also expected to be profitable. This indication of the profitable ranges might prove useful to the firm in assessing the *sensitivity* of profit to deviations from the planned level of output. Sensitivity analysis is discussed in more detail in Chapter 13.

Both break-even charts and flexible budgets have their advantages. It seems probable that a combination of the two techniques will lead to better decisions being made than if either method is used in isolation. Graphical analysis could be used to establish the general ranges within which production is at its most profitable, and flexible budgeting could be applied to 'sharpen up' the figures.

It is also possible to use a chart to illustrate the effect of different prices on the returns expected. If Burnden charged £5.50 instead of £5 per unit, this would change the total revenue line on the chart and would show a different break-even point and possibly a different level of output which maximises profit.

8.5 An alternative approach to cost–volume–profit analysis

In our discussion of the construction and interpretation of break-even charts, we have stressed the critical assumption of linearity, in relation to both variable costs and fixed costs. The break-even and profit–volume graphs presented in this chapter not only make the same linearity assumption about costs but also assume that selling prices remain unchanged whatever the output level.

How realistic are these assumptions? It may be argued that, if taken to extremes, they conflict with economic reasoning. For instance, an economist might argue that the firm would have to reduce its unit selling price in order to increase its level of sales volume. Consider the graphical presentation of the alternative CVP chart shown in Figure 8.4.

This chart does not assume linearity of costs and revenues, but rather assumes that both costs and revenues are curvilinear. The total revenue curve begins to slope upwards less steeply as price reductions become necessary, and then slopes downwards as the adverse effect of price reductions outweighs the beneficial effects of increased sales volume in terms of total revenue. This total revenue curve reflects the idea of declining marginal revenue – that in order to sell more it will be necessary to reduce price. The total cost curve is curvilinear because costs rise at a slower rate as efficiency increases and then more rapidly as diminishing returns occur. Note that this chart shows two break-even points, X and Y. (Because of the curvilinear cost and revenue functions, it is possible to have more than two break-even points.)

If we now superimpose the conventional (linear) break-even chart on the alternative (curvilinear) graph, as in Figure 8.5, we can see more clearly the possible similarities and differences between the two approaches. Within the relevant range of output levels, the two graphs show a similar relationship. Outside this range, it would be dangerous to assume such a relationship. The difference between the two graphs is the result of their differing assumptions about the behaviour of costs and revenues, and consequently of profit. The conventional graph implies that profit will grow to infinity, or at least to the constraining point of maximum capacity, whereas the alternative graph is based on what is perhaps the more realistic assumption that profit will be influenced by the effect of cumulative price reductions and the diminishing returns of cost factors.

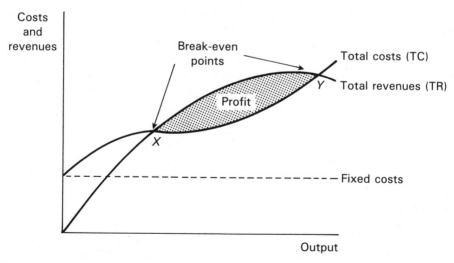

Figure 8.4   Alternative CVP chart.

Figure 8.5 Comparison of alternative CVP graphs.

8.6 Multiproduct firms

Before leaving our analysis of cost–volume–profit relationships, we shall examine briefly the effects of relaxing one of the simplifying assumptions made throughout this chapter: namely, that the firm produces only one product. Are the techniques of break-even analysis and flexible budgeting as useful and simple to apply to multiproduct firms as to those manufacturing a single product? Provided that none of the firm's input factors is in short supply, there seems to be no reason why the techniques should not be equally useful and straightforward. All that is required is a separate break-even or flexible budgeting analysis of each product.

Two particular problems may arise if this approach is followed. First, there may be interdependences between the production or demand functions of two or more of the firm's products: that is, the demand for, or cost of manufacturing, a product may be affected by the demand for or level of production of some other product. If this is the case, it will be necessary to consider the interdependent products together. This should present no particular problems if the output mix of the products is determined by the nature of the interdependence. The combination of interdependent products may be dealt with as though it were a single product. If the product mix is not determined independently, it will be difficult to deal satisfactorily with different products on one graph.

Second, there is the question of how the fixed costs of the firm should be dealt with. Should these be allocated on some basis between the various products for inclusion in the individual break-even charts and flexible budgets? Following the principles developed in this and the previous chapter for dealing with fixed costs, the answer will depend upon their nature. If the costs clearly relate to a particular product and would not be incurred if that product were not to be manufactured, then they should be regarded as fixed costs of the product and included in the analysis relating to it. If, on the other hand, the costs are in the nature of general overheads, created by the existence of the firm itself rather than of any particular product, then to allocate them to individual products will be misleading and may lead to incorrect output decisions. Initial output decisions should be made for each product, regardless of general fixed costs. Then a budget should be prepared for the firm as a whole, based on the optimal output levels for each product and incorporating the general fixed costs of the firm, to ensure that the predicted contributions from the individual products are sufficient to cover the non-allocatable fixed costs. The construction of a break-even chart for the firm *as a whole* seems unnecessary in these circumstances, and may be confusing as it depends upon a prior management decision on optimal output mix which management may not be able to make rationally without a cost–volume–profit analysis.

CHAPTER SUMMARY

Understanding the behaviour of costs and revenues allows managers to estimate the effects of decisions. The relationships between revenues from sales, the operating level, the performance of activities and related expenditure, particularly the split between the fixed and variable elements of costs, can be expressed through break-even charts, contribution margin analysis and flexible budgets. These tools provide useful information for evaluating the choice between alternative levels of operation and the effects of changes in operations on expected profitability. Management planning can be helped by analysis of the break-even level of activity: that is, where total revenues are equal to total costs, the level of activity required to generate a target profit, and the critical points at which cost expenditures change. In all cases the usefulness of the analysis depends on the validity of the assumptions made about the pattern of cost and revenue behaviour.

REVIEW QUESTIONS

1. 'The assumption of linearity of costs negates much of the usefulness of the accountant's work in the area of cost–volume–profit analysis.' Discuss.

2. Explain and discuss the usefulness of the contribution margin and the margin of safety.

3. Compare and contrast the break-even chart and the profit–volume chart as providers of useful information to management.

4. Discuss the economist's contribution to cost–volume–profit analysis.

5. Discuss the practical problems involved in using break-even charts and profit–volume charts for multiproduct firms.

EXERCISES

8.1 Wagner plc manufactures an instrument which has a variable cost structure as follows:

	£
Materials	30.00
Labour	7.50
Variable overhead	3.00
	40.50

The instruments sell at £67.50 each and the company expects a sales revenue from this product in the current year of £1,012,500. Fixed overhead expense attributable to this product is budgeted at £105,000. A wage agreement with the employees states that a 10% increase will be paid to labour in the forthcoming year, while the managing director believes that material prices will rise by 7.5%, variable overhead by 5%, and fixed overhead by 3%, from the beginning of the new financial year.

(a) Calculate the new selling price if the contribution ratio is to be maintained.

(b) Calculate the sales volume required in the forthcoming year if price remains the same and profit is to be maintained. (Solution at end of text.)

8.2 Power Ltd's condensed income statement for 19X2 is as follows:

		£
Sales (100,000 units)		1,000,000
Cost of goods sold		600,000
Gross margin		400,000
Selling expenses	150,000	
Administrative expenses	100,000	250,000
Net profit (before income taxes)		150,000

The budget committee has estimated the following changes for 19X3:

30%	increase in number of units sold
20%	increase in material unit cost
15%	increase in direct labour cost per unit
10%	increase in variable indirect cost per unit

5%   increase in indirect fixed costs

8%   increase in selling expenses, arising solely from increased volume

6%   increase in administrative expenses, reflecting anticipated higher wage and supply price levels (any changes in administrative expenses caused solely by increased sales volume are considered immaterial)

As inventory quantities remain fairly constant, the committee considered that, for budget purposes, any change in inventory valuation can be ignored. The composition of the cost of a unit of finished product during 19X2 for materials, direct labour and production overhead, respectively, was in the ratio of 3 to 2 to 1. In 19X2, £40,000 of the overhead was for fixed costs. No changes in production methods or credit policies were contemplated for 19X3.

(a) From the data above, compute the *unit sales price* at which Power Ltd must sell its only product in 19X3 in order to earn a budgeted profit (before income tax) of £200,000.

(b) The sales manager is unhappy about the prospect of an increase in selling price and wants to know how many units must be sold at the old price to earn the £200,000.

(c) One of the company directors believes the estimated increase in sales is over-optimistic and wants to know what annual profit will be if the selling price determined in (a) is adopted but the increase in sales volume is only 10%. (Solution at end of text.)

8.3   Michelangelo Ltd manufactures a single product which sells at £1.20 per unit. The variable cost of this product is 60p per unit. At present the fixed expenses of the organisation are £30,000 p.a. Michelangelo is currently selling its full productive capacity of 100,000 units p.a. at what the company's directors believe is the optimum price–volume relationship for the product. However, they are considering selling the product under an additional brand name. While being virtually identical from the manufacturing point of view, brands will be differentiated by the packaging and the marketing approaches adopted. Sales of the existing and the new brand when both are priced at 90p per unit are expected to total 300,000 units.

The introduction of the additional brand will require the firm to increase its productive capacity. To do this will increase Michelangelo's fixed costs to £60,000 p.a. However, as this will involve some re-equipment, there will be economies of operation arising which will reduce variable costs to 50p per unit.

(a) Present the above information graphically.

(b) For both the existing situation and the proposed scheme calculate: (i) the break-even point; (ii) the profit; (iii) the margin of safety in units; and

(iv) the sales required under the proposed scheme to maintain the present profit position. In relation to these situations, discuss whether the proposed scheme will improve the company's position.

(c) Briefly discuss the criticisms that might be made of the conventional linear break-even graph. Do these criticisms invalidate its use in practical situations?

8.4   It is 19X6. Mr Normanton, the managing director of Normanton Manufacturing Ltd, is concerned that, while there has been a rapid increase in demand in the company's rather unstable industry in recent years, Normanton has not been able to match the growth of its main rival, Cairns Ltd. He is also worried because raw materials, which currently account for half of the variable manufacturing costs for both companies, are about to be increased in price by 10%, and he is aware that the manufacturing process employed by Cairns Ltd uses less raw materials.

The managing director has been able to obtain the following actual or estimated figures for the two companies:

	Normanton	Cairns
19X3 sales (units)	60,000	58,000
19X4 sales (units)	80,000	90,000
19X5 sales (units)	100,000	118,000
Fixed manufacturing overheads (£)	385,000	490,000
Variable manufacturing costs per unit (£)	3.60	2.40
Fixed selling and administrative expenses (£)	165,000	160,000
Variable selling costs per unit (£)	1.20	1.40

All administrative costs are fixed for both companies. The selling price has remained constant at £12 per unit since January 19X3, but both companies are planning to increase it to £12.50 following the price increase in raw materials. Neither company carries significant levels of stocks or work in progress.

(a) Write a note to the managing director commenting on the effect on the break-even point and the profitability of different levels of sales of the differences in the manufacturing processes adopted by Normanton Manufacturing Ltd and Cairns Ltd.

(b) Calculate the break-even point in units and the number of units which must be sold to achieve profits of £150,000, for both companies, *after* the increase in raw materials and selling prices.

(c) Outline briefly the main limitations of cost–volume–profit analysis.

8.5   Cong Printers Ltd publishes a weekly newspaper. Its profit and loss account for the year ended 31 August 19X3 was as follows:

	£	£
Sales revenue (50 issues)		200,000
Advertising revenue		200,000
		400,000
Paper	150,000	
Payments to journalists	100,000	
Depreciation	40,000	
Distribution costs	30,000	
Other expenses	30,000	
		350,000
Profit		50,000

The board is considering two means of increasing profitability for the year ending 31 August 19X4. The first plan would involve the publication of 50 issues of a midweek edition. Market research suggests that this would achieve 80% of the 10,000 circulation of the existing weekend paper, and have to sell at only 35p. In order to maintain sales of the existing paper at present levels, its price would be held stable at 40p. In the absence of the midweek edition, this would be raised to 44p to help offset the anticipated increase for the coming year of 20% in the cost of paper and 15% in the rate of pay for journalists.

Advertising would cover eight pages in the midweek edition, as opposed to ten in the existing paper, though the total number of pages would remain the same. Advertising rates would average £350 per page. The average rate of £400 per page for the existing edition would be maintained, though if the midweek edition were not introduced, this would be increased to £450.

If the midweek paper is published, paper costs will be increased in proportion to the extra volume of pages printed, and journalists' pay will be increased by £45,000. Half of the distribution costs and other expenses will be increased in proportion to the increased volume of pages published; the balance of these costs, and depreciation, will not be increased, either through price changes or because of the increase in the level of activity.

The alternative scheme involves offering the facilities of the company for printing programmes, advertising handouts and other miscellaneous work. This work would require the hiring of a manager at £12,000 per year, and paper and other operating costs would be, on average, 50% of revenue from printing. Revenue from this activity is very uncertain, and the board has estimated the following probability distribution:

15% chance	£36,000
50% chance	£64,000
35% chance	£80,000

(a) Calculate the estimated additional profit from publishing the midweek edition.

(b) Calculate the level of revenue needed under the second scheme to produce an estimated additional profit equal to that from publishing the midweek edition.

(c) Discuss how the board might decide between the two alternative schemes, given the probability distribution provided for the second scheme and assuming that the estimates made under the first scheme were almost certain to be correct.

Note

1.

	£
Variable costs	90,000
Step fixed costs	50,000
Total costs	140,000
Sales revenue	150,000
Profit	10,000

Pricing decisions

In previous chapters we have developed the notion that the long-run objective of an organisation should be to generate surplus cash from its operations: that is, to maximise the discounted present value of future net cash inflows. In this context, surplus cash represents the residual after deducting the total cash costs of operations from the total cash revenues from operations. We have also looked in some detail at how we might classify, analyse and predict costs so as to improve decision making – but we have spent little time on an examination of the other part of the equation: namely, the determination of total revenues. Yet perhaps the most important operating decisions of all are concerned with the establishment of selling prices for an organisation's goods and services. It is the volume of sales multiplied by the selling price which determines the total cash inflows. In the long run, an enterprise's total cash inflows must exceed its total costs if the enterprise is to survive. In this chapter we look at how accounting data might be used by management in making selling price and output level decisions. Our analysis is conducted from two separate viewpoints, depending upon the market for the enterprise's goods. We might identify the two market situations as ones:

● where demand for the firm's goods can be reasonably well estimated;

● where it is very difficult to predict demand.

Cost information may be used to support decisions about prices, but such information will be useful for this purpose only if it reflects an appropriate understanding of cost drivers and the pattern of cost incidence. For the purposes of presenting the analysis of pricing decisions in this chapter, we will refer to cost behaviour mainly in terms of fixed and variable costs, but it should be remembered throughout that estimating product costs (and identifying fixed and variable elements) involves analysis of a wide range of factors which might influence the incidence of costs. (See Chapter 7 for a fuller discussion of this issue.)

In practice, many companies may have little difficulty in pricing their products. Under certain market conditions a single market price, or at least a relatively narrow range of market prices, will exist for a product and customers will pay that price and no more. Hence the company will simply charge the market price. Such a situation might be found in particular industries where small firms are competing with a few very large companies who exercise effective price control. The small firms have little choice but to accept the prices determined by the pricing policies of the large companies. The oil and chemical industries are examples of industries which are dominated by a few very large companies. A similar situation will exist where there is a highly competitive market for a product. If any one firm attempts to charge more than the market price, customers will go to another supplier. Furthermore, the pressures of competition will tend to drive the market price down, so that it is likely that all firms will be charging a price close to their long-run marginal production costs. Hence any attempt to charge below the market price is likely to spell financial failure for a firm. Supermarket chains and discount warehouses are examples of highly competitive sectors of the economy.

9.1 Pricing decisions in context

Before we analyse the accountant's contribution to pricing, we consider the organisational context within which pricing decisions are taken. The price to be charged for a product is one element in the organisation's *marketing strategy*. That strategy will be designed to achieve the organisation's goals, which we have assumed to be best represented by cash maximisation. If the organisation produces many different products, it has the problem of deciding which marketing strategy to pursue so that cash is maximised for all products.

The selling price chosen for each product is an important part of the marketing strategy. For instance, certain prices may be lowered to attract customers away from competitors; others may be raised if it is thought that no significant loss of market share will occur. However, the choice of selling price is not the only tactical device available to managers in designing the organisation's marketing strategy. The quantity of a particular product which the organisation will be able to sell will depend also on the promotional strategy adopted, including the extent and nature of advertising, on the design and quality of the product, on the intensity of the selling effort expended and on the selection of distribution channels. Although these are strictly matters for the marketing staff rather than for the accountant, it should be evident that marketing and financial implications are heavily interdependent. For example, the design of the product will affect its manufacturing cost, and the intensity of selling effort will affect selling and distribution costs. It is essential that the marketing and accounting staff liaise frequently while the marketing strategy is being developed.

Other factors will also influence the relationship between the selling price charged and the quantity demanded. These will be reflected in the *price elasticity of demand* for the firm's products (i.e the responsiveness of changes in demand to changes in price). If demand for a product is price elastic, relatively small changes in price will result in relatively large changes in demand. If demand is price inelastic, the quantity demanded will be relatively unaffected by changes in selling price. The extent of demand elasticity depends on a variety of factors. For example: How necessary is the product? – the more necessary it is, the more inelastic will be the demand for it. What are current consumer tastes and how are they likely to change over time? – products which are highly susceptible to consumer taste, such as fashion goods, are likely to have elastic demand over time. How readily available are substitute products? – the more readily available are acceptable substitutes, the more elastic will be the demand for the product. How competitive is the market within which the product is sold? – the more competitive the market, the more elastic the demand for the product.

Finally in this section, we consider one situation where it is likely to prove particularly difficult to predict demand: that is, where a *new product* is to be manufactured and sold. The problem is likely to be acute if the new product is dissimilar to any product previously sold by the producing firm or other firms. Such a situation arose at the start of the microchip technology revolution when firms were considering applications of the new technology (digital watches, electronic calculators, multimedia computers, etc.) which had not been possible, at least at a comparatively low cost, using previously available methods. In such situations, firms will undertake market research. For example, they might engage in *test marketing*: that is, selling the new product in a number of different (and perhaps quite small) areas, possibly at a different price in each area, in an attempt to collect information concerning the likely demand for the product at various prices. When the new product is eventually launched fully, the selling organisation may also pursue particular *pricing strategies*, designed to maximise cash returns over the life of the product. For example, in the early part of the product life, before other firms have developed the technology necessary to compete, the firm might follow a *skimming* pricing strategy. It will set a high initial price for the product and progressively lower it as the market broadens and competitors emerge. Such a strategy was evident in the early days of personal computer development. Alternatively, if a firm is attempting to enter an already established market, it might pursue a *penetration* pricing strategy: in other words, it will set a low initial price in an attempt to acquire a substantial share of the market, and subsequently increase the price as its market position strengthens. Such a strategy has been evident among later entrants to the personal computer market, such as Amstrad.

On some occasions with a new product, a firm may be fairly sure of the price at which it will be able to sell the product – for example, because it is to be sold in a mature market – but needs to know the maximum or *target cost* at which manufacture and sale of the product will be profitable. Production of new models of refrigerator or washing machine are examples of such a situation.

The brief discussion above should have made it clear that decisions concerning the pricing of goods and services are not the sole preserve of the accountant. It is beyond the scope of this chapter to investigate marketing and other strategic areas in more detail. Rather, we shall discuss how accounting information might provide one useful input to pricing decisions by looking at both optimal pricing decisions, where firms have a reasonably clear idea of the relationship between selling price and demand, and methods based primarily on cost, which may be of use where the selling price–demand relationship is very uncertain or unknown.

9.2 Optimal price setting

Most firms operate in an environment where the selling prices charged for their products are in some way (intuitively or formally) related to the quantities demanded by customers. Generally speaking, the lower the selling price of the product, the more units of the product that will be taken up by the market. We might term this relationship the firm's *demand schedule* or *demand function*. The precise quantification of this relationship is generally very difficult to determine in practice, particularly as it is likely to be changing over time.

The firm's *supply schedule* refers to the costs incurred in producing and selling the units of output sold. The supply schedule is usually easier to estimate than the demand schedule, primarily because the firm has more control over its costs than it has over the demand for its products, and thus can predict costs with more confidence. Nevertheless, if demand and supply schedules can be drawn up, the firm will be in a position to attempt to derive (simultaneously) both its optimal output level and its optimal selling price – information vital in pursuing the goal of cash maximisation. We can derive optimal selling prices by any (or all) of three methods: graphical analysis, flexible budgets, or simple differential calculus.

Suppose that a firm, Ewood plc, makes one product. Ewood plc has a relatively simple cost function, comprising total fixed costs of £8,000 per annum and a variable cost of £30 which is incurred for each additional unit produced and sold over a very large range of levels of output. The present selling price for the product is £70, at which price 300 units are demanded annually. The sales manager of Ewood plc estimates that each successive £10 increase in price will result in a drop in annual demand of 100 units; similarly each successive £10 reduction in price will cause an increase in demand of 100 units. It is possible to charge intermediary prices within each £10 range with proportionate changes in demand.

To derive the optimal selling price we first calculate total cost and total revenue functions for the product, regardless of which of the three methods we are going to use. The total cost function is a straightforward calculation, based on the level of fixed costs and the variable cost per unit of output:

$$\text{Total cost} = \text{TC} = £8,000 + £30x \tag{9.1}$$

where x is the annual level of demand and output.

Calculation of the total revenue function is more difficult. It must be done in two stages. First, selling price (SP) is expressed as a function of the level of output. At present, selling price is £70 and output is 300 units. Each increase or decrease in price of £10 results in a corresponding decrease or increase in demand of 100 units. If the selling price were increased by £30 (i.e. to £100) demand would be zero. Thereafter, to increase demand by *one* unit, selling price must be reduced by £10/100 units or 10p. Hence the maximum selling price attainable for an output of x units is:

$$\text{Selling price} = \text{SP} = £100 - £0.1x \tag{9.2}$$

This selling price equation determines the slope of the line of Ewood plc's demand schedule, as shown in Figure 9.1. Point A on Figure 9.1 represents the current situation, where, at a selling price of £70, 300 units are demanded.

Second, total revenue is expressed in terms of the selling price equation. This is an easier calculation. As total revenue is the product of the selling price per unit and the number of units sold, the equation for total revenue is:

$$\text{Total revenue} = \text{TR} = \text{SP}x = (£100 - £0.1x)x = £100x - £0.1x^2 \tag{9.3}$$

Figure 9.1 Ewood plc: demand schedule.

We can now calculate the optimal output level and selling price using each of our chosen methods.

Optimal pricing using graphical analysis

The relationship between selling price, demand and total revenue can be tabulated as shown in Table 9.1. The bell-shape total revenue curve is depicted in Figure 9.2.

We can calculate total costs for Ewood plc in the same manner, as in Table 9.2. This is shown graphically in Figure 9.3.

Finally, we can determine the relationship between output and profit for Ewood plc as in Table 9.3.

This relationship between revenue, cost and profit can be shown graphically as in Figure 9.4. Figure 9.4 is a form of break-even chart (introduced in Chapter 8) in which the slope of the total revenue line is curvilinear, whereas total costs are assumed to be linear in relation to output.

Table 9.1 Ewood plc: price, demand and revenue information

Price (£)	Demand and output (units)	Total revenue (£)
100	0	0
90	100	9,000
80	200	16,000
70	300	21,000
60	400	24,000
50	500	25,000
40	600	24,000
30	700	21,000
20	800	16,000
10	900	9,000

Table 9.2 Ewood plc: cost and output information

Units of output	Variable costs (£)	Fixed costs (£)	Total cost (£)
100	3,000	8,000	11,000
200	6,000	8,000	14,000
300	9,000	8,000	17,000
400	12,000	8,000	20,000
500	15,000	8,000	23,000
600	18,000	8,000	26,000
700	21,000	8,000	29,000
800	24,000	8,000	32,000
900	27,000	8,000	35,000

Table 9.3 Ewood plc: revenue, cost and output information

Output (units)	Total revenue (£)	Total cost (£)	Profit (loss) (£)
100	9,000	11,000	(2,000)
200	16,000	14,000	2,000
300	21,000	17,000	4,000
400	24,000	20,000	4,000
500	25,000	23,000	2,000
600	24,000	26,000	(2,000)
700	21,000	29,000	(8,000)
800	16,000	32,000	(16,000)
900	9,000	35,000	(26,000)

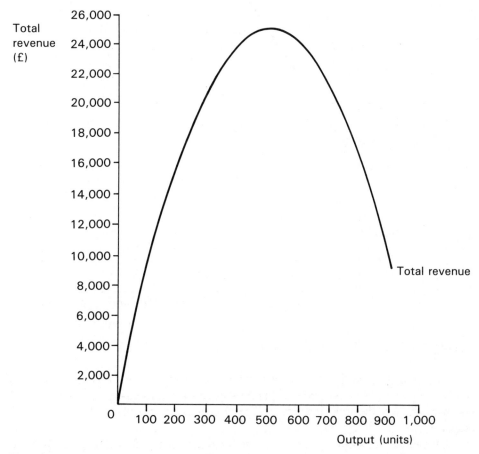

Figure 9.2 Ewood plc: total revenue function.

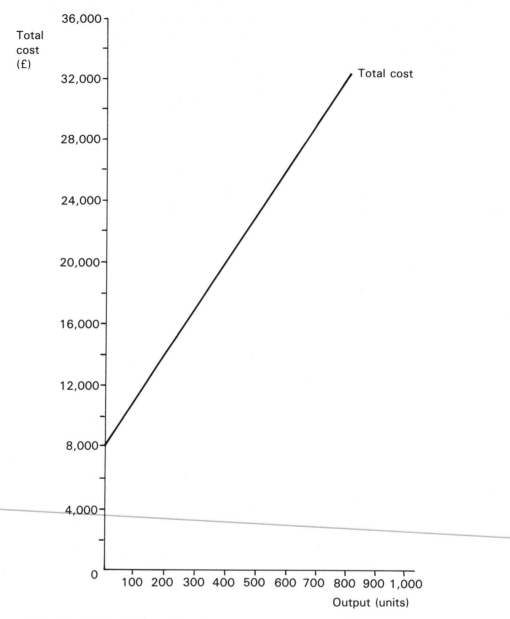

Figure 9.3 Ewood plc: total cost function.

The optimal output level is the point at which the highest profit is achieved. This is shown by point *y* on the graph in Figure 9.4, and it represents the greatest vertical distance between the total revenue and total cost lines at a level of 350 units of output.

An alternative form of presentation is to use a profit–volume graph (also introduced in Chapter 8) to explain the relationships of costs, revenues and profits.

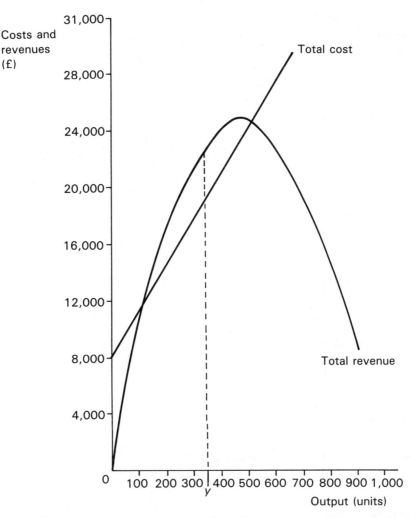

Figure 9.4   Ewood plc: costs, revenues and profits.

Figure 9.5 shows the profit–volume graph for Ewood plc. It can be seen from the profit–volume graph that the optimal output level is approximately 350 units.

Having calculated the optimal output level, we are now in a position to answer the other part of our original question – what is the optimal selling price for Ewood plc? This we can find by substituting the optimal output level (350 units) in the selling price equation (equation (9.2)):

$$SP = £100 - £0.1\,(350)$$
$$SP = £65$$

The optimal selling price for Ewood plc is £65 per unit, the maximum price at which 350 units can be sold.

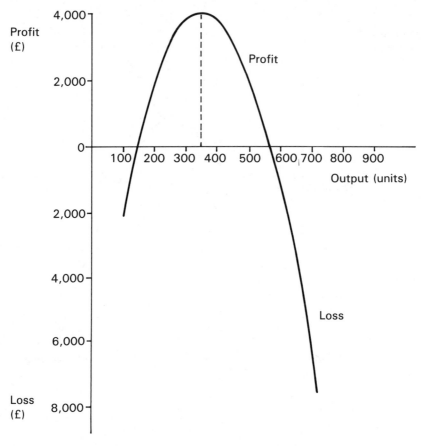

Figure 9.5   Ewood plc: profit–volume graph.

Flexible budgeting

As an alternative to the use of graphical analysis, the technique of flexible budgeting, introduced in Chapter 8, may be used to determine the optimal selling price and output level. The flexible budgets for Ewood plc are prepared on the basis of the estimated total cost function (£8,000 + £30x), and the estimated total revenue function (£100x − £0.1x^2) derived from the demand schedule shown in Figure 9.1. Table 9.4 shows the flexible budgets prepared for different levels of output. The budgeted figures show that the optimal output level is 350 units and the optimal selling price is £65. In order to be sure that the optimal price–output combination has been discovered, it may be necessary to prepare further budgets for output levels just above and just below 350 units to ensure that they produce lower expected profits than does the output of 350 units.

Table 9.4 Ewood plc: flexible budgets

	Output level (units)						
	100 (£)	200 (£)	300 (£)	350 (£)	400 (£)	500 (£)	600 (£)
Variable costs (£30 per unit)	3,000	6,000	9,000	10,500	12,000	15,000	18,000
Fixed costs	8,000	8,000	8,000	8,000	8,000	8,000	8,000
Total costs	11,000	14,000	17,000	18,500	20,000	23,000	26,000
Sales revenue (£90 per unit)	9,000 (80)	16,000 (70)	21,000 (65)	22,750 (60)	24,000 (50)	25,000 (40)	24,000
Profit/(loss)	(2,000)	2,000	4,000	4,250	4,000	2,000	(2,000)

Optimal pricing and simple calculus

The optimal output level is represented by the point at which *marginal cost* (the change in total cost as a result of making one additional unit) is equated to *marginal revenue* (the change in total revenue resulting from the sale of one additional unit). In effect the decision rule is that production should be increased so long as incremental benefits exceed incremental costs. This condition is satisfied until marginal cost equals marginal revenue. Beyond this point, increases in production will give rise to extra costs greater than the extra benefits, resulting in a fall in total profits, assuming that marginal revenue does not increase again relative to marginal cost.

Marginal cost and marginal revenue equations may be derived using differential calculus, and the resulting equations may be solved to determine the optimal output level.

$$\text{Total cost} = £8,000 + £30x \tag{9.1}$$

$$\therefore \quad \text{Marginal cost} = \frac{dTC}{dx} = £30$$

$$\text{Total revenue} = £100x - £0.1x^2 \tag{9.3}$$

$$\therefore \quad \text{Marginal revenue} = \frac{dTR}{dx} = £100 - £0.2x$$

At the optimal output level $\dfrac{dTC}{dx} = \dfrac{dTR}{dx}$

$$\therefore \quad £30 = £100 - £0.2x, \quad x = 350 \text{ units}$$

The optimal output level is 350 units. The highest selling price at which this output can be sold is found, as before, by substituting for x in the selling price equation (equation (9.2)):

$$SP = £100 - £0.1(350)$$
$$\therefore \quad SP = £65$$

9.3 Evaluation of optimal price-setting methods

If the application of calculus can derive the optimal selling price so speedily, why do we need to examine either the graphical analysis or the flexible budgeting methods?

The answer to this question lies with the uses to which the information will be put. While managers will be interested in the optimal selling price and output level derived from the estimated functions, they will be interested equally in the *sensitivity* of profit to changes in output and changes in selling price. For example,

Ewood plc currently charges a unit price of £70 at which annual demand is 300 units. Both graphical analysis and flexible budgeting reveal that this present policy may be expected to produce a profit of £4,000, only £250 less than that obtainable from the optimal price–output combination. The managers of Ewood plc might decide that the costs involved in changing selling price, such as the costs of preparing new price lists for customers, are greater than the additional profit of £250 that may be expected from a change of selling price. Differential calculus does not give this information, whereas the provision of information on the sensitivity of profit to changes in costs and revenues is the essence of both the graphical and flexible budgeting approaches.

In addition, both graphs and flexible budgets can handle more easily cost and revenue functions which are not in a convenient form for algebraic manipulation (e.g. step-variable cost functions), and may present relevant data to management more clearly and comprehensively than do algebraic methods. Indeed, both sorts of representation of most aspects of business activity are very common in practice, presumably because of their clarity of exposition.

In practice a combination of the three methods may prove to be the most helpful way of calculating and explaining optimal output levels and optimal selling prices.

As we noted earlier, there will be considerable uncertainties associated with the estimates; in particular with demand estimates. This will be the case especially where a new product is being analysed. Even with existing products, the analysis may suggest radical changes to selling prices and/or output levels. In such cases it may be wise to implement these gradually, as a means of increasing management's level of confidence in the demand relationship predictions. For example, if the above analysis for Ewood plc had suggested halving the current price, it might be prudent to try initially a £5 or £10 reduction to see if the effects on demand are as predicted by the equation.

9.4 Cost-plus pricing

The approaches described in the previous section are based on the notions of supply and demand. In many situations, however, firms may find it extremely difficult, even with the support of their marketing departments, to predict how many units can be sold at particular selling prices: for example, where a new product is to be manufactured. In cases such as these, price analysis must be supported by other methods which rely primarily on the determination of costs. As we have seen in previous chapters, however, analysing the behaviour of costs (Chapter 6) and attributing costs to particular products (Chapter 7) are complex tasks. The form of cost analysis that is appropriate to support pricing decisions will depend upon the situation – whether management is pricing its normal products or whether special non-recurrent orders are being priced.

The rationale for looking at costs when deciding prices is that, in order to survive and operate profitably, a firm must set price at a level which will generate at least sufficient revenues to cover costs. In the extreme, a firm could determine price solely on the basis of a cost-plus formula. In practice, however, most managers have at least an intuitive understanding of market conditions and so will tend to use a cost-plus calculation *as the first step* in price determination, but will include consideration, often in informal or implicit ways, of market demand conditions. In the light of these conditions, the price initially calculated using the cost-plus formula would be amended.

An example of the form that a cost-plus calculation might take is given in Table 9.5. The formula might be applied to a single job or to a whole product line. In Table 9.5 the direct costs of the job or product (i.e. those directly identifiable with the job or product) are estimated and to these is added an amount to recover production overheads (sometimes including depreciation), which may include both variable and fixed costs. A mark-up is also added, to cover selling and administrative overheads and profit, often designed to reflect what the decision maker regards as a 'reasonable' level of profit.

The use of such a formula is appealing. It looks objective and accurate and is relatively easy to apply. Furthermore, it enables management to delegate pricing decisions to subordinates. But the formula suffers from a number of defects and to apply it without affording them proper consideration may lead to suboptimal pricing decisions.

First, the inclusion of direct costs in the formula may be criticised. Frequently, they are interpreted as costs that are easily traceable to a specific job or product. They are not necessarily the same as variable costs and may not correspond to changes in the firm's cash flows. Similarly, if the overhead costs in the formula are fixed, they will have to be paid whether or not the job being priced is undertaken. They are not avoidable costs but allocation may lead to their being treated as if they were. A firm may quote a cost-plus price for a contract that results in the contract going elsewhere even though the firm would have been justified in quoting a lower price, sufficient to cover total incremental cost, thereby winning the contract.

Table 9.5   Example of cost-plus calculation

	£	£
Direct costs:		
Labour	4,780	
Materials	1,860	
Machine depreciation	2,600	9,240
Production overheads:		
80% on direct costs*		7,392
Total cost		16,632
Profit mark-up:		
20% on total cost		3,326
Price		19,958

*The overhead allocation is normally a predetermined percentage of one or, as in this example, all of the items included as direct costs. It may be based on money values or on some other unit measure, e.g. labour hours.

A cost-plus approach such as that in Table 9.5 can thus contravene the principles of relevance established in Chapter 5, which direct attention to the changes in cash flows associated with decisions. For long-term pricing decisions, overhead costs (which are fixed in the short run) may be relevant because in the long run all costs are avoidable. It does not follow that the sort of crude allocation method normally employed in the cost-plus formula is the best way of taking account of such costs.

There are other reasons for doubting the wisdom of overhead allocation. These have been discussed in Chapter 7 (see pages 146–8) and include the difficulty of identifying the measure of operations to be used as a basis for allocation and of establishing the relationship between that base and the costs to be allocated. An activity-based costing approach to attributing costs to products will normally result in very different overhead allocations from the type of blanket rate methods traditionally used in costing and illustrated by the '80% on direct costs' line in Table 9.5.

The profit mark-up seems to imply an attempt to ensure that the firm makes a 'reasonable profit'. It is unlikely that this will accord with the objective assumed in this text of maximising the cash resources of the organisation. This latter goal is most likely to be achieved if all projects showing an expected surplus of revenue over incremental costs are accepted.

The final defect to be noted here reflects a direct contrast with the economist's approach to pricing. Because the cost-plus formula pays no regard to demand conditions, the formula will produce the same answer whether the firm is operating in a highly competitive market or in a near monopolistic position. A seller cannot set both price and sales volume without reference to the demand function for the particular product. The sales volume will normally depend, at least in part, upon the price set, and the relationship between selling price and demand will depend, among other things, upon the type of market in which the firm operates.

In many cases the difficulty encountered in estimating a firm's demand curve inhibits the use of the type of analysis for setting prices which we discussed in the previous section. The cost-plus solution to this problem is simple: ignore it. However, this approach contravenes a basic principle of good decision making: it is preferable to obtain an answer that is approximately right than one that is precisely wrong. Most decisions are beset with difficulties and to ignore them will almost inevitably lead to suboptimal courses of action being pursued.

In the context of pricing decisions, we should recognise that difficulties exist in forecasting demand conditions. Management experience and intuition may well make an important contribution to the decision. However, that is no reason to ignore the other information needed to set prices: the relevant cost of particular courses of action and the associated rules for ascertaining the minimum price that should be set if a product is to be offered for sale. This information will at least provide some assistance to the price setter in determining pricing policies.

9.5 Contribution margin pricing

Many of the deficiencies of cost-plus pricing can be overcome by the use of contribution margin pricing. This is especially the case in relation to short-term pricing decisions. In essence, this approach tries to establish a price that is at least great enough to cover all incremental costs associated with the production and sale of a product.

Contribution margin pricing enjoys at least two advantages over full cost-plus pricing. First, the focus on incremental costs avoids the problems of allocating fixed costs to products, and second, the contribution approach provides information about cost–volume–profit relationships, thereby making it easier to develop pricing formulae. As an example of contribution margin pricing, consider the following data for Deepdale plc presented in a 'conventional' form in Table 9.6 as a first step in determining selling prices.

The total cost for each of the three products, £16, £15.50 and £22 respectively, is an average total cost, which entails the allocation of fixed overheads. To this total cost has been added a profit margin determined by management. If business activity is poor, it may well prove to be in Deepdale plc's interest to sell its three products at prices lower than those determined by average costs. How much lower can be shown by applying the contribution margin approach. By rearranging the data we can first identify the incremental costs, in this case presumed to be the total direct and variable costs, associated with each of the three products, as shown in the table below:

	Product A (£)	Product B (£)	Product C (£)
Direct material	3.00	4.00	5.00
Direct labour	2.50	2.00	3.50
Variable production overheads	1.50	2.00	1.50
Variable selling costs	1.00	0.50	0.75
Incremental costs	8.00	8.50	10.75

It can be readily seen that, if the company cannot sell its three products at their cost-plus prices, it will still make a *contribution* towards fixed costs and profit if it sells product A at any price in excess of £8, product B at any price in excess of £8.50, and product C at any price in excess of £10.75. These three amounts, £8, £8.50 and £10.75 respectively, might be referred to as *minimum acceptable prices* for the products as they just cover all the incremental costs. They would not, of course, represent the actual prices charged in normal conditions for the firm's regular products. Such a pricing policy would quickly lead to bankruptcy, as there would be no contribution to fixed costs or profit. The actual prices to be charged for the products will be higher than the minimum prices, and must take into account other factors such as the degree of competition and the level of demand, insofar as these can be estimated.

Let us pursue this argument a little further. Suppose, for example, Deepdale plc receives a one-off special order from a customer who wishes to buy 500 units of product A at a price of £10 per unit. The cost-plus price of A is £18.40 per unit. Should the special order be accepted? If management applies the cost-plus criterion to this offer, it will reject the offer, as it will 'lose' £8.40 per unit on the order

Table 9.6 Deepdale plc: product selling price data (1)

	Product A (£)	Product B (£)	Product C (£)
Direct material	3.00	4.00	5.00
Direct labour	2.50	2.00	3.50
Total direct cost	5.50	6.00	8.50
Production overheads:			
Variable	1.50	2.00	1.50
Fixed	5.00	4.00	7.00
Total cost of production	12.00	12.00	17.00
Selling costs:			
Variable	1.00	0.50	0.75
Fixed	1.20	1.20	1.70
Fixed administrative cost	1.80	1.80	2.55
Total cost	16.00	15.50	22.00
Profit margin (%)	2.40 (15)	1.55 (10)	4.40 (20)
Cost-plus selling price	18.40	17.05	26.40

(i.e. £18.40 less £10). If, however, management accepts the offer, what will happen? Five hundred units will be sold at a price of £10 per unit and the incremental costs of producing and selling each unit will be £8; a contribution of £2 per unit, or £1,000 in total, will be generated towards the fixed costs and profits of Deepdale plc. It seems that Deepdale plc should accept the special order. However, there are caveats which should be observed. Specifically, management might ask the following questions:

1. Is this special order likely to use limited plant capacity which could be better employed manufacturing goods saleable at normal prices? If so, then the order is using the firm's scarce resources and, as we shall see in Chapters 11 and 12, further analysis of the problem is necessary.

2. Can the special sale be made without reducing sales at normal selling prices? For example, other customers for product A may also expect to buy it for £10 per unit if they become aware of sales to one customer at this price.

3. What will be the likely advantages and disadvantages of the sale on future relationships? The new customer may be so pleased with the purchase that other of the firm's products are purchased at prices well in excess of marginal cost. On the other hand, the new customer may expect future purchases of the firm's products to be at special 'reduced' prices.

If the answers to the above questions suggest that the overall effect is likely to be disadvantageous, perhaps Deepdale plc should not proceed with the order. It should still be stressed, however, that the contribution margin approach will always be based on the underlying notion of a minimum price. Whether or not that price is ever charged will depend upon the other qualitative factors to be considered by management, which will vary from one pricing decision to another.

In addition, the contribution margin approach rests on the distinction that is drawn between fixed and variable costs. We have used these classifications in order to demonstrate the rationale of the approach, but the difficulties of classifying costs in practice should not be underestimated. All cost-based approaches to pricing depend on the quality of cost analysis provided and how well it reflects the pattern of cost behaviour affecting the firm. The difficulties of cost analysis and cost allocation, and the use of activity-based costing methods as an attempt to provide more accurate information on the relationship between production and the incidence of costs, were discussed in Chapter 7.

To conclude our discussion of cost-based pricing, let us return again to the data for Deepdale plc, presented in rearranged cost–volume–profit form in Table 9.7. Table 9.7 shows three possible price structures (denoted by P_1, P_2 and P_3 respectively) for the three products A, B and C. We might delineate these possible prices as follows:

P_1 is the *minimum short-run price*, represented by the variable (incremental) costs of production and sale. Fixed costs are not covered by price P_1, as they will be incurred anyway, and thus are not relevant to short-run decisions. P_2 is a *minimum long-run price*, based in this instance on a predetermined level of fixed costs and an (arbitrary) allocation method. It should be stressed that other allocation methods will yield other minimum long-run prices, all of which will be arbitrary to some extent. In the long run, both variable and fixed costs must be recovered from selling prices if the firm is to generate sufficient cash flows to survive. We might say that in the long run all costs, however classified, are incremental costs. P_3 is the *normal desired long-run price* for each product. It includes an expected profit margin reflecting management's quantified perception of the various factors (e.g. possible total demand, elasticity of demand, quality of the product) unique to each product.

Table 9.7 Deepdale plc: product selling price data (2)

	Product A (£)	Product B (£)	Product C (£)
Variable costs:			
Direct material	3.00	4.00	5.00
Direct labour	2.50	2.00	3.50
Production overheads	1.50	2.00	1.50
Selling costs	1.00	0.50	0.75
P_1 total variable cost	8.00	8.50	10.75
Fixed costs:			
Production overheads	5.00	4.00	7.00
Selling costs	1.20	1.20	1.70
Administration	1.80	1.80	2.55
P_2 total cost	16.00	15.50	22.00
Profit margin (%)	2.40 (15)	1.55 (10)	4.40 (20)
P_3 cost-plus selling price	18.40	17.05	26.40

The possible range of prices for each product is:

	Product A (£)	Product B (£)	Product C (£)
P_1 = minimum short-run price	8.00	8.50	10.75
P_2 = minimum long-run price	16.00	15.50	22.00
P_3 = normal long-run price	18.40	17.05	26.40

The range gives management some idea of its flexibility in setting prices. For instance, if Deepdale plc is selling B in a monopolistic market, then it may be able to obtain a price near to £17.05, the desired long-term price; if, for example, there is a great deal of competition for C, then Deepdale plc may have to be satisfied with a price no greater than £22, and possibly less.

CHAPTER SUMMARY

Accounting information will rarely be the sole determinant of price, but it does provide one part of the total information that management will need to set prices. In this chapter we have reviewed two main areas in which accounting can offer guidelines on alternative prices and benchmarks to support pricing decisions: optimal price-setting methods and cost-based methods.

Optimal pricing can be used where the firm is able to estimate its demand schedule: that is, where it is able to take account of the market conditions in an explicit and formal way. Combining demand information with analysis of the structure of the firm's costs allows managers to identify the optimal combination of price and output, where the surplus generated from operations will be maximised. Where adequate information about the demand schedule is not available, cost-based methods can be used to support pricing decisions. The usefulness of cost-based approaches depends on the validity of the analysis of the behaviour of the firm's costs, particularly regarding the classification and treatment of fixed and variable costs and the methods by which costs are attributed to products. Nonetheless, used appropriately, cost information can help identify minimum short-run and long-run prices.

In practice, cost-based methods give a pragmatic means of analysing price structures as a starting point for the pricing decision. The eventual pricing decision is likely to be the result also of a consideration of broader marketing strategies which involve the use of information outside the normal realm of the accountant. Nevertheless, the accountant's contribution in providing timely and relevant cost information and in analysing the implications of alternative selling price–output combinations is an essential ingredient of the whole process.

REVIEW QUESTIONS

1. 'Supply and demand models of pricing are too difficult to put into practice.' Discuss.

2. Discuss the relationship between optimal output levels and optimal selling prices.

3. 'Pricing should be related to competitive market situations, rather than to internal cost structures.' Discuss.

4. Discuss some of the possible dangers facing an organisation associated with contribution margin pricing.

5. Discuss any possible relationships between 'short-run' and 'long-run' pricing policies.

EXERCISES

9.1 Mr Sisley runs a small printing business. Each job is undertaken according to special instructions from the customer. Mr Sisley uses a system recommended by his trade association to fix the price he charges to his customers. He estimates what he paid for the paper used (he keeps large stocks of paper) and adds a standard percentage for 'consumables' (ink etc.). He estimates the number of labour hours required for the job and values them at the appropriate wage rate; he adds a standard percentage to cover fixed overhead costs. The sum of all these items gives a 'total cost' for the job and he adds 10% to total costs for his profit. The standard percentages are set equal to the actual percentage relationships between corresponding total costs during the previous financial year.

Actual results for last year ran as follows:

		£
Sales		266,000
Cost of paper used	24,000	
Consumables	3,000	
Wages	120,000	
Fixed costs	96,000	243,000
Net profit		23,000

Last year Mr Sisley's employees were fully occupied. During the current year just ending, however, business has fallen by 15% – measured in labour hours required. No one has been laid off. Mr Sisley has simply paid for idle time. Total wage costs for the current year and total fixed costs are the same as last year; cost of paper used is £22,000 and cost of consumables £2,250. No special prices have been charged on any jobs during the year. Mr Sisley is surprised to find, however, that he has made a loss on his business even though each job has shown a satisfactory profit.

(a) Prepare a calculation showing the amount of the loss for the current year.

(b) Explain how the loss has arisen and comment critically on Mr Sisley's pricing system. (Solution at end of text.)

9.2   Schmitt plc, which is a good customer of Schein Ltd, has asked Schein to produce 400 units of a special variation of one of the standard products that it buys from Schein. The estimated full cost of producing each unit of the standard product is £90, of which £60 is variable cost and £30 is allocated fixed cost. The selling price is £108 per unit. Although Schein is not geared to make the modifications required, it decides for 'customer relationship' reasons to agree to go ahead and supply the order. It will be possible to modify up to 100 of the special units each 40-hour week, without disrupting regular production, but special machinery will be required for the purpose. There are three alternative ways of obtaining this machinery. Details are as follows:

1.   *Adapting existing machinery*
The existing machinery which could be adapted is not being used at present, although it is envisaged that in approximately three months it will be required in its present form for a contract currently being negotiated. Costs of adapting this machinery would be £4,500, and after the order has been completed it would cost £5,400 to remove the adaptations and replace worn parts, etc., in order to return the machine to its current value. The machinery which could be adapted originally cost £30,000 five years ago and is being depreciated at £3,000 p.a. A special insurance policy would have to be held while it was operated in its adapted form, the fixed annual premium associated with this being 2% of the value of the machine when adapted. The current value of the machine is £9,000. Variable operating costs associated with using the adapted machinery would be: labour £9 per hour and maintenance £4.50 per hour.

2.   *Hiring specialist machinery*
The charge for hiring suitable machinery, which includes maintenance and insurance, but no labour costs, is £15 per production hour with a minimum hire charge of £900 per week.

3.   *Purchasing specialist machinery*
To buy a new machine would cost £15,000. Operating, maintenance and insurance costs would be on the same basis as for the adapted one. The manufacturers of the machinery estimate that it loses value at the rate of £6 for every unit produced, and on this basis they are prepared to repurchase any machinery sold by them, after deducting a further 10% of the residual value to cover transaction expenses.

(a) Prepare a report to the managers of Schein Ltd, advising them which of the alternative courses of action would be most beneficial, based upon the given information. Indicate ways in which your recommendation might be further improved. In your report suggest a price to be charged to Schmitt plc for the modified product, mentioning the factors which should be considered before a final decision is taken.

(b) Suppose that Schmitt plc was willing to place a continuing order for the modified product. In this new situation, broadly explain the alterations needed to produce a long-run cost analysis of the alternatives. (Solution at end of text.)

9.3   Ravel Ltd manufactures two products, the renoir and the whistler. Each product is produced in a separate department. The company's budget for next year runs as follows:

	Renoir		Whistler
Selling price per unit (£)	40.00		50.00
Variable cost per unit (£)	25.00		30.00
Contribution per unit (£)	15.00		20.00
Planned production (and sales)—(units)	38,000		7,000
Total contribution (unit contribution × planned sales) (£)	570,000		140,000
Less Fixed departmental overhead costs (£)	370,000		250,000
Departmental contribution to general fixed costs (£)	200,000		(110,000)
Total contribution (£): Renoir		200,000	
Whistler		(110,000)	
		90,000	
General fixed costs (£)		80,000	
Budgeted profit (£)		10,000	

Fixed departmental overhead costs for either product could be avoided if the particular product were not produced. At all positive production levels they are fixed in total for each product.

The company is concerned that the whistler is apparently being produced at a loss and asks your advice. You learn that the company has recently commissioned a market research survey for both its products. The following figures are included in the survey report:

	Renoir				Whistler			
Selling price (£)	20	30	40	50	25	50	75	100
Maximum quantity likely to be demanded at price shown (000s units)	80	60	40	20	10	8	6	4

(a) Calculate the production levels for the renoir and the whistler, likely to maximise the company's profit in the coming year.

(b) Prepare a statement showing the improvement in expected profit if your suggested production levels are implemented. Include a note of any reservations you have about your figures.

9.4 Princess plc produces a single product, the connaught. The connaught is perishable and no stocks are kept. During the previous month Princess's results were as follows:

	£000	£000
Sales (100,000 units)		400
Less Cost of goods sold:		
Basic wages	10	
Bonus	45	
	55	
Materials	200	255
Gross profit		145
Less Sales commission	50	
General administration	15	65
Profit		80

The company pays its labour force a basic wage per month irrespective of production level and a bonus (currently at the rate of 45p per unit produced). The sales commission is paid to a marketing company which sells the connaught on behalf of Princess. General administration is the only fixed overhead incurred by the company. For some time past there have been serious problems associated with materials usage. Recently a machine has become available which allows a higher-quality material to be used, and this will reduce waste. The effect is expected to be a halving of materials costs. The machine cannot be bought, but can only be leased from the manufacturer on a monthly basis. The monthly rental is £55,000.

Princess has just completed a market research survey to clarify the conditions of demand for the connaught. The survey found that if price per unit were set at £5.00 no sales would be made. Alternatively, if the connaught were distributed free to customers, the maximum distribution would be 500,000 units. If price were increased by 1p, sales would fall by 1,000 units at all prices within the stated range.

If the machine were leased, it is estimated that basic wages would remain the same, but the bonus rate would increase to 50p per unit. However, there would be no change in general administration costs or in the sales commission arrangements.

The objective of the company is to maximise monthly profits, but hitherto the company has not used a formal pricing policy designed to ensure the achievement of that objective, but has relied upon the judgement of the sales manager.

(a) Prepare calculations to determine whether or not Princess should lease the machine.

(b) Determine the range of prices over which Princess might expect to make profits if it decides to lease the machine.

(c) Comment upon the significance of your calculations in (a) and (b).

9.5   During the financial year beginning 1 August 19X4, Commercial Printers Ltd has been operating to full capacity. All customers have been charged according to the company's standard pricing formula. The charge for a typical day's printing work can be calculated as follows:

	£
Paper, 18,000 sheets at 10p per sheet	1,800
Ink and other consumables, at 1.1111p per sheet	200
Wages	1,600
Overheads (all fixed) (150% of wages)	2,400
Total estimated cost	6,000
Add 20% for profit	1,200
Charge to customer	7,200

For the second half of the year, the company expects demand to slow down, and it is believed that, if prices are maintained at present levels, the company may lose a substantial amount of business. The following estimates have been prepared of the number of days' work (out of a maximum 125 days available) that would be obtained at different price levels.

Price (£)	7,200	5,700	4,200
Days' work obtained	60	90	120

The company is uncertain as to whether the fall-off in demand will be permanent. If it is not permanent, the directors wish to continue to pay all employees full time, even though there may be insufficient work for them. Otherwise they will lay off employees as necessary to respond to the fall in demand.

(a) Calculate the price at which profits will be maximised or losses minimised, the number of days' work obtained at that price, and the profit or loss for the six months ending 31 July 19X5:

  (i) on the assumption that the existing workforce will remain employed throughout the period; and

  (ii) on the assumption that the existing workforce will be laid off as necessary, without cost, to reflect the amount of work undertaken.

(b) Write a memorandum for the directors, explaining why it might be desirable to charge a price below the 'total estimated cost' for a typical day's work.

(c) Comment briefly on the reasons why cost-plus pricing may be used despite its theoretical shortcomings.

Relevant information for operating decisions

AIMS AND OBJECTIVES

☐ To apply the concepts and methods introduced in previous chapters to an analysis of various short-term operating decisions, including:

Dropping or adding a product or segment
Joint product decisions
Make or buy decisions.

In earlier chapters we have stressed the importance of the differential future cash flow concept in determining whether costs and/or benefits are relevant for management decisions. This is true whatever the time period of the decision: that is, whether the decision is long-term, involving the commitment of resources to extend productive capacity, or is an operating decision involving the best use of existing capacity.

The pricing and output applications described in the preceding two chapters are largely concerned with a general analysis for established or continuing operations. Management may also be faced with a variety of special decision problems which are one-off or infrequent, and which require specific evaluation: for example, whether to launch a new product and invest in new machinery, and the choice between buying in computer software or developing it in-house. In this and the four succeeding chapters we shall look in more detail at how the notion of relevant costs might be applied to some specific types of decision facing the firm. This chapter will consider the financial evaluation of a number of special types of decision. In each case we shall see that the application of the principles of relevance established in Chapter 5, together with the related idea of contribution introduced in Chapter 8, will lead to the provision of appropriate information for the decision. The following two chapters will examine the effects of limitations in the availability of resources for operations, and Chapters 13 and 14 will examine long-term investment decisions.

10.1 The nature of operating decisions

We might classify operating decisions as having two distinguishing characteristics. They usually involve time periods of less than one year (hence the need to take account of the time value of money is reduced) and are concerned with the use of existing physical resources. Examples of operating decisions might be as follows:

1. Which products should be produced? How many units of each product should be produced?

2. Should existing products be abandoned?

3. Should component parts for final products be manufactured internally or bought from outside suppliers?

4. How should scarce capacity be best used?

The analysis of these sorts of decisions proceeds in two stages. First, the accounting information, in the form of relevant future cash flows, is prepared. This is the more straightforward aspect of the analysis. Second, qualitative factors are identified as being important, and in some cases may overrule a decision based purely on monetary figures. Our concern here is with the development of the accounting information relevant to operating decisions, but, where appropriate, we will try to identify qualitative factors which are of obvious significance. As in all decision making, a large number of non-financial considerations may be important alongside the financial evaluation, and these factors can be very complex in special decision contexts. For example, the decision to accept a special order might be influenced by the desire to establish a presence in a new market or to create a relationship with a new customer, and the decision to relocate operating facilities might have to consider the welfare consequences for the existing workforce and local community. From the perspective of accounting measurement, however, the priority remains the same – to provide financial information which is relevant to the specific decision that has to be taken and which can be combined with other forms of information in the overall evaluation.

10.2 Dropping a product or segment

The usefulness of differential cash flows can be seen clearly in situations where management is faced with the choice of reducing (or adding to) its product range. This choice will be quite a common one for managers of multiproduct firms.

Let us begin the analysis by presuming that Bloomfield plc makes three products, A, B and C, income statements for which are presented in Table 10.1. On the basis of the given figures for Bloomfield plc in Table 10.1, management might think that it would be in the interests of the company to drop product C. After all, the income statement for the company shows that C makes a loss, whereas both A and B make a profit. But would the dropping of C be a wise decision? Suppose that for whatever reason Bloomfield plc will not produce any additional units of A and B, or alternatively, that sales of A and B would be unaffected by dropping C. How will the analysis now look? A comparison of the costs and revenues for Bloomfield plc under both alternatives (i.e. keeping or dropping C) may reveal that a different conclusion is warranted. The figures are shown in Table 10.2. The most important column is the final one, which shows the differential cash flows to the firm. If C is dropped from the range, the total cash inflow, here presumed to be the same as total net profit, is reduced by £7,000. This is made up as follows:

	£
Cash outflows avoided by dropping product C:	
Variable costs avoided	30,000
Separable fixed costs avoided	5,000
	35,000
Less Cash inflows lost	42,000
Differential loss in revenue	(7,000)

The decision to drop C would, at this stage, be unwise. This could have been seen clearly had the income statement for Bloomfield plc been recast so as to deal differently with the non-separable fixed costs. The bottom line of the income statement, showing the profit or loss for the individual products, is arrived at after allocating fixed costs which, by their very nature, can be allocated only on an arbitrary basis. A different format for the income statement of Bloomfield plc which avoids the problems of allocation and shows separately the contribution to general fixed costs for each product is presented in Table 10.3.

But is this the end of the story? Should management simply accept the revised conclusion that production of C is worthwhile because of its contribution of £7,000 to total fixed costs and profit? Presumably C utilises factory space. Perhaps this

Table 10.1 Bloomfield plc: income statement for the year to 31 December 19X1

	Product A	Product B	Product C	Total
Sales (units)	2,000	4,000	6,000	12,000
	(£)	(£)	(£)	(£)
Sales	20,000	32,000	42,000	94,000
Less Variable costs	8,000	12,000	30,000	50,000
Contribution margin	12,000	20,000	12,000	44,000
Less Separable fixed costs*	2,000	3,000	5,000	10,000
Less Non-separable fixed costs allocated on the basis of sales units	2,500	5,000	7,500	15,000
Profit/(loss)	7,500	12,000	(500)	19,000

*The separable fixed costs of producing each product are avoidable if manufacture of the product is discontinued.

Table 10.2 Comparison of cash flows under alternative decisions

	Keep A, B and C (£)	Keep A and B and drop C (£)	Differential cash flows (£)
Sales revenue	94,000	52,000	42,000
Less Variable costs	50,000	20,000	30,000
Contribution margin	44,000	32,000	12,000
Less Separable fixed costs	10,000	5,000	5,000
Less Non-separable fixed costs	15,000	15,000	0
Net profit	19,000	12,000	7,000

Table 10.3 Bloomfield plc: income statement for the year to 31 December 19X1

	Product A (£)	Product B (£)	Product C (£)	Total (£)
Sales	20,000	32,000	42,000	94,000
Less Variable costs	8,000	12,000	30,000	50,000
Contribution margin	12,000	20,000	12,000	44,000
Less Separable fixed costs	2,000	3,000	5,000	10,000
Product contribution	10,000	17,000	7,000	34,000
Less Non-separable fixed costs				15,000
		Net profit		19,000

space could, even temporarily, be rented out. The question then is: how much rent would Bloomfield plc need to receive in order to make it profitable to drop C? The answer is obviously at least £7,000 p.a., as this is the minimum amount which would compensate for the loss of C's contribution. The same argument in terms of rental forgone might be applied equally to A or B, where the minimum amounts acceptable would be £10,000 and £17,000 respectively. If in fact renting out the space used by C for £7,000 p.a. were the only alternative given up by production, we would term the amount of £7,000 the *opportunity cost* of keeping C for the next year. Further, if a rent in excess of £7,000 were offered to Bloomfield plc then, based purely on the quantifiable factors of the decision, the offer should be accepted. However, consideration must be given to other aspects involved in the decision (e.g. how is C's labour force to be deployed; what will happen to the plant and equipment used to produce C?).

10.3 Joint product decisions

A single manufacturing process often entails the simultaneous production of two or more separate, identifiable outputs. These outputs are referred to as *joint products* if they have significant sales value and *by-products* if they have small sales value in relation to the main products. The process which generates the products is termed a *joint process*. The essential characteristic of a joint process is that none of the products resulting from the process can be produced without also producing all the other products in the joint group, although it may be possible to vary the proportions. For example, refining crude oil can produce many different grades of petrol and fuel oil; the processing of animals can produce many different cuts of meat, as well as fats and hides. A pork chop cannot be produced without producing the rest of the pig!

A critical decision which faces manufacturers of joint products, and which concerns us here, is whether to sell the products when they emerge from the joint process at what is termed the *split-off* point, or whether to process them further and incur additional, but separable, processing costs. The diagrammatic representation in Figure 10.1 may clarify the decision. Figure 10.1 shows a possible situation in which three separate joint products, A, B and C, and one by-product, D, can be produced from a single joint process. If we assume that there is a ready market for the products at the point of split-off, the question then arises as to whether additional processing should be incurred to produce A_2, B_2 and C_2, or whether the

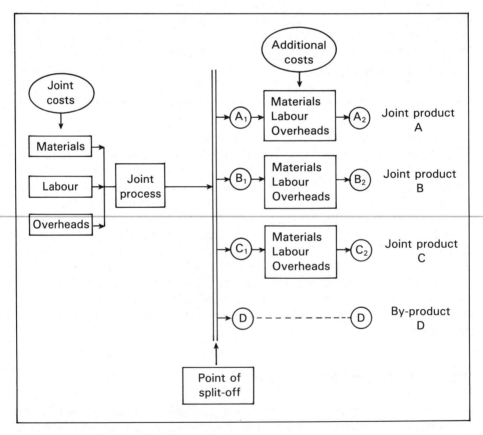

Figure 10.1 Joint products and by-products.

products should be sold in their existing state as A_1, B_1 and C_1. The analysis should be conducted in terms of differential cash flows. The decision to process further a joint product depends neither upon the amount of joint costs (fixed or variable) incurred in the initial joint process, since having already been incurred they are irrelevant to future actions, nor on the way these may be assigned to individual products for stock valuation purposes. The decision to process further depends simply upon whether the additional revenue from sale is justified by the additional costs involved.

Consider the following example. Boundary plc produces two products, D and E, by means of a joint process. Both products have an intermediate market and thus can be sold at the split-off point. For every 100 kg of material used in the joint process, there is an output of 80 kg of D and 20 kg of E. The data relevant to selling prices and costs are:

	Product D	*Product E*
Selling price at the split-off point	£320(£4 per kg)	£160(£8 per kg)
Costs of additional processing	£200(£2.5 per kg)	£60(£3 per kg)
Selling price at final stage after processing	£560(£7 per kg)	£200(£10 per kg)

Should D and/or E be processed further? Analysing each in turn:

Product D: Further process or immediate sale?

	Immediate sale (£)	*Further process* (£)	*Difference* (£)
Sales revenue	320	560	240
Additional costs	0	200	200
Additional profit/(loss)	320	360	40

Product E: Further process or immediate sale?

	Immediate sale (£)	*Further process* (£)	*Difference* (£)
Sales revenue	160	200	40
Additional costs	0	60	60
Additional profit/(loss)	160	140	(20)

The differential analysis reveals that D should be processed further as the additional revenue per unit of £3 (£7 – £4) is greater than the additional cost per unit of £2.50, whereas E should be sold after split-off as the additional revenue of £2 per unit (£10 – £8) is less than the additional cost of £3 per unit.

We have not yet addressed ourselves to the question of whether the joint process should be operated in the first place. There is obviously no point in making decisions about the possible worth of incurring additional costs if it is unprofitable to make the products initially. Let us refer back to the example of Boundary plc and assume the following additional data. Each month the joint process incurs avoidable fixed costs of £1,000 and a variable cost per 100 kg batch for labour and raw materials used of £400. Further assume that ten batches are processed each month. We can now determine whether it is profitable to operate the joint process by analysing the data as follows:

	Product D (£)	Product E (£)	Total (£)
Sales (10 batches):			
Product D after additional processing (10 batches × £560)	5,600		5,600
Product E sold at split-off (10 batches × £160)		1,600	1,600
			7,200
Less Additional costs of processing product D (10 batches × £200)	2,000		2,000
Surplus before costs of joint process	3,600	1,600	5,200
Less Additional costs of joint process:			
Avoidable fixed costs	1,000		
Variable costs (10 batches × £400)	4,000		5,000
Monthly surplus from whole process			200

The 'marginal' additional monthly surplus of £200 shows that the operation of the entire process appears to be worthwhile. If, of course, the monthly surplus for the process had been a negative amount (i.e. a loss had been incurred), then it would be unwise to proceed, even though both D and E show surpluses before deducting avoidable joint process costs.

10.4 Make or buy decisions

As a further example of the use of differential cash flow analysis to assist decisions about operations, consider the choice between buying supplies of a good or service and producing them within the firm. This has become a common question in many businesses, particularly concerning service functions such as computer systems – where buying off-the-shelf software might be compared with developing customised systems in-house. In the public sector many organisations have been required by government to undertake exercises on the contracting out of services, such as refuse collection in local authorities, in order to establish if it is better to purchase these services from an independent supplier or to operate the service within the authority itself.

Table 10.4 Bloomfield plc: make or buy decision

	Production (£)	Purchase for resale (£)	Differential flows (£)
Cost of production			
Variable cost	12,000	–	
Separable fixed cost	3,000	–	
Purchase @ £4/unit	–	16,000	
Total	15,000	16,000	1,000
Sales revenue	32,000	32,000	–
Net product contribution	17,000	16,000	+1,000

Returning to the example of Bloomfield plc, let us suppose that the firm is able to acquire supplies of product B from an overseas supplier at a cost of £4.00 per unit for the volume of 4,000 that Bloomfield expects to sell. Would it be worthwhile for Bloomfield to cease production of B and simply purchase supplies for resale?

This opportunity can be evaluated by comparing the flows associated with production with those expected for purchase and resale, as in Table 10.4. If Bloomfield ceases production of B, total costs of £15,000 will be avoided. The costs of purchase for resale will be £16,000 (£4 × 4,000), which is higher than the costs avoided and would suggest that production should be continued, because the purchase alternative would have a negative effect on Bloomfield plc's cash flows.

Note, however, that a full evaluation of the opportunity requires consideration of all the consequences of the decision. For example, if by ceasing production, factory space would be released which Bloomfield plc could rent, generating an income of £2,500, that additional cash flow would be relevant to the make or buy decision. When this flow is taken into account, the alternative of purchase for resale can be seen to be worthwhile, as it increases Bloomfield's return by £1,500 (production cash flow = –£15,000, purchase cash flow = –£16,000 + £2,500 (rental) = –£13,500). As with the other types of operating decision that have already been discussed, a wide variety of other qualitative factors would also be relevant to a make or buy or contracting out decision. Bloomfield plc would have to consider factors such as whether the quality of products will be equivalent to its own production, whether this can be guaranteed, whether continuity of supply can be assured and whether imported goods will be as easy to sell.

10.5 Pricing an additional order

A final example of how the analysis of differential cash flows can be useful for the purposes of decision making is the evaluation of the minimum price at which accepting an additional special order would be worthwhile. This example has already been illustrated in section 9.5 of the preceding chapter on contribution margin pricing, and readers should review the discussion in that section. The approach adopted is consistent with that applied to other decisions in this chapter, in that it focuses on the changes in the flows of revenue which will make a decision to incur certain costs worthwhile. The minimum price that can be set for an incremental order is that amount which covers the incremental costs of satisfying the order. Any price above incremental cost will be making a contribution to the generation of profit.

CHAPTER SUMMARY

This chapter has looked at the application of the concept of relevance to the production of information that can guide management on a number of operating decisions which are unusual in nature or which arise infrequently. We have discussed what is the relevant accounting information in deciding whether to drop a line of business, dealing with joint products and choosing between production and purchase, and have also referred to the considerations covered in the previous chapter for pricing an incremental order.

In all cases what is relevant information is determined by looking at the differential flows associated with alternative courses of action – that is, what changes as a result of a decision on any particular opportunity. The differential costs and benefits are the relevant information for decision making. In measuring these costs and benefits, all the consequences of a decision must be identified, including the effects from constraining or creating other opportunities for the firm. In the following two chapters we expand our analysis to the impact of scarce resources on the information required to make operating decisions.

REVIEW QUESTIONS

1. 'Whatever the nature of the business decision, only differential future cash flows are relevant to the decision.' Discuss.

2. Give some specific examples of business decisions in which *qualitative* factors would probably determine the future outcome, and explain how such factors might affect the decisions.

3. Discuss some of the *social* implications of dropping a segment or division of a business. How should these implications be included in the decision process?

4. Discuss some possible disadvantages that might arise from the allocation of joint costs to individual products.

5. 'The results of short-term decisions determine the organisation's future.' Discuss.

EXERCISES

10.1 Shown below is a statement of profitability for the first quarter of 19X4, for two products manufactured by Clarice plc:

	A	B	Total
Volume of production and sales	1,000	800	
	(£)	(£)	(£)
Unit selling price	175	140	
Revenue	175,000	112,000	287,000
Manufacturing costs:			
Fixed/set-up costs for individual products	35,000	29,000	64,000
Variable A @ £60	60,000		
B @ £65		52,000	112,000
	95,000	81,000	176,000
Joint costs allocated in proportion to other manufacturing costs	19,000	16,200	35,200
Selling and administrative costs, allocated in proportion to revenue	26,250	16,800	43,050
Total costs	140,250	114,000	254,250
Product profit/(loss)	34,750	(2,000)	32,750

Provide recommendations for management, supported by appropriate calculations, in response to the following questions:

(a) What minimum price would make acceptance of an order for an additional 200 units of A worthwhile?

(b) As product B is recorded as making a loss, should production be terminated?

(c) Other manufacturers are willing to supply both A and B at the levels required, at a unit cost of £150 and £110. If production ceases, Clarice could offer the factory space for rent at £35,000 per quarter. Would this alternative be beneficial for the company? (Solution at end of text.)

10.2 The directors of Nicholson Department Store Ltd are concerned at the poor results achieved in its toy department. They have noted that it has earned an income of only £0.06 per £1 of sales, considerably less than the target set by the company. They are considering the closing of the department.

The income account of the department for the year just ended runs as follows:

	£	£
Sales		297,200
Less Cost of sales		191,200
Gross profit		106,000
Less		
Wages of sales assistants (2 @ £16,000)	32,000	
Salary of supervisor	21,000	
Establishment costs of the department (heating, repairs, insurance, etc.)	12,000	
Rent of store – allocated to department on basis of floor area occupied	10,000	
General overhead costs of store – allocation in proportion to sales in each department	12,000	87,000
Net income for the year		19,000

If the department were closed, the space it occupied could be used either for an extension of the clothing department, or for storage of inventory (in which case rent of £16,000 per annum for warehouse facilities could be saved). You are also given the following information:

1. The gross profit earned in the toy department would be expected to remain at the same level in future years. If the clothing department were extended, it would be expected to increase its sales by £180,000 and earn a gross profit of 50% on sales.

2. If the department were converted to storage, the sales assistants would be transferred to other departments at their present wages. This would avoid the need to employ new assistants at a wage of £14,000 per annum each to make good normal losses of staff. If the department were turned over to clothing, the assistants would be employed in the extended department at their present wages and no additional assistants would be required.

3. In either event, the supervisor of the department would be redundant; the new department would come under other supervisors, already employed. In accordance with company policy, however, the supervisor would not be dismissed but would be found employment in general administrative duties, at the present salary.

4. Establishment costs of the department would be:

   if converted to storage £6,000 p.a.
   if converted to clothing £8,000 p.a.

5. If the department were converted to storage, general administrative costs for the store would fall by £2,000. Otherwise, they would continue at the present level.

6. It is to be assumed that there would be no material capital expenditure associated with any of the possibilities.

(a) Prepare calculations to indicate to the board of directors the best course of action. You may make and specify any reasonable assumptions that you consider necessary for your answer and you may add a *short* note on any considerations not reflected in your calculations.

(b) Prepare a short note on the suitability of judging departments by their net income per £1 of sales. (Solution at end of text.)

10.3 Aurea plc has been invited to tender a price for an order for 2,500 Gallions. Aurea only produces this product to order and currently has no other orders in process.

The production requirements for Gallions are as follows:

(1) *Materials*
Three types of material are used in production:

	Amount used per unit	Latest purchase price	Resale value	Current price to buy
Material A	12 kg	£2.50	£1.00	£2.75
Material B	4 kg	£7.00	£5.50	£8.50
Material C	6 kg	–	£6.50	–

Material A is used extensively throughout Aurea's range of products. Current stocks are 40,000 kg and it is freely available in the market.

Material B is used infrequently. Aurea has 4,000 kg in stock which it was planning to sell due to its perishable nature.

Material C is a by-product from another processing department. It is sometimes sold on the open market, but most manufacturers produce for their own use, and Aurea does not have an alternative source of supply. Aurea currently uses this material in a product earning £58 contribution per unit and using 8 kg per unit.

(2) *Labour*
For each unit produced, six hours of one type of skilled labour are required. Aurea currently pays these workers at a rate of £10/hour. Although they are fully occupied at present, it is estimated that these workers could be persuaded to work 17,000 hours of overtime at one and a half times the normal wage rate. No more skilled workers can be recruited, so other production time required will have to be transferred from a product which is priced at £48 per unit with variable costs of £38, requiring one hour's labour per unit.

(3) *Overheads*

The overheads incurred depend on the overall level of operations of the plant. Without this contract the plant will be operating at 70% capacity and incurring variable overheads of £6 per hour. The contract would extend operations to 82.5% of capacity and produce efficiencies in variable overheads leading to a rate of £5.60/hour.

Aurea also has a policy of recovering fixed overheads by allocating them to production costs on the basis of £3 per labour hour.

Calculate the minimum price at which Aurea could bid for the contract.

10.4 Salazar Separators plc produce four products – maz, mez, miz and moz – by subjecting input chemical material (known as krudex) to an analytical process. The output proportions are maz 40%, mez 30%, miz 20% and moz 10%. The company has capacity to process 30,000 gallons of chemicals per four-week period.

An output of 20,000 gallons per four-week period represents the sales demand at prevailing prices which are:

Maz	£3.00 per gallon
Mez	£3.50 per gallon
Miz	£4.00 per gallon
Moz	£6.00 per gallon

and requires an input of 20,000 gallons of krudex which costs £1.50 per gallon. The labour cost of processing 20,000 gallons is £10,000. The company's fixed overhead at 50% to 100% of capacity working is £10,000 per four-week period. Variable overhead has been found to be closely related to direct wages and an absorption rate of 50% thereof is applied.

The company is considering whether to subject any or all of the four products to further processing in order to produce more refined products which would be known as supermaz, supermez, supermiz and supermoz, and which would command higher prices, namely:

Supermaz	£3.50 per gallon
Supermez	£3.80 per gallon
Supermiz	£6.00 per gallon
Supermoz	£8.00 per gallon

Sales demands for the super products are not expected to exceed those for the products they would replace. For technical reasons, it is not possible to produce both the original and the refined versions of any of the four products during a four-week period, though one or more of the products can be produced in the refined version and the others in the original version.

Additional material and labour costs for the more refined process have been estimated as follows:

	Supermaz (£)	Supermez (£)	Supermiz (£)	Supermoz (£)
Activating ingredients (of no significant weight or volume)	2,000	3,000	2,000	1,500
Direct wages	1,000	3,000	1,000	1,000

Present a report, submitting information on the basis of which a decision could be made as to whether to undertake the additional processing under consideration, and state your recommendations.

10.5 Arts plc produces sports and casual T-shirts with unusual printed designs and colours. Production involves three main processes following receipt of the cotton cloth, all of which are undertaken in-house: dyeing the material to Arts special colours, manufacture of the shirts and printing with the final design. Cotton Stitchers plc has approached the management of Arts with an offer to take the dyed cloth, manufacture the required T-shirts and return them for final printing, at a cost of £3.00 per T-shirt. Arts plc management estimate that the current variable cost for manufacture of T-shirts is £2.50. They also estimate that if the firm were to concentrate its activities on dyeing and printing only, there would be savings of £40,000 in fixed costs.

(a) Assuming that Arts plc is currently operating with a relatively stable demand for 50,000 T-shirts per year, should management accept the offer for external manufacture by Cotton Stitchers?

(b) At what level of production would the relative advantage of in-house production and purchasing the service from Cotton Stitchers change?

Three years ago, Arts plc invested in new advanced printing machinery to accommodate expected demand for more complicated printing finishes. The machinery is not being fully used as that demand has not materialised, and it is no longer anticipated that the additional facilities offered by the machinery will be required. The company management are concerned about the continued high operating costs of the advanced machinery, which amount to £5,000 (including depreciation), as against an estimated operating cost of £3,700 (including depreciation) for more modest machinery which could be purchased as a replacement.

Comparative details for the two types of machinery are as follows:

	Existing machinery	Replacement machinery
Purchase price (£)	12,000	4,500
Current market value (£)	3,000	4,500
Estimated life	3 years	3 years
Estimated scrap value in 3 years	nil	nil
Annual depreciation (£)	2,000	1,500

(c) Provide calculations to support a decision whether or not to replace the advanced machinery.

The effect of scarce resources on short-term decisions

AIMS AND OBJECTIVES

☐ To explain the meaning of scarce resources and examine their impact on short-term decisions.

☐ To describe linear programming formulations to solve decision problems where more than one resource is scarce.

☐ To explain how to solve linear programming problems graphically.

☐ To discuss the limitations and assumptions of linear programming.

So far in our analysis we have assumed that there are no restrictions on the input factors needed for production. We have, for example, assumed that materials, machinery and labour are readily available and can be bought or hired in the desired quantities. In practice, however, it is quite likely that this assumption will not hold. A required input is described as a *scarce resource* if the firm has insufficient supplies of it to accept all opportunities which are expected to generate positive contributions. Scarce resources restrict the firm's feasible production plans and our analysis should therefore account for these constraints. It is no longer sufficient simply to evaluate whether or not an available opportunity is worthwhile in terms of generating a positive contribution. Rather, the analysis must also incorporate *comparison* between worthwhile opportunities and investigation of production plans involving different combinations of possible products, to ensure that the limited available resources are allocated in the most beneficial way. We will examine the mode of analysis required in two stages: first, by assuming that only one resource is scarce; and second, by extending the analysis to cope with the situation in which more than one resource is scarce.

Where only one resource is scarce, products competing for its use must be *ranked* so that the most efficient use is made of the scarce resource. To achieve the maximum contribution overall, the firm should develop a plan which obtains the maximum contribution from each available unit of the scarce resource, and this aim is achieved by ranking products according to the contribution they produce per unit of the scarce resource they require. The following example explains the procedure.

Prenton plc is considering its production plan for the next year. Four products, P, Q, R and S, are available for production and sale. The data relevant to the products are given in Table 11.1. Which products should Prenton plc produce? If no resources are in short supply, Prenton plc should produce all four products up to the level of their respective demands, as each one makes a positive contribution to fixed costs and profit.

Suppose now that Prenton plc is unable to obtain sufficient labour for next year to produce all four products to their demand limits (i.e. 120,600 labour hours). In fact only 41,500 labour hours are expected to be available. It is now necessary to analyse the relationship between contribution earned and resource used: that is, to see how efficiently the four products use available labour. The ranking according to their contributions per labour hour is shown in Table 11.2. Table 11.2 shows that R, showing a contribution of £12.5 per labour hour, uses labour hours most efficiently and should be produced to its demand limit. Product S is the second most efficient and should also be produced to its demand limit. This process continues until all the 41,500 available labour hours have been used. Between them R and S require 29,800 labour hours (R requires 14,400 (600 × 24) and S 15,400 (1,100 × 14)). This leaves 11,700 available for Q, the third best on the ranking. But to produce Q to its demand limit would require 20,800 labour hours (800 × 26) which is more than the amount available. Production of Q is therefore restricted to 450 units (11,700 ÷ 26), and no labour hours remain to produce any units of P. The optimal plan for Prenton plc is set out in Table 11.3.

The optimality of the plan may be tested by considering the effect of transferring one of the scarce labour hours currently being used to help to produce

Table 11.1 Prenton plc: product data

		P		Q		R		S
Selling price (£)		1,150		750		800		650
Less Labour (£10 per hour)	700		260		240		140	
Materials (£5 per kg)	100	800	295	555	260	500	370	510
Contribution per unit (£)		350		195		300		140
Labour required per unit (hours)		70		26		24		14
Maximum expected demand at above selling price (units)		1,000		800		600		1,100

Table 11.2 Ranking of products on the basis of contribution per labour hour

Product	Contribution per unit (£)	Labour hours per unit	Contribution per labour hour (£)	Ranking
P	350	70	5.0	4
Q	195	26	7.5	3
R	300	24	12.5	1
S	140	14	10.0	2

Table 11.3 Prenton plc: derivation of the optimal plan

Product	Units produced	Labour hours required	Contribution (£)
R	600	14,400	180,000
S	1,100	15,400	154,000
Q	450	11,700	87,750
P	0	0	0
		41,500	421,750

one unit of Q (the least acceptable product included in the plan) to P (the only and therefore the best product excluded from the plan). We presume for illustrative purposes that all products are divisible and hence that we can measure contributions for fractions of products. Is the substitution worthwhile? The effect on total contribution will be as set out below:

	£
Increase in contribution from P through gain of one labour hour	5.0
Fall in contribution from Q through loss of one labour hour	7.5
Net decrease in contribution	2.5

The substitution is not worthwhile. Similarly it will not be worthwhile to substitute P for either of R and S, both of which use scarce labour hours more efficiently than Q.

The plan we have drawn up is the best available. We must stress here that we would *not* have obtained the same answer if we had ranked the four products according to their unit contributions, because that ranking does not take account of the relative usage of the scarce resource. In the case of Prenton plc it is interesting to note that P, which has the highest unit contribution (£350), also produces the lowest contribution per hour of labour, the scarce resource. Product S, on the other hand, has the lowest unit contribution (£140) but the second highest contribution per labour hour. In simple terms, the reason why contribution per unit of the scarce resource is a more appropriate means of evaluating products than is unit contribution is that ultimately a firm wishes to maximise its total contribution. So if Prenton plc had 140 labour hours available for production of either P or S, it could make either 2 units of P, giving a total contribution of £700 (2 × £350) or 10 units of S, giving a contribution of £1,400 (10 × £140). Although P has the higher unit contribution, this is more than compensated for when labour is scarce by the fact that more units of S can be produced using a given number of labour hours. The same sort of reasoning would, of course, apply if the scarce resource in question were something other than labour time: for example, raw materials, machine hours, factory space or even cash.

11.2 Decision making with more than one scarce resource

Let us now extend the analysis by addressing the problem of decision making for a firm that is faced with constraints on the availability of at least two resources (e.g. labour and machinery). We have seen that it is possible to apply a ranking criterion based on contribution per unit of scarce resource to determine the best production plan if only one resource is in short supply. Can we apply the same criterion if two resources are scarce? The answer is that we can apply the ranking method, but it will give us the optimal answer only if it results in the same ranking for each constraining factor. If the rankings based on the use of different scarce resources differ, then it will not be clear how management should proceed in selecting production alternatives. Rather than allocating resources to products in a single rank order, it will be necessary to consider different combinations of available products to ensure that all resources are being used to their best advantage. The best plan could be obtained by examining all possible combinations of product selection, but the sheer number of calculations involved will usually make this approach infeasible. What is needed is a method of analysis which limits the number of possible combinations of products to be examined, and which ensures that the optimal plan is included in the set examined. In effect a method is needed to account for the relative use of scarce resources by different products. Such a method is provided by the technique of *linear programming*.

11.3 Linear programming: formulation

Linear programming is the most simple of the mathematical programming techniques available to the decision maker. It is widely used in fields other than production planning, but it is this function, as an aid to the solution of business decision problems, that is of particular interest to us here. In order to illustrate the formulation, and subsequently the solution, of linear programming problems, we make use of an example.

Carrow plc manufactures two products, the widget and the didget. Each widget which is sold produces a contribution of £5 and each didget £4. All input factors required to manufacture the two products are readily available at their market prices with the exception of labour time, storage space and a special component, the justin. In the coming year Carrow plc expects to have available a maximum of 30,000 labour hours, 12,000 ft^2 storage space and 33,000 units of justin.

Each widget requires 15 labour hours, an average of two square feet of storage space per annum and 10 units of justin. Each didget requires 8 labour hours, an average of four square feet of storage space per annum and 12 units of justin. No restriction is expected on the demands for the two products. Carrow plc is seeking a production plan for the coming year that will maximise total contribution to fixed costs and profit from the two products. There is to be no production for stock.

Letting x_1 equal the number of widgets to be produced and sold in the coming year, and x_2 equal the number of didgets, we may formulate the problem as a linear programme:

Maximise $C = \quad 5x_1 + 4x_2$ \hfill (11.1)

Subject to
$$\left.\begin{array}{r} 15x_1 + 8x_2 \le 30,000 \\ 2x_1 + 4x_2 \le 12,000 \\ 10x_1 + 12x_2 \le 33,000 \end{array}\right\} \quad (11.2)$$

$$\left.\begin{array}{r} x_1 \ge 0 \\ x_2 \ge 0 \end{array}\right\} \quad (11.3)$$

(11.1) is known as the *objective function* and is normally an equation (model) describing total profit or, more precisely, total contribution. We wish to maximise the value of this expression (C). In this case, total contribution is the sum of the contributions from widgets (£5 per unit multiplied by x_1 units) and didgets (£4 per unit multiplied by x_2 units). It is the object of the linear programming solution to find optimal values for x_1 and x_2, the quantities of each product to be produced and sold.

The other expressions are inequalities that define the *constraints* to be observed in maximising the value of the objective function. The constraints under (11.2) represent restrictions on the availability of input factors (resources). For example, 30,000 – the right-hand side of the first constraint – is the total amount of labour hours expected to be available in the coming year. The left-hand side of the constraint defines total labour hours required: 15 hours for each of the x_1 widgets to be produced and 8 hours for each of the x_2 didgets. Hence the constraint requires that total labour hours used ($15x_1 + 8x_2$) must be less than or equal to total labour hours available (30,000). Similarly the available amount of storage space and justin must not be exceeded.

In the case of Carrow plc, no constraints are expected on the demands for the two products. Demand constraints could easily be incorporated into the linear programming formulation. For example, suppose that Carrow plc expected to be able to sell no more than 1,500 widgets and 1,600 didgets during the coming year. As there is to be no production for stock, the company will not want to produce more of either product than it is able to sell, and the demand constraints will be:

$x_1 \le 1,500$
$x_2 \le 1,600$

The constraints included under (11.3) are known as *non-negativity constraints*. They are technical requirements to ensure that negative production quantities for any of the products are not included in the optimal plan. Other refinements are possible within the general formulation and, provided the expression may be stated in a linear form, there is usually no reason why they should not be incorporated. The description 'linear programming' merely reflects that the equations and inequalities included are linear (i.e. they may be represented by straight lines – see Chapter 8 for examples of linear cost–volume–profit charts).

Linear programming, then, is suitable for solving problems where the objective is to maximise (or minimise) the value of some linear function subject to constraints (expressed as linear inequalities) which must not be violated.

11.4 Linear programming: solution

There are a number of techniques available for the solution of linear programming problems. All but the simplest problems are normally solved on a computer and it is not proposed to discuss the methods used in detail here.[1] Simple linear programming problems – for example, where only two products are to be considered – may be solved with the aid of a graph. As this method of solution also serves to illustrate a number of the principles involved in more complicated methods of solution, we shall apply it to the example of Carrow plc. Recall the linear programming formulation of the production problem facing the company:

$$
\begin{array}{lll}
\text{Maximise } C = & 5x_1 + 4x_2 & \text{(objective function)} \\
\text{Subject to} & 15x_1 + 8x_2 \leqslant 30{,}000 & \text{(labour constraint)} \\
& 2x_1 + 4x_2 \leqslant 12{,}000 & \text{(storage space constraint)} \\
& 10x_1 + 12x_2 \leqslant 33{,}000 & \text{(justin constraint)} \\
& x_1 \ , \ x_2 \geqslant 0 & \text{(non-negativity constraints)}
\end{array}
$$

The first step in the graphical solution is to plot the various constraints. In Figure 11.1 we start by drawing axes representing possible production levels of widgets and didgets, x_1 and x_2. Any point on the graph represents a production plan. For example, point A represents a production of 3,000 widgets (x_1) and 4,000 didgets (x_2). Our first task is to define a region, known as the *feasible region*, which covers all points, or solutions, that yield production plans not violating any of the constraints.

Consider first the two non-negativity constraints: $x_1 \geqslant 0$ implies that the solution must lie on or to the right of the x_2 axis. Similarly $x_2 \geqslant 0$ implies that the solution must lie on or above the x_1 axis. The boundary lines describing the other three constraints will all be linear as the constraints themselves are expressed as linear inequalities. If an input is utilised up to the limit imposed by the available amount of the resource, the inequality describing the constraint will become an equality. For example, if labour is fully utilised then the values of x_1 and x_2 will be such as to satisfy the equation

$$15x_1 + 8x_2 = 30{,}000$$

There is an infinite combination of values of x_1 and x_2 which satisfy this equation. To construct the line which connects them all, we need only calculate two of the combinations as we know the line is straight. The two we shall calculate are shown as points B and C in Figure 11.1. Point B represents a value of zero for x_2 and consequently the expression above reduces to $15x_1 = 30,000$, i.e. $x_1 = 2,000$. Point C represents a value of zero for x_1 and hence a value of 3,750 (30,000/8) for x_2. By connecting these two points we construct a line representing the boundary imposed by the labour constraint; the solution must lie to the left of and below this line. By a similar process we may construct constraint lines for storage space and for the special component justin. The lines are shown in Figure 11.1.

To be acceptable a solution must not violate any of the five constraints. All such solutions lie within the shaded area, designated the feasible region, on the graph in Figure 11.1. They are known as *feasible solutions*. Any production plan represented by a point outside the feasible region will violate at least one of the constraints and will not be acceptable.

The next step is to find the solution, from within the feasible region, that is *optimal*, i.e. that gives the highest value to the objective function. To do this we shall make use of what are normally known as iso-profit lines. An iso-profit line connects all points on the graph that represent production combinations yielding the same profit. As our assumed objective is to maximise total contribution to fixed costs and

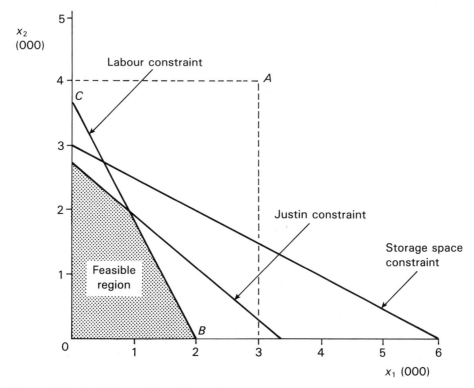

Figure 11.1 Definition of feasible region.

profit, our lines will connect all points representing production combinations producing the same total contribution: that is, giving a constant value to the objective function. For example, the broken line DE on the graph in Figure 11.2 links all solutions that yield a total contribution of £20,000.

The construction of the line is similar to the method used to construct the constraint boundary lines; as the line is straight (because the contribution per unit for each product is constant at all production levels) we need only calculate two points lying on it to be able to draw the whole line. For simplicity we choose the two points representing a zero production of one product and a balancing figure for the production of the other. For the £20,000 constant contribution line, if $x_2 = 0$ then x_1 must equal 4,000 (£20,000/£5), and if $x_1 = 0$ then x_2 must equal 5,000 (£20,000/£4). Similarly, we might construct an iso-profit line for a contribution of £10,000. This is the broken line FK in Figure 11.2.

There is an infinite number of (parallel) constant contribution lines, all having a negative slope equal to the ratio of the contribution from a widget to the contribution from a didget (5/4). The objective is to discover the product combination represented on the highest contribution line: that is, the one which will yield the highest total contribution. From the graph it is apparent that line HJ is the highest profit line attainable that includes a product mix not outside the feasible region ($0GIF$, as drawn in Figure 11.2). The line HJ is tangential to the feasible region at point I. It is a

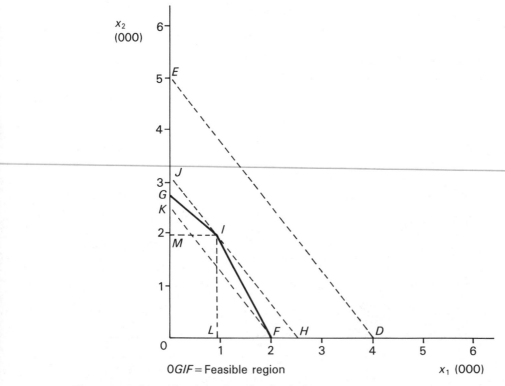

Figure 11.2 Identification of optimal solution.

general rule of linear programming solutions that the optimum will lie somewhere on the boundary of the feasible region: for any point within, but not on the boundary of, the feasible region, there exists another on the boundary having a greater contribution. Unless the iso-profit lines have the same slope as one of the constraint boundary lines, there will always be a unique solution at the intersection of two constraint lines, as at the intersection of the labour and justin constraint lines in our example.

The solution represented by point I is optimal. It is within the feasible region and yields a higher contribution than any other point in the feasible region. We might ascertain the production plan it represents by reading from the graph the value of x_1 and x_2 ($0L$ and $0M$ respectively). However, this method may lack precision and as an alternative we might utilise our new-found knowledge that the optimal plan involves using labour and the special component justin to their available limits. In other words, the inequalities describing these two constraints in the initial linear programming formulation become equalities at the optimal point, i.e.

$$15x_1 + 8x_2 = 30,000$$
$$10x_1 + 12x_2 = 33,000$$

Solving these as simultaneous equations we obtain values of $x_1 = 960$ and $x_2 = 1,950$. The optimal plan, then, is to produce 960 widgets and 1,950 didgets.[2]

Let us check that this plan will not lead to the violation of any constraints. The usage of the scarce resources implied by the plan is shown in Table 11.4. None of the constraints is violated. This confirms the feasibility of the plan. The total contribution expected from the plan may be determined by substituting the optimal values of x_1 and x_2 into the objective function:

Total contribution = £5(960) + £4(1,950) = £12,600

The optimality of this contribution could be confirmed by checking that there is no feasible substitution that would lead to a higher total contribution. Subject to the limitations of the method (discussed in the next section), the solution obtained by linear programming should be optimal.

Using the graphical framework, we might have calculated the optimal solution differently. As we know that the optimum solution(s) will lie at one of the corner points of the feasible region, we might simply have calculated the contribution at each of these points and chosen the one with the highest contribution, thus avoiding the need for iso-profit lines. Alternatively, we could have dispensed with the graph altogether and calculated the values of x_1 and x_2 at the corner points by solving simultaneously all possible pairs of constraint equations, including the non-negativity constraints. After discarding solutions that violated other constraints, the

Table 11.4 Usage of scarce resources

Labour	15(960) + 8(1,950) = 30,000
Storage space	2(960) + 4(1,950) = 9,720
Justin	10(960) + 12(1,950) = 33,000

solutions remaining would have represented the production plans at all corner points of the feasible region. From among them, we would have chosen the combination of x_1 and x_2 that yielded the highest contribution.

11.5 Limitations and assumptions of linear programming

There are a number of limitations to the linear programming approach, some of which stem from the assumptions implicit in the technique. The usefulness of linear programming models for decision making depends upon how well they simulate the conditions under which the firm operates.

As we have seen, linear programming models assume linear relationships between the variables. As such, they suffer similar limitations to the linear break-even charts discussed in Chapter 8. This has a number of practical implications. For example, one implicit assumption is that, whatever the quantity of a particular product offered for sale, up to the level of any demand constraint which is included in the model, the selling price remains constant. The usual economic assumption is that the greater the number offered for sale, the lower will be the average price obtainable in the market (except in rarely found perfect markets). If a firm feels that it will be able to sell up to X units at a price of £Y, it may include a constraint to this effect in its linear programming model. However, the optimal solution may suggest an output less than X units, and it may be that the firm could sell this lower output at a price in excess of £Y. If the price is increased accordingly, the original plan may no longer be optimal. In this situation, the first formulation may be revised in the light of the first solution and the procedure repeated until a satisfactory position is reached.

A further implication of the linearity assumption is that each unit of output of a particular product requires a constant amount of each input factor: that is, each successive unit of an input factor used on a particular product produces the same output quantity of that product. In the case of labour it is assumed that the workforce is equally efficient in all situations, ignoring the possibility that labour needs time to 'warm up' at the start of a production run, or that people become more weary and less efficient towards the end of the run, and so on.

Furthermore, the model depends upon our being able to divide the total cost function of the firm into fixed and variable elements. Where step cost functions exist (see Chapter 6), they must be treated with care. Some may be reasonably approximated by a linear function, while others may, within defined ranges, be regarded as fixed. Where neither of these treatments seems appropriate, some improvisation may be necessary. For example, the programme may be run at different maximum output levels, corresponding to the points at which steps in total costs occur; step costs would be ignored in the formulation but adjusted manually in comparing contributions at each output level.

It is implied also that, however many units of an input factor are bought, up to any constraint that may be assumed, the same price will be paid for each unit. This may fail to take account of discounts for bulk buying, increased prices as the available supply diminishes, and so on. Where these implied assumptions are not representative, or reasonably representative, of the actual conditions facing the firm, the use of a linear programming model may be inappropriate.

The linear programming solution may not be optimal if the input cost and price data used do not represent the relevant costs of the particular factors. For example, to maximise product contributions calculated on a historical cost basis may lead to a solution that is inconsistent with the maximisation of current cash resources.

We have not dealt explicitly with the problem of uncertainty. In practice, linear programming is a most useful aid to analysing the uncertainty problem. Once the initial programme is formulated, say on the basis of 'best estimates', the values of individual elements may be altered and the programme re-run rapidly on a computer to determine the effect of the change on total contribution. This sensitivity analysis enables the firm to form an opinion as to the sensitivity of total contribution to environmental changes or estimating errors in the value of individual input factors. Because much of the decision-making cost is in the initial formulation of the problem, rather than in its solution, the incremental cost of undertaking the sensitivity analysis may be relatively low.

There are a number of other factors that may need to be considered. It is frequently the case that the solution to a linear programming problem involves fractional units of products (for example, with slightly different constraints the solution to the Carrow plc problem could have involved production of 960.5 widgets). It may be that the assumption that fractional units of products can be produced and sold is invalid. If so, the optimal solution will have to be in terms of integer output levels. Where fairly large output levels are involved, this may be achieved by rounding down any fractional output levels to the nearest whole number. Where small output levels are envisaged and each output unit is large relative to the total, such a process of rounding may not lead to a solution that is a good approximation to the optimum, and a more refined form of programming may be required. This is known as *integer programming* and involves the inclusion of extra constraints to prohibit solutions involving fractional output levels.[3]

A further factor that was ignored in handling the problem of Carrow plc was the possibility of interdependence between the demands for widgets and didgets. Demand for the products, on the one hand, may be complementary. An example would be a firm manufacturing propelling pencils and the leads that are used in them. A fall in the number of pencils sold may lead to a fall in the number of leads demanded. Alternatively, the products may be substitutes for each other, when a fall in the number of one product sold will be associated with a rise in the demand for others. An example would be an organisation manufacturing more than one sort of breakfast cereal. The implicit assumption of linear programming is that the demand functions for the various products under consideration are independent of each other. Where this is not a valid assumption, a more refined mathematical programming approach is required.

An analogous problem may arise where there are interdependences between the input factors required to manufacture two or more of the products. For example, a farmer cannot produce milk, meat and hides independently of each other. They all come from the same input factor, the cow, and the final amounts produced are interrelated. In situations like this, the basic programming model may require development by the addition of extra constraints. Often, however, if the implied assumptions discussed in this section do not hold, we must resort to one of the non-linear programming techniques that are available.[4]

Finally, we mention three further points that are not strictly limitations of linear (and other) programming techniques, but rather are warnings to exercise care in their use. Similar caveats apply to many other mathematical business problem-solving techniques, as we have seen in previous chapters. The first concerns the existence of costs and benefits that are not readily quantifiable and hence cannot be easily incorporated into the linear programming formulation. For example, the firm may lose customer goodwill if it fails to produce a full line of products. It may be possible to treat this as a demand interdependence problem if the necessary quantification can be achieved. On the cost side, there is the possibility of industrial action if the optimal plan involves laying off part of the labour force. The uncertainties involved make it difficult to predict the likelihood and potential cost of a strike, for example. It may be that the firm wishes to ensure that the plan selected does not involve reducing the number of people employed on production below a specified minimum. In the case of Carrow plc, for example, a constraint is already included limiting the maximum number of labour hours. Suppose the firm also requires that a minimum of 18,000 hours be worked to reduce the probability of industrial action. This could be achieved by inserting a further constraint

$$15x_1 + 8x_2 \geqslant 18{,}000$$

which would ensure that at least 18,000 labour hours were required in the production plan.[5]

The second point is that linear programming will only yield a solution that is optimal for the available input data. Any opportunities that are not included in the formulation cannot be considered. It is important for the decision maker to ensure that a satisfactory range of feasible opportunities is taken into account, unless there is some obvious reason for excluding any of them.

The final point concerns the implied rigidity of the constraints. As we are using a precise mathematical technique to solve our problem, the input data must also be precise. A limit of 30,000 labour hours is interpreted in the solving of the problem at its face value, and not, for example, as $30{,}000 \pm 10\%$. In practice, it is likely that the constraints will have some degree of flexibility, particularly if the possibility of paying increasing prices for further supplies is not rejected.

At first sight, the limitations of linear programming seem imposing. Yet many of them stem from the implied assumption of linear cost functions, and a number of statistical studies have presented evidence suggesting that within fairly wide relevant ranges firms are confronted with cost functions that may be reasonably approximated by linear expressions.[6] In addition, many firms are already using linear programming techniques on a wide variety of business problems, with apparently satisfactory results.[7]

CHAPTER SUMMARY

Scarce resources restrict the firm's ability to exploit all available worthwhile opportunities. It is therefore important that decision analysis takes account of the effects of the existence of scarce resources on the courses of action that management should choose. The methods that should be used to do this depend on the number of constraints there are on production.

Where only one resource is scarce, competing alternatives should be ranked on the basis of contribution generated per unit of scarce resource used, in order to maximise the total amount of contribution earned. When the firm is faced with more than one limiting factor, no unambiguous ranking of the independent production opportunities available can be guaranteed. Rather it is necessary to look at the way different combinations of products make use of all the scarce resources and generate contribution. This analysis can be achieved through the technique of linear programming, which provides a mathematical method for expressing the relationship among opportunities, the firm's objective and the constraints on pursuit of that objective. As its name implies, linear programming assumes linear relationships between variables, and its usefulness is limited to the extent to which this assumption reflects the pattern of the firm's operations.

REVIEW QUESTIONS

1. When is a resource said to be scarce? Distinguish between short-term and long-term scarcity.

2. Explain in words how you would formulate and solve a linear programming problem.

3. 'The results of linear programming are only as good as the assumptions of the model used.' Discuss.

4. 'The results of short-term decisions determine the organisation's future.' Discuss.

EXERCISES

11.1 Spohr's accountant has drawn up the following statement to help the managing director in his decision on what to produce during the coming month:

	Product					
	A	B	C	D	E	F
Selling price (£)	135	177	123	129	153	135
Cost (£): Materials	30	45	36	54	81	72
Labour	36	45	30	24	18	15
Variable overheads	9	9	9	9	9	9
Fixed overheads	36	45	30	24	18	15
	111	144	105	111	126	111
Profit per unit (£)	24	33	18	18	27	24
Ranking	3=	1	5=	5=	2	3=
Estimated maximum demand per month (units)	500	700	600	1,000	400	600

Labour is all of one grade and earns £6 per hour; Spohr can hire only 11,000 labour hours during the coming month. All other resources can be obtained in the desired quantities. Materials are valued at expected cost; none is held in stock at present. Fixed overheads are charged at 100% of labour cost under the company's costing system.

(a) Criticise the accountant's statement as a basis for product selection and suggest an output plan for the coming month. Indicate how confident you are that your suggestion is optimal.

(b) Suppose that the price of materials has increased dramatically during the past month and that Spohr holds very large stocks purchased before the increase. Explain briefly how such materials should be valued for output decisions. (Solution at end of text.)

11.2 Mussorgsky Ltd manufactures two products, the hi and the fi. It sells the hi at £130 and the fi at £160. At these prices, the company is able to sell as many units of each product as it can produce. The variable cost of each hi is £90 and of each fi, £100. The company also incurs annual fixed costs of £95,000, the amount of which is unaffected by the production levels of hi and fi.

In the coming year Mussorgsky Ltd expects to have available only 28,000 hours of skilled labour time and 66,000 hours of machine time. The company does not expect to be able to exceed these amounts during the coming year. All other input factors are expected to be available in any likely quantities. Each hi produced requires 7 hours of skilled labour time and 33 machine hours. The requirements for each fi are 14 hours of skilled labour time and 22 machine hours.

The company wishes to determine a production plan which will maximise its expected profit for the coming year. No stocks of hi or fi are held at present and there is to be no production for stock during the coming year.

(a) Formulate the above problem as a linear programme.

(b) Calculate the optimal production levels for hi and fi during the coming year, and the company's expected profit if the optimal plan is implemented.

(c) Outline the limitations of linear programming in solving problems such as this in practice. (Solution at end of text.)

11.3 Paganini Ltd is drawing up production plans for the coming year. Four products are available:

	Product			
	A	B	C	D
Selling price per unit (£)	220	212	388	344
Cost of materials per unit (£)	68	100	152	88
Labour hours per unit – Grade A	10	6	–	–
Grade B	–	–	10	20
Grade C	–	–	12	6
Variable overheads (£)	24	28	20	24

Fixed overheads of the firm amount to £142,000 per annum. Each grade of labour is paid £6 per hour, but skills are specific to a grade so that an employee in one grade cannot be used to undertake the work of another grade. The annual supply of each grade is limited to the following maxima:

Grade A – 9,000 hours
Grade B – 14,500 hours
Grade C – 12,000 hours

There is no effective limitation on the volume of sales of any product.

(a) Calculate the product mix which will maximise profit for the year, and state the amount of the profit.

(b) Calculate the minimum price at which the sale of product A would be worthwhile.

(c) Calculate the amount by which profit could be increased if the supply of Grade A labour were increased by one hour.

(d) Describe briefly the limitations of the technique you have used in answering (a).

11.4 Pamina owns a small, highly skilled business which manufactures flutes and sets of pan-pipes. The following data are relevant to the two products:

	Flute (F)	Set of pan-pipes (P)
Selling price per unit (£)	120	100
Variable cost per unit (£)	80	70
Contribution per unit (£)	40	30
Raw materials required:		
Special wood	1 'length'	2 'lengths'
High quality metal	0.2 kg	0.1 kg
Direct labour required (hours)	20	20

Estimates of the resource quantities available in a year are:

Special wood	1,000 'lengths'
High quality metal	100 kg
Direct labour	12,000 hours

(a) Advise Pamina how many flutes and sets of pan-pipes she should produce each year in order to maximise her profit.
(If a graphical solution is used, plot the number of flutes on the vertical axis.)

(b) Pamina has been discussing her selling prices with a musical friend, who remarked that she should be able to sell a set of pan-pipes for the same price as a flute, i.e. £120 per set. Show how this new selling price would affect the optimal production quantities calculated in (a), and calculate the improvement in profit that would result.

(c) Discuss the limitations of the method of solution that you have used in parts (a) and (b).

11.5 Cumberland Manufacturing Ltd produces four products. Details of the sales price, material costs and labour requirements for each of the four products are provided below:

	Product			
	1	2	3	4
Sales price per unit (£)	65	27	60	46
Material cost per unit (£)	14	10	10	18
Labour hours per unit:				
Grade A	3	–	2	–
Grade B	–	2	–	4
Grade C	6	–	9	–

Each labour hour costs £4. The supply of all three categories of labour is restricted, and they are not interchangeable. The total number of hours available per month is as follows:

Grade A   6,000 hours
Grade B   10,000 hours
Grade C   18,000 hours

The company expects to be able to sell all units produced.

(a) Calculate the production plan which will maximise contribution for the month, and calculate the amount of contribution under this plan.

(b) Calculate the effect upon your answer to part (a) of the availability of an additional 900 hours of each grade of labour (consider the effect of additional hours of each grade separately).

(c) Discuss briefly any factors which you think might restrict the confidence of managers in the optimal plan calculated in answer to part (a).

Notes

1. Those interested in a further examination of the methods available for solving more complex problems might refer to W. J. Baumol, *Economic Theory and Operations Analysis*, 4th edn, chapter 5, Prentice Hall, 1977, for the simplex method, or B. V. Carsberg, *Introduction to Mathematical Programming for Accountants*, chapters 4 and 5, Allen and Unwin, 1969, for an alternative description of the method, based on repeated substitution.
2. The simultaneous equations may be solved by multiplying through the first equation by 1.5 and subtracting from the answer the second equation. So:

$$22.5x_1 + 12x_2 = 45,000$$
$$10x_1 + 12x_2 = 33,000$$
$$\overline{12.5x_1 + 0 = 12,000} \qquad \text{so } x_1 = 960$$

Substituting this value for x_1 into the original first equation gives:

$$15(960) + 8x_2 = 30,000 \qquad \text{so } x_2 = 1,950$$

3. A detailed study of mathematical approaches is outside the scope of this text. For a good introduction to integer programming see Baumol, op. cit., chapter 8.
4. A good introduction to non-linear programming can be found in Baumol, op. cit., chapter 7.
5. If the requirement is merely that the labour should be employed for a minimum of 18,000 hours (not necessarily on productive work), the original constraint limiting the maximum number of labour hours becomes

$$15x_1 + 8x_2 \leq L$$

and the following additional constraints are included:

$$L \leq 30,000$$
$$L \geq 18,000 \text{ (or } -L \leq -18,000)$$

In addition, it will be necessary to amend the objective function to recognise the fact that the first 18,000 hours of labour employed is now a fixed cost.

6. See, for example, J. Johnston, *Statistical Cost Analysis*, McGraw-Hill, 1960, particularly chapters 4 and 5.
7. For examples of some applications, see P. G. Moore and S. D. Hodges (eds), *Programming for Optimal Decisions*, Part 2, Penguin, 1970.

Dual prices and opportunity costs

AIMS AND OBJECTIVES

☐ To explain the concept of internal opportunity cost when one or more than one resource is scarce.

☐ To illustrate the calculation of internal opportunity cost using dual prices with one scarce resource and with two or more scarce resources.

☐ To discuss the meaning, limitations and applications of dual prices.

In the previous chapter we considered means of determining an optimal production plan where one or more of a firm's resources is scarce. In this chapter we consider ways of measuring the opportunity costs of scarce resources, and the limitations and applications of such measures. To enable the reader to relate the arguments back to the analysis in the previous chapter, we continue to use the examples from that chapter: namely, Prenton plc, to demonstrate the single scarce resource problem, and Carrow plc, to demonstrate the multiple scarce resource problem.

The most important message of this chapter is that the opportunity cost (the relevant cost for decisions) of using a scarce resource may be greater than the incremental cash flow directly associated with its purchase. Use of a scarce resource involves not only the cost of buying it, but also the possibility that, because supply of the resource is limited, its use on one project may mean that another project cannot be undertaken even though it might have produced a contribution towards fixed costs and profit. It is this contribution forgone which provides the basis for measuring the *internal opportunity cost* of using a scarce resource.

12.1 Internal opportunity cost with one scarce resource

In order to illustrate the concept of internal opportunity cost with one scarce resource, we return to the example of Prenton plc, introduced on p. 220. The relevant information relating to the company's production problem is reproduced in Table 12.1.

The figures in Table 12.1 show that the last product accepted into the optimal plan was Q, which has a contribution per labour hour of £7.5. It will not pay Prenton plc to substitute any other new product (say T, U or V) for Q unless it yields a contribution per labour hour of at least £7.5 (over and above the cash cost of one labour hour). This amount is the marginal return per labour hour within the framework of the optimal plan, and may be described as the *internal opportunity cost* of one labour hour. It is the reduction in contribution that will result from removing one labour hour from production of Q, and therefore a cost that must be taken into account when evaluating any alternative use of that labour hour.

Internal opportunity cost requires some clarification. Consider the value to Prenton plc of one labour hour. If Prenton plc were deprived of one labour hour, production of Q (the marginal product) would have to be reduced by 1/26 of a unit, as it takes 26 labour hours to produce one unit of Q. We assume that it is possible to produce fractions of a product. The effect on total contribution of this loss of one labour hour would be:

		£
Fall in total sales revenue [1/26 × £750]		28.85
Less Saving on materials not used in producing		
one unit of Q [1/26 × £295]	11.35	
Saving of one labour hour	10.00	21.35
Internal opportunity cost or fall in total		
contribution		7.50

An identical answer (of £7.50) would be obtained if we considered the additional contribution that would result from an extra labour hour.

Table 12.1 Prenton plc: product data

	P		Q		R		S
Selling price (£)		1,150		750		800	650
Less Labour (£10 per hour)	700		260		240		140
Materials (£5 per kg)	100	800	295	555	260	500	370	510
Contribution per unit (£)		350		195		300	140
Labour required per unit (hours)		70		26		24	14
Maximum expected demand							
(units)		1,000		800		600	1,100
Contribution per labour hour (£)		5		7.5		12.5	10
Ranking		4		3		1	2
Units produced		0		450		600	1,100
Labour hours required (total							
available is 41,500)		0		11,700		14,400	15,400

Thus we can say that the *total opportunity cost* of one (scarce) labour hour, which determines its contribution to the optimal plan, is made up of two elements:

	£
Cash cost per labour hour (given)	10.00
Imputed internal opportunity cost (derived)	7.50
Total opportunity cost	17.50

This leads to an important decision rule in situations of scarce resources: a firm should accept new products into its production plan only if they yield positive contributions when the scarce resources they use are included at their total opportunity costs. The inclusion of scarce resources at these costs should ensure that they are always used efficiently.

The use of internal opportunity costs is often required in decisions involving the choice between buying in a component from an outside supplier or producing it within the firm: that is, *make or buy decisions*. If there is spare productive capacity, the choice is simple: it is worth buying a component only if the additional cash flows incurred in production are greater in total than the buying-in price, as we saw in the example in Chapter 10 (p. 211). If, however, the firm has no spare productive capacity, then other work must be displaced if the components are to be manufactured internally. In this case the comparison should be between the buying-in price and the additional cash flows from production plus the contribution lost because of the work displaced (the internal opportunity cost). The following example provides a further illustration of a typical make or buy decision, to demonstrate the need to take into account internal opportunity cost.

Bootham plc's accountant has estimated the cost per unit of making a component as:

	£
Direct material	50
Direct labour (4 hours)	25
Variable overhead	10
Fixed overhead	30
Total cost	115

The same component can be bought for £90. Should Bootham plc make or buy the component assuming:

- there is spare capacity;

- there is no spare capacity?

The additional cash flows entailed in making the product are material + labour + variable overhead = £85, which is less than the buying-in price of £90. If there is spare capacity, the decision should be to make the component. Note that fixed overhead is omitted from the calculation of the price of manufacture, as it is not an additional cost.

If there is no spare capacity, then it will be necessary to determine the contribution which could otherwise be earned per hour of production, as this will be forgone in order to make the component and is thus a relevant cost of the decision. For example, assume Bootham plc's normal production is taken up with a product for which the following unit details are relevant:

		£
Selling price		50
Less Direct materials	12.50	
Labour (2 hours)	12.50	
Variable overhead	5.00	30
Contribution		20

Of the resources required for production, labour is in short supply. As it requires two labour hours to produce the normal product, then for every scarce labour hour used in making the component Bootham plc forgoes a contribution of £20/2 = £10 from normal production. In other words, labour is at present earning for the firm a contribution of £10 for every hour worked. The company must ensure that labour earns at least this amount if it is taken off normal production to work on the new component. Thus the full opportunity cost of labour is not represented by its cash cost. Because labour is in short supply, the real cost is the cash cost plus the internal opportunity cost, and any new production should be charged this total opportunity cost to ensure that labour is allocated efficiently. The total opportunity cost of manufacturing one component for Bootham plc now becomes:

		£
Direct material		50
Variable overhead		10
Labour:		
Cash cost (4 hours × £6.25)	25	
Internal opportunity cost		
(4 hours × £10)	40	65
Total opportunity cost		125

When the internal opportunity cost for labour, represented by the contribution lost from displaced production (assumed to be its best alternative use within the firm), is brought into account, the decision is to buy the component, as the buying-in cost of £90 is lower than the total opportunity cost of manufacture of £125.

We should not leave the make or buy problem without mentioning some of the more obvious qualitative factors which may influence the decision. Suppose

Bootham plc has no spare capacity and hence decides to buy rather than to make. One factor the company should consider is whether the future supply of the component is likely to be reliable. Unforeseen delivery problems could lead to production difficulties if the bought-in component is to be used within the firm, or to loss of custom if it is to be sold. In either case, the company is likely to suffer a loss of contribution. Another factor is whether the quality of the bought-in component will always be satisfactory and, if it is not, whether Bootham plc will be able to exert pressure on the supplier to improve the quality. Inferior quality may lead to high wastage rates if the component is used on internal production, or to customer dissatisfaction and consequent loss of future business if it is sold externally.

A third factor relates to the stability of the bought-in component's price. At current prices, buying seems a better alternative than making. But if the buying-in price increases more rapidly in the future than internal manufacturing costs, then the position may change. A similar argument may be made in respect of labour capacity. Although there is no current spare capacity, this situation may not persist. If spare labour capacity is expected in the near future, it may be better for the company to make the component and suffer a short-term cost in terms of lost contribution, in return for the gains which would be expected in the longer term from making rather than buying when there is spare labour capacity.

12.2 Internal opportunity cost with two or more scarce resources

In the previous chapter we considered means of determining an optimal production plan where two or more of a firm's resources are scarce. In section 12.1 it was demonstrated that, in the case of a single scarce resource, the internal opportunity cost of one unit of that resource is given either by the extra return which could be secured if one extra unit were available or by the decline in contribution that the firm would suffer if it were deprived of one unit of the resource. We now turn to the problem of determining internal opportunity costs of resources where more than one is scarce.

Within the linear programming framework (see Chapter 11) there is a way of determining the marginal contribution of each scarce resource towards fixed costs and profit. This marginal return is known normally as the *dual price* or *shadow price* of the particular resource. Given the type of formulation used in the previous chapter, the dual price of a resource measures by how much total contribution will fall if the available amount of that resource falls by one (small) unit. If the linear programme is solved on a computer, the dual price is normally readily available. Its calculation is part of the method usually used on computers for solving linear programming problems. However, we shall continue with the graphical method of solution to illustrate the principles involved in calculating dual prices, and the economic meaning which may be ascribed to them.

Let us continue with the case of Carrow plc, whose linear programming problem was formulated as follows:

$$\text{Max } C = 5x_1 + 4x_2 \qquad \text{(objective function)}$$

s.t.
$$15x_1 + 8x_2 \leqslant 30,000 \quad \text{(labour constraint)}$$
$$2x_1 + 4x_2 \leqslant 12,000 \quad \text{(storage space constraint)}$$
$$10x_1 + 12x_2 \leqslant 33,000 \quad \text{(justin constraint)}$$
$$x_1, \quad x_2 \geqslant 0 \quad \text{(non-negativity constraints)}$$

We shall consider the effect on total contribution of reducing the availability of each of the three scarce input resources in turn. The total contribution from the original optimal plan was £12,600 (p. 227). In the first instance we shall consider the effect of reducing the availability of each resource by 1,000 units to avoid the infinitesimal figures that would result from a reduction of only one unit. To find the reduction that would be caused by a reduction of a single unit we may, in this case, divide the calculated loss in total contribution by one thousand. This method would not be valid if such a substantial reduction in resource availability were to lead to a change in the marginal product combination or in those resources representing an effective constraint on production (in the case of Carrow plc, labour hours and units of special component justin), but the principles illustrated may be applied to smaller changes. The original constraint lines are shown on the graph in Figure 12.1. The dotted lines represent the boundaries that would be operative if the available amounts of each resource were to be reduced by 1,000 units.

Labour hours

Suppose that Carrow plc expects to have available only 29,000 labour hours in the coming year. The expected availability of the other two scarce resources is unchanged. The boundary line of the feasible region represented by the labour constraint will move downwards and to the left. It is apparent from the graph in Figure 12.1 that the new optimal production plan is represented by point I', where the revised labour constraint line and the original justin constraint intersect. To determine the production plan represented by this point we solve the following simultaneous equations:

$$15x_1 + 8x_2 = 29,000$$
$$10x_1 + 12x_2 = 33,000$$

This gives values of 840 for x_1 and 2,050 for x_2. The production plan is summarised in Table 12.2, which also shows that the new plan produces a total contribution of £200 less than the original. Correspondingly, a reduction of one hour in the amount of labour time available would lead to a fall in the value of the optimal plan of £0.2.

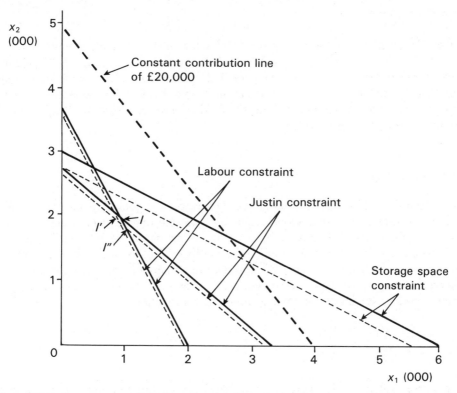

Figure 12.1 Carrow plc: original and revised constraint lines.

Table 12.2 Carrow plc: production plan revised for reduction in available labour

	Quantity	Contribution per unit (£)	Total contribution (£)
Widgets	840	5	4,200
Didgets	2,050	4	8,200
Revised total contribution			12,400
Original total contribution			12,600
Decrease due to a reduction of 1,000 in available labour hours			200
Decrease caused by a reduction of one in available labour hours			£ $\dfrac{200}{1,000}$ = £0.2

Storage space

It can be seen from Figure 12.1 that a reduction in the available storage space of 1,000 ft^2, the other two constraints remaining at their original levels, would not affect the optimality of the original plan. The optimal point would be I on the graph in Figure 12.1 and the total contribution would be £12,600. It follows that a reduction of one square foot in the available storage space would also lead to no fall in the value of the optimal plan.

Special component justin

A reduction of 1,000 units in the number of justin components available, amounts of labour time and storage space originally available remaining unchanged, would lead to an optimal plan represented by point I'', as may be seen from Figure 12.1. The boundary line of the feasible region described by the justin constraint moves downwards and to the left. The new optimum lies where the revised justin constraint intersects the original labour hours constraint. The relevant values of x_1 and x_2 are determined by solving the following simultaneous equations:

$$15x_1 + 8x_2 = 30,000$$
$$10x_1 + 12x_2 = 32,000$$

This gives values of 1,040 for x_1 and 1,800 for x_2, implying the production plan shown in Table 12.3. This plan yields a contribution £200 less than the original one. Correspondingly, a fall of one unit in the availability of justin would lead to a decrease of £0.2 in total contribution.

Table 12.3 Carrow plc: production plan revised for reduction in available justin

	Quantity	Contribution per unit (£)	Total contribution (£)
Widgets	1,040	5	5,200
Didgets	1,800	4	7,200
Revised total contribution			12,400
Original total contribution			12,600
Decrease due to a reduction of 1,000 in available units of justin			200
Decrease caused by a reduction of one in available units of justin		£ $\dfrac{200}{1,000} = £0.2$	

Table 12.4 Carrow plc: dual prices of resources

Resource	Fall in total contribution if amount available decreases by one unit (dual price) (£)
Labour time	0.2
Storage space	0.0
Special component justin	0.2

The reductions in total contribution caused by falls of one unit in the available supplies of the three scarce resources are summarised in Table 12.4. The figures measure the marginal return yielded by a single unit of each resource within the framework of the optimal plan. Their use as measures of the internal opportunity cost of the resources is discussed in the next section.

12.3 Interpretation of dual prices

It is worthwhile to note first the equivalence of the dual price of a scarce resource and its marginal return (when it is the only scarce resource), as discussed in section 12.1. The latter is no more than a special case of a dual price and could equally well have been determined by solving the single scarce resource problem as a linear programme. Both measure the amount by which total contribution would fall if the firm were deprived of one unit of the scarce resource. Provided the scarce resource remains an effective constraint on production, both also measure the amount by which total contribution would rise if an additional unit of the resource were available. As we noted earlier, when we discussed the opportunity cost of using a single scarce resource, the total opportunity cost of using a marginal unit of a resource is the sum of its external price and its internal opportunity cost. The latter is given by its dual price.

Two further observations on dual prices may be of interest. We have seen that costs that are fixed regardless of the decision to be taken have no relevant external cost. However, if these costs represent a scarce resource, there may be a relevant cost attached to that resource: the total opportunity cost of using one unit will equal its dual price.

In the problem of Carrow plc, the dual price of storage space was zero (Table 12.4). The same is true of any resource that does not represent an effective constraint on production, even if the available supply of the resource is expected to be limited.[1] Neither a marginal increase nor a marginal decrease in the available amount of the resource will lead to any change in the optimal plan. The cost of using such a resource is its relevant external cost, which reflects the only sacrifice involved in utilising it.

12.4 Limitations of dual prices

As dual prices are the products of a linear programming framework, they suffer the same limitations and are based on the same assumptions as are relevant to linear programming (see pp. 228–30). Within these limits, they are useful indicators of the internal opportunity cost of using scarce resources.

However, there is a further reason for caution when dual prices are being used. They measure contribution changes resulting from marginal increases or decreases in resource availability. A large increase in the availability of a particular resource may mean that it is no longer an effective constraint on production and its dual price becomes zero. Consider the case of Carrow plc finding a supplier which is willing to provide up to an extra 11,000 units of the special component justin. The company has to decide how much over and above the market price previously charged it would be willing to pay for extra units. It might be argued that, as the dual price of a resource measures the maximum amount a firm would be willing to pay, over and above the external opportunity cost, to obtain one further unit of that resource, then Carrow plc should be willing to pay a premium of up to 20p (the dual price) for each of the extra 11,000 units of justin.

If we recalculate the optimal plan, reflecting the increased availability of justin but ignoring, at present, the surcharge that will be paid on all units used over 33,000, then the increase in total contribution will measure the maximum amount, over and

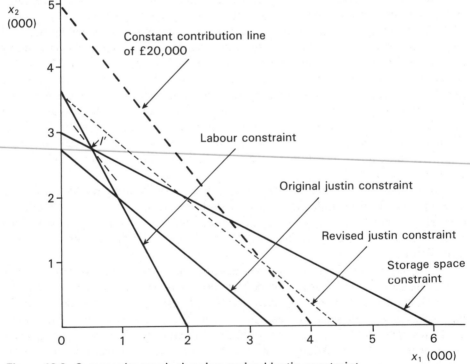

Figure 12.2 Carrow plc: graph showing revised justin constraint.

Table 12.5 Carrow plc: production plan revised for increase in available justin

	Quantity	Contribution per unit (£)	Total contribution (£)
Widgets	545.5	5	2,728
Didgets	2,727.3	4	10,909
Revised total contribution			13,637
Original total contribution			12,600
Increase in total contribution			1,037

above the present market price, that Carrow plc should be willing to pay for however many extra units of the special component are required. The revised justin constraint boundary is shown as a dotted line in Figure 12.2, and it is clear from the graph that justin is no longer an effective constraint. The optimal point is now I' where the labour time and storage space constraints intersect. The relevant values of x_1 and x_2 are found by solving the following simultaneous equations:

$$15x_1 + 8x_2 = 30,000$$

$$2x_1 + 4x_2 = 12,000$$

This gives values correct to one decimal place of 545.5 for x_1 and 2,727.3 for x_2, implying the revised production plan shown in Table 12.5.

The extra contribution under the new plan is £1,037, and the plan requires an extra 5,183 units of justin.[2] The extra 5,183 units required increase total contribution by £1,037, an average of £0.2 per unit. The extra contribution obtainable from each unit of justin up to the amount required under the new plan remains equal to the dual price of 20p. But any units obtainable above this level do not increase total contribution at all, since justin is no longer an effective constraint. Consequently it assumes a dual price of zero.

Dual prices alone are of little help in tackling problems like this, where the change in resource availability is not marginal. The example suggests that we need to re-solve the problem incorporating the revised constraint(s) and compare the new optimal solution with the original plan.

12.5 Applications of dual prices

Provided the limitations mentioned in the previous section are borne in mind, dual prices, discriminately applied, have a number of uses. First, they provide an indication of which constraints are the most severe. In the original example of Carrow plc, whose dual prices are given in Table 12.4, it does not seem worthwhile endeavouring to find new storage space. The zero dual price attached to this resource indicates that it is not an effective constraint on production. The company might usefully seek ways of relieving each of the other constraints, for a relaxation of either of them will lead to an increase in total contribution. It may be misleading to argue that, since the special component justin and labour time both have the same dual price, it is, in some sense, equally worthwhile to relieve either of them. The units chosen for measuring the constraint will affect the size of the dual price. For example, had we chosen labour weeks of 35 hours each instead of labour hours as the measure of labour time, the dual price would have been 35 times higher, i.e. £7, considerably greater than the justin dual price. The dual price per unit of the resource will be a good indicator of where effort should be directed to relieve constraints only if the expected cost per unit of relaxation is the same for each resource constraint.

A second application of dual prices may arise when new opportunities, not in the original plan, are presented for consideration. Dual prices reflect the best marginal use of resources within the framework of the optimal plan, and, to be acceptable, a new opportunity should use the resources at least as profitably as this marginal use; in a situation of scarce resources the new opportunity, if accepted, will displace one or more of the opportunities included in the optimal plan. The new opportunity is a worthwhile substitute if it yields a surplus when the resources it requires are valued at total opportunity cost, including the dual price values of any scarce resources needed. However, dual prices alone will not reveal precisely how the production levels of opportunities within the optimal plan should be adjusted: to determine this the firm must adopt some approximate method or re-formulate and re-solve the linear programme. The dual prices act merely as a screening device for new opportunities, a useful function as it avoids the firm having to re-run the linear programme for every new opportunity that emerges.

A third use arises when all decisions are not taken by a central decision-making body with access to the linear programme. Decentralised decision making may be in evidence particularly in divisionalised firms where each division enjoys a certain amount of decision-taking autonomy. To reduce the chance that resources are used suboptimally, they should be charged to those responsible for decisions at their total opportunity cost. As this includes the dual price value of scarce resources, only projects at least as efficient as those included in the optimal plan should be accepted. Problems facing divisionalised firms are discussed in Chapter 18.

CHAPTER SUMMARY

In earlier chapters we have established certain principles for the recognition of relevant costs when evaluating particular decisions. These include the need to recognise all incremental flows that result either directly or indirectly as a consequence of the decision. When an organisation's ability to accept opportunities is constrained by the existence of scarce resources, new products should be evaluated by costing the use of each resource at its total opportunity cost, which comprises the cost of acquiring the resource plus the contribution forgone by not using that resource on the best available alternative (the internal opportunity cost). Valuing scarce resources on the basis of total opportunity cost will generally ensure they are allocated in the most efficient manner.

When more than one resource is scarce, the internal opportunity costs are measured by the dual prices which are produced as part of a linear programming solution. Dual prices measure the marginal return associated with each resource. The information provided by dual prices may help management in identifying which constraints are having the most severe effect on contribution earned, in screening new opportunities to identify whether or not they should be incorporated in production plans, and in pricing the use of resources in decentralised organisations. However, dual prices are based on marginal changes in resource availability and will not give an accurate guide when major changes in the availability of a scarce resource are being considered.

REVIEW QUESTIONS

1. Discuss the importance of internal opportunity cost in the context of managerial decision making.

2. Suppose that management has decided to make a product internally rather than buy it on the open market, which appears to be the cheaper option. Discuss some possible reasons for this apparently irrational choice.

3. Explain what you understand by the dual (or shadow) price of a resource. What role does it play in determining the opportunity cost of using the resource?

4. Discuss the usefulness of dual prices in managerial decision making and explain their limitations. Illustrate your answer by reference to particular decisions.

5. List the major places so far in this book where the linearity assumption has been discussed. What conclusions do you draw about the importance of the linearity assumption?

EXERCISES

12.1 Zemlinsky plc, a manufacturer of scientific instruments, has been working on the manufacture of blue noise detectors under a contract with the government of Utopia. The government has just cancelled the contract and paid compensation of £50,000. The company has now 1,000 partly completed detectors on hand. It sees two alternative courses of action: (a) completion of the detectors and their sale to the Ruritanian government for £200 each, or (b) sale of the detectors for scrap in their present state for £20 each. You are given the following additional information:

  1. Zemlinsky has spent £60,000 on the scientific development of the detectors; the resulting plans and specifications could be sold for £35,000 if and only if the detectors were sold for scrap.

2. 1,000 lb of material X has been purchased for production of the detectors at a cost of £30 per lb: 300 lb has already been used in production. The remaining 700 lb is in stock and could not be used in its existing state on other work in the company. It could be sold for £25 per lb; alternatively it could be put through a special process at a cost of £5 per lb and used as a substitute for material A, which has a current price of £32 per lb. Material A is in common use by Zemlinsky.

3. 5,000 lb of material Y has been purchased for production of the detectors at a cost of £10 per lb. 3,000 lb has already been used and 2,000 lb is in stock. Each finished detector requires 10 lb of Y. If the detectors are scrapped, the material in stock will have to be sold as there is no alternative use for it in the company. The current buying price of Y is £12 per lb, but it could be sold for only £6 per lb and Zemlinsky would have to pay removal costs of £8 per lb in the event of sale.

4. Each detector requires 7.5 hours of grade A labour. Zemlinsky has increased its labour force to provide the required time. 2,500 hours (out of the required total of 7,500 hours) have already been used. Grade A labour is paid £6 per hour. If the manufacture of detectors is discontinued, the labour will be used on less skilled work and save the employment of additional persons at a wage of £5 per hour (dismissal of the employees would be contrary to company policy).

5. Each detector requires 10 hours of grade B labour, which has a current wage rate of £7 per hour and which is in short supply. Each hour spent on the detectors would make it necessary to give up other work earning a surplus of £1 after charging all costs including wages. No grade B labour has yet been used.

6. Under the company's costing system, all jobs are assigned an additional cost, equal to 75% of direct labour cost, to cover overheads. The manufacture of the detectors has not and will not cause any actual increase in overhead costs.

Prepare calculations showing which course of action is preferable. Describe the ingredients of your calculations clearly. Mention *two* factors which might influence the decision, but which are not reflected in your calculations. (Solution at end of text.)

12.2 Susanna is in charge of a small chemical plant which uses two surplus by-products (code-named A10 and B11) transported by pipeline from a large refinery. The daily supply of the two by-products is limited to 25 tonnes of A10 and 37.5 tonnes of B11, any surplus being collected by a local dealer. The dealer pays Susanna £90 per tonne for A10 and £70 per tonne for B11. The plant managed by Susanna converts the by-products into two new chemicals sold under the names of siroe and ezio. Both chemicals are in great demand and Susanna can sell as much as she produces. Given below are details of the two chemicals:

	Siroe	Ezio
Tonnes of A10 required for 1 tonne	1	3
Tonnes of B11 required for 1 tonne	3	1.5
Plant hours required for 1 tonne	1	1
Selling price of 1 tonne (£)	540	660

The plant is currently operated for 13 hours per day and the production costs for siroe and ezio are both £80 per hour. The plant has to be kept operational for the remaining 11 hours of each day at a cost of £20 per hour. The net costs of disposing of the waste products from the production process are included in the £80 per hour production cost figures.

(a) Calculate how many tonnes of siroe and ezio Susanna should produce in order to maximise the profits of the plant. Calculate the contribution that will result if your suggestion is followed.

(b) Calculate the dual prices of the resources used.

(c) Discuss the likely practical usefulness of the calculations undertaken in parts (a) and (b). (Solution at end of text.)

12.3 Macke Ltd manufactures a high-fidelity amplifier, one of the components of which is loudspeaker B717. A specialist loudspeaker manufacturer has quoted £30 each for the supply of the 5,000 B717s which will be required during the forthcoming year. You have been asked to advise the board whether to accept the quotation or continue to manufacture, and have ascertained the following facts:

1. The costs of producing the 4,000 B717s used last year were:

	£
Direct material	104,000
Direct wages	28,000
Plant depreciation	4,800
Plant insurance	4,400
Plant maintenance contract	5,200
General fixed overhead apportioned to this production	20,000

2. The following unit cost increases are anticipated for the forthcoming year if the company continues to manufacture B717s:

Direct material   £1.20
Direct wages   40p

3. If it is decided to discontinue the production of B717s, then the plant currently used will be sold.

4. If the B717s are purchased, the following costs will be incurred in addition to the basic price charged by the supplier:

Inspection and storage   £8,000 p.a.
Carriage and insurance   £2 each

(a) Prepare a statement to enable you to advise the board whether to continue manufacturing B717s or to buy them.

(b) Prepare a summary of any other matters that the board should consider in arriving at its decision.

12.4   Vivaldi plc is considering its production plan for 19X8. At present it manufactures and sells four products, A, B, C and D. Some of the company's resources are expected to be in short supply during 19X8, and the directors are considering ceasing production of one or more of the existing products in order to make the most efficient use of available resources. The company accountant has produced the following statement to help the directors make a decision:

	A (£)	B (£)	C (£)	D (£)
Variable costs per unit:				
Materials: XK7 (units)	(3)6.00	(4)8.00	(1)2.00	(5)10.00
Others	41.00	65.00	38.00	21.00
Labour: Skilled (hours)	(2)30.00	(1)15.00	(3)45.00	(2)30.00
Unskilled (hours)	(2)20.00	(6)60.00	(1)10.00	(3)30.00
Variable overheads	42.00	54.00	26.00	63.00
	139.00	202.00	121.00	154.00
Selling price per unit	200.00	250.00	160.00	220.00
Contribution per unit	61.00	48.00	39.00	66.00
Fixed costs (40% of variable costs)	55.60	80.80	48.40	61.60
Profit/(loss) per unit	5.40	(32.80)	(9.40)	4.40

Total fixed costs are not expected to be affected in 19X8 by any decision regarding particular products. However, the company accountant argues that, as all products are expected to yield positive contributions, some other method must be used to eliminate one or more of them. The accountant suggests that the most profitable products are those that recover a fair share of fixed costs. Consequently, fixed costs have been allocated to each product at a rate of 40% on total variable costs. This percentage is based on the company's accounts for 19X6, which showed total variable costs of £2,000,000 and total fixed costs of £800,000. The accountant recommends that products B and C should not be produced in 19X8 as they do not recover a fair share of fixed costs; only products A and D should be manufactured.

The directors are uneasy about discontinuing both B and C in 19X8 and seek advice from a firm of consultants. The consultants recommend the use of linear programming to solve the problem, and duly formulate the programme taking account of scarce resources expected and including as the objective function the maximisation of total contribution, using the unit contribution figures from the accountant's statement.

The solution to the linear programme reveals the following dual prices for 19X8:

Material XK7	£5 per unit
Skilled labour	£8 per hour
Factory space	£10 per yd^2 per annum

Usage of factory space during 19X8 is expected to be:

Product A	3 yd^2 per annum per unit
Product B	2 yd^2 per annum per unit
Product C	1 yd^2 per annum per unit
Product D	4 yd^2 per annum per unit

The dual prices of all resources other than the three mentioned above are zero.

(a) On the basis of the information given, which products should Vivaldi plc plan to produce in 19X8? (Note: You are *not* required to calculate production quantities.) Give your reasons.

(b) Explain the economic significance of dual prices and discuss the limitations to their usefulness.

12.5   Liza Beck runs a small but successful pottery business. She has only two products, an ornate bowl and a classically proportioned jug. At the present moment she is producing 10 bowls and 15 jugs each week. One of the reasons that her production is limited is that she does not want to spend more than 7.5 hours per day making pottery in a five-day working week; each bowl and each jug requires 1.5 hours of her time. There is also a limited amount of kiln space available to fire the pottery. A bowl takes up 1.5 times as much space as a jug, and the total capacity of the oven is equal to 30 jugs or 20 bowls. Liza uses a special clay in order to give her pottery its distinctive feel. This clay is in much demand and Liza is only able to obtain a maximum of 84 lb per week. A jug requires 3.5 lb of the clay, whereas a bowl requires 2.4 lb. At the present, Liza sells her bowls for £11.80 each and her jugs at £16 each. The clay costs equal £2 for each bowl and £3 for each jug. Her weekly fixed costs total £25.

(a) Calculate the number of bowls and jugs that Liza should manufacture and calculate the improvement in her profit. (If you use a graph as part of your solution, plot the number of *jugs* on the *vertical* axis.)

(b) Explain what is meant by the term 'dual price' (or shadow price) and indicate which of the three constraints in your solution has a zero dual price.

Notes

1. Strictly, the supply of all of a firm's resources will be limited in an absolute sense by the amount of the resource available in the world. For practical purposes, however, a resource need only be regarded as scarce if its supply is limited within the range of any production plan a firm is likely to adopt.
2. Each widget requires 10 units of justin and each didget 12 units. Under the new production plan shown in Table 12.5, a total of 38,183 units of justin are required ($10[545.5] + 12[2,727.3]$). The previous plan required the maximum then available of 33,000 units, and hence an additional 5,183 units are needed.

Long-term decisions: the net present value rule

In previous chapters we have discussed the analysis of costs and benefits for particular short-term decisions. These decisions will, of necessity, entail the use of such assets as factories and plant and equipment, the purchase of which, at some earlier date, constituted a decision by the firm to commit resources for a long time period. Thus the ability of the firm to operate at different levels of activity is determined largely by the nature of the long-term (or fixed or capital) assets at its disposal. Decisions on the acquisition (and disposal) of long-term assets provide the operational context within which short-term activities can be undertaken and adjusted. For example, a firm cannot produce beyond a certain level unless it invests further funds in productive equipment; it may not be able to exploit new market opportunities if it fails to invest in new technology; it may fail to take advantage of prospective customers in the USA unless it contemplates the purchase of an American company.

The process of assessing the desirability of long-term investments is known as *capital budgeting*. This area of management decision making is important because it generally involves the commitment of significant organisational resources for a long period of time, in ways that it may be difficult to adjust and with consequent risks – for example, of being overtaken by technological advances. Long-term investments constitute the basis for the firm's future success, and must be evaluated in a way consistent with the firm's objectives. In this chapter and the next, we look at different methods available to evaluate long-term investments.

Throughout this book we have assumed that the firm's main objective is to maximise the (present value of) cash flows from its operations. This chapter is devoted to the technique of capital investment appraisal which is most consistent with this objective – net present value. We describe the principles involved in net present value, the mechanics of the quantitative analysis, and how additional factors such as the sensitivity of the analysis to particular estimates, limits on the amount of capital available and the effects of inflation can be taken into consideration. The next chapter looks at a number of alternative methods and also at evidence on how capital budgeting is undertaken by managers in practice.

13.1 The investment decision process

Firms often express their long-term strategic aims in a variety of different ways. For example, media and publishing group Pearson plc devoted the front cover of its 1993 annual report and accounts to a strategy statement: 'Our strategy is to be a major international provider of media content, renowned for distinctive products that deliver information, education and entertainment in ways that people want them.' ICI has a similar statement on page 1 of its annual report for 1994: 'Our objective is to maximise value for our shareholders by focusing on businesses where we have a market leadership, a technological edge and a world competitive cost base. We will promote a culture of continuous improvement in everything we do.' Comparing these two statements, the ICI strategy gives more information about the methods by which the company intends to pursue its objective. Indeed the notes following this statement give more detail still on strategic direction, referring to priorities such as 'providing unrivalled, international service to its customers', 'increasing the Group's presence in the fast growing markets of Asia Pacific' and 'investing in research and technology'. Someone reading the ICI financial statements might find it difficult to judge the extent to which unrivalled service is given but should be able to get some information on whether Asian Pacific activity is growing and how far the commitment to research is matched by expenditure.

Whether disclosed externally or not, firms must find ways of converting their broad statements of strategy and objectives into more specific and more operational aims. The commitments to particular objectives must be translated into operating activities. The modern, competitive firm is continually on the lookout for opportunities which are consistent with its strategy, and the stage of evaluating the financial costs and benefits of opportunities which meet strategic objectives may in fact be of a relatively low level of importance in the investment decision process. Consider Figure 13.1, which offers a possible sequence of five stages in that process.

Stage 1 — Search for investment opportunities consistent with strategy

Stage 2 — Screen projects for possible further investigation

Stage 3 — Define projects more clearly via initial estimates and feasible alternatives

Stage 4 — Evaluate alternatives

Stage 5 — Decide whether to accept or reject the alternatives

Figure 13.1 The investment decision process.

The diagram seeks to show that capital investment decision making is not an instantaneous process. Investments do not appear out of thin air. Thus at stage 1, ICI's search for opportunities consistent with its concern to grow in the Asia Pacific region has led to decisions involving 'enlarging a plant in Taiwan and building a new plant in Pakistan', taking 'a 2.5% share in the flotation of the Yizheng Chemical Fibre Company' and plans 'to build a new factory in Indonesia to help meet rising demand in Asia Pacific'. But how do we know if the investment opportunities in stage 1 should undergo rigorous evaluation techniques to determine their acceptability? Two intermediate steps are necessary. Before a major evaluation is undertaken, preliminary screening should try to iron out potential problems relating, *inter alia*, to the feasibility of the project, the level of risk involved and the availability of resources to carry out the project.

After the project has been filtered and deemed worthy of further investigation (i.e. it has passed stage 2), it is likely that a more detailed specification will be made. This will entail an analysis of the project's technical and financial characteristics, and will probably necessitate engineering expertise. The nature and sophistication of this analysis will, to a large extent, depend on the type of project. Thus, for example, new strategic proposals may have ill-defined technical characteristics, but may be thought necessary to keep the firm at the cutting edge of business (e.g.

investments in advanced manufacturing systems); projects which simply replace labour with capital (e.g. the installation of robotic equipment) may be capable of well-defined specifications; replacement projects, which seek to replace existing assets with similar ones, may also be easy to specify; welfare projects, such as the installation of air-conditioning to improve the immediate working environment, may be justified if they meet certain minimum cost requirements.

It is only after the investment has been found, screened and defined that the accountant's functional role becomes significant. It is at the evaluation stage that the accountant draws together the cash flow analysis relating to the costs and benefits of the project and seeks to determine its financial acceptability. Information relating to production, sales, purchasing and organisational costs, and the effects of external factors on these, will probably be compiled by the accountant in discussion with those in charge of the functional areas to which the project relates. Thus quantification of the additional sales revenue generated by the project will reflect the judgements of both the sales director and the management accountant; production costs and capacity use will be determined by the production director and the accountant, and so on. If the financial analysis suggests the project is worthwhile, the decision at stage 5 may well be acceptance of the investment.

13.2 The timing of cash flows

Having set out the five-stage process, we should stress here that the evaluation criteria for long-term investment decisions differ from those applicable to short-term decisions in only one important respect. When cash flows arise in different periods, it is necessary to incorporate into the analysis a means of taking account of the differences in their timing. The importance of the time value of money and the underlying rationale of the net present value (NPV) method were explained in Chapter 3. In essence, the difference between short- and long-term decisions is one of time; and the biggest technical problem in long-term decision making is how to deal with the time factor (including the impact of risk and uncertainty) in the analysis.

In other respects, the principles appropriate for both short- and long-term decisions are identical. Both are directed to the same overall goal (to maximise the present value of cash resources) and both use the differential future analysis principle for determining relevant cash flows (i.e. whatever the time period covered by the decision, only cash flows that change as a result of a decision are relevant to that decision).

Let us suppose that a firm is considering the possible purchase for £2 million of a new machine which is likely to enhance its operating capacity considerably. How should the firm decide whether purchase of the machine is worthwhile? The first thing to note is that, although the uncertain benefits from the machine will arise in the future, the decision must be made now. Future benefits are always uncertain, because the future is always uncertain. (See Chapter 4 for a discussion of the problems of risk and uncertainty in decision making.) The decision involves a trade-off between the uncertain future returns and the certain present cost of £2 million.

Management should use a method of analysis which deals with all costs and benefits of the decision in terms of the present, when the decision has to be taken. This complicates the analysis. Suppose management's best estimates of the quantifiable benefits (inflows less outflows) from the investment are £400,000 p.a. for ten years. Is purchase worthwhile? If we simply add up the ten annual money cash inflows, we can see readily that the total of £4 million is greater than the £2 million cost of the machine.

But such a simplistic approach completely ignores the point that future cash benefits are less attractive than present ones, because cash has a value dependent upon the time at which it arises. This time value arises from the existence of opportunities to lend and borrow at positive rates of interest. To incorporate the time value of money, we use a *discount factor*, based on the firm's relevant interest rate or *cost of capital*, to bring all future cash flows to the present decision date. How we might derive a cost of capital for the firm on which to base such a discount factor will be examined later in this chapter; for now we assume that the cost of capital is 10% p.a. How does this change the analysis? Will the purchase of the machine still be worthwhile? The annuity discount factor for ten years at 10% p.a. is 6.145;[1] thus the discounted present value of the yearly future cash flows is £400,000 × 6.145 = £2.458 million, which is greater than the investment cost of £2 million. Purchase of the machine is worthwhile. The machine has a positive NPV (the difference between the discounted future net cash inflows and the investment cost) of £458,000. Although purchase is worthwhile, the net benefit of £458,000 is considerably smaller than the gain of £2 million calculated from undiscounted cash flows.

Note that the application of the NPV method yields a *cash* figure, the maximisation of which is consistent with the organisation's assumed overall objective. In the absence of scarce resources, an organisation should accept all opportunities with positive net present values and reject those with negative net present values. We can summarise the NPV decision criterion as involving the following three basic steps:

1. Estimate the date and amount of the relevant future cash inflows and outflows (including the investment cost) arising from each decision alternative.

2. Discount these cash flows at an appropriate discount rate.

3. Decide whether the alternative(s) is acceptable, by use of the NPV rule.

We now turn to a consideration of each of these three basic steps.

13.3 Estimation of cash flows

Cash flows and accounting profits

All cash inflows and outflows which change because of the undertaking of a project are relevant to the project, and should be discounted to determine its present value. Strictly this means that not only should all relevant operating cash revenues and costs be included, but also any changes in taxation payments and investment grants which arise through undertaking the project.

It is very important to remember that all relevant cash flows should be included in a project assessment, on the date at which they arise, irrespective of the period to which they relate. For example, suppose that a firm buys an asset for £15,000 which will produce additional net cash inflows of £8,000 p.a. for three years. After three years the asset will be worthless. For purposes of external reporting, the firm uses straight-line depreciation for all its assets.[2] We might draw up yearly income statements for the asset as in Table 13.1, based on conventional accounting procedures for measuring income (we assume that all net cash inflows will be included in income in the year in which they are received).

The purpose of the depreciation charge in conventional accounting is to spread the cost of the asset, £15,000, over its estimated three-year life. It allocates the cost against the revenue to which it relates, in order to produce a yearly income figure. Other possible depreciation methods could involve different patterns of charges to the income statement, and hence different yearly income figures. If, for example, the firm uses the 'sum of the years' digits' method,[3] the yearly income statement shown in Table 13.2 would result for the same asset.

The point of these two examples is very simple. Irrespective of the accounting depreciation method used, and the accounting income reported, the estimated cash inflow arising from the asset will be £8,000 p.a., and the estimated cash outflow will be £15,000, the purchase price of the asset. These are the only cash flows associated with the machine, and the only amounts to be included in the NPV calculation for managerial decision purposes. The allocation of the investment cost of £15,000 may be necessary to measure accounting income for external reporting purposes: as we

Table 13.1 Income statements using straight-line depreciation

	Year 1 (£)	Year 2 (£)	Year 3 (£)
Net cash inflows	8,000	8,000	8,000
Less Depreciation $\frac{£15,000}{3}$	5,000	5,000	5,000
Net income	3,000	3,000	3,000

Table 13.2 Income statements using sum of the years' digits depreciation

	Year 1 (£)	Year 2 (£)	Year 3 (£)
Net cash inflows	8,000	8,000	8,000
Less Depreciation	7,500	5,000	2,500
Net income	500	3,000	5,500

explained in Chapter 5, it is not necessary, and indeed it may be misleading, to include a non-cash allocation such as depreciation in internal decision-making calculations. Managerial decision analysis makes no distinction between capital and income items. The purpose of managerial decision making is to maximise the present value of future cash flows, not allocated accounting profits.

The range of possible cash flows

Because many of the cash flows associated with long-term investment decisions arise far into the future, the prediction of their exact amount is often very difficult. The use of single-point estimates of future cash flows is unlikely to be an adequate means of describing their uncertainty. We might more usefully attempt to incorporate elementary probability theory into our analysis, so as to produce expected cash flows. The following example explains how we might do this. (Chapter 4 deals in some detail with expected values.)

Griffin plc is contemplating an investment project, the cash flows from which are uncertain. On the basis of management's expectations, a range of probable cash flows has been drawn up. This suggests that there is a 20% probability of a yearly net cash inflow of £7,000, a 50% probability of £8,000 p.a., and a 30% probability of £10,000 p.a. What is the expected yearly future cash flow for Griffin plc?

Possible cash flows p.a. (£)	Probability of occurrence
7,000	0.20
8,000	0.50
10,000	0.30
	1.00

The expected yearly cash inflow is the sum of each possible cash flow, multiplied by the probability of its occurrence. Thus, the expected cash flow is $7,000(0.20) + 8,000 (0.50) + 10,000(0.30) = £8,400$.

The percentage figures used to assess the probability of the cash flows may be based on past experience of similar projects. Alternatively, if no similar investment has been undertaken previously, as will inevitably be the case with investments at the leading edge of technology, the estimates will be 'best guesses' which incorporate all the available evidence on factors which determine cash flows: for example, the anticipated level of demand for the product being sold and the likely changes in the firm's levels of costs associated with the investment.

The impact of working capital

The decision to undertake a long-term investment will frequently involve necessary outlays on current assets (e.g. stocks and amounts owing by customers) and current liabilities (e.g. amounts owing to suppliers) in order to support the higher level of activity brought about by the new investment. For example, additional cash may be needed to fund the higher levels of raw materials, finished goods and amounts owing by customers resulting from new activity levels: in turn, some of the finance may be provided by suppliers. If these items of current assets and liabilities (which make up the additional *working capital* required) are needed for the entire life of the investment, then the working capital will not be released until the project is finished, and calculations of the acceptability of the investment must incorporate the cash flows associated with changes in working capital.

13.4 The cost of capital

Use of the NPV method entails the determination of an appropriate interest rate or discount rate to discount future cash flows to their equivalent present value. This discount rate is usually referred to as a *cost of capital*; this is a simple concept to understand, but notoriously hard to measure. Indeed there are many conflicting views on just how the cost of capital should be computed.

Our view is that the cost of capital should measure the minimum return required by providers of long-term funds. Most firms raise their long-term funds from two main sources, *equity capital* and *debt capital*. Equity capital represents the funds provided by the owners of the firm. Payments made to the owners of equity capital (called *dividends*) vary according to, among other things, how well the firm is doing. No dividends can be paid to equity holders until the firm has met its obligations to the providers of debt capital, although there is then no limit on the amounts which can be paid, subject to the firm having sufficient income and cash resources from which to make the payment. The equity capital itself is rarely repaid until the firm is liquidated.

The returns paid to debt holders (called *interest*), on the other hand, are usually fixed by contract, and must be paid regardless of the size of the firm's income or cash resources. Furthermore, much debt capital is *redeemable*: that is, a date (or dates) is specified by which the capital must be repaid. If no provision is made for repayment, the debt is termed *irredeemable*. Failure to pay interest or repay capital on the due dates often results in control of the firm being passed to the debt holders.

As debt capital and equity capital carry different levels of risk relating both to interest and dividend payments and to capital repayment, they often have different costs. In other words, the holders of debt capital generally require a lower return than do the holders of equity capital, because the interest paid to them and the repayment of their capital both take preference over payments to the owners of equity capital. Thus to calculate a cost of capital which incorporates both the cost of equity capital and the cost of debt capital, it is necessary first to calculate the individual costs of the different sources, and second to combine them into a weighted average cost of capital. We deal with each stage in turn.

Cost of equity capital

There are a variety of models available for calculating the cost of equity capital – the minimum return required by shareholders. We will discuss the two most widely advocated models, the dividend growth model and the capital asset pricing model (CAPM).

Dividend growth model

Under this model the cost of equity capital is derived from the basic valuation model which we first introduced in Chapter 3. This model defines the value of equity capital as the present value of the future dividend stream. It can be expressed as:

$$V_E = \frac{d_1}{(1 + K_E)} + \frac{d_2}{(1 + K_E)^2} + \frac{d_3}{(1 + K_E)^3} + \cdots + \frac{d_n}{(1 + K_E)^n}$$

where V_E is the present value of equity capital, *ex div* (i.e. just after a dividend has been paid); d_1 is the dividend to be paid after one year, d_2 is the dividend to be paid after two years, and so on; K_E is the cost of equity capital or the minimum annual return required by the providers of equity capital; and n is the last time at which a dividend will be paid. If the dividend stream is expected to be constant throughout all future periods, then, as n (the time period) approaches infinity, the valuation model may be simplified to a perpetuity, i.e.

$$V_E = \frac{d}{K_E}$$

Rearranging to derive the cost of equity gives:

$$K_E = \frac{d}{V_E}$$

Suppose the market value of equity is £200,000, and the firm intends to pay dividends of £20,000 p.a. indefinitely. What is the cost of equity capital?

$$K_E = \frac{d}{V_E} = \frac{£20,000}{£200,000} = 0.1 \text{ or } 10\%$$

If dividends are expected to grow at a constant per annum rate (g) over future periods, the basic valuation model becomes:

$$V_E = \frac{d_0(1 + g)}{(1 + K_E)} + \frac{d_0(1 + g)^2}{(1 + K_E)^2} + \cdots + \frac{d_0(1 + g)^n}{(1 + K_E)^n}$$

As n approaches infinity, the valuation model can be simplified to:

$$V_E = \frac{d_0(1+g)}{K_E - g} = \frac{d_1}{K_E - g}$$

Rearranging to derive the cost of equity gives:

$$K_E = \frac{d_1}{V_E} + g$$

Suppose the market value of equity is £420,000, the dividend just paid is £20,000 and the expected future growth rate is 5% p.a. What is the cost of equity capital?

$$K_E = \frac{d_1}{V_E} + g = \frac{£20,000(1.05)}{£420,000} + 0.05$$

$$= 0.1 \text{ or } 10\%$$

Capital asset pricing model

Under the CAPM, the approach to the cost of equity capital is very different. Here the cost of equity capital is calculated by reference to the return required in a single period by the company's investors. This return comprises two elements – an element which is risk free and thus represents a fixed minimum level of return, and an element (or premium) which depends on the relative risk associated with the performance of the company's shares. This split of return into a riskless and risky element is a very useful way of understanding why different investments offer different returns. The greater the level of risk, the higher the promised return. In principle it is not difficult to calculate these two parts of the shareholder's return. The risk-free rate can be defined as the current return from long-term government securities (e.g. the return on Treasury bills). This return is risk free in the sense that it is most unlikely that the government will default on its borrowing commitments. The relative risk of the company's shares is determined by relating two factors:

- the average return available from all listed shares (i.e. from the market portfolio); and

- the relative risk of the company's shares compared to the average for all listed shares.

The CAPM formula which is used to derive the cost of equity by incorporating the above data is as follows:

$$K_E = r_f + (r_m - r_f)\beta$$

where K_E is the cost of equity capital, r_f is the return on a risk-free security (e.g. on Treasury bills), r_m is the return on the market portfolio (e.g. the return on the *Financial Times* All Share Index); and β is the variability of the company's return in relation to that of the market portfolio.

Let us see how it works. Suppose the current return on Treasury bills is 10%, the return on the FT All Share Index is 19% and the variability of the company's return, as determined by a series of past observations, is 80% or 0.8 that of the market (i.e. if the FT All Share Index were to increase by 10%, this particular company's return would increase by 8%). We can calculate the cost of equity capital for the company – the minimum return required by shareholders – as follows:

$$K_E = r_f + (r_m - r_f)\beta$$
$$= 0.10 + (0.19 - 0.10)0.8$$
$$= 0.10 + (0.9)0.8 = 0.172 \text{ or } 17.2\%$$

It can be shown that, if the capital market is in equilibrium, these two models should give similar results, though some slight differences may occur because of their respective time horizons: that is, the CAPM is a single-period model, whereas the dividend valuation model covers periods longer than one year.

The following example shows in more detail how different costs of equity capital can be calculated for the same company.

Ayrsome plc is an all-equity-financed company whose shares are listed on the London Stock Exchange. It has paid dividends per share over the past five years of 7.5p, 8.3p, 8.7p, 10.4p and 12p. Its current market price per share is £2.40. The company's financial analyst has collected data on the returns on Ayrsome plc's shares and those on the FT All Share Index over the past five years, and has estimated the company's beta factor as 0.7. The analyst has also estimated the average return on the All Share Index to be 15% and the return on Treasury bills to be 8%.

With the above information we can calculate Ayrsome plc's cost of equity capital under each of the two methods as follows:

1. *Dividend growth model*

$$K_E = \frac{d_1}{V_E} + g$$

$d_1 = 12p(1 + g)$, where g (see below) is 12.5%

$$= 12p(1.125)$$

$V_E = £2.40$

$g = \sqrt[4]{12/7.5} = 12.5\%$

$$K_E = \frac{12(1.125)}{240} + 0.125 = 0.181 \text{ or } 18.1\%$$

2. CAPM

$$K_E = r_f + (r_m - r_f)\beta$$
$$= 8 + (15 - 8)0.7 = 12.9\%$$

What meaning can we derive from these very different estimates? We might begin by stressing the inherent differences between the two models.

The CAPM is a single-period model and therefore the rate obtained is the return expected over the next time period. The K_E estimated using the dividend growth model is the average return in perpetuity. It should also be remembered that strictly both models depend on the existence of a perfect capital market. Where market imperfections exist, it cannot be assumed that they will affect both models equally or in the same way. It is possible that some of the difference observed is due to the effect of such imperfections.

In addition, the difference in the observed results may be caused by defects in one or both of the models and/or errors in their application. A major reservation with respect to the growth model is its very assumption of constant dividend growth. While there is some evidence to show that firms attempt to pursue stable dividend policies, such an assumption inevitably represents a weakness in the model. There are further problems in estimating the values of the variables included in the calculation of K_E. The greatest difficulties are associated with determining the dividend growth rate. Past growth patterns may be an indicator of future growth, but they must be interpreted with care. The data given in the question are typical. Although average growth over the period has been 12.5%, this has not occurred in any year. Actual growth rates over the four-year period have been 10%, 5%, 20% and 15%.

The major reservation in principle with the CAPM is the assumption that required returns are entirely determined by the company's beta factor. One way of regarding the beta factor is as a reward for the risk which is determined by the movement of the company's share price with the movement of the market index: that is, as a reward for the risk which cannot be diversified away. This is consistent with the assumption of a perfect capital market in which rational and risk-averse investors will not hold risk that can be diversified away. However, if the capital market is imperfect, it is possible that share prices may be influenced by more than undiversifiable risk. Other assumptions underlying the CAPM may give rise to further reservations about the results. In particular the CAPM assumes that shares are completely characterised by information about their expected single-period return and the standard deviation of possible returns about the expected return. In other words, information about return and standard deviations is all that is required by the market in arriving at a share price. If, in practice, other factors influence share prices then the results from the CAPM may be suspect.

Further, the estimate of beta is based on historic data. For decision-making purposes beta values should be based on *what is going to happen*, not what has happened.

One further consideration must be borne in mind in comparing the results. The CAPM return of 12.9% is calculated without direct reference to the current market value of the ordinary shares in Ayrsome plc. In the dividend growth model, the share price, V_E, should be the equilibrium value. If the current value is not in equilibrium, this could explain the difference between the two results. If the CAPM result is 'correct', Ayrsome is currently undervalued and would be a good investment.

Cost of debt capital

The cost of debt capital is easier to determine than the cost of equity because the annual interest payments and the final capital repayment (if any) are fixed by the terms of the contract. The cost of debt, K_D, can be determined from the following valuation expression:

$$V_D = \frac{C}{(1 + K_D)} + \frac{C}{(1 + K_D)^2} + \cdots + \frac{C + R}{(1 + K_D)^n}$$

where V_D is the current market value of debt, *ex interest* (i.e. just after an annual interest payment has been made); C is the annual interest payment; R is the capital amount payable on redemption at time n; and n is the number of years to redemption.

If the debt capital is irredeemable, the redemption payment is zero and n approaches infinity. The valuation expression simplifies to:

$$V_D = \frac{C}{K_D}$$

Rearranging gives the formula for the cost of irredeemable debt capital:

$$K_D = \frac{C}{V_D}$$

Suppose that a firm has issued £500,000 of 8% irredeemable debt capital, which now has a market value of £440,000. The next annual interest payment of £40,000 (8% of £500,000) is due shortly. In order to estimate the cost of the debt capital, it is first necessary to calculate its *ex interest* value by subtracting the current interest payment due from the current market value. This gives an estimate of what the value will be just after the interest has been paid, and complies with the *ex interest* assumption in the valuation expression. The revised value may then be included in the cost of capital formula:

$$K_D = \frac{£40,000}{£(440,000 - 40,000)} = 0.1 \text{ or } 10\%$$

If debt capital is redeemable, no simple rearrangement of the valuation expression is possible and the cost of debt must be found by trial and error. A simple computer program will usually complete the calculation very quickly. The valuation expression may be rewritten using the symbols $A_{\overline{n}|}$ and $V_{\overline{n}|}$, introduced and explained in the appendix to Chapter 3:

$$V_D = C \times A_{\overline{n}|} K_D + R \times V_{\overline{n}|} K_D$$

In words, the *ex interest* value of redeemable debt is equal to the present value of the annual interest payments (the present value of an annuity of £C per annum for n years) plus the present value of the redemption payment, £R.

Suppose that a firm has issued £1 million of 7% debt, redeemable in 20 years at £102%: that is, each £100 of debt will be redeemed for £102. The current market value of the debt, *ex interest*, is £50%. What is the cost of the debt capital? The current total market value of the debt is £500,000 (£50 multiplied by 10,000 units of £100 each). Annual interest payments are £70,000 (7% of £1 million) and the redemption payment is £1.02 million (£102 multiplied by 10,000 units of £100 each). Substituting these numbers in the simplified valuation expression gives:

$$£500,000 = £70,000 \times A_{\overline{20}|} K_D + £1,020,000 \times V_{\overline{20}|} K_D$$

We must find the value for K_D which sets the right-hand side of this equation equal to £500,000 (the current value of the debt).

At 15%: (£70,000 × 6.2593) + (£1,020,000 × 0.0611) = £500,473
At 16%: (£70,000 × 5.9288) + (£1,020,000 × 0.0514) = £467,444

The cost of redeemable debt capital is just over 15%. If a more accurate indication than this is required, we may use a procedure known as *linear interpolation* to estimate where the cost lies between 15% and 16%. This procedure is explained in the next chapter (p. 291).

The weighted average cost of capital

Having computed the costs of the specific sources of capital, it is then necessary to weight the costs according to the market values of the sources of capital. Market values and not book values should be used because they are both current and observable. Furthermore they measure the amount sacrificed by investors in a company as a result of their continuing to own equity or debt which could otherwise be sold at its market value. In other words, they indicate the opportunity cost to investors of being investors in that particular company. The need to use a weighting arises because the aim of the cost of capital calculation is to offer a minimum acceptable return for *all* projects undertaken by the firm. If projects were expected to earn returns which corresponded to the cost of *individual* sources of capital – for example, if each project were financed by a specific loan taken out for that purpose – a firm might increase its cheapest source of capital, debt capital, to unreasonable levels. This would ultimately imperil the position of equity shareholders (as interest payments would bite more deeply into the profits available for dividends), who would increase the return they required from their investment to compensate for their additional risk. This could mean that a firm's overall cost of capital would increase, or at least would not decrease, if it issued substantial amounts of apparently cheap debt. Also, any attempt to match the uses and sources of long-term funds would result in different discount rates for projects which might otherwise be identical.

The weighted average cost of capital (WACC) can be derived by substituting the values for K_E (cost of equity) and K_D (cost of debt) into the following formula:

$$\text{WACC} = \left[K_E \times \frac{V_E}{V_T} \right] + \left[K_D \times \frac{V_D}{V_T} \right]$$

where V_E is the total market value of equity; V_D is the total market value of debt; and V_T is the total market value of debt and equity.

We are now in a position to show how we might compute the weighted average cost of capital for a firm. We will use the following data for Portman plc for the purpose. Portman plc has a capital structure as follows:

3 million ordinary (equity) shares of £1 each	£3,000,000
7% debt (redeemable at par in seven years' time)	£1,300,000

The ordinary shares have a current market value of £3 each *ex div*; an annual dividend of £900,000 has just been paid. Dividends have grown steadily at 6% p.a. over past years, and are expected to grow at the same rate in future years. The debt has a current market value of £77.177% *ex interest*.

Using the formulae for each specific source of capital, Portman plc's weighted average cost of capital is as follows:

1. *Cost of equity (using the dividend growth model)*

$$K_E = \frac{d_1}{V_E} + g = \frac{£900,000(1.06)}{3,000,000 \times £3} + 0.06$$

$$K_E = 0.106 + 0.06 = 0.166 \text{ or } 16.6\%$$

2. *Cost of debt*

$$V_D = \frac{C}{(1 + K_D)} + \frac{C}{(1 + K_D)^2} + \cdots + \frac{C + R}{(1 + K_D)^n}$$

$$1,300,000(0.77177) = 91,000 \times A_{\overline{7|}}K_D + 1,300,000 \times V_{\overline{7|}}K_D$$

at 12% $V_D = 91,000 (4.5638) + 1,300,000 (0.4523) = £1,003,300$

$$= £1,300,000 (0.77177)$$

$$\therefore K_D = 12\%$$

3. *Weighted average cost of capital*

Total market value of equity	£9,000,000
Total market value of debt	£1,003,300
Total market value of Portman plc	£10,003,300

$$\text{WACC} = 16.6\% \times \frac{9,000,000}{10,003,300} + 12\% \times \frac{1,003,300}{10,003,300} = 16.14\%$$

The illustration shows that the minimum rate to be used by Portman plc in project appraisal is 16.14%. A word of caution: note that such a rate will be applicable to all projects only if all projects are subject to the same degree of risk. If different projects attract different levels of risk, more sophisticated treatment may be necessary. One possibility is to use portfolio analysis, which was introduced and explained in Chapter 4.

13.5 The net present value decision rule

Having determined the relevant future cash flows, and derived a weighted average cost of capital, the firm is now in a position to decide whether the project should be undertaken, based on a calculation of its net present value. The following example shows how such a decision might be reached.

Layer plc is considering the introduction of a new product to add to its present range. A feasibility study costing £7,000 has been carried out. This suggests that a selling price of £5 per unit should be set, at which price demand is expected to be 50,000 units p.a. Manufacture requires a new machine costing £200,000, which will be worthless when demand for the product ceases in four years' time. Variable costs of producing the new product are estimated at £3 per unit; additional overheads will be £25,000 p.a. if manufacture takes place. The directors estimate that Layer plc's cost of capital is 10% p.a.

Table 13.3   Schedule of future cash flows

	£
Net cash inflows:	
Annual contribution £(5 − 3) × 50,000	100,000
Less Annual fixed costs	25,000
	75,000
Present value of annual cash inflows:	
£75,000 × $A_{\overline{4}|}$ 10%	
=£75,000 × 3.17	237,750
Net present value of investment:	
Present value of cash flows	237,750
Less Cost of machine	200,000
Net present value	+ 37,750

If we assume that all cash inflows and outflows will arise on the final day of each year, with the exception of the cost of the machine which will be payable at the start of the first year, we can prepare a schedule to determine the worth of the proposed investment, as in Table 13.3. The investment shows a discounted NPV of +£37,750 and thus is acceptable. Note that the cost of the feasibility study of £7,000 is ignored in the calculations as it has already been incurred.

However, because the estimated cash flows arise over a future period of four years, the directors may wish to know how 'wrong' they can be in their estimates of each of the variables before NPV becomes negative and the project unacceptable. This is obviously important as it may reveal which variables are most critical to the success of the project.

13.6 Sensitivity analysis

A useful technique for determining how sensitive the NPV is to errors in estimation is known as *sensitivity analysis*, which we introduced in Chapter 4. This involves calculating the expected NPV (or contribution or other measure of worth) of a project on the basis of most likely outcomes, and subsequently investigating the implications of various deviations of actual outcomes from forecast. For example, the value that a particular variable will take if the NPV expected from the project is to be reduced to zero may be ascertained and the difference in value expressed as a percentage of its most likely value. This provides an indication of the sensitivity of the project's expected NPV to changes in the value of individual variables, and points to those estimates in which a small deviation may be critical for the success or failure of the project. These estimates should be examined most carefully before a decision is made on the project. The increased availability of sophisticated inexpensive computers has made this method generally practicable.

We shall illustrate the usefulness of sensitivity analysis by examining in turn the sensitivity of Layer plc's new project's NPV of £37,750 to errors in estimating some of the variables which contribute to the NPV – selling price, annual volume of sales, variable cost per unit, annual fixed costs and the life of the product.

For each of these components of the NPV figure, we shall calculate the percentage change in its value which can occur before the NPV becomes zero. This is known as the *sensitivity margin* (SM). First, in order to provide a basis for assessing the various sensitivity margins, it is helpful to calculate the break-even annual net cash flow and the break-even annual contribution:

$$\text{Break-even annual net cash flow} = \frac{\text{Investment cost}}{\text{Discount factor}} = \frac{£200,000}{3.17} = £63,091$$

$$\begin{aligned}
\text{Break-even annual contribution} &= \text{Break-even annual net cash flows} \\
&\quad + \text{Annual fixed costs} \\
&= £63,091 + £25,000 \\
&= £88,091
\end{aligned}$$

We can now calculate the various sensitivity margins:

1. *Selling price*

   Break-even selling price = x, where
   $£(x - 3) \times 50{,}000 = £88{,}091$
   $\therefore \quad x = £4.76$

   The selling price can fall from £5 to £4.76 and the product will still break even. This reveals a sensitivity margin (SM) of

   $$\frac{£(5 - 4.76)}{£5} = 0.048 \text{ or } 4.8\%$$

2. *Annual volume of sales*

   Break-even annual volume = x, where
   $£(5 - 3) \times x = £88{,}091$
   $\therefore \quad x = 44{,}045$

   The annual sales volume can drop by 5,955 units (i.e. from 50,000 to 44,045), and the product will still break even. Thus the SM is

   $$\frac{50{,}000 - 44{,}045}{50{,}000} = 0.119 \text{ or } 11.9\%$$

3. *Variable cost per unit*

   Break-even variable cost = x, where
   $£(5 - x) \times 50{,}000 = £88{,}091$
   $\therefore \quad x = £3.24$

   Variable cost per unit can increase from £3 to £3.24. The SM for variable cost per unit is

   $$\frac{£(3.24 - 3)}{£3} = 0.08 \text{ or } 8\%$$

4. *Annual fixed costs*

   Fixed costs can rise by $£(75{,}000 - 63{,}091) = £11{,}909$ before NPV = 0. The SM for annual fixed costs is therefore

   $$\frac{£11{,}909}{£25{,}000} = 0.476 \text{ or } 47.6\%$$

5. *Product life*

The NPV for the current four-year life is £37,750. Suppose only a three-year life was anticipated. In that case NPV would be $-200,000 + 75,000A_{\overline{3}|}$ 10% $= -£13,250$ (where $A_{\overline{3}|}$ 10% $= 2.49$). The break-even product life is somewhere between three and four years. If NPV changes linearly with product life, we may estimate the break-even life as follows. The increase in NPV as product life increases one year, from three to four years, is £51,000 (from $-£13,250$ to $+£37,750$). Thus the increase in product life above three years necessary to give an NPV of zero is 13,250/51,000 of one year. The break-even life is $3 + (13,250/51,000) = 3.26$ years. The SM is $(4 - 3.26)/4 = 0.185 = 18.5\%$.

What conclusions can we draw from the sensitivity analysis applied to the new product? We can say initially that the NPV is most sensitive (the lowest percentage SM) to errors in the estimation of selling price, where only a 4.8% error is needed to eliminate the positive NPV. The margins of error on variable cost per unit (8%) and annual sales volume (11.9%) are also critical and particular attention should be directed to these estimates. Note that the estimate of annual fixed costs is not particularly critical – in fact it may be increased by as much as 47% before the project becomes unacceptable.

There are, however, certain factors which should be considered when interpreting the results of sensitivity analysis, and indeed of net present value calculations in general. First, the final investment decision must depend ultimately upon the particular risk of the project and the firm's attitude to it. Second, sensitivity analysis ignores the possibility of combination errors which could arise because two or more components of the overall calculation are interdependent. For example, the sensitivity margins on sales volume and selling price should not be viewed in isolation from each other, as it is likely that they are connected closely (see Chapter 9). Third, different acceptable safety margins may be applicable to each component, depending upon the decision maker's confidence in the various estimates. For example, a 2% safety margin on a rent payment which is fixed by contract may be more acceptable to a firm than a 20% margin on the costs of raw materials which are purchased in extremely volatile markets. In summary, we might say that sensitivity analysis is intended as an aid in investment decisions, not as a definitive answer to the problem of risk and uncertainty.

$\boxed{13.7}$ The problem of scarce capital

One problem that frequently arises in practice is concerned with the acceptance of long-term investments when the amount of available capital is rationed. Capital rationing can be said to occur when a company has more projects showing a positive net present value when discounted at the prevailing cost of capital than can be financed from available funds.

It is, however, important to distinguish between two different types of capital rationing, sometimes termed 'hard' and 'soft' rationing. The distinction between the two is determined by the cause of the rationing (i.e. by what is meant by 'availability of funds'). Thus if the company wishes to impose its own constraints on the level of capital expenditure, the situation is one of soft rationing. However, when the constraint is imposed externally by the capital markets, hard rationing is taking place. In this situation the company cannot raise the necessary additional finance for acceptable projects at any price.

Why might a company choose to impose internal rationing? It may seem irrational not to accept projects with positive net present values when discounted at the cost of capital. But such seeming irrationality may be necessary to comply with the company's objectives. Perhaps the owners are quite happy with their existing returns and have little desire to expand via new capital investments; perhaps funds are available but managerial ability to manage the new investments is not; perhaps also the reluctance to raise external funds for 'good' projects may be due to the fear of loss of control over the running of the company. There is much evidence that companies do impose internal restrictions on their capital budgets, and thus there is a necessity to understand how the choice of investments might be made in such circumstances.

Whether hard rationing really exists is a more debatable issue. It has been argued that hard rationing is no more than a temporary imperfection in the market for funds, and is due to lack of information on the part of those seeking finance – in other words, any company which puts enough effort into looking for finance, and is prepared to pay the prevailing rates, will find a supplier. The contrary view is that, for small expanding companies at least, access to finance for investment is difficult because of gaps in the institutional framework of the provision of funds. A 1982 study by Pike bears out these findings. In examining constraints on 126 companies' investment programmes, Pike observed the following as being the most significant:

	%
Lack of profitable investment opportunities	19.8
General economic uncertainty	18.7
Unwillingness to increase level of borrowings	19.0
Lack of capital available	8.7
Lack of trained managers to implement investment opportunities	7.4

Source: R. H. Pike, *Capital Budgeting in the 1980s*, CIMA, 1982.

For our purposes the question is how the NPV criterion should be modified to incorporate this scarcity of capital, be it hard or soft. The following illustration considers the problem.

Sincil plc is considering its capital expenditure programme for 19X0 and 19X1. The company's directors have reduced their initial list of projects to five, the expected cash flows of which are set out in Table 13.4.

Table 13.4 Expected cash flows from projects

Project	Cash flows			
	19X0 (£)	19X1 (£)	19X2 (£)	19X3 (£)
A	−60,000	+30,000	+25,000	+25,000
B	−30,000	−20,000	+25,000	+45,000
C	−40,000	−50,000	+60,000	+70,000
D	0	−80,000	+45,000	+55,000
E	−50,000	+10,000	+30,000	+40,000

None of the five projects can be delayed. All are divisible (i.e. cash outlays may be reduced by any proportion and inflows will then be reduced in the same proportion). All cash flows arise on the first day of the year. The minimum return required by shareholders of Sincil plc is 15% p.a. Which projects should Sincil plc accept if the capital available for investment is limited to £100,000 on 1 January 19X0 but readily available at 15% p.a. on 1 January 19X1 and subsequently?

The problem may be solved in two steps: first, we calculate the NPV of each project; and second, we use these NPVs to determine the allocation of the £100,000 investment capital.

Step 1 – calculation of NPV

A $-60,000 + 30,000(0.87) + 25,000(0.76) + 25,000(0.66) = +1,600$
B $-30,000 - 20,000(0.87) + 25,000(0.76) + 45,000(0.66) = +1,300$
C $-40,000 - 50,000(0.87) + 60,000(0.76) + 70,000(0.66) = +8,300$
D $0 - 80,000(0.87) + 45,000(0.76) + 55,000(0.66) = +900$
E $-50,000 + 10,000(0.87) + 30,000(0.76) + 40,000(0.66) = +7,900$

All five projects show positive NPVs and, under conditions of no capital rationing, all would be accepted. However, by totalling the cash required at 19X0, we can see that Sincil plc needs £180,000 capital at 1 January 19X0 to undertake all five projects. Only £100,000 is available and no project can be delayed. How should Sincil plc allocate the £100,000 capital? Project D may be accepted as it has a positive NPV and requires none of the scarce capital. The remaining four projects should be ranked on the basis of the NPV they produce per £ of investment required at the date on which capital is rationed: that is, on 1 January 19X0. The procedure is analogous to that described in Chapter 11 for allocating a single scarce resource. The aim is to apply available capital to those projects which use it most efficiently: in other words, those that produce the highest NPV for each £ of scarce capital they require.

Step 2 – ranking on the basis of NPV per £ of investment cost

Project	NPV per £ of outlay on 1 January 19X0	Ranking	Fraction accepted	Capital needed on 1 January 19X0 (£)
A	$\dfrac{1,600}{60,000} = 0.027$	4	0	0
B	$\dfrac{1,300}{30,000} = 0.043$	3	1/3	10,000
C	$\dfrac{8,300}{40,000} = 0.207$	1	1	40,000
E	$\dfrac{7,900}{50,000} = 0.158$	2	1	50,000
			Total available capital	100,000

The application of the ranking per £1 of investment outlay thus gives us a criterion for choice in situations of scarcity. Sincil plc should accept projects D, C and E completely, and one third (presuming projects are divisible) of project B. Project A should be rejected, even though it shows a positive NPV; more efficient uses are available for the capital which would be required to undertake it.

This method of allocating scarce capital is valid only if no other resources needed by the firm, including capital at any time other than 1 January 19X0, are scarce. Otherwise it is necessary to use mathematical programming methods to deal with problems of scarcity, similar to the linear programming method discussed in Chapter 11. The following example of Valley plc shows how this might be done.

Valley plc is financed entirely by ordinary shares. Its effective cost of capital, net of tax, is 10% per annum. The directors of Valley plc are considering the company's capital investment programme for the next two years, and have reduced their initial list of projects to four. Details of the projects are set out in Table 13.5.

None of the projects can be delayed and all projects are divisible. No project can be undertaken more than once. Valley plc is able to invest surplus funds in a bank deposit account yielding a return of 7% per annum, net of tax.

Which projects should Valley plc accept if capital available immediately is limited to £500,000, capital available after one year is limited to £300,000 and capital is available thereafter without limit at a cost of 10% per annum?

We can now draw up a mathematical programming formulation to help the directors choose projects on the basis of capital scarcity at different points in time. Let a, b, c and d be the proportions of projects A, B, C and D accepted, and x be the amount in £000 placed on deposit immediately. The resultant formulation would

Table 13.5 Cash flows (net of tax) and NPVs (£000)

Project	Immediately	After 1 year	After 2 years	After 3 years	NPV
A	−400	+50	+300	+350	+156.3
B	−300	−200	+400	+400	+149.3
C	−300	+150	+150	+150	+ 73.0
D	0	−300	+250	+300	=159.3

be as follows:

Maximise $156.3a + 149.3b + 73.0c + 159.3d - 0.027x$

Subject to $400a + 300b + 300c + x \leqslant 500$

$200b + 300d \leqslant 300 + 50a + 150c + 1.07x$

$a, b, c, d, x \geqslant 0$

$a, b, c, d \leqslant 1$

We can interpret the formulation as follows. The objective function is to maximise the positive net present values of the four projects (a, b, c and d). To complete the information in the objective function, it is necessary to calculate the NPV (at 10%) per £1 of external investment for one year:

	£
Amount received after one year from £1 invested at 7%	1.07
Discounted at 10%: 1.07×0.909	= 0.973
Less Original investment	= 1.000
NPV per £1	= −0.027

We now have to consider the two cash availability constraints. The cash available immediately is £500,000. All projects except D require immediate cash outflows. The first constraint is thus:

$400a + 300b + 300c + x \leqslant 500$

The cash limit after one year is £300,000, by which date the investment of surplus funds will include one year's interest at 7% to augment the cash available. Projects A and C also generate inflows on that date. Projects B and D both require further outflows. The constraint thus becomes:

$200b + 300d \leqslant 300 + 50a + 150c + 1.07x$

The final two sets of constraints, a, b, c, d, $x \geqslant 0$, and a, b, c, $d \leqslant 1$, reflect the situation that projects are divisible but cannot be undertaken more than once. Solution of the linear programme would give the optimal plan for Valley plc.

13.8 The impact of inflation on long-term decisions

Throughout our analysis of long-term decision making we have made no explicit reference to the possible impact of inflation on the estimates of future cash flows and on the cost of capital. This has been a deliberate omission. It is necessary to understand the basic method of long-term decision making before adding any refinements. But of course in any real-world situation, the existence of inflation is likely and presents a problem to decision makers. Quite apart from the difficulty of predicting future levels of inflation and, more particularly, their effect on the prices of resources used by the firm, decision makers face the problem of how to incorporate inflation into project appraisal. For instance, should inflation be incorporated into estimates of future cash flows? Or into the cost of capital rate? Or both? This section briefly tackles these particular issues.

Brisbane plc is considering a project which will cost £30,000, have a life of three years, and reduce labour costs by £12,000 p.a. for each of the three years. The company's cost of capital is 10% p.a. For simplicity, assume that labour costs are paid annually in arrears. No increases in any prices are expected in the future.

In this case the project is marginally unacceptable, as follows:

$$\text{NPV} = -£30,000 + £12,000 \; A_{\overline{3}|} \; 10\%$$
$$= -£30,000 + £29,842 = -£158$$

Now suppose that general inflation is anticipated at 5% p.a. compound and that all specific prices (i.e. all the costs of Brisbane plc) are expected to change in line with general inflation. In other words, no real relationships change. The existence of expected inflation will affect both the cash flows and the cost of capital.

The initial investment outlay of £30,000 remains unchanged as it occurs at the decision date, but the three yearly cost savings of £12,000 must be increased in money terms to reflect the expected increase in labour costs of 5% p.a. Thus the cost savings become:

Year 1 £12,000 × (1.05) = £12,600
Year 2 £12,000 × (1.05)^2 = £13,230
Year 3 £12,000 × (1.05)^3 = £13,892

With the existence of inflation, a larger return than previously will be required by suppliers of funds, to compensate them for the loss of purchasing power of their funds. Thus if the return required after one year on each pound supplied is £1.10 without inflation, it will be necessary to pay £1.10(1.05) = £1.155, if inflation is expected at 5% p.a. compound, implying a discount rate of 15.5% p.a.

The appraisal of the project may now proceed as previously using cash flow estimates and a discount rate which incorporates inflation. The NPV is computed as follows:

Year	Cash flows (£)	Discount factor at 15.5%	Present value (£)
0	− 30,000	1.0000	− 30,000
1	+12,600	$\dfrac{1}{(1.155)} = 0.8658$	+10,909
2	+13,230	$\dfrac{1}{(1.155)^2} = 0.7496$	+9,917
3	+13,892	$\dfrac{1}{(1.155)^3} = 0.6490$	+9,016
		Net present value	−158

The calculation of the NPV shows that in this case nothing has changed relative to the original situation, because all prices are affected equally by the existence of inflation. The measuring scale is different, but the NPV is still the same. The project is still marginally unacceptable.

The illustration gives us a basis for clarifying some basic ideas of long-term decision making under inflation. Cash flows which are estimated as actual cash sums to be paid or received in future periods are referred to as *money cash flows*; a discount rate which converts money cash flows into present values and which allows for both the time value of consumption potential (i.e. the time value of money if no inflation is expected: in our example, 10% p.a.) and the effect of inflation (in our example, 5% p.a.) is referred to as a *money discount rate* (in our example, 15.5%). In most countries, virtually all interest rates are expressed in money terms, with no distinction being made between that part of the rate which represents the time value of consumption potential and that part which represents compensation for expected inflation. Because no split is readily available between the two components of the money discount rate, it is usually more convenient to undertake NPV calculations in money terms – discounting money cash flows at a money discount rate – than to attempt to disaggregate the observed money interest rate into its two component parts and adopt an alternative NPV calculation.

Nevertheless, it is possible, even if not preferable, to express cash flows in *real* terms (i.e. in units having a constant purchasing power), and to discount these at a *real discount rate*. We might define a real cash flow as the cash amount we would have to pay now, in today's pounds, to buy the same amount of goods as we will be able to buy with any given future cash amount when we receive it. The real discount rate is computed by:

$$K = \frac{i - h}{1 + h}$$

where K is the real discount rate, i is the money discount rate, and h is the expected rate of inflation.

We can use our basic example to illustrate the computation in real terms of the NPV. The figures are as follows:

Year	Money cash × flows (£)	Deflation factor = at 5%	Real cash × flows (£)	Real discount = factor at 10%*	Present value (£)
0	− 30,000	1.0000	−30,000	1.0000	− 30,000
1	+12,600	$\dfrac{1}{(1.05)} = 0.9524$	+12,000	0.9091	+10,909
2	+13,230	$\dfrac{1}{(1.05)^2} = 0.9070$	+12,000	0.8264	+9,917
3	+13,892	$\dfrac{1}{(1.05)^3} = 0.8638$	+12,000	0.7513	+9,016
				Net present value	−158

$$*K = \frac{0.155 - 0.05}{1 + 0.05} = 0.1 \text{ or } 10\%$$

The NPV is still −£158, as in the previous computation when money cash flows and a money discount rate were used. This demonstrates that NPV calculations may be carried out either in money terms or in real terms. Provided that inflation is dealt with correctly in computing cash flows and discount rates, both methods will yield the same answer. The essence of the argument is consistency: money cash flows to be discounted at a money rate, real cash flows at a real rate. However, as we have noted, it is usually preferable to undertake calculations involving inflation by using money cash flows and money discount rates for two main reasons. First, the use of money discount rates avoids the necessity of splitting the discount rate into an inflationary element and an element for the real rate, and thus necessitates fewer calculations. Second, and more importantly, money interest rates are the ones used in almost all financial dealings and can thus be observed, whereas real rates cannot, as they are determined by (possibly variable) predictions of inflation.

One final point of great importance warrants mention. In our simple example we have assumed that all prices change in line with general inflation, and consequently that cash flows in real terms are identical to cash flows at current prices. In practice, it is quite likely that inflation will affect different resources in different ways, and thus that real relationships between resources will change. Let us alter our example to make it somewhat more realistic. Suppose now that specific wage rates are expected to increase at 8% p.a., although the general rate of inflation is still expected to increase at 5% p.a. Money and real costs of capital are as previously (15.5% and 10% respectively). Our analysis in *money* terms for Brisbane plc will now be as follows:

Year	Cash flows at current × prices (£)	Specific inflation = at 8%	Money × cash flows (£)	Money discount = factor at 15.5%	Present value (£)
0	−30,000	1.00	−30,000	1.0000	−30,000
1	+12,000	1.08	+12,960	0.8658	+11,221
2	+12,000	$(1.08)^2$	+13,997	0.7496	+10,492
3	+12,000	$(1.08)^3$	+15,116	0.6490	+ 9,810
				Net present value	+1,523

The new calculation, incorporating the differential impact of inflation on the labour costs saved and on the cost of capital, results in a positive NPV of £1,523 and a sign for acceptability. The sign has changed from negative to positive because the cost of labour is increasing over time *relative* to other prices, and hence cash savings are increasing in real terms. The same conclusion would, of course, hold if the appraisal were undertaken using real cash flows – as opposed to savings at current prices – and a real discount rate. The point of the more realistic example using differential price change rates is this: if we had simply estimated cash savings at current prices (i.e. £12,000 p.a.) and applied a real discount rate (i.e. 10%), the answer would have shown a negative NPV of £158, and the project would probably have been rejected. This would be a wrong decision because the benefits of the labour cost savings would be underestimated. For purposes of investment appraisal under inflation, it is essential that net benefits (the cash flows) are expressed in terms comparable with the discount rate. Calculating net benefits on one basis and the discount rate on a different basis may well lead to incorrect investment recommendations.

Finally, let us suppose that Brisbane plc is tackling a trickier problem. The company is deciding whether to introduce a new product with a three-year life. The investment cost will be £60,000 at 1.1.19X0, and 10,000 units of the product are expected to be sold each year for £10 in current prices. Because of severe competition in the market, Brisbane plc expects price increases to be limited to 3% per annum. Brisbane plc's money cost of capital is 12% per annum. The following variable costs per unit, expressed in current prices, will be incurred:

	£
Labour	2.00, increasing at 4% p.a.
Raw material	3.00, increasing at 6% p.a.
Overhead	1.50, increasing at 4% p.a.

The example poses a variety of costs, prices and inflation rates. To determine whether the project should be accepted, we should compute the relevant money cash flows over its life and discount them at the money discount rate. Of vital importance is tabulating and ordering the data in an easily understandable way, to ensure we compare like with like. We might proceed as follows:

Brisbane plc	Money cash flows (£)			
	1 Jan. 19X0	31 Dec. 19X0	31 Dec. 19X1	31 Dec. 19X2
Investment cost	(60,000)			
Revenue:				
$100,000 \times (1.03)$		103,000		
$100,000 \times (1.03)^2$			106,090	
$100,000 \times (1.03)^3$				109,273
Labour:				
$20,000 \times (1.04)$		(20,800)		
$20,000 \times (1.04)^2$			(21,632)	
$20,000 \times (1.04)^3$				(22,497)
Raw material:				
$30,000 \times (1.06)$		(31,800)		
$30,000 \times (1.06)^2$			(33,708)	
$30,000 \times (1.06)^3$				(35,730)
Overheads:				
$15,000 \times (1.04)$		(15,600)		
$15,000 \times (1.04)^2$			(16,224)	
$15,000 \times (1.04)^3$				(16,873)
Net cash flow	(60,000)	34,800	34,526	34,173
Discount factor at 12% per annum	1	0.8928	0.7972	0.7118
Present values	(60,000)	31,069	27,524	24,324

Net present value is +£22,917 and the project is worthwhile.

CHAPTER SUMMARY

Capital budgeting is the process of evaluating long-term commitments of resources in the acquisition of capital assets. The role of accounting is to provide detailed cash flow analysis on the costs and benefits of potential capital projects in order that their financial acceptability can be determined. This is part of an overall investment process which includes searching for strategic opportunities and screening possibilities before detailed evaluation commences.

In this chapter we have described the net present value approach to evaluating capital projects. The advantage of this approach is that it is linked directly to the measurement of present value or wealth, and therefore with our assumed objective of management decision making – the maximisation of the present value of the firm's net cash inflows. It is this attribute which makes the NPV rule so attractive as a criterion for the evaluation of capital investment opportunities. Under certain circumstances, a firm which accepts a project with a positive NPV should enjoy an immediate increase in its value, equal to the amount of the project's NPV.

The quality of investment decisions depends in part on the quality of estimates produced in looking to what is inevitably an uncertain future. In undertaking net present value analysis, care must be taken in estimating the future cash flows which provide the basis of project evaluation, and the cost of capital which is used as the discount rate to equate flows at different points in time. In particular, the effects of inflation on cash flows and on the cost of capital must be dealt with in a consistent manner. Money flows should be discounted at the money cost of capital, and flows expressed in real terms at the real cost of capital. Sensitivity analysis may be used to test implications of deviations from the forecasts used in the principal NPV analysis, and can help identify those factors that are most crucial to the success of a project. When capital rationing occurs, competing investment projects can be ranked on the basis of their present value per £ of investment outlay.

REVIEW QUESTIONS

1. Contrast the type of information required for long-term decisions with that required for short-term decisions. Are there any essential differences?

2. Why is it necessary to build a discount factor into long-term decision making?

3. Discuss some of the difficulties of measuring the firm's weighted average cost of capital.

4. 'Sensitivity analysis is a most powerful technique in project appraisal.' Discuss.

5. Compare and contrast the different methods available for dealing with inflation in investment decisions.

EXERCISES

13.1 Poulenc and Nielsen each own 50% of the issued ordinary share capital of Mozart Ltd, but neither plays any part in its management. The company presently has £30,000 available on bank current account, which it is proposing to invest in a project expected to produce cash inflows of £8,000 after one year, £10,000 after two, and £17,000 after three. No other cash flows are expected to be associated with the project. If the £30,000 is not used on this project, it will be paid out as a dividend to Poulenc and Nielsen. If the project is accepted, the cash inflows it produces will be paid out in full as dividends as they arise.

Nielsen is in agreement with the company investing in the proposed project, but Poulenc wishes to take his wife on a world cruise and claims that the company is not acting in his best interests if it fails to pay the money as dividend to enable him to do so. Mozart Ltd is able to both lend and borrow funds freely at 5% p.a.

(a) Calculate the net present value of the proposed project to Mozart Ltd.

(b) Explain whether the company is acting in the best interests of *both* its shareholders by accepting the project if

   (i) Poulenc and Nielsen may both borrow freely at 5%;

   (ii) Poulenc and Nielsen may both borrow freely at 10%.

(c) Comment briefly on the implications of your answers to (a) and (b) above for capital investment theory. (Solution at end of text.)

13.2   Reger plc is considering the introduction of a new product, the trump, to its range. A feasibility study, recently undertaken at a cost of £10,000, suggests that a selling price of £50 per unit should be set for the trump.

Manufacture of the trump would require a specialised machine costing £150,000. The machine is expected to be capable of producing trumps for an indefinite period, although due to its specialised nature it is not expected to have any resale or scrap value when production of trumps ceases. Variable costs of manufacturing trumps are estimated at £30 per unit, and overhead costs are estimated at a fixed level of £40,000 p.a., avoidable only if no trumps are manufactured or sold. At a selling price of £50, it is estimated that 5,000 trumps will be demanded and sold each year. Demand for trumps is expected to cease after four years.

All expenses and revenues will be paid or received in cash at the end of the year in which they arise, with the exception of the cost of the machine which will be payable at the beginning of the first year in which trumps are manufactured. The directors of Reger plc estimate the company's cost of capital at 10% p.a.

(a) Calculate the net present value expected from the introduction of the proposed new product, based on the estimates given.

(b) Prepare a statement showing in percentages how sensitive the net present value is to errors of estimation in each component of your calculation in (a).

(c) Comment briefly on the results of your calculations in (a) and (b). (Solution at end of text.)

13.3 Nono plc is financed by three types of capital:

1. 1 million 50p ordinary shares, each having a current market value of £5.20 *cum div*. The current annual dividend, which is due to be paid shortly, is 20p per share. The dividend has grown steadily in the past at a compound annual rate of 15% and is generally expected to continue doing so indefinitely.

2. £200,000 irredeemable 8% debt, having a current value of £50% *ex interest*.

3. £2 million 10% debt, redeemable in 20 years at a price of £110%. The current market value is £80% *ex interest*.

Nono is considering a new project having the same risk characteristics as existing projects, which would require an immediate outlay of £150,000 and would produce annual net cash inflows of £30,000 indefinitely.

Prepare calculations showing whether acceptance of the new project is worthwhile.

13.4 Vitali Ltd is considering the replacement of a group of machines used exclusively for the manufacture of one of its products, the yeti. The existing machines have a book value of £65,000 after deducting straight-line depreciation from historical cost; however, they could be sold for £45,000 only. The new machines would cost £100,000. Vitali expects to sell yetis for four more years. The existing machines could be kept in operation for that period of time if it were economically desirable to do so. After four years, the scrap value of both the existing machines and the new machines would be zero.

The current costs per unit of manufacturing yetis on the existing machines and the new machines are as follows:

	Existing machines (£)		New machines (£)
Materials	22.00		20.00
Labour (8 hours @ £5)	40.00	(4 h @ £5)	20.00
Overheads (8 hours @ £2.40)	19.20	(4 h @ £7.20)	28.80
Total cost	81.20		68.80

Overheads are allocated to products on the labour hour rate method. The hourly rates of £2.40 and £7.20 comprise £1 and £2.50 for variable overheads and £1.40 and £4.70 for fixed overheads, including depreciation.

Current sales of yetis are 1,000 units p.a. at £90 each; if the new machines were purchased, output would be increased to 1,200 units and selling price would be reduced to £80. Vitali requires a minimum rate of return on investment of 20% p.a. in money terms. Materials costs, overheads and selling prices are expected to increase at the rate of 15% p.a. in step with the index of retail prices. Labour costs are expected to increase at the rate of 20% p.a. Assume that annual receipts and payments would arise annually on the anniversary of the installation of the new machinery.

(a) Give calculations to show whether purchase of the new machines would be worthwhile.

(b) Explain briefly your treatment of inflation.

13.5 Sati Ltd is considering which, if any, of four projects to accept. The cash flows, which are all paid out or received at the end of the year in question, are shown below. All the projects are regarded as equally risky. The company's capital budget for year 0 is restricted to £6 million; at later times funds will be readily available at the firm's cost of capital rate of 10% p.a. All the projects must be commenced at time 0 or abandoned; they cannot be postponed. Parts of a project may be accepted, but no project can be accepted more than once.

Projects	Initial investment (£000)		Receipts (£000)			
Years	0	1	1	2	3	4
A	1,000	2,000	–	1,500	1,500	1,500
B	5,000	–	2,000	2,000	2,000	2,000
C	4,500	–	1,750	1,750	1,750	1,750
D	1,750	1,400	–	1,500	1,500	1,500

(a) Provide reasons and calculations showing which, if any, of the projects should be adopted by Sati Ltd.

(b) If it were anticipated that the amount of funds available for capital investment in future years would be limited, would your answer differ? Explain *briefly* the techniques available to solve the multi-period rationing case.

Notes

1. See the appendix to Chapter 3 for an explanation of compounding and discounting factors.
2. That is, the cost of an asset is written off against income in equal parts for each year of its life.
3. Using the sum of the years' digits method of depreciation, the cost of the asset is spread between accounting periods in the ratio $n:n-1:n-2...:1$, where n is the original life expectancy of the asset. So for an asset with an expected life of three years, the ratio is 3:2:1, i.e. 1/2 in the first year, 1/3 in the second year and 1/6 in the third year.

Long-term decisions: internal rate of return and other methods

AIMS AND OBJECTIVES

☐ To describe and evaluate the internal rate of return method of investment appraisal.

☐ To describe and evaluate the payback method, with and without discounting.

☐ To describe and evaluate the accounting rate of return.

☐ To summarise existing evidence concerning the methods used in practice to make long-term decisions.

☐ To explain the importance of and the procedures for undertaking post-audits of capital investments.

In the previous chapter we discussed the net present value (NPV) approach to long-term capital investment decisions. We believe that technically it is the best approach currently available, because it is linked directly to the measurement of present wealth or value. NPV is, however, only one of many possible approaches to long-term decision making. In this chapter we consider a number of alternative methods which are to be found in practice and contrast them with the NPV method. First, we consider one appraisal method (the internal rate of return) which incorporates the time value of money, and then we consider two methods (the payback method and the accounting rate of return) which normally do not. Finally we look at evidence on how managers actually evaluate investments and compare practice with theory.

14.1 The internal rate of return

The internal rate of return, or yield, method, entails the discounting of future cash flows to the present date, and as such bears some similarity to the NPV method. The internal rate of return (IRR) of a project may be defined as the discount rate at which the present value of all future cash flows, positive and negative, is equal to the investment cost of the project. Phrased differently, we may say that the IRR method, unlike the NPV method, does not seek to generate a cash figure to determine whether an investment should be undertaken, but rather it seeks to find the discount rate at which the NPV of a project is zero. It signals acceptance or rejection of an investment in percentage terms, not in cash terms. Because it is a relative measure, expressing net returns as a percentage of investment cost, it takes no account of the absolute size of a project's required investment cost or of its cash returns. This is an important difference between the NPV and IRR methods, and we shall return to examine its implications later in this chapter.

To be acceptable under the IRR criterion, a project must have an internal rate of return greater than some other rate, which we might term a 'hurdle' or 'cut-off' rate. This rate should be the same as the discount rate suggested for use in NPV calculations – that is, the weighted average cost of capital (WACC) – which reflects all long-term sources of funds used by a firm.

Internal rates of return are usually determined by a process of trial and error. (Computers perform the necessary calculations very speedily.) Consider the following cash flow profile for a particular project, + and − denoting positive and negative flows respectively:

Year 0	Year 1	Year 2	Year 3
−£9,514	+£1,000	+£5,000	+£9,000

What is the internal rate of return of the project? The answer is not obvious, so we might begin by choosing any discount rate as the potential IRR. (Remember: we are trying to find a rate which equates cash inflows of £1,000 in year 1, £5,000 in year 2 and £9,000 in year 3 with one cash outflow, the project cost of £9,514 at the start of year 1.) Let us begin by choosing a rate of 10% p.a. The NPV of the project at this rate is:

$$-9{,}514 + 1{,}000(0.909) + 5{,}000(0.826) + 9{,}000(0.751) = +£2{,}284$$

However, we are trying to find a discount rate which shows neither a positive nor a negative net present value. Thus 10% is too low. Let us try a rate of 15%. The NPV for the project now becomes:

$$-9{,}514 + 1{,}000(0.870) + 5{,}000(0.756) + 9{,}000(0.657) = +£1{,}049$$

15% is still too low. Let us try 20%:

$$-9{,}514 + 1{,}000(0.833) + 5{,}000(0.694) + 9{,}000(0.579) = 0$$

By trial and error we have found that the IRR of the project is exactly 20%. To determine whether this is an acceptable project, we of course need the additional information on the hurdle rate. If the hurdle rate is less than 20%, the project should be undertaken; if it is greater than 20%, the project should be rejected.

In general, the IRR for any project is represented by r in the following equation:

$$\frac{a_1}{(1+r)} + \frac{a_2}{(1+r)^2} + \cdots + \frac{a_n}{(1+r)^n} - I_0 = 0$$

where $a_1, a_2 \ldots a_n$ are the cash flows at the end of years 1, 2 ... n respectively and I_0 is the project cost payable immediately. Using the actual cash data from our example, we can rewrite the equation as

$$\frac{1,000}{(1.2)} + \frac{5,000}{(1.2)^2} + \frac{9,000}{(1.2)^3} - 9,514 = 0$$

This can be interpreted roughly to mean that, if cash flows of £1,000, £5,000 and £9,000 are received at the end of years 1, 2 and 3 of a project's life, then, if the initial cost is £9,514, the project is 'yielding' a percentage return of 20% p.a. Hence the common use of the term 'yield' to mean the same as internal rate of return.

In situations where management must decide whether to accept or reject a single project, the IRR criterion always gives the same advice as NPV, provided that the cash flow pattern is *orthodox* (i.e. that one or more cash outflows is followed by a series of cash inflows).

Figure 14.1 depicts the NPV of a project with an orthodox cash flow pattern, expressed as a function of the discount rate. The intercept of the NPV line with the

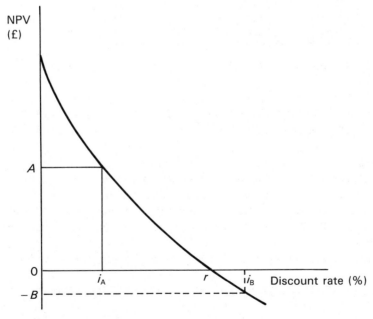

Figure 14.1 The relationship between IRR and NPV.

horizontal axis is denoted by point r. This point is the project's IRR (i.e. the rate at which the project shows a zero net present value). For any point on the graph where the NPV is positive (to the left of point r and above the horizontal axis), the cost of capital must be less than the IRR (point r). For example, if the cost of capital is i_A, the project's NPV is positive and equal to £A. Similarly for any point on the graph where the NPV is negative (to the right of point r and below the horizontal axis), the cost of capital must be greater than the IRR (point r). For example, if the cost of capital is i_B, the NPV is negative and equal to $-$£B.

Thus both methods, NPV and IRR, give the same solutions to most normal accept/reject decisions. However, there are situations in which the application of the two methods is not so straightforward, and which may lead to conflicting advice. We now examine some of these situations and explain why the NPV method is, in each case, to be preferred.

14.2 Mutually exclusive projects

Suppose that Loftus plc is in a situation where it has three possible investment projects, but it may accept only one of these three. The firm's cost of capital is 10% p.a. The cash flow profiles of the three projects are as follows:

| Project | Cash flows (£) | | | |
	Year 0	Year 1	Year 2	Year 3
A	−9,514	+1,000	+5,000	+9,000
B	−9,514	+7,000	+5,000	+1,000
C	−9,514	+4,500	+4,500	+4,500

Let us begin by computing the NPVs of the three projects, as follows:

A $-9,514 + 1,000(0.909) + 5,000(0.826) + 9,000(0.751) = +£2,284$
B $-9,514 + 7,000(0.909) + 5,000(0.826) + 1,000(0.751) = +£1,730$
C $-9,514 + 4,500(2.487)$ $= +£1,677$

The answer is clear and unambiguous. As the projects are mutually exclusive, Loftus plc should accept A, as it has the highest net present value of the three available projects, when discounted at the cost of capital of 10% p.a.

Now let us see how the IRR rule would rank the three projects. Project A gives an IRR of exactly 20%, as we have seen from our previous illustration of the computation of the IRR.

The IRR for project B is more difficult. Trying a rate of 20%, we have:

$-9,514 + 7,000(0.833) + 5,000(0.694) + 1,000(0.579) = +£366$

This shows that 20% is too low. (Figure 14.1 shows that NPV usually decreases as the discount rate increases.) Trying a rate of 25%, we have:

$$-9{,}514 + 7{,}000(0.800) + 5{,}000(0.640) + 1{,}000(0.512) = -\pounds202$$

The negative NPV found when applying a rate of 25% shows that the IRR must lie somewhere between 20% and 25%. Where it lies may be approximated by using the technique of *linear interpolation.*

The solution is only approximate as it is based on the assumption that NPV changes linearly as the discount rate changes, an assumption which is not strictly correct, as can be seen from the graph in Figure 14.1.[1] IRR is estimated as follows. For a 5% increase in the discount rate (from 20% to 25%), NPV falls by £568 (from +£366 to −£202). We have to calculate what increase in the discount rate is needed to reduce NPV by £366, i.e. to zero. This increase is added to 20% to find the IRR. If a 5% increase leads to a fall of £568 in NPV, the increase necessary for a fall of £366 is (5 × 366/568). The IRR for project B is approximately:

$$20 + \left(5 \times \frac{366}{568}\right) = 23.22\%$$

The IRR for project C is easier to determine, as the yearly cash flows are constant. It is solved as follows:

$$9{,}514 = 4{,}500\ A_{\overline{3}|}\ r$$
$$A_{\overline{3}|}\ r = 2.114$$

Using interpolation, we have:

$$A_{\overline{3}|}\ 19\% = 2.140$$
$$A_{\overline{3}|}\ 20\% = 2.106$$

$$IRR = 19 + \frac{2.140 - 2.114}{2.140 - 2.106} = 19.76\%$$

The IRRs and NPVs of the three projects are:

Project	IRR (%)	NPV (£)
A	20.00	+2,284
B	23.22	+1,730
C	19.76	+1,677

The rankings of A and B are clearly quite substantially different. If Loftus plc uses the NPV rule, it will choose A; if the IRR rule is used, it will choose B. In this situation the choice of NPV or IRR is critical. But why has this situation arisen at

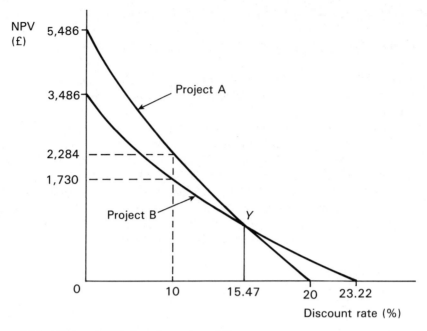

Figure 14.2 NPV and IRR of projects A and B.

all? The answer is because the two methods do not always rank projects in the same way, and in any situation in which the choice of one project precludes the acceptance of others, the ranking of projects is vital.

Figure 14.2 illustrates the nature of the problem. The graph shows the NPVs of A and B as functions of the discount rate. The two functions intersect at point Y where the discount rate is 15.47% p.a. For discount rates below 15.47%, the NPV rule favours A; for rates greater than 15.47%, B is better. What meaning can we ascribe to these figures?

Let us begin by looking at the differences between the cash flows of A and B. These are as follows:

	Year 0	Year 1	Year 2	Year 3
Project A	−9,514	+1,000	+5,000	+9,000
Project B	−9,514	+7,000	+5,000	+1,000
Difference	0	−6,000	0	+8,000

The cash flow from B is greater by £6,000 in year 1, and the cash flow from A is greater by £8,000 in year 3. Suppose Loftus plc provisionally accepts A. What would happen if it did this? In cash flow terms, it would *give up* the incremental return of £6,000 from B in year 1 to receive an extra £8,000 in year 3. Would this be worthwhile? The answer is that it would if the extra return were greater than the firm's cost of capital (here 10%). To answer this, we need to compute the return on the additional cash outflow of £6,000 which will generate a cash inflow of £8,000 in two years' time. Thus the return (r) is derived from the formula:

$$6,000 = \frac{8,000}{(1+r)^2} \quad \text{where } r = 15.47\%$$

The return of 15.47% represents the point at which the two NPV curves intersect, as shown by Figure 14.2 (i.e. the discount rate at which both projects have the same NPV and at which Loftus plc would be indifferent between them). As 15.47% is greater than the firm's cost of capital of 10%, the firm should invest in project A rather than B.

Because the very nature of the NPV method ensures that the additional cash flows are compared with the cost of capital, it accounts for the size of the investment in its recommendations. The IRR method does not account for size in its recommendations. IRR measures the average annual return earned on the amount remaining invested in the project at the start of each year. Hence, in our example, although project A earns a lower average return (20.00%) over its life than does B (23.22%) it does so on a higher average sum invested. Much more of the capital invested in B is repaid after only one year (£7,000) than is the case with A (£1,000); hence A is preferable. This preference is quite rational – most people would rather have a return of 50% p.a. on an average annual investment of £1,000, than a 100% return on an average annual investment of £100.

14.3 The problem of unorthodox cash flows

Up to now we have discussed the IRR criterion in the context of orthodox cash flow patterns, in which negative investment outflows are followed by positive cash inflows. In these cases a unique IRR can always be calculated. There are, however, investment projects in which the cash flow signs change from positive to negative and vice versa during the life of the project. For example, consider the case where replacement of equipment is concentrated into only a few years of a project's life; or where a mine has to be made safe (involving cash costs) after excavations have been completed. In these cases technical problems may arise with the use of the IRR: for example, there may be more than one IRR for a project or, alternatively, there may be no meaningful IRR at all. Consider the following two projects with attendant cash flows:

| Project | Cash flows (£) | | |
	End of Year 0	Year 1	Year 2
D	−2,000	+5,100	−3,150
E	+1,000	−2,000	+2,000

The internal rates of return (r) are as follows:

$$\text{Project D} \quad -2,000 + \frac{5,100}{(1+r)} - \frac{3,150}{(1+r)^2} = 0$$

where $r = 5\%$ or 50%

$$\text{Project E} \quad +1,000 - \frac{2,000}{(1+r)} + \frac{2,000}{(1+r)^2} = 0$$

$$1,000(1+r)^2 - 2,000(1+r) + 2,000 = 0$$
$$1,000 + 2,000r + 1,000r^2 - 2,000 - 2,000r + 2,000 = 0$$
$$1,000r^2 = -1,000$$
$$r^2 = -1$$
$$r = \sqrt{-1}$$

It is difficult to imagine how a decision maker could not be confused by these solutions. A hurdle rate for D of anywhere between 5% and 50% may indicate acceptance or rejection. Whatever the hurdle rate for E, it is hard to see how an internal rate of return of $\sqrt{-1}$ could lead to any conclusion as to acceptability! We might note here that both D and E still generate unambiguous net present values. Project D has a positive net present value at all costs of capital between 5% and 50%, and E has a positive net present value at any discount rate. In view of the technical difficulties associated with IRR, it is always preferable to use NPV to evaluate projects with unorthodox cash flows.

14.4 The payback method

It would be wrong to assume that all managers use the relatively sophisticated discounted cash flow techniques embodied in both the NPV and the IRR methods. In practice, other less sophisticated and, as we shall see, less 'correct' methods are used to evaluate long-term investments, and the use of discounting techniques in managerial decision making is substantially an innovation of the 1960s and 1970s. It is important to bear in mind that non-discounting methods have been employed in practice for many years and continue to be so. The simplest of the non-discounting methods is known as the payback method.

The payback criterion involves estimating the time period, usually the number of years, over which the cost of any particular investment is 'paid back'. This time period – the *payback period* – is then compared to some standard period to decide whether the project is to be accepted. If a number of projects are being ranked, the most acceptable will be the one which has the shortest payback period. The method thus looks at the return *of* investment, rather than the return *on* investment, and the criterion for choice is expressed as a period of time rather than as either a cash figure or a percentage. Consider three projects, K, L and M, with the following cash flows:

	Project K	Project L	Project M
Initial cost (£)	−15,000	−15,000	−15,000
Cash flows by year:			
Year 1	+1,000	+1,000	+11,000
Year 2	+3,000	+3,000	+3,000
Year 3	+11,000	+11,000	+1,000
Year 4	0	+10,000	+10,000

All have payback periods of three years. Are they equally worthwhile?

We might make the following observations about the three projects. First, under a strict interpretation of the payback rule, management would be indifferent as between the three projects, as each pays back its initial investment cost of £15,000 in three years. Yet it should be immediately obvious that differences exist between the projects for two reasons:

1. The cash flows from K cease at the end of the payback period (at the end of year 3), whereas the cash flows from L and M continue for one year after the end of the payback period.

2. The cash flows from M are much larger in the earlier years, and therefore are more attractive than the cash flows of L or K, in view of the time value of money.

This example illustrates the two main problems with the use of the payback method. It ignores both the existence of cash flows arising after the payback period, and the timing of the cash flows within the payback period. Why then is this method used in practice when it has such major faults? The answer may well be that, because payback does not entail the use of the mathematical methodology of discounting, it may be easy, and not too misleading, to apply it to small investment projects where the prediction of longer-term cash flows is not critical to the acceptance decision, or where the pattern of later cash flows is assumed to be similar to that of early years. Even if discounting methods are to be used, payback may be a rough screening device which gives some clue at an early stage whether the project is likely to be acceptable. If it becomes evident after using the payback rule that there is very little chance of acceptance of the project, then the more detailed and time-consuming calculations are avoided. This is particularly true for projects whose cash flows are subject to great uncertainty in the longer term. A short payback period may provide some assurance that acceptance of the project is unlikely to have serious consequences for the firm. However, use of the payback method is no substitute for the application of more refined methods of handling risk, such as those discussed in Chapters 4 and 13.

Discounted payback

It is possible to adapt the payback method to take account of the time value of money by discounting the cash flows before calculating the payback period. This *discounted payback* method will establish the period over which the investment becomes worthwhile: that is, the time taken before the present value of the inflows covers the present value of the outflows. It does not, however, remove the other fundamental weakness of payback, the failure to account for flows after the payback period, and so will not show how worthwhile a project is.

14.5 The accounting rate of return

The accounting rate of return is another non-discounting method of project appraisal which enjoys quite wide acceptance. It has several synonyms: for example, 'unadjusted' rate of return, 'book' rate of return or, most simply, return on investment (ROI).[2] The accounting rate of return (ARR) can also be computed in many different ways, all of which rely on traditional accounting profit numbers, rather than on cash flow numbers. The ARR may, for instance, be computed by dividing a prospective investment's annual net profit by either the total investment cost, or the average book value of the investment. Because the ARR method necessitates the use of accounting profits, accrued revenues and costs, rather than yearly cash flows, enter the calculations. Accounting profits also involve depreciation charges, which are non-cash items.

Assume a project (fixed asset) with an initial cost of £100,000, an estimated life of five years and nil scrap value, which is to be depreciated using the straight-line method (i.e. at the rate of £20,000 p.a.). The asset is expected to generate operating cash flows of £30,000 p.a. The accounting rate(s) of return can be computed as follows:

$$\text{ARR on total investment} = \frac{30,000 - 20,000}{100,000} = 10\%$$

$$\text{ARR on average investment} = \frac{30,000 - 20,000}{100,000 \div 2} = 20\%$$

The faults of the method are obvious. It uses accounting profits rather than cash flows, and it does not consider the time value of money (i.e. profits arising in the final year of the asset's life are weighted equally with profits arising in the first year). Further, like the IRR method, the ARR method deals in ratios, and thus says nothing about the size of the projects. As we have seen in the IRR section, this can present problems if projects are mutually exclusive.

Consider the following data on two alternative projects, P and Q, both of which have an initial investment cost of £100,000 and are expected to last for three years, at the end of which each investment will be worthless. The cost of capital is 10%.

1. *Net yearly cash flows*

	P (£)	Q (£)
Year 1	70,000	20,000
Year 2	50,000	30,000
Year 3	10,000	80,000

We will examine their potential acceptability under the NPV and the ARR methods.

2. *Net present value method*

Project P $\quad -100{,}000 + 70{,}000(0.909) + 50{,}000(0.826) + 10{,}000(0.751)$
$= +£12{,}440$

Project Q $\quad -100{,}000 + 20{,}000(0.909) + 30{,}000(0.826) + 80{,}000(0.751)$
$= +£3{,}040$

Clearly P is the more acceptable project.

3. *Accounting rate of return method (based on total investment cost)*

$$\text{ARR} = \frac{\text{Annual cash flow} - \text{Annual depreciation}}{\text{Total investment cost}}$$

Project P $\quad \text{ARR} = \dfrac{\dfrac{70{,}000 + 50{,}000 + 10{,}000}{3} - \dfrac{100{,}000}{3}}{100{,}000}$

$$\text{ARR} = \frac{43{,}333 - 33{,}333}{100{,}000} = 10\%$$

Project Q $\quad \text{ARR} = \dfrac{\dfrac{20{,}000 + 30{,}000 + 80{,}000}{3} - \dfrac{100{,}000}{3}}{100{,}000}$

$$\text{ARR} = \frac{43{,}333 - 33{,}333}{100{,}000} = 10\%$$

Using ARR, the two projects are indistinguishable, as each shows a return of 10%. Furthermore, both apparently produce a return no higher than the cost of capital. This shows that incorrect decisions can be taken by using the ARR method, based on arbitrary accounting profits, caused by arbitrary depreciation figures and other accounting allocations.

14.6 | Long-term decisions in practice

We have looked in some detail at various methods which might be used to decide on the worth of long-term projects. Some are technically sophisticated, some are costly to implement and some, which are neither sophisticated nor costly, are intuitively appealing. Whatever their apparent merits and demerits, it would be wrong to conclude this chapter by failing to mention which methods are used by corporate decision makers. The methods used for evaluation of capital investments in practice have been the subject of a number of research studies over the last 20 to 30 years, in many different countries. The primary interest of researchers has been to establish whether there is wide acceptance by decision makers of apparently superior methods, and to ask why methods other than those suggested by theory might be used in practice.

Without referring to a large number of individual studies in detail, it is possible to mention several major findings which require some explanation or comment.

Multiple methods

Surveys of practice have typically found that managers tend to use more than one technique when assessing a possible capital investment. This finding has been reported in successive surveys of UK managers and also in international surveys, although the pattern of preference for different techniques and between quantitative and qualitative methods does vary between countries.[3] This behaviour may reflect a desire to assess projects from a number of different points of view and to apply multiple criteria before acceptance. It might also be the case, however, that managers recognise the need to make the strongest possible case for investments they are proposing, and utilise different techniques in order to present their recommendations to best advantage.

Reliance on qualitative judgement

Several studies have shown that managers place considerable reliance on qualitative criteria in their analysis and justification of investments. For example, Kim and Song[4] reported that higher proportions of managers regarded qualitative factors as 'extremely important' for investment justification than quantitative methods. The effect of an investment on the firm's ability to compete in the marketplace was seen as extremely important by 52% of Korean managers, 43% of US and 41% of Japanese, and operational performance improvements were seen as extremely important by 49% of Korean managers and 46% of Japanese, although by a much lower figure of 18% of US managers. In the UK in a survey in 1982,[5] Pike noted that considerable weight appeared to be placed on judgemental issues, 63% of his respondents indicating qualitative judgement to be 'important' or 'very important' in decision making.

The pre-eminence accorded to qualitative judgement might seem somewhat surprising. But should we really be surprised to find that managers use their judgement extensively in making decisions which shape the firm's future? Throughout this book we have frequently stressed that the qualitative aspects of business decisions are very important, even if difficult to quantify. So why might 'qualitative judgement' be of primary importance in long-term decision making? Managers may use non-quantitative reasoning because of particular strategic considerations affecting the firm or perhaps because of the uncertainty attached to the outcomes of long-term decisions. It is likely that the results of such decisions will be affected by some unexpected features – and thus exclusive reliance on numerical forecasts might expose managers to criticism if those forecasts are not met. In other words, judgemental decision making may be in the managers' own interests.

Preference for IRR over NPV

Earlier in this chapter we sought to demonstrate that NPV is to be preferred to IRR because in a number of situations IRR will give recommendations which are inconsistent with maximising the present value of future cash flows. However, as illustrated by the figures in Table 14.1, surveys of practice have consistently revealed more frequent use of IRR. For example, based on a survey of 300 UK manufacturing companies, Drury *et al.* reported that IRR was used 'always' or 'often' by 60% of respondents, but NPV by only 45%, while Pike found that 75% of his sample firms used IRR at some time but only 68% NPV.

Table 14.1 Use of quantitative methods of investment appraisal

	Kim and Song			Pike and Wolfe		Drury et al.
	Japan	USA	Korea	UK		UK
				% using		
	% regarding extremely or very important			total	always or mainly	% using always or often
Payback	86	71	75	92	71	67
Accounting rate of return	53	46	68	56	28	43
Internal rate of return	20	69	75	75	55	60
Net present value	28	64	60	68	37	45

Sources: R.H. Pike, 'An empirical study of the adoption of sophisticated capital procedures and decision-making effectiveness', *Accounting and Business Research*, **18**(72), Autumn 1988; C. Drury, S. Braund, P. Osborne and M. Tayles, *A Survey of Management Accounting Practices in UK Manufacturing Companies*, ACCA Research Occasional Paper, Chartered Association of Certified Accountants, 1992; and Il Woon Kim and Ja Song, 'US, Korea and Japan: accounting practices in three countries', *Management Accounting* (US), August 1990.

How are we to explain this apparent conflict between the prescriptions of theory and the choices of decision makers? We probably cannot argue that decision makers are unfamiliar with the arguments concerning the merits of the methods. Academic writers have been presenting the case for NPV in more or less sophisticated fashion for the last 30 years, and it is not likely that all of these presentations have remained unheard and unread. Perhaps the explanations lie not at a technical level, but rather at a more practical level, one which reflects the comparative ease of understanding the data. Here we offer, in no particular order, three possible explanations for the practical superiority of IRR over NPV.

First, in contrast to the NPV rule, the IRR method does not require an explicit cost of capital calculation at the *start of the analysis*, although the *final* decision on acceptability should be based on a comparison of the IRR and the cost of capital. What may happen in practice is that the IRR is measured finally against a series of possible hurdle rates (whether costs of capital or otherwise) chosen on a subjective basis. Thus use of the IRR allows the manager to incorporate qualitative judgement into the analytical framework. A series of possible hurdle rates could also be tested using NPV, by calculating a range of NPVs at different discount rates. However, this procedure may well appear more cumbersome and less readily understandable to a manager.

Second, there is evidence to suggest that managers may be more 'at home' in dealing with percentage measures than with absolute cash flows when comparing investments and investment returns. The use of IRR allows them to make use of this familiarity.

Finally, and somewhat more tentatively, we suggest that many managers may prefer IRR because it enables them to allow for the different risk levels associated with particular investments, by examining the differences in the margins of safety as measured by the difference between the IRR and the required return. Although this appears a rather more unsophisticated treatment of risk than others we described in Chapter 4, it is easier to implement and allows a more obvious use of qualitative managerial judgement, an attribute which we have seen to be attractive to many managers.

Use of non-discounting methods

While surveys taken over the last 30 years do suggest an increasing recognition of discounted cash flow appraisal methods, the figures in Table 14.1 also reveal considerable continued reliance on techniques which do not involve discounting. The preference for non-discounting approaches is most apparent in the figures for Japan, but payback also appears to be very popular in other countries, including the UK.

How are we to explain the continued popularity of the non-discounting methods? A number of factors may be suggested for this situation. For example, many managers may feel that the uncertainty inherent in the cash flow estimates renders complex evaluation methods superfluous. Why make an elaborate analysis when the underlying data themselves are unreliable? At least payback has the advantages of simplicity and understandability. It may also be the case that the popularity of payback is in part due to management's concern with short-term liquidity rather than longer-term profitability. In particular, with investment in modern technology, managers may feel that a short payback reduces the risk of being overtaken by further technological developments before investment can be considered again. Finally, we might stress that one theoretical justification for the use of discounting depends both on the existence of a perfect capital market and on the belief that share prices represent the present value of the anticipated dividend stream. It is possible that the capital market is imperfect (or at least that managers believe it to be so) and that the value of shares is affected by (short-term) variables other than anticipated dividends. This point is worth exploring further, as it may do much to explain the continued importance in investment appraisal not only of payback, but of other profit-based measures such as ARR.

Insofar as managers believe that variables such as reported profits, asset cover and current ratios influence share prices, they ignore at their peril the effects of long-term decisions on these variables. Nor should we forget that many managers have their own compensation and bonuses tied to the firm's (or the division's) performance, as measured typically by a variant of the accounting rate of return, the return on investment (ROI). ROI (which is discussed more fully in Chapter 18) is by far the most popular method used to evaluate performance within the organisation. There is an obvious incentive for managers to accept projects which are successful when evaluated by the same criteria (ARR or ROI) as those against which they themselves are assessed. This may be the case even if these criteria give different signals (and therefore entail the choice of different projects) from those given by the NPV method.

At the root of the conflict may well lie the managers' belief that they are constrained in their long-term decision making by the short-term view adopted by the capital markets. They are less willing to accept long-term projects which do little to enhance short-term profits. Long-term projects with long gestation periods, which depress accounting profits in the early years, may make the firm vulnerable to bids from third parties or may otherwise threaten the positions of managers, if these lower accounting profits have adverse effects on the share price. The moral may be that if investors worry about the quality and quantity of short-term profits then, to maintain the company's share price (and their own positions), so should the managers. An illustration of the manager's dilemma when accounting profits and present values conflict is given in an appendix to this chapter.

14.7 Post-audit of capital investments

Before completing this chapter, mention should be made of the practice of *post-auditing* (or post-implementation audit) of capital investment projects. This procedure involves comparing the actual outcomes associated with a project with the results originally expected and on which the investment decision was taken.

A post-audit of investments can be beneficial to management in a number of ways. It can help to provide control information about asset acquisition and utilisation which may allow adjustments to be made while a project is still being implemented, or other corrective action to be taken. Post-audit can also help future decision making by allowing judgements to be formed on the quality and accuracy of the estimation process used when the project was evaluated. In addition, the knowledge that post-auditing will take place may improve the quality of information for the original decision. Managers often have incentives to give optimistic predictions of the benefits an investment will bring: for example, if they are keen to obtain the latest technological development. The knowledge that their estimates will be audited against actual outcomes, and that variations will have to be explained and justified, can act as a constraint against over-optimistic predictions. However, care should be taken to ensure that post-auditing is perceived as fair and that it does not discourage managers from proposing risky but potentially beneficial innovations.

When undertaking a post-audit of a capital investment, the same techniques as were applied in the original investment decision should be used for comparing actual and expected results. This should mean looking at cash flows rather than the effects on accounting profits. The timing of the review should enable a realistic assessment of actual benefits to be made, and it may be appropriate to carry out the exercise more than once. Estimates of future flows should be revised from their original amounts in the light of experience and new information since the project began. Ideally, a post-audit review should be undertaken for all significant capital projects, although clearly it will be of most importance with larger investments.

The main difficulties in undertaking post-audits are in identifying the actual flows related to a capital investment. It can be extremely difficult to quantify some benefits – for example, an improvement in productivity because of investment in staff working conditions – or to isolate the flows linked to the investment in one particular asset from the rest of the production facility, and the information may not be collected in the same form as that used for the original investment proposal.

Evidence on the use of post-auditing is varied but suggests that this practice is increasing, certainly among the larger UK companies. For example, surveys of practice have reported an increasing proportion of large UK companies using post-audits, from 47% in 1985 to 67% in 1988 and 77% in 1990.[6] However, it also appears that the form of review undertaken concentrates on the capital costs rather than the associated benefits. For example, in a survey of medium-sized businesses, McIntyre and Coulthurst[7] reported that, while 87% of those surveyed compared actual and predicted costs on all or most investment projects, a much lower figure, only 47%, carried out a similar comparison for the benefits of the investments. It is possible that firms review expenditure as part of a concern for cost control but do not engage in the full review of both costs and benefits that is implied by post-auditing.

CHAPTER SUMMARY

This chapter has expanded in two ways our consideration of management accounting methods which might be used in the analysis of long-term capital investments. First, we have reviewed alternative appraisal methods to the NPV approach described in Chapter 13 as the best way theoretically to make decisions that are consistent with an objective of maximising wealth. Second, we have commented on the use of different methods by corporate managers as revealed in surveys of practice.

A summary comparison of the alternative methods we have discussed is set out in Table 14.2. We would reiterate that the NPV method should be used in all cases which demand relatively complex and sophisticated treatments. This conclusion is based on the grounds that the NPV method:

- is clear, simple to understand and unambiguous;

- focuses on the maximisation of the present value of future cash flows, which is the objective assumed for business decision making;

Table 14.2 Comparison of alternative methods of capital investment appraisal

Method	Decision rules*	Basis of rule	Limitations
Net present value	Accept all projects with a positive NPV. Rank highest NPV first.	Wealth-maximising objective. Cost of capital calculation can be used for the discount rate. Timing, amount and duration of cash flows can be identified.	Relative returns of projects are not shown. Limited treatment of uncertainty and risk.
Internal rate of return	Accept projects exceeding the target rate of return. Rank highest IRR first.	Target rate can be established. Timing, amount and duration of cash flows can be identified.	Ignores absolute £ value of return. Limited treatment of uncertainty and risk. Multiple rates of return possible.
Payback	Accept projects if payback shorter than target. Rank quickest payback first.	Speed of recovery of investment is most important. Timing, amount and duration of cash flows can be identified. Risk is lower with quicker payback.	Ignores cash flows after payback period. Ignores timing of flows within the payback period and hence the time value of money. Limited treatment of uncertainty and risk.
Accounting rate of return	Accept projects exceeding target rate of return. Rank highest ARR first.	Effect on accounting profits, relative to book value of investment, is most important. Pattern of recognition of profits can be identified.	Ignores cash flows. Ignores the time value of money. Subject to distortion through accounting policies. Uncertainty and risk ignored.

* Accept/reject and ranking rules assuming no capital rationing.

- uses a discount rate (the cost of capital) which reflects the returns required by the suppliers of funds; and

- avoids the many technical problems of the IRR method, and accounts for the time value of money, which is ignored in non-discounting methods.

Surveys of practice have shown that managers tend to use more than one method of investment appraisal, that qualitative judgement is relied upon as well as quantitative techniques, and that rate of return and non-discounting methods remain popular. These findings highlight the importance that behavioural, psychological and other contextual factors can have on management decision making in practice, and on the role that is played by procedures based on accounting profits.

Even though the NPV method appears not yet to have gained the wide acceptance by business which it deserves, this situation may change as managers come to realise that the use of the method leads to optimal decision making, at least in the sense that the present value of the firm's cash resources will be equal to or larger than the present value of cash resources resulting from the use of any other method.

APPENDIX
Accounting profit v. present value: an example

The following example relating to project choice illustrates the sort of dilemma faced by managers when determining the figures to place reliance on for a choice between competing capital investment possibilities.

Mr Race, the chief executive of Course plc, is concerned about the share price of his company, fearing that, unless it improves over the next two years, the company may be subject to an unwelcome takeover bid. Mr Race is currently choosing between two alternative ways (A and B) of marketing a new product. The sales of the product will last for four years. A market research survey has suggested that the annual net cash receipts (R) for the new product, before advertising and special packaging costs, will be the same whichever marketing alternative is chosen, and will be determined by the equation

$$R = 600,000y - 100,000y^2$$

where y represents the relevant year: for example, in the second year $(y = 2)$, $R = £800,000$. The equipment required by each marketing alternative has a four-year life and zero scrap value, and costs £1,000,000 for alternative A and £800,000 for alternative B. The initial two years' advertising costs will be the same for both alternatives: namely, £400,000 in the first year and £200,000 in the second year. For alternative A, the advertising costs compared to the second year will increase at 20% p.a. compound for the third and fourth year. No further advertising costs will be incurred in alternative B after the second year. Alternative B necessitates the use of special display packaging, the cost of which is equal to 20% of the annual net cash receipts (R).

The purchase of the equipment will take place on the first day of the first financial year, and all other cash flows can be assumed to take place on the last day of each financial year. The effective after-tax cost of capital of Course plc is 10%.

On the basis of the above data, which alternative should Mr Race choose: A or B? Let us begin our analysis by determining the effect of each alternative on the reported profitability of Course plc. Tables 14.3 and 14.4 show the profits generated by alternatives A and B over the four-year period of the investment.

Though both alternatives show an accounting loss in the first year, the net improvement in profitability over the first two years, the period of Mr Race's expressed concern, is much greater for alternative A. Alternative A increases reported profit by £200,000 in the first two years; alternative B by only £40,000. The signal given to Mr Race might be to choose alternative A, as this is likely to have a more favourable short-term impact on the company's share price. But how would the alternatives be ranked under our preferred NPV criterion? Would the same preference be expressed? Tables 14.5 and 14.6 show the NPV calculations over the full life of the projects.

Table 14.3 Alternative A: effect on profits (£000)

	Years							
	1		2		3		4	
Net revenues (£)		500		800		900		800
Less Advertising (£)	400		200		240		288	
Depreciation (£)	250	650	250	450	250	490	250	538
Net profit (£)		(150)		350		410		262

Table 14.4 Alternative B: effect on profits (£000)

	Years							
	1		2		3		4	
Net revenues (£)		500		800		900		800
Less Advertising (£)	400		200		—		—	
Packaging (£)	100		160		180		160	
Depreciation (£)	200	700	200	560	200	380	200	360
Net profit (£)		(200)		240		520		440

Table 14.5 Alternative A: net present value calculation (£000)

	Periods				
	0	1	2	3	4
Machine cost (£)	(1,000)				
Operating cash flows (£) (Net revenues *less* advertising)	–	100	600	660	512
Net cash flow (£)	(1,000)	100	600	660	512
Discount factor at 10%	1.000	0.9091	0.8264	0.7513	0.6830
Present values of cash flows (£)	(1,000)	91	496	496	350
	Net present value +£433,000				

Table 14.6 Alternative B: net present value calculation (£000)

	Periods				
	0	1	2	3	4
Machine cost (£)	(800)				
Operating cash flows (£) (Net revenues *less* advertising and packaging)	–	–	440	720	640
Net cash flow (£)	(800)	–	440	720	640
Discount factor at 10%	1.000	0.9091	0.8264	0.7513	0.6830
Present values of cash flows (£)	(800)	–	364	541	437
	Net present value +£542,000				

Examination of the results shown in Tables 14.5 and 14.6 reveals clearly Mr Race's dilemma. The NPV model, which discounts the cash flows arising over the project's entire life, signals alternative B as the appropriate choice. If Mr Race wishes to maximise the wealth of Course plc's shareholders, he should choose alternative B. The relative benefits of alternative B are the superior cash flows in the later years related to the lower investment cost. Reconciliation of conflicts such as these are major problems for corporate managers, and we should not ignore such problems. Perhaps shareholders in Course plc might prefer alternative A if they also believed the future independence of their company to be more secure via the short-term benefits produced by this investment. Perhaps also Course plc has shareholders who have invested for short-term capital gains rather than for a longer-term dividend stream – in which case they might also prefer alternative A. But for the purpose of developing a theory of long-term decision making, we must presume that shareholders are primarily interested in the long-term future of the organisation, and that they expect to receive a stream of dividends as reward for their investment. On this basis it is difficult to argue against the NPV method.

REVIEW QUESTIONS

1. Explain the situations in which the IRR technique may lead to different conclusions from the NPV method. Are these situations likely to arise often?

2. Many studies have shown that, in practice, IRR is preferred to NPV. Why is this? Do you believe that accounting writers should rethink their theories in the light of such practices?

3. 'Any appraisal technique which uses discounting is likely to be more effective than any technique which does not.' Discuss.

4. 'The accounting rate of return is riddled with inconsistencies such as to make its usefulness very doubtful.' if you accept this proposition, why do you think that the accounting rate of return is still used in practice?

5. 'The future is so uncertain that the use of any technique which requires the precise identification of future yearly cash flows is an unwarranted luxury. In inflationary times, such techniques are simply academic.' Discuss.

EXERCISES

14.1 Marc plc is considering the selection of one of a pair of mutually exclusive investment projects. Both would involve purchase of machinery with a life of five years. Project 1 would generate annual cash flows (receipts less payments) of £200,000; the machinery would cost £556,000, and have a scrap value of £56,000. Project 2 would generate annual cash flows of £500,000; the machinery would cost £1,616,000 and have a scrap value of £301,000.

Marc uses the straight-line method for providing depreciation. Its cost of capital is 15% p.a. Assume that annual cash flows arise on the anniversaries of the initial outlay, that there will be no price changes over the project lives, and that acceptance of one of the projects will not alter the required amount of working capital.

(a) Calculate for each project:

(i) the accounting rate of return (ratio, over project life, of average accounting profit to *average book value of investment*) to nearest 1%;

(ii) the net present value;

(iii) the internal rate of return (DCF yield) to nearest 1%;

(iv) the payback period to one decimal place.

(b) State which, if any, project you would select for acceptance, giving reasons for your choice of criterion to guide the decision. (Solution at end of text.)

14.2 Strauss Ltd is considering three projects, each of which, if accepted, would commence on 1 January 19X7. Cash flows expected from the projects are as follows:

	Project		
	A (£)	B (£)	C (£)
1 January 19X7	−5,000	−10,000	−6,000
31 December 19X7	+4,000	+ 1,000	+2,200
31 December 19X8	+1,500	+ 1,000	+2,200
31 December 19X9	+1,100	+13,900	+2,200

Projects A and B are mutually exclusive (i.e. only one of them may be accepted). The company's accountant has calculated the approximate internal rate of return of each project as follows:

Project A   20%
Project B   18%
Project C   5%

The accountant advises that project A should be accepted rather than B as it has a higher internal rate of return, and that C should be accepted as it shows a positive rate of return. Strauss Ltd is able both to lend and borrow funds freely at 10% p.a.

(a) Prepare calculations showing which projects Strauss Ltd should accept. If your recommendations differ from those of the accountant, explain and justify the differences.

(b) Prepare revised calculations so that the internal rate of return method of appraisal and the method you have used in (a) above, lead to the same conclusions. (Solution at end of text.)

14.3 Moore plc manufactures and sells a wide range of consumer durable goods. The sales of one of its products, alpha, have been increasing in recent years. The current selling price of each alpha is £40 and the variable costs are £35 per unit. Fixed costs directly attributable to alpha are currently £140,000.

Over the next four years it is anticipated that the sales will be as follows:

	Unit sales
Year ended 31 December 19X7	73,000
19X8	81,000
19X9	89,000
19Y0	97,000

Selling prices will increase by 5% each year over this period, whereas variable costs will increase by 7% p.a. and fixed costs by 5% p.a.

In anticipation of the management accountant presenting figures which may show a decline in profits for alpha, the sales manager has proposed an extensive advertising campaign to boost sales of this product. Such a campaign would cost an additional £150,000 at the beginning of the first year and a further £50,000 at the beginning of the second year. The expected benefits are reflected in the revised sales forecast as follows:

	Unit sales
Year ended 31 December 19X7	93,000
19X8	107,000
19X9	112,000
19Y0	118,000

After 19Y0 alpha is expected to be superseded. The sales increase would require an additional investment in working capital of £80,000 during the first year and a further £20,000 during the second year. This working capital would all be disinvested during the final year in which alpha is made and sold.

The general manager is willing to consider such a campaign, although there is some concern as to how this will be reflected in the annual profitability statements, particularly in the years when additional advertising expenditure will be incurred. It is company practice to charge all advertising and sales promotion expenditure to the current income statement and not to defer the expense.

(a) Prepare a statement showing the estimated profitability of alpha over the next four years, assuming the additional advertising expenditure is not incurred.

(b) Prepare a statement showing whether or not the increased advertising expenditure can be justified in the light of the company's target return on investment of 15% p.a.

(c) Prepare a statement showing the profitability of alpha over the next four years, assuming the advertising campaign is undertaken.

14.4 Mrs Capricorn is proposing to purchase a machine to manufacture widgets. She plans to manufacture 10,000 widgets per annum and sell them at £2 per unit; materials and other variable costs would amount to 50p per unit and there would be no fixed costs. The machine would cost £40,000 and have a life of five years, after which it would be sold for scrap for £1,000. The machine would require an overhaul at the end of year 3 at a cost of £10,000. Assume that sale proceeds and variable costs arise at the end of each year. Mrs Capricorn requires a return of 7% p.a. on investment; she does not expect there to be any change in relevant prices over the foreseeable future.

(a) Prepare a calculation showing whether the purchase of the machine is worthwhile.

(b) Assume that Mrs Capricorn can borrow and lend as much as she wants at 7% p.a. She decides that she will arrange her affairs so that she spends the same amount on living expenses each year and has £40,000 in hand for the purchase of a new machine in five years' time. Calculate how much she can use for living expenses each year.

(c) Prepare a calculation of accounting profits (according to usual conventions), balance sheets and rates of return on capital employed over the life of the asset, assuming that Mrs Capricorn implements the plan found in your answer to (b).

(d) Comment on the usefulness of conventional accounting calculations for purposes of investment decision making.

14.5 Stadler is an ambitious young executive who has recently been appointed to the position of financial director of Paradis plc, a small listed company. Stadler regards this appointment as a temporary one, enabling him to gain experience before moving to a larger organisation. His intention is to leave Paradis plc in three years' time, with its share price standing high. As a consequence, he is particularly concerned that the reported profits of Paradis plc should be as high as possible in his third and final year with the company.

Paradis plc has recently raised £350,000 from a rights issue, and the directors are considering three ways of using these funds. Three projects (A, B and C) are being considered, each involving the immediate purchase of equipment costing £350,000. One project only can be undertaken and the equipment for each project will have a useful life equal to that of the project, with no scrap value. Stadler favours project C because it is expected to show the highest accounting profit in the third year. However, he does not wish to reveal his real reasons for favouring project C and so, in his report to the chairman, he recommends project C because it shows the highest internal rate of return. The following summary is taken from his report:

Project	Net cash flows (£000) Years 0	1	2	3	4	5	6	7	8	Internal rate of return (%)
A	−350	100	110	104	112	138	160	180	–	27.5
B	−350	40	100	210	260	160	–	–	–	26.4
C	−350	200	150	240	40	–	–	–	–	33.0

The chairman of the company is accustomed to projects being appraised in terms of payback and accounting rate of return, and is consequently suspicious of the use of internal rate of return as a method of project selection. Accordingly, the chairman has asked for an independent report on the choice of project. The company's cost of capital is 20% and a policy of straight-line depreciation is used to write off the cost of equipment in the financial statements.

(a) Calculate the payback period for each project.

(b) Calculate the accounting rate of return for each project.

(c) Prepare a report for the chairman with supporting calculations indicating which project should be preferred by the ordinary shareholders of Paradis plc.

(d) Discuss the assumptions about the reactions of the stock market that are implicit in Stadler's choice of project C.

Notes

1. Our interpolation is based on NPVs at 20% and 25%. Greater precision would be achieved by undertaking further calculations prior to interpolation to find the two integer discount rates that give NPVs closest to zero: the lower discount rate will give a positive NPV and the higher one a negative NPV.
2. The term 'return on investment' is also sometimes confusingly used to refer to the internal rate of return.
3. See, for example, R. H. Pike and M. B. Wolfe, *Capital Budgeting in the 1990s*, Chartered Institute of Management Accountants, 1988; C. Drury, S. Braund, P. Osborne and M. Tayles, *A Survey of Management Accounting Practices in UK Manufacturing Companies*, ACCA Research Occasional Paper, Chartered Association of Certified Accountants, 1992; and Il Woon Kim and Ja Song, 'US, Korea and Japan: accounting practices in three countries', *Management Accounting* (US), August 1990.
4. Op. cit.
5. See R. H. Pike, 'A review of recent trends in capital budgeting processes', *Accounting and Business Research*, Summer 1983.
6. Figures taken, respectively, from: D. Holmes and B. Neale, 'Auditing for fullest control', *Accountancy Age*, 25 April 1987; Pike and Wolfe, *Capital Budgeting*, op. cit.; and B. Neale and D. Holmes, *Post Completion Auditing*, Pitman, 1991.
7. A. D. McIntyre and N. J. Coulthurst, *Capital Budgeting Practices in Small and Medium-Sized Businesses: A Survey*, Chartered Institute of Management Accountants, 1986.

The budgeting process

AIMS AND OBJECTIVES

☐ To explain the importance and goals of budgeting.
☐ To explain the relationship between budgeting and planning.
☐ To describe the procedures for preparing budgets.
☐ To explain and discuss the relationship between budgeting and control.
☐ To discuss the effects of budgeting on motivation.

In previous chapters we have examined in some detail the types of decision, both short- and long-term, typically undertaken by management, and we have set out the criteria to be used to ensure that such decisions are consistent with the assumed goals of the organisation. Throughout these chapters we have stressed the importance of the concept of differential analysis as the basis of managerial decision making. Our primary aim has been to look at individual decisions in isolation, so as to highlight the main principles of decision analysis. We have not considered explicitly the interdependences which exist between the different functions within an organisation, or the information needed by management when implementing decisions and controlling subsequent operations.

In practice, managerial decisions frequently have implications for a number of functions of a business: for example, marketing, production, purchasing and financing. Such functions do not operate independently of each other. Decisions which utilise these functions are interdependent decisions. For example, suppose that the management of a manufacturing firm decides to sell x units of product Y. Unless the firm holds large stocks of Y and docs not wish to replace these stocks when they are used, the decision to sell will involve a decision to produce more units of Y, which in turn may entail a further, simultaneous decision to purchase raw materials, hire labour and incur overhead costs, each of which will affect the firm's financial resources.

A vitally important task for management is to co-ordinate these various interrelated aspects of decision making. Co-ordination helps, first, to ensure that the final results are consistent with the organisation's goals and, second, to prevent suboptimisation within the organisation by ensuring, as far as is possible, that individual managers are working towards the same end. This is a difficult and time-consuming task. Individual managers may pursue targets which appear good for themselves, but which, from the firm's viewpoint, are not optimal. For example, the manager of the assembly department may wish to buy components externally rather than rely on internal manufacture, perhaps because external components are currently cheaper than the price charged to the assembly department by the manufacturing department. However, for the firm as a whole this choice may be suboptimal when other social and economic factors are considered. We consider this particular issue in Chapter 18.

One way for management to co-ordinate activities is to prepare detailed and explicit financial plans of action for specific future periods, both for individual units within the firm, such as manufacturing and assembly divisions, and for the firm as a single entity. These detailed plans are usually referred to as *budgets*, and the co-ordinating activity is usually termed the *budgetary process*. The overall plan for the firm is termed the *master budget* or *comprehensive budget*. Essentially budgeting involves *modelling* the organisation's activities – quantifying the expected physical and financial consequences associated with implementing decisions over a given period. Budgets stand as plans of action and targets for actual operations.

In the discussion that follows, we will most commonly refer to budgeting in a manufacturing firm, but this process is of equal importance in service firms and non-profit organisations, although the principal focus of the budget will reflect their different operating contexts. In manufacturing, the main issue is following through the relationship between the expected level of sales activity and the different aspects of the productive process – acquiring materials and capital assets, policy on inventory, etc. In a service organisation, the critical factor is more likely to be the relationship between intended sales activity and the availability of the necessary staff and skills. Services such as consultancy cannot be stored in inventory to deal with fluctuations in demand, so planning to have the required staff available at the right time is of critical importance for success. In non-profit organisations, the principal budgeting issue is planning the relationship between revenue received and expenditure allocations. For example, a local authority must plan its spending in different areas, such as leisure services and housing, to be consistent with expectations of revenue that will be received from local taxes, government grants, etc., and a charity must budget its allocation to different projects to fall within expectations of donations that will be received.

15.1 The role of budgeting

The general objective of budgeting is to provide a formal, quantitative and authoritative statement of the firm's plans, expressed in money terms. (We will discuss the validity of purely financial budgets in the final section of this chapter.) This rather wide-ranging statement covers a multitude of different possible contributions that budgeting can make to the management process. At least six points, some of which are overlapping, are worthy of further analysis.

1. *Budgeting forces managers to plan.* The existence of formal budgets compels busy managers to think coherently about their position in the firm and their contribution to its future. Thus budgeting forces managers to stand back from their regular activities and to consider the goals of the firm, as well as the more detailed ways of achieving them. Awareness of broader goals and environmental conditions can enhance managers' perspectives on operating activities.

2. *Budgeting reveals new data about the firm's future and thus reduces the risks inherent in its operations.* For example, the extent of the different, and joint, claims on resources from managers of decentralised activities may not be obvious until they are brought together in the budget. This may then show the existence of scarce or surplus resources, which, in turn, may lead to improved measures (e.g. opportunity costs) of the costs of using such resources.

3. *Budgeting encourages communication and the co-ordination of activities.* Budget procedures allow information about the proposed activities of the firm to be communicated to different managers in different locations, and may thus help in the reconciliation of claims to, and availability of, significant resources. In addition, where responsibilities are geographically and functionally separate, it may be difficult to communicate the performance targets expected of individuals – formal budgeting seeks to mitigate this problem. Whether or not all employees should participate in the setting of such targets is an important issue which we discuss later in this chapter.

4. *Budgeting provides a guide to action.* The physical process of budgeting of itself gives information to management about the feasibility and appropriateness of particular activities, and helps identify factors that are critical to success in meeting targets. If activities are seen to be infeasible or inappropriate, the signal is given for corrective action, and once the budget has been approved, managers are given a clearer indication of the tasks and targets expected of them.

5. *Budgeting acts as a basis for measuring and evaluating performance.* This aspect of budgeting is regarded by many writers as being its most important feature. The preparation and subsequent agreement of the budget offers a benchmark against which the performance of all entities within the firm, as well as the firm itself, can be measured. Comparison of budget plans with actual experience gives feedback information on the quality of planning, changes in the environment and the efficiency of operations. Managers can be held responsible for their own particular portion of the overall budget. Budgets thus facilitate management by exception, as it is necessary for managers to investigate only those aspects of performance which are significantly different from expectations.

6. *Budgeting aids goal congruence.* The process of planning and controlling is an iterative process which helps greatly to marry the firm's goals with those of its

individual parts: that is, it helps the achievement of goal congruence between each part of the firm (the managers and the divisions) and the firm itself.

Because of these important functions, budgeting is sometimes said to have a 'sense-making' role in organisations: in other words, the budget conveys much more than just the formal financial numbers, giving a representation of how the organisation sees its activities. Decisions about what is included in, and what is omitted from, the budget implicitly communicate information about organisational values and priorities. For example, if senior management state that the firm's strategy is based

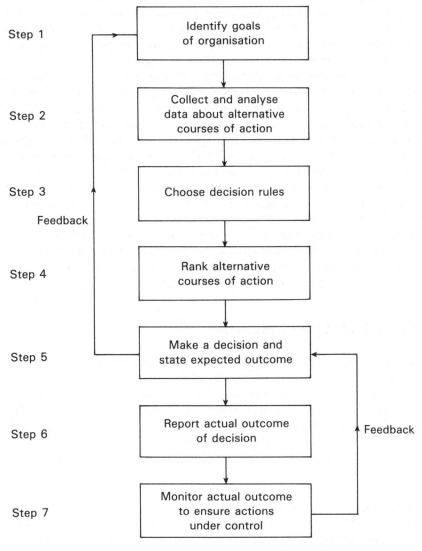

Figure 15.1 Framework for managerial planning, decision making and control.

on product innovation, but at the same time reduce the budget for research and development, staff will doubt the integrity of that claim. Similarly, the success of actual operations will be interpreted with reference to the budget. Terms such as 'over budget' and 'under budget' may suggest particular value judgements about performance, but they are entirely dependent on the figures set in the budget, and the judgements will be valid only if the budget itself is appropriate.

In order to understand the budgetary process more clearly, we should explain how it fits into the overall framework for managerial planning, decision making and control, which we first set out in Chapter 1. The framework is produced again here (see Figure 15.1). The budgetary process begins with step 5 of the managerial framework: once decisions have been taken to commit resources to specific plans of action, forecasts are made of the expected outcomes of these plans, in the form of budgets. Budgets thus embody the expected outcomes of particular decisions; and because decisions take account of the interdependences within the organisation, budgets include the impact of these interdependences.

As we have just seen, the use of budgets is integral to the *planning process*. But the importance of budgeting does not stop with planning. In order to ensure that plans are correctly implemented, that stated targets are reached and that information is available to aid future planning, actual performance must be regularly reported and monitored, by comparison with expected performance (steps 6 and 7 of the framework). These two steps are commonly known as the *control process*. Thus the use of budgets is important also as an aid to performance evaluation and control. We might also add a third main use of budgets as a device for *motivation*: that is, as an influence on the way in which individuals participate in the organisation. The subsequent sections of this chapter look in turn at the contribution of budgeting to planning, control and motivation. In Chapter 16 we describe the steps involved in preparing a master or comprehensive budget for the firm. Chapter 17 looks in more detail at the control information provided by analysis of the variances between budget and actual performance, and Chapter 18 looks at budgeting and planning in decentralised organisations.

15.2 Budgeting and planning

In order to aid the pursuit of organisational goals, explicit, formal plans should be drawn up. If this is not done, managers can use only crude, intuitive measures to judge whether their operations are successful, and their targets achieved. Budgets represent the financial expression of formal plans, and, as with successful planning, successful budgeting should also be formalised. But what is planning? This is a difficult question to answer easily, as firms engage in different forms of planning. We might classify business plans as falling under one of the following headings:

1. *Operating plans*. These are short-term plans which relate directly to the achievement of the firm's objectives. Thus the annual production and sales plans, as well as the plans to finance them, would be examples of operating plans. As we will see, most of the firm's budgeting activities are taken up with short-term operating plans.

2. *Administrative plans.* These are 'tactical' plans concerned with the creation of the organisational structure, under which budgets and performance levels can be determined for appropriate functions.

3. *Long-term strategic plans.* These plans are concerned with the long-term development of the firm's strategy, and are likely to be expressed in quite general terms.

The objectives of the budget, and the means of attaining them, should be stated explicitly. The level of sophistication and detail of any budget should be a function of the size of the organisation and also the position of the particular budget within the organisation. For example, the top management of a large organisation is not likely to wish to consider detailed budgetary data concerning proposed expenditure on spare parts in one of many factories within the organisation; rather it might wish to concern itself with the proposed total expenditure for the forthcoming period for the whole factory. This implies a structure of responsibility centres within the organisation, each accountable for a specific level of detail within the total budgetary process. We look at this notion of responsibility accounting and its corollary activity, management by exception, in the next section dealing with budgeting and control. It is very important to point out here that, as with other aspects of the planning and control process, the benefits of any system of budgeting should be judged in relation to the costs of setting up and operating the system. No managerial activity should be viewed in isolation from its attendant costs and benefits. There are, however, two interdependent aspects of the relationship between budgeting and planning which we should consider in more detail: the method by which budgets are prepared, and the time periods covered by budgets.

The preparation of budgets

Budgets do not appear out of thin air; they represent the product of much organisational thinking and, often, internal dissension. Most large organisations commit considerable human resources to the preparation of budgets. A budget director or controller, who usually takes no part in the detailed preparation of individual budgets, is responsible for overall budget preparation and co-ordination, often being assisted by a budgeting committee consisting of members of top management from each of the organisation's functional divisions. The task of the committee is to set general guidelines to be followed by individual managers in building up their own budgets, to resolve differences among them, and to submit a final comprehensive budget for approval by the board of directors.

In effect, budgeting constitutes a system of authority within the organisation. The structure of budget organisation and responsibility is important. Budgeting is a complicated process and in practice seldom starts with a 'clean sheet'. Such general factors as last year's budget and actual level of performance, the profit or return on investment objectives of the firm, and the relative bargaining strengths of interested groups will influence the process. Ideally these influencing factors will result in a budgeting procedure which sets targets that are neither over- nor under-demanding, so that challenges are offered but fears of unfavourable variances are calmed. We will discuss these issues further in the final section of this chapter.

As can be imagined, only infrequently will figures be immediately accepted without controversy. Rather, an iterative process is involved by which the plans, intentions, ambitions and constraints of individual managers throughout the organisation are submitted, reviewed, changed and ultimately, by reason of the authority of the budget controller and the budget committee, agreed. Budgeting, in short, is a bargaining process in which individual goals are traded off for (it is hoped) the overall benefit of the organisation, and, as in most bargaining situations, the end product is often radically different from the original submission. The end product of the whole budgeting process takes the form of the organisation's expected position at some future point in time (a *budgeted balance sheet*) and the means of reaching that position (a *budgeted income statement*). A statement of the sources and applications of the organisation's funds may accompany the two main statements. The budgeting process will typically begin well in advance of the period covered by the budget. For example, the preparation of detailed budgets for a firm with a year end of 31 December may well begin in the summer of the previous year, and be completed by October of that year. The budget statements are usually vague single-valued estimates of the future, derived from individual budgets for sales, purchases, cash flow, etc., and as such are static. We query the usefulness for control purposes of such static budgets in the following section.

In preparing detailed budgets, it must be recognised that the activities of the organisation are likely to be limited by certain constraints. In consequence, the recognition of both the level of constraints and the time at which they are likely to arise is of critical importance. For example, if 4,000 units of a particular product can be produced with the available equipment and workforce, but only 3,000 units can be sold, then obviously the principal limiting factor for the firm is the level of consumer demand. In this case, it will be necessary to prepare first the sales budget and then the other budgets in the light of estimated sales. Similarly, situations may arise in which productive capacity or short- or even long-term cash may prove to be the constraining factor. If one constraint cannot be relaxed, all budgets must be geared to the one representing the constraining factor. If it is anticipated that two or more constraining factors are likely to be in force simultaneously, the procedure is more complicated, although the underlying principles are similar, and the organisation should use an optimising technique such as linear programming (see Chapter 11) to derive its best budgetary plan.

The time periods covered by budgets

Budgets are financial plans for future periods. But which future periods? In general, planning horizons will depend largely on the uncertainty of the business environment and management's need for control information. It is normal, however, to distinguish between two types of budget, short-term and long-term, because they may seek to serve different purposes and because the level of detail they incorporate may differ widely.

Short-term budgets

These are related to current conditions and usually cover a period of one year. Such annual budgets are, in turn, broken down into quarterly, monthly, four-weekly or even weekly periods. The actual level of disaggregation of the annual budget is a function of the particular business, but at least some disaggregation is usually necessary. For instance, management will wish to monitor progress throughout the year, and to take any corrective action as soon as possible rather than wait until the end of the year when the final results are known. Equally, management will need information during the year to adjust current budgets for the remainder of the period if the situation warrants such changes.

Although the time period chosen for a short-term budget is often one year, this may vary from firm to firm. For example, the appropriate period for a short-term budget of a firm engaged in the fashion trade may be considerably less than one year, whereas a similar budget for a construction company may be prepared for a longer period.

In general the period selected will depend upon such factors as the following:

1. *The life cycle of the firm's products.* The shorter the life cycle, the more frequent will be the need for operating decisions and budgets.

2. *The type of customer.* In industries where buying and selling relationships are very close (e.g. between food manufacturing and food retailing), both parties may prefer to enter into longer-term contracts to encourage stability.

3. *The stability of demand for the firm's product.* Most firms have some degree of seasonality of sales, and thus the season (e.g. the Christmas season for retailing) may influence the budget period as much as the financial year.

4. *The existence of any constraints on operations.* As we have discussed, certain constraints (e.g. shortage of labour, materials or funds) may necessitate more regular control reports and, if of sufficient severity, a rescheduling of operations.

5. *The characteristics of the industry.* Some production processes involve such a level of technological sophistication that short-term alterations to budget will be impossible.

The above discussion suggests that, at the very least, the importance of the multipurpose budget demands that revisions should be frequent enough to accommodate situations in which the original assumptions in the budget, in relation both to the current and to future periods, have proved to be invalid. The necessity and direction of such revisions will be determined in large part by the stability of the firm's environment, but failure to revise budgets properly may diminish quickly their relevance to managerial decision making.

One means of incorporating regular revisions is by way of a rolling or continuous budget. A continuous budget is formulated initially for a period of, say, one year. As each monthly, four-weekly or quarterly period passes, two actions take place within the budgetary process. First, a budget for the corresponding period of the following year is prepared, thus ensuring that a short-term budget is always in existence for the immediate future 12 months. Second, the budget for the following 11 months (or 48 weeks or three quarters if appropriate) is revised in the light of the results of the period which has just elapsed (in particular, of any changes in expectations regarding costs, etc.), thus ensuring that the current budget is revised constantly and kept up to date.

Long-term budgets

These are budgets which relate to the development of the business over many years and, as such, are unlikely to be changed very often. They reflect a long-run appreciation of the firm's objectives and are usually drawn up in very general terms covering, *inter alia*, the nature of the business, its position in the industry, the expected level of inflation and its impact on the business. The targets covered by long-term budgets are often expressed as overall company goals – for example, to produce a return on shareholders' funds of 20%. Achievement of this target will in turn entail the setting of more detailed sub-goals for individual divisions and managers. Thus, to achieve the 20% return on shareholders' funds, the production department's goal might involve a target quota of 10,000 components per week.

Long-term budgets are typically drawn up for a period of between three and ten years, and will deal particularly with the firm's likely requirements for long-term assets, and the appropriate mix of debt and equity finance.

15.3 Budgeting and control

A second major purpose of budgeting is its usefulness for control purposes. The control process follows the planning process: that is, once plans have been agreed, decisions are implemented and reports are prepared to determine whether events are going according to plan. We might say that the control process involves three sequential, but interrelated stages: the recording of actual performance, the comparison of actual performance with expected performance and, as a linking stage, the provision of regular feedback to allow continual monitoring of events. These three steps are brought together in Figure 15.2, which shows an abbreviated view of the control process.

Differences between budgeted and actual performance are termed *variances*. The generation of variances provides the feedback which entitles us to term the whole process a control system. Notice that the diagram of the *control process* takes the appearance, via the feedback mechanism, of a loop, or continuous process. This is because any time scale has been omitted from the diagram. The budget for the current period is compared with the actual performance of the current period and the variances are calculated accordingly. These variances will be useful both as a spur to immediate, remedial action if actual performance is less good than expected and also as input into the budgetary process for future periods. We now examine each of the three aspects of the control process in more detail.

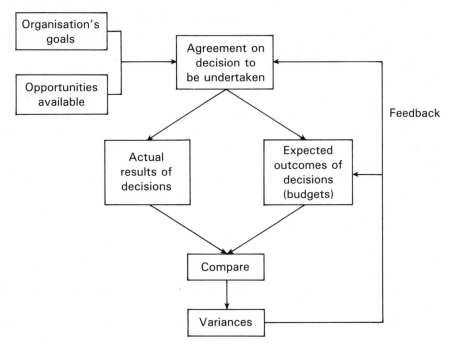

Figure 15.2 The control process.

Recording actual performance

We have seen that the decisions giving rise to the formulation of plans and budgets are carried out for different areas of activity within the organisation. If such budgets are to be used to assess and evaluate individual performance, managers need some criteria to determine exactly what constitutes a particular area of activity. To achieve this end, budgets should reflect *areas of responsibility* within the firm, so that individuals are charged *only* with those costs and revenues for which they can be held responsible: that is, for those costs and revenues which they control. Thus we might define a responsibility area, or centre, as an area of activity within an organisation which has control over particular resources for a specified period.

It is vital that such areas are explicitly defined, so that managers and employees know precisely what is expected of them. Conceptually, this is easy to acknowledge; in practice it is very difficult to apply. The difficulty lies in determining which costs should be assigned to specific responsibility centres. We can do no better than to cite guidelines for deciding which costs should be assigned to responsibility centres (first drawn up in the USA in 1956):[1]

1. If the person has authority over both the acquisition and the use of the services, he should be charged with the cost of such services.

2. If the person can significantly influence the amount of cost through his own action, he may be charged with such costs.

3. Even if the person cannot significantly influence the amount of cost through his own action, he may be charged with those elements with which the management desires him to be concerned, so that he will help to influence those who are responsible.

Responsibility centres are usually cost centres, profit centres or investment centres. The nature of the organisational structure will determine the type(s) of responsibility centre. A *cost centre* is the smallest area of responsibility for which costs are accumulated: for example, a single department of a firm employing few people. A manager in charge of a cost centre is held accountable only for the controllable costs of his or her centre. He or she has no control over, and is therefore not accountable for, revenues earned. A *profit centre*, such as an autonomous division within a firm, is a section of business for which both costs and revenues are accumulated. Thus, a manager in charge of a profit centre is responsible for the profit, or contribution margin, earned by his or her section of the business. The manager of an *investment centre* is responsible for the return on the assets under his or her control. We will deal more fully with some of the problems caused by accounting for divisional responsibility centres in Chapter 18.

Table 15.1 provides an example of a reporting system based on the notion of responsibility accounting. For purposes of simplicity, it deals only with the costs for which each centre is responsible. In this example, there are four levels of responsibility within the organisation. The managing director is responsible for the running of the whole organisation (Level 1), and so receives reports concerning the four functional areas of the firm – general administration, finance, production and sales. The reports show both the monthly and accumulated figures for the organisation's budget, and the variances which have arisen to date. Obviously, the managing director will wish to look only at those variances representing significant departures from plan and so demanding his or her attention. Other variances can, if necessary, be examined by subordinates. This is known as *management by exception*. It assumes that where actual outcomes are close to plan there is less need to investigate performance than where the gap is large.

We shall demonstrate the notion of responsibility accounting by tracing responsibility for the costs of one of the functional areas, production, from Level 2 to Level 4. The production director's cost budget is made up by reference to the five areas directly under his or her control. Table 15.1 shows that factory A contributes costs of £51,000 to an overall monthly cost budget of £125,000. The total budget of factory A (Level 3) is then broken down further into the budgets for the three departments within the factory which are under the control of the factory supervisor. We can see that the manufacturing department of factory A contributes costs of £18,000 to the total budget of £51,000. Finally, the total budget of the manufacturing department of factory A is broken down (Level 4) into the elements of production within the department, for which the departmental supervisor is responsible. The system of responsibility accounting is intended to generate control reports which reflect the decentralisation of authority within the firm. In our example we have delineated four levels of managerial responsibility, from board

Table 15.1 Responsibility accounting reporting system

Overall responsibility		Budget		Variance* F(U)	
		This month (£)	Year to date (£)	This month (£)	Year to date (£)
Managing director	*Level 1 Managing director's monthly performance report*				
	General administration costs	X	X	X	X
	Financial director	X	X	X	X
	Production director	125,000	470,000	(7,630)	(40,150)
	Sales director	X	X	X	X
	Total controllable costs	174,000	666,000	(7,480)	(39,750)
Production director	*Level 2 Production director's monthly performance report*				
	Manufacturing administration costs	X	X	X	X
	Factory A	51,000	193,000	(4,000)	(19,000)
	Factory B	X	X	X	X
	Factory C	X	X	X	X
	Supervision: personnel and scheduling	X	X	X	X
	Total controllable costs	125,000	470,000	(7,630)	(40,150)
Factory supervisor	*Level 3 Factory A's monthly performance report*				
	Manufacturing dept	18,000	78,000	(3,600)	(9,800)
	Assembly dept	X	X	X	X
	Packing dept	X	X	X	X
	Total controllable costs	51,000	193,000	(4,000)	(19,000)
Department supervisor	*Level 4 Manufacturing dept's monthly performance report*				
	Machine operators	X	X	X	X
	Direct materials	X	X	X	X
	Material handlers	X	X	X	X
	Other variable overheads	X	X	X	X
		18,000	78,000	(3,600)	(9,800)

* F signifies a favourable cost variance, i.e. actual is less than budget; U signifies an unfavourable variance, i.e. actual is greater than budget.

level to department foreman. The system has the advantage of allowing responsible officials to react speedily to any changes in their own area of responsibility, with the result that the flow of reports through the firm will allow corrective action to be taken at the appropriate level.

Comparison of actual and expected performance

When a single, fixed budget (e.g. the organisation's master budget) is prepared for planning purposes, the level of activity used to determine the costs and revenues relevant to the budget will reflect the level which is most likely to be attained. But fixed budgets may not serve equally well for control purposes. For control purposes it is necessary to compare like with like: that is, to compare actual and budgeted costs at the level of activity achieved during the period. This ensures that valid comparisons and inferences can be made when the budgeted activity level is not attained. If the organisation's output tends to vary across a range of levels, then a number of different, flexible budgets should be prepared (see Chapter 8). They show the effects on costs (and contributions) of producing at various activity levels, and thus put the management in a better position to evaluate performance and take appropriate action. The key to flexible budgeting is, as we have seen, understanding the firm's pattern of cost incidence, and in particular the separation of fixed and variable costs. Only if the flexible budget is based on a valid understanding of the relationship between operating activities and costs being incurred (for example, through cost driver analysis) will it be possible to gauge the impact of changes in the activity level on the period's results.

In practice this split may not be easy to achieve. Very few of the firm's costs are 'fixed' over the long term, and very few costs are 'variable' in the short term. The time period chosen in preparing the flexible budget is therefore very influential in determining the usefulness of the control system's output and thus its ultimate success. In addition, these problems of cost classification are likely to be accentuated in the future as many organisations replace labour with capital, and invest more heavily in high-technology equipment. Situations can be envisaged in which the only short-term variable costs under the manager's control will be represented by raw material and energy costs. It is certainly difficult to describe the minimal labour force employed to supervise the workings of robots and flexible manufacturing systems as being variable in relation to the level of production. And as firms plan their production around computer-integrated manufacturing systems, the classification of labour as 'direct' may cease to have any relevance at all. These problems emphasise the need for management to ensure that the way in which costs are classified, and their behaviour is predicted for budgeting, is based on a thorough analysis of the relationship between the firm's activities and cost incidence.

The following example explores the issue of budgeting for control. Bramall plc produces one product, and activity levels vary widely from month to month. The following statement shows Bramall plc's production budget based on an average level of output of 20,000 units per four-week period, and the actual results for a four-week period during October:

	Budgeted production for 4-week period	Actual production for 4-week period
Number of units produced	20,000	17,600
Costs	(£)	(£)
Variable labour costs (£1 per unit)	20,000	19,540
Variable cost of small parts (4p per unit)	800	1,000
Other variable costs (21p per unit)	4,200	3,660
Fixed costs	18,000	16,000
Total costs	43,000	40,200

The arithmetic difference, or total variance, between the total costs expected (£43,000) and the costs actually incurred for the same period (£40,200) is £2,800. As costs incurred are less than those expected, we might say initially that this difference of £2,800 represents a favourable (F) variance. But before we make that statement, we must ask ourselves why we have prepared these figures, and how we should use the differences which they reveal. If we are trying to assess the effectiveness of the production manager in controlling his costs *once the planning decision to produce 17,600 units has been made*, then the favourable variance of £2,800 is meaningless. Why is this? Simply because we are failing to compare similar aspects of the same decision. For control purposes we should compare the actual costs of producing 17,600 units with the budgeted costs of producing the same number of units. If we do this, as in Table 15.2, a very different pattern is revealed.

Table 15.2 shows the breakdown of the total variance of £2,800 into two separate variances for which different managers may be responsible. These separate variances arise because the budget has been 'flexed' to the actual level of activity. The difference between the original budget of 20,000 units and the flexed budget of 17,600 units gives rise to a *budget revision variance* or *volume variance*. This variance reflects the expected change in costs due to the change in activity level. As the revised budget entails a fall in production of 2,400 units, Bramall plc expects a reduction in costs of £3,000 (i.e. 2,400 units at £1.25 per unit). The cost per unit avoided represents the variable cost of production, £1 plus 4p plus 21p. Fixed costs are not expected to change with the level of activity and so remain at £18,000 in the revised budget. The second variance, representing the difference in costs at the actual level of activity, is the *control variance*. This tells top management whether the production manager has been able to meet the revised budget (i.e. control the revised level of costs) for the actual level of activity. We shall discuss how we might determine the causes of, and thus the responsibility for, these different kinds of variance in Chapter 17.

We can now see that the production manager exceeded his budget for the production of 17,600 units by £200: that is, the control variance is unfavourable (U).

Table 15.2 Bramall plc: budgeting for control[*]

	Original (fixed) budget 20,000 units	Revised (flexible) budget 17,600 units	Actual results 17,600 units
Costs:			
Labour costs (£1 per unit)	20,000	17,600	19,540
Small parts (4p per unit)	800	704	1,000
Other variable costs (21p per unit)	4,200	3,696	3,660
Fixed costs (£)	18,000	18,000	16,000
Total costs (£)	43,000	40,000	40,200

3,000 (F)   200 (U)

Budget revision variance	Control variance	
2,400 units at £1.25	Cost of labour	1,940 (U)
= £3,000 (F)	Cost of small parts	296 (U)
	Cost of other variable overheads	36 (F)
	Expenditure on fixed costs	2,000 (F)
		200 (U)

[*] See Table 15.1 for definition of F and U.

A breakdown of the control variance reveals that the variable costs of both labour and small parts were greater than expected, whereas the cost of other variable overheads was lower than budgeted. Expenditure on fixed costs was considerably less than expected. It is apparent that attention should be directed to the labour variance: not only is it large within the context of the labour budget, but it also seems worthy of investigation within the context of the total budget. Attention should also be paid to the fixed cost variance. It is possible that the original budget for fixed costs was set at too high a level and that a more realistic figure might improve the quality of future plans.

Provision of feedback information

Timely and regular feedback is vital to a successful control system, as an aid to both managers and employees. For example, managers need speedy information on significant deviations from budget in order to take effective action to correct such deviations and to amend future plans, in so far as deviations signify a change in longer-term circumstances; employees need equally speedy information to know whether or not they have achieved their targets, and whether their performance is satisfactory. Delay in giving information on employee performance may lead to a loss of motivation, to the detriment of future performance.

The regularity with which control information is generated determines in large measure the success of the entire control process. Regularity will be largely dependent upon the activity under consideration and on the position of the activity within the entire organisation. For example, departmental supervisors will require feedback immediately if machinery breaks down, or materials are faulty; plant supervisors will require daily information on the levels of output reached; whereas for the performance of divisions within the organisation, and the performance of the organisation as a whole, the provision of formalised monthly reports will usually be adequate. But we must stress again that reports of variances do not necessarily tell the management why deviations have occurred; nor do they offer advice as to how deviations are to be acted on. For example, suppose that the production department of a large manufacturing organisation reports a favourable variance on labour cost. Is this necessarily an indication to top management that labour efficiency has increased and that the supervisor responsible should be encouraged to sustain the situation? The answer depends upon the cause of the variance and on its consequence elsewhere. It may be that the favourable variance has been achieved by labour working more quickly but less carefully than budgeted, with the result that material wastage is substantially greater than was expected. The unfavourable variance in respect of material usage should be compared to the favourable variance on labour cost before it is decided to continue with the new increased speed of working. It is one of management's most important tasks to interpret and evaluate variance information.

15.4 Budgeting and motivation

All budgeting processes involve relationships between people – for example, manager–employee, director–manager and manager–manager relationships – and all interpersonal relationships generate, to some extent, behavioural effects. Thus budgeting entails behavioural effects. The present state of knowledge concerning the behavioural implications of accounting is such that even very broad generalisations can be dangerous. Individuals, whatever their formal position within the organisation, differ in their behaviour in any given situation, and organisational settings vary widely from firm to firm.

The earlier sections of this chapter may have given the impression that budgeting is a somewhat mechanistic exercise. We described it there as a means of stating individual and collective expectations, and of ensuring operational and administrative control. We suggested its purpose might include planning, evaluating performance, reducing uncertainty, achieving goal congruence, providing a guide to action and communicating and co-ordinating activities. In practice many of these courses are likely to be in direct conflict. Requests for additional funds from individual managers may be mutually incompatible, especially when resources are limited. This problem is accentuated when managers, in the expectation that their requests will be cut back, propose overly optimistic budgets. The final agreed budgets may be determined as much by the managers' political skills as by the merits of their cases. This involvement in the process is likely (and perhaps intended) to influence the individual behaviour and action of the participants. As we earlier intimated, this conflict of aims is likely to be at its most acute when budgets are used both for planning and for motivation. We now consider this issue further.

In determining the basis to be used in evaluating performance for any budget period, two related behavioural questions have given rise to considerable debate and elicited much research output.[2] First, how tightly should budgets be set in order to induce maximum performance from employees? Second, what degree of employee participation in the budgeting process should be encouraged?

To clarify some of the issues under these two headings, we shall say something about the forms of organisational structure which can exist within individual firms. In order to illustrate the main points, it is useful to identify two forms of organisational structure which lie towards opposite ends of the spectrum of possible structures: the *classical* and the *modern* structure.[3] The classical structure supposes the existence of formal relationships within a hierarchical organisation, which exists simply to maximise profits. Employees, who are characterised as being basically inefficient and antagonistic to management, are presumed to be motivated purely by monetary rewards. The classical idea views the imposition of pressure upon an alien workforce as being the best way to achieve the desired results.

The modern view of organisational structure views matters from a different perspective. The firm is seen as being a partnership or coalition of managers and employees who are not motivated solely by notions of profit and cash, but also by psychological and social needs. This view recognises that individuals within an organisation have different goals and levels of aspiration, and it is only by harnessing these to the particular situations facing the organisation that an increased sense of commitment to the goals of the organisation is achieved. (See Chapter 1 for an extended discussion of this view.) The modern view incorporates the idea of *budgetary slack*, representing a degree of padding introduced into budgets so as to guard against possible failure to attain targets. It is deemed necessary to do this because failure to attain budget levels is seen as a social stigma which affects the individual in such a way that it reduces aspiration levels, goals and, eventually, performance.

Slack exists within even the most efficient and well-run organisations. It exists because human nature requires it to exist. It is argued that if individuals are given no room to manoeuvre within a budgetary constraint, then conflict will quickly arise between the individual's personal goals and those of the firm. The type of organisational structure possessed by the firm, whether classical, modern or some intermediate structure, will have a direct bearing on the behavioural questions we have raised.

Consider now the first of the two questions posed above: how tightly should budgets be set so as to encourage maximum performance? For example, if budgets are set at too high a level, individuals may become discouraged in their tasks and not attempt to meet targets; alternatively, if budgets are pitched at too low a level, individuals may become self-satisfied and inefficient, and thus perform below their real potential.

The setting of budgets should therefore seek to reflect individuals' need for achievement and their perception of the probability of succeeding, together with the level of reward appropriate for the level of success, while, at the same time, recognising individuals' need to avoid failure, and the cost to the firm of such failure. It is a delicate balance. The above analysis suggests that the relationship between budgets and performance should recognise the aspiration levels of individuals. To be good motivators, budgets must be closely linked to such aspiration levels and incorporate personal perceptions of success and failure. Two types of budget are frequently referred to in this context: ideal budgets and currently attainable budgets.

Ideal budgets are intended to act as a powerful incentive to performance by making no allowance for such mitigating factors as machine breakdowns, material shortages or labour strikes. In effect, they assume that the firm can operate at maximum capacity with maximum efficiency. Under normal operating conditions they are not likely to be achieved. Research has shown that ideal budgets are unlikely to represent the best form of motivation if the employees view them as being unreasonable and unachievable.[4]

Currently attainable budgets represent those which can reasonably be achieved under normal working conditions. They allow for normal breaks and suppose less than perfect efficiency. The problem for managers is to define 'reasonable achievement' and 'normal working conditions' in such a way that the standards set are tight enough to prevent inefficiency, while at the same time generating a feeling of satisfaction on achievement. It is a difficult feat to accomplish. Evidence suggests that defined, quantitative targets are more likely to induce higher levels of performance. Aside from the technical problems involved, it requires from the management a thorough knowledge of the workforce, much previous experience in the area and, most of all, a great deal of common sense.

The research studies on budgeting and behaviour raise a potentially serious problem, to which we briefly referred earlier. It may be desirable to set the budget at a particular level in order to motivate the individual to achieve some other level: for example, to set the budget slightly above reasonable expectations. Such a budget may elicit maximum performance from the employee, but it will not be a suitable basis for planning what is likely to be achieved. Thus it may be inconsistent to use the same budget for both planning and motivational purposes.

The second question we posed earlier was: what degree of employee participation in the budgeting process should be encouraged? We should perhaps begin by defining our terms. Participation is a process of joint decision making in which the interests of all participants are fairly reflected, and where the outcome is a decision to which all parties are committed. Participation in the setting of budgets should improve performance where group decision making results in the reconciliation of goals and commitment to budgets. There is now a considerable body of research showing that in general better performance can be expected from employees if they have some say in the construction of the budgets to be used to evaluate their performance (i.e. that participative budgets are more likely to succeed than are authoritative, imposed budgets).[5] Indeed, common sense suggests that participation by individuals who have detailed knowledge of the particular problems associated with any given task is likely to increase the realism of budgets. But as with most topics which involve the interaction of human relationships, the relationship between the optimum level of participation and the optimum level of performance is not without complexities. A word of caution is warranted, prompted by recent research in this area. Researchers have found that, *inter alia*:

1. Participation may not be 'real', in the sense that the purpose of joint discussions may simply be a ratification of previous management decisions.

2. The results of participation in the budgeting process may be of less benefit to non-numerate managers. The important point underlying this caveat is that the communication and understanding of financial information may be of equal benefit to all parties only when all have equal competence in its analysis.

3. Participation will be more effective in situations where changes in the working environment are possible. In machine-controlled settings, where most decisions are programmed, the effect of participation is minimal.

One other issue should be addressed before we leave our initial discussion of budgeting. Throughout this chapter we have assumed budgets to be expressed purely in financial terms. But need we necessarily rely only on monetary measures? Certainly there are compelling arguments for monetary measures – after all, budgets are a part of the firm's management control system, and control information is inevitably expressed quantitatively. It is also reasonable to demand consistency of measurement between internal targets and budgets and objectives expressed in financial terms (e.g. maximisation of the firm's cash flows). Further arguments for the use of monetary measurements might include the following:

1. Much of the quantitative information used in budgeting is already produced by the management accounting system for other purposes: for example, for reporting to shareholders.

2. Such measurements are easily understood by managers and relate directly to the firm's reward structure.

3. Such measures represent the only common basis on which the comparative performance of managers, and divisions, can be analysed.

4. Production of non-monetary statements may prove to be a very costly exercise.

But should we simply accept these views without challenging their underlying assumptions? At their heart is the implicit assertion that monetary measures are the most relevant available. We might argue, however, that certain important concepts of the firm's, and the manager's, performance cannot easily be measured in money terms, and that we should therefore try to develop different or additional measures. Indeed the nature of the existing budget system may well demand this if, in seeking to meet budget targets, costs are incurred, which by their nature are not easily measurable and which therefore do not appear directly in the budget statements.

The possible range of non-monetary or qualitative measures which could be introduced into the budget system varies considerably in ease of measurement. For example, such items as the amount of time devoted to training, labour turnover rates, and levels of absenteeism can be relatively easily measured; whereas the measurement and interpretation of individual attitudes and interpersonal judgements is complicated by the lack of appropriate evaluation methods. Perhaps the best situation is to argue for a compromise – the inclusion of relevant non-monetary measures (e.g. those relating to quality, reliability, service, satisfaction of employees) as supplementary information to conventional budget statements. After all, budgets themselves are no more than output statements, and do not normally offer a detailed explanation of actual performance. The introduction of more qualitative measures more accurately reflects the complexity of the managerial environment and the notion that performance must encompass a variety of objectives rather than a single monetary target.

CHAPTER SUMMARY

Budgeting assists management in the tasks of co-ordinating operations following decisions about activities, communicating priorities throughout the organisation, and forming a judgement on the adequacy of actual performance. The budget helps to determine how decisions taken are actually implemented in practice, influences expectations throughout the organisation, and sets targets against which actual results will be judged. We have discussed the use of budgets with respect to planning, control and motivation. Adequate planning depends on appropriate choices about the structure of the budget and the time periods to be covered. Calculating variances by comparing budget and actual amounts, and investigating the causes of variances where necessary, can contribute to the control of operations. Because of these roles, the budget process itself is extremely important and must be undertaken with due recognition of the effects that setting budget figures will have on the behaviour and motivation of staff at all levels.

As we have seen, budgets seek to serve many different and often conflicting aims and, as such, it is unlikely that all will be achieved with equal success. To prevent dissatisfaction with the system, a priority ranking of the budget's aims may be useful. Such a ranking should involve a review of budgeting procedures and may result in better data for future budgeting decisions and an improvement in the attitudes of managers to the whole budgeting process.

We have also attempted to portray budgeting as a complex process which is not susceptible to simple economic models or simple accounting rules, but whose influence, as a system of authority, pervades organisational behaviour. Its role is well summarised by Cyert and March:

> Within rather large limits, the organisation substitutes the plan for the world – partly by making the world conform to the plan, partly by pretending that it does. So long as achievement levels continue to be satisfactory, budgeting decisions are exceptionally dependent on decisions of previous years, with shifts tending to reflect the expansions and inclinations of subunits rather than systematic reviews by top management.[6]

REVIEW QUESTIONS

1. Specify and comment on the objectives of budgeting.

2. Outline the differences and similarities between budgets for planning and budgets for control.

3. 'Budgetary control can provide a bridge which links the resources of an organisation to the behaviour of the people within the organisation.' Discuss.

4. 'Responsibility accounting is the essence of a successful managerial control system.' Discuss.

5. 'Planning and control systems do not themselves exercise control. That is the prerogative of management.' Explain how management might use such systems for control purposes.

EXERCISES

15.1 An important concept in management accounting is that of responsibility accounting.

(a) Define the term 'responsibility accounting'.

(b) What are the conditions that must exist for there to be effective responsibility accounting?

(c) What benefits are said to result from responsibility accounting?

(d) Listed below are three charges found on the monthly report of a division manufacturing and selling products primarily to outside companies. Divisional performance is evaluated by the use of return on investment, i.e. the ratio of profit to total assets. You are to state which, if any, of the following charges are consistent with the responsibility accounting concept. Support each answer with a brief explanation.

   (i) A charge for general corporation administration at 10% of division sales.

   (ii) A charge for the use of the corporate computer facility. The charge is determined by taking actual annual computer department costs and allocating an amount to each user based on the ratio of departmental hours of use to total corporate hours of use.

   (iii) A charge for goods purchased from another division. The charge is based upon the competitive market price for the goods.

15.2 As the management accountant in a company producing, selling and distributing a wide range of products, you are considering possible improvements in the current system of budgetary control. The existing system of annual budgets produces unrealistic variances because of the rapidly changing conditions in which the company operates. As an alternative you are proposing to adopt a system of continuous budgeting on a quarterly cycle.

Write a report to your financial director explaining the procedure required to operate the proposed continuous budgeting system, and indicate the benefits likely to arise.

15.3 As the newly appointed controller of Telemann Foods, you have been asked to design a budgetary control system for the firm. Being of some experience, you have witnessed the introduction of budgetary control systems in several organisations and feel that a carefully considered framework is an essential first step if such systems are going to be successful. The technical detail of budgetary control (e.g. the methods of variance calculation) should, you have found, follow only after such a framework has been considered.

Telemann Foods are take-away restaurants whose profits have been growing by 40% annually for the last five years. There are now 29 restaurants located in England. Each is run by a manager who has considerable freedom in relation to the type of food sold, its selling price, the nature and extent of advertising, and staffing policies. Because of the variety in types of location and the nature of local competition (which is generally intense), each restaurant is encouraged to have its own style and character. The central organisation of Telemann Foods provides the finance to set up and sustain each take-away restaurant. It also purchases the supplies and food for the restaurant, and provides accounting, legal and administrative services for the restaurants.

All managers are paid a basic salary of £25,000 per year, and commission, computed quarterly, amounting to 20% of the excess of their store's profits over the budget profit. (At present, the budgetary control system merely comprises a quarterly meeting of each store manager with the chief executive of Telemann Foods, when agreement is reached as to the next quarter's profit budget.)

Develop a framework for the design of a budgetary control system. Use the above information about Telemann Foods in your analysis, and indicate the nature of any further information which you might need to complete your design.

Notes

1. Report of the Committee on Cost Concepts and Standards, *The Accounting Review*, April 1956, p. 190.
2. See, for example, G. H. Hofstede, *The Game of Budget Control*, Tavistock, 1968; C. Argyris, 'Human problems with budgets', *Harvard Business Review*, January/February 1953; A. G. Hopwood, *Accounting and Human Behaviour*, Prentice Hall, 1976.

3. See E. H. Caplan, *Management Accounting and Behavioural Science*, Addison Wesley, 1971.
4. See Hofstede, op. cit.; A. G. Hopwood, *An Accounting System and Managerial Behaviour*, Saxon House, 1973.
5. See the references quoted in note 2 above.
6. R. M. Cyert and J. G. March, *A Behavioral Theory of the Firm*, Prentice-Hall, 1963.

The master budget and the cash budget

AIMS AND OBJECTIVES

☐ To explain how the master budget is prepared and to discuss its component parts, including:

    The sales budget
    The production budget
    The capital expenditure budget
    The cash budget
    The budgeted income and expenditure account.

☐ To explain and illustrate the use of short-term cash budgeting.

In the previous chapter we discussed how managerial decisions can often involve the simultaneous use of factors which draw on the marketing, sales, production, purchasing and financial aspects of business; and we stressed the importance of management's task of co-ordinating all these various, interrelated aspects of decision making. This chapter considers how the ultimate production of this co-ordinating activity, the master plan or master budget for the firm, is pieced together. The master budget represents the firm's blueprint for the forthcoming period(s). It brings together the various individual budgets prepared within the organisation.

No organisation of any size or complexity should proceed without an overall plan, and, in practice, most large organisations prepare some form of master budget. The master budget will rarely be a single statement, but rather will comprise a large number of interrelated statements for different aspects of the organisation's activities. The format may vary (there is no standard mode of preparation), and should reflect the underlying structure of the organisation and its operations. Thus a manufacturing company could be expected to have, *inter alia*, sales budgets for different product groups, advertising budgets and plant maintenance budgets while a local authority will have budgets structured around areas of activity such as housing, planning, parks, etc. Broadly we may distinguish two main types of budget statement:

1. *Operating budgets*, which deal with all operational activities for the budget period, such as production, purchasing, administration and research. Later in the chapter we will discuss the following types of operating budget:

    (a) sales budget, representing revenue from forecasts of likely demand;

    (b) production budget, comprising the various requirements to produce the desired level of goods;

    (c) capital budget, indicating expenditure on acquiring capital assets in the operating period currently being planned, and also the longer-term capital spending programme;

    (d) general and administrative budget, covering all the non-production and non-sales aspects of operations.

2. *Financial budgets*, which will comprise:

    (a) the cash budget, which is concerned with financing requirements for the budget period;

    (b) the budgeted income statement, which summarises the plans included in the operating budgets;

    (c) the budgeted balance sheet, which expresses expectations about the overall financial position at the end of the period.

The need to prepare a master plan is usually cited as a prerequisite for success. It is useful because, as we argued in the previous chapter, it both sets out the organisation's targets for the coming period in a quantifiable, easily understood form, and provides a basis for co-ordinating the organisation's detailed operating budgets, which are essential ingredients of the control process.

16.1 Preparation of the master budget

The preparation of a master budget is rarely an easy task. The speed with which agreement can be reached on the final budget figures depends upon the size of the organisation, the number of different responsibility centres, the degree of divisionalisation and so on. But even within a small organisation, detailed discussion, argument and persuasion may be necessary at all levels before the master budget can be drawn up. The art of preparing the master budget lies in the ability of the budget committee to piece together at minimum cost and maximum agreement the various parts of the corporate jigsaw.

The analogy with a jigsaw is worth pursuing. The most time-consuming part of putting together a jigsaw is knowing where to start. The more pieces in the jigsaw, the harder is this task. Likewise in preparing the firm's master budget the most difficult tasks for the budget committee may lie in knowing which of the individual functional budgets (e.g. sales, purchasing, production) to use as the starting point for the total plan. Preparation of the budget may entail a number of different submissions before final agreement is reached. The procedure might thus involve an initial budget for an individual responsibility centre, which may be revised prior to submission to the budget committee. This committee may in turn require further amendments on seeing the budgets from other centres.

Management will usually be aided in its choice of the initial jigsaw pieces by recognising that the range of the firm's activities is likely to be inhibited by certain constraints; more specifically that there is likely to be at least one critical factor which determines the firm's appropriate output level. It is a primary function of management to determine the nature of this critical factor(s) and decide whether the costs of alleviating the constraint(s) are worth incurring. The critical factor could be one of many: for example, the firm may suffer restrictions on its productive capacity, its supply of labour, its availability of cash or, perhaps most likely in a competitive situation, the demand for its products at a particular price. For purposes of exposition this chapter will presume demand quantity to be the constraining factor, and thus the sales budget will determine, within reasonable bounds, the levels of the other functional, allied budgets. A sales forecast is frequently the starting point for budgeting because it represents a key estimate of the level of operating activity from which many other factors follow, such as manufacturing, purchasing and operating expenses. (If there is more than one constraining factor, a more refined technique such as mathematical programming will be necessary for piecing together the jigsaw.)

Figure 16.1 The relationship between budget statements.

Figure 16.1 illustrates the relationships between the various budget statements in the periodic budgeting process, assuming that the critical variable which is the starting point of the estimation process is a sales forecast. In the remainder of this chapter we show how, in a much simplified situation, management may gradually build up a master budget for the firm, following the flows implied in this diagram. The example of Windsor plc is used for illustrative purposes throughout the chapter. Windsor plc produces and sells only two products, Y and Z. Its actual balance sheet as at 31 December 19X0, is shown in Table 16.1. The balance sheet is a statement of a firm's position at a particular point in time, usually at the end of an accounting period. It shows the firm's assets, conventionally at their original cost adjusted for depreciation where appropriate, less liabilities. The difference between assets and liabilities represents the interest in the firm of the providers of long-term funds (see pp. 262–70).

The master budget often leads to summary financial statements in the form of a budgeted income statement and a budgeted balance sheet. As such, it provides a forecast of what the firm's published income statement and balance sheet will look like for the period covered by the budget. This may be of interest to managers, as the published income statement and balance sheet will be one means of communication between those responsible for running the firm (the managers) and others with an interest in its performance (e.g. shareholders and other providers of long-term funds). Insofar as the master budget is intended to forecast the contents of the firm's

Table 16.1 Windsor plc: balance sheet as at 31 December 19X0

	£	£	£
Fixed assets (at cost *less* depreciation)			260,000
Current assets:			
Stocks of finished goods at 'full' cost:			
500 units of product Y at £7.50	3,750		
500 units of product Z at £7.50	3,750		
	7,500		
Work in progress	8,000		
Raw materials at cost:			
5,000 kg at £1.00	5,000	20,500	
Debtors (accounts receivable)		24,000	
Cash		22,500	
		67,000	
Less Current liabilities (creditors)		12,000	
Net current assets			55,000
Total net assets			315,000
Represented by:			
Issued share capital			240,000
Retained income			75,000
Total long-term funds			315,000

published accounting reports, it should be prepared on the same basis as will be the published accounting statements. Hence the conventions used in preparing the budgeted income statement and balance sheet for inclusion in the master budget will often be identical to those used in preparing the firm's external accounts.

We discussed some of these conventions briefly in Chapter 5 (pp. 94–6) and pointed out that, whatever their merits in external reporting, they often result in figures that are only partly relevant to managerial decision making. In particular, the use of historical costs and the allocation of fixed costs between products may not provide measures of the relevant costs of using resources. Our main purpose in this chapter is to illustrate how a master budget might be built up from a series of subsidiary budgets. For convenience, we adopt accounting conventions that are often used in the preparation of external accounting reports. However, it is crucial to recognise that the resulting figures may not be the best available for internal decision making; the figures most relevant for that purpose have been discussed in previous chapters. In other words, our main purpose in this chapter is to forecast the impact on a firm's income statement and balance sheet of decisions taken on the bases we have recommended previously. We begin by looking at the various operating budgets referred to earlier and then discuss the financial budgets and how these relate to the expectations and plans for operations.

16.2 Sales budget

The sales budget for an organisation is derived from estimates of the demand for (and the ability to supply) its different products at particular prices. These estimates are, in turn, determined on the basis of sales forecasts. Thus sales forecasting precedes sales budgeting.

The purpose of sales forecasting is to estimate the organisation's sales revenue for the budget period. Two interdependent factors make up sales revenue: the volume of sales and the selling price(s) – we examined the relationships between the two in Chapter 9. Some of the variables which may affect the organisation's pricing policy are:

- extent of market competition;
- general economic and industrial conditions;
- organisational cost structure.

Sales volume will be determined both by the chosen pricing policy and by some or all of the following additional factors, some of which may be uncontrollable:

- level and effectiveness of advertising and other promotional policies;
- quality of the sales force;
- past sales volume, and the relationships with suppliers and customers;
- any seasonal and cyclical influences;
- decisions of competitors.

The sales forecaster might use the above variables to predict, first, the level of regular business, comprising contracts already placed and the normal demand of regular customers; second, the level of non-regular business, comprising the likely demand from new customers and other non-repetitive sources (i.e. although certain individual transactions may not be repeated regularly, the total amount of such business may be stable from year to year); and finally the level of unstable business or unexpected demand which, by its very nature, is difficult to forecast.

Sales forecasting procedures can be very sophisticated and a detailed discussion of them lies outside the scope of this text.[1] However, we note below some approaches that a forecaster might use in deriving his or her expectations:

1. *Assessments by sales department staff.* Estimates of sales demand might be made by the individual salespersons and subsequently be passed upwards for consideration by the sales managers. This approach has the advantage that individual salespersons can offer advice on the basis of detailed knowledge of the particular factors peculiar to their own areas.

2. *Mathematical analysis of past sales figures.* The purpose of such an analysis, of whatever degree of sophistication, is to indicate trends in the relationship between selling price and quantity demanded and, where possible, patterns of seasonal variation. This information can then be adjusted for known factors, such as the level of future advertising or changes in the degree of market competition, to produce future sales forecasts.

3. *Senior management judgement.* The meeting of the senior management team, which might include representatives of production management, purchasing and administration, as well as senior sales executives, may bring a wider variety of expertise to the forecasting exercise.

On the basis of sales forecasts we can draw up the sales budget for Windsor plc as per Table 16.2. Note that, although the 'conventionally' calculated production cost of the two products is the same (£7.50), their selling prices differ. This is a common occurrence in practice. It may result from certain products being advertised more heavily than others, from differences in the competitiveness of markets in which different products are sold, or from differences between the relevant incremental costs of products, even though their costs calculated according to normal accounting conventions are the same.

Table 16.2 Windsor plc: sales budget for the year to 31 December 19X1

	Units to be sold	Price (£)	Total sales revenue (£)
Product Y	40,000	10.00	400,000
Product Z	16,000	12.50	200,000
			600,000

Table 16.3 Windsor plc: selling expenses budget
for the year to 31 December 19X1

	£
Sales commission (5% × £600,000)	30,000
Salaries	27,000
Travelling expenses	15,000
Advertising and promotion	23,000
	95,000

When the sales budget has been prepared, it is a relatively straightforward task to estimate the appropriate selling and distribution costs: that is, those costs which depend upon the level of sales. The make-up of the selling expenses budget is shown in Table 16.3. Of the items making up the selling expenses budget, only sales commission (5% of £600,000) varies directly with sales revenue; the remainder of the costs are fixed for the following year, although their actual amounts are, to a large extent, determined by the expected volume of sales.

16.3 Production budget

In order to meet its sales demand, the organisation requires a continually available stock of saleable finished goods. It must attempt to plan its manufacturing cycle so as to ensure the availability of stock. Production planning is of particular importance if the organisation has seasonal peaks in its sales levels. It is also likely that the management will wish to have a minimum stock of finished goods at any point in time, not only to meet future sales targets, but also to meet unforeseen orders and to alleviate possible difficulties in meeting existing orders if any production breakdowns occur. In recent years, however, many companies have looked closely at their production and stock relationships to try to minimise the level of stock and work in progress held by the firm, thereby saving warehouse and interest costs. Attempts to make suppliers deliver raw materials only when the firm needs them (known as just-in-time delivery) cut down dramatically the need for excess buffer stocks. To accomplish this properly, the firm must reorganise its production activities – usually via computer-aided techniques.

Hence we might say that the production budget for the period (the amount of finished goods to be produced during the period) is determined by the sales budget and by the stock of finished goods required by the organisation. If we further suppose, as in the case of Windsor plc, that the organisation possesses a stock of finished goods at the start of the period, we can generalise the number of units to be produced by solving the following simple equation:

Units to be = Units to + Units to be in − Units in opening
produced   be sold   closing stock   stock

Table 16.4 shows Windsor plc's production budget in units for the year to 31 December 19X1, on the assumption that 1,200 units of Y and 800 units of Z are required at the year end, and that there will be no change in the quantity or cost of work in progress (i.e. partially completed units), which will remain constant at £8,000.

Having determined the required levels of production for the year, the management can now proceed to determine the costs of producing the required units of finished product. In practice it is unlikely that levels and costs of production will be determined independently of each other. For ease of exposition we presume such independence. We will classify the costs of production under three separate headings, raw materials, direct labour and manufacturing overhead, each of which gives rise to a separate budget. Capital expenditure needed to support production is discussed in section 16.4.

Raw materials budget

In Windsor plc's case we assume that there is only one type of raw material which is used in the production of both Y and Z. It is a major task of the purchasing manager to ensure that raw materials are available whenever required. This may entail 'bulk buying' at particular times during the year, with the attendant possibility of holding large raw materials stocks which take up extra warehouse space and have a cost to the firm in terms of the finance which is invested in them. However, one result of bulk buying may be the ability to negotiate a lower price for the materials purchased, which thus acts as a countervailing benefit to the extra storage and finance costs. The raw materials budget might therefore be useful for estimating the warehouse space needed and for determining reorder levels, as well as agreeing any constraints on raw material expenditure.

We assume that both products use 2 kg of raw material to produce a single unit, and that the price to be paid for the raw material is £1 per kg. We also assume that management requires 7,000 kg of raw material to be in stock at the year end. We can now prepare the raw materials budget for the year as per Table 16.5.

Table 16.4 Windsor plc: production budget (in units) for the year to 31 December 19X1

	Y (units)	Z (units)
Budgeted sales (as per Table 16.2)	40,000	16,000
Budgeted closing stock	1,200	800
Total requirements	41,200	16,800
Less Opening stock (as per Table 16.1)	500	500
Required production	40,700	16,300

Table 16.5   Windsor plc: raw materials budget for the year to 31 December 19X1

	Units of production	Quantity required per unit (kg)	Total quantity required (kg)	Price per unit (£)	Total cost (£)
Needed for production of:					
Y (as per Table 16.4)	40,700	2	81,400	1.00	81,400
Z (as per Table 16.4)	16,300	2	32,600	1.00	32,600
Total to be used in production			114,000		114,000
Add Budgeted closing stock			7,000	1.00	7,000
Total requirement			121,000		121,000
Less Opening stock (as per Table 16.1)			5,000	1.00	5,000
Total to be purchased			116,000		116,000

Direct labour budget

If the organisation does not make different specialised products, direct labour requirements (i.e. labour which is readily traceable to particular units of production) can be determined from previous experience or by using time and motion studies. These figures can then be applied to the production target to ascertain labour requirements. If the production mix is intricate, the determination of direct labour cost is trickier, as labour is then regarded as a 'pool' to support production generally. Direct labour budgets might be used for a variety of purposes, among the most important of which are:

● to help the development of recruitment policies;

● to identify training and education needs;

● to provide a framework for wage negotiations, for both skilled and unskilled labour.

We assume that production of each unit of Y and Z is expected to require 15 minutes of direct labour (i.e. 4 units can be produced per hour), and that the rate payable is £12 per hour. This yields a budget for direct labour as shown in Table 16.6.

Table 16.6   Windsor plc: direct labour budget for the year to 31 December 19X1

	Units of production	Labour hours per unit	Total hours	Total budget at £12 per labour hour (£)
Y (as per Table 16.4)	40,700	1/4	10,175	122,100
Z (as per Table 16.4)	16,300	1/4	4,075	48,900
			14,250	171,000

Table 16.7 Windsor plc: manufacturing overhead budget for the year to 31 December 19X1

	£	£
Fixed costs:		
Power	3,600	
Supervision	22,000	
Maintenance	13,500	
Rent, rates and insurance	25,000	
Depreciation	10,000	74,100
Variable costs:		
Indirect labour (57,000 units at £1 per unit)		57,000
Power (57,000 units at 20p per unit)		11,400
Total		142,500

Table 16.8 Windsor plc: cost of goods sold budget for the year to 31 December 19X1

	From Table	£	£
Materials (to be used in production)	16.5		114,000
Direct labour	16.6		171,000
Manufacturing overhead	16.7		142,500
			427,500
Add Stock of finished goods at 1 January 19X1 (as per Table 16.1)			7,500
			435,000
Less Stock of finished goods at 31 December 19X1			
Y, 1,200 units at £7.50* per unit		9,000	
Z, 800 units at £7.50* per unit		6,000	15,000
Cost of goods sold (56,000 units as per Table 16.2 at £7.50* per unit)			420,000

*The calculation of the 'full' unit cost of finished goods is as follows:

		£
Raw materials (2 kg at £1 per kg)		2.00
Direct labour (1/4 hour at £12 per hour)		3.00
Manufacturing overheads £142,500		2.50
(as per Table 16.7) 57,000 units		
		7.50

The method of stock valuation which allocates total manufacturing overhead to products is known as full or absorption costing. Under this method, which is widely used for external reporting, some fixed manufacturing overheads are carried forward to the next period as part of closing stock. The determination of the basis of allocation is an arbitrary choice and thus different bases can lead to different unit costs of finished goods. As we noted earlier, this method of stock valuation may not be the best available for managerial decision making. (See Chapter 7 for a fuller discussion.)

Manufacturing overhead budget

Manufacturing overhead represents those expenses which, unlike raw materials and direct labour, cannot easily be identified with separate units of production. However, some manufacturing overhead, which in the case of Windsor plc is represented by indirect labour and a part of the total cost of power, varies with the level of production and must be assigned both a basis of allocation and a rate of allocation. We assume in our example that indirect labour and a part of the total cost of power are variable costs and are allocated to production on the basis of a budgeted level of activity of 57,000 units of production, as calculated in Table 16.4; and that indirect labour is charged at a rate of £1 per unit of production, and power at 20p per unit of production. The remaining manufacturing overhead is composed of fixed costs. Table 16.7 shows the make-up of the manufacturing overhead budget for the year. Depreciation is calculated using the straight-line method and represents a writing off of part of the original cost of fixed assets.

The total production costs may now be summarised in a cost of goods sold budget, shown in Table 16.8. This is effectively a summary statement in the overall process of preparation of the master budget.

16.4 Capital expenditure budget

The capital expenditure budget will usually be prepared for a longer period than other budgets, say from three to five years, and is used to indicate the expenditure required to cover both capital projects already in place and those to be undertaken. Thus the budget should be geared to the current production budget, future expected levels of output and the long-term development of the business, and the industry, as a whole. It may be convenient to classify projects in the capital expenditure budget under separate headings, for example:

- cost reduction and replacement expenditure;

- expenditure on the expansion of existing product lines;

- new product expenditure;

- health, safety and welfare capital expenditure.

The reason for making this differentiation lies in the method(s) of appraisal used for their justification. The first three categories are susceptible to the types of capital investment appraisal technique discussed in Chapters 13 and 14, whereas projects in the last category arise generally from policy decisions of top management, or from sources such as mandatory government regulations.

The administration of the capital budget is usually separate from that of the other budgets. Indeed in most large companies there is a capital projects committee which has overall responsibility for the authorisation and monitoring of capital projects, and for the preparation of the capital budget. Thus, for example, projects

Table 16.9 Windsor plc: capital expenditure budget for the year to 31 December 19X1

Project number	Estimated date of payment		Cost (£)
153	30 January	Replace machine M75	25,000
154	31 May	Purchase new machine N23	10,000
		Total capital expenditure	35,000

costing over £100,000 may require authorisation by the board of directors, those between £50,000 and £100,000 may need approval by divisional management, and those below £50,000 may be approved by individual divisional managers. The capital expenditure budget for Windsor plc for 19X1 is set out in Table 16.9.

16.5 General and administrative expenses budget

In most organisations there is a block of costs, often relatively fixed in amount in the short term, which relate to the non-production and non-sales aspect of business. Table 16.10 itemises these costs for Windsor plc.

16.6 Cash budget

Having prepared detailed budgets for each of the functional aspects of the business, we now draw up one of the most important budgets of all – the cash budget. The ability of the firm to generate cash flow represents its ability to pay dividends, and to succeed and grow in the future. The preparation of the cash budget aids management in its planning and in its desire to minimise unwanted, and non-productive, cash balances, while at the same time ensuring that, wherever possible, expensive borrowing to overcome short-term deficiencies is not incurred. Most organisations draw up their cash budgets on, at least, a monthly basis, and we will show how this can be done in the concluding section of this chapter; for the purposes of determining the master budget of Windsor plc, we show simply the

Table 16.10 Windsor plc: general and administrative expenses budget for the year to 31 December 19X1

	£
Office wages	21,000
Executive salaries	35,000
Office supplies	4,000
Miscellaneous	5,000
Total	65,000

Table 16.11 Windsor plc: cash budget for the year to 31 December 19X1

	From Table	£
Opening cash balance (per opening balance sheet)	16.1	22,500
Add Receipts:		
Collections from customers		
(sales less £6,000 increase in debtors)	16.2	594,000
Total cash available		616,500
Less Payments:		
For materials		
(purchases less £5,000 increase in creditors)	16.5	111,000
For selling expenses	16.3	95,000
For direct labour	16.6	171,000
For manufacturing overhead*	16.7	132,500
For capital equipment	16.9	35,000
For general expenses	16.10	65,000
Total cash needed		609,500
Closing cash balance		7,000

*Note that the cash payment for manufacturing overheads excludes the depreciation expense of £10,000, as depreciation is a non-cash item.

total cash amounts for the full year. We assume in our analysis that debtors (amounts owed by customers) will increase over the year by £6,000, and that creditors (amounts owed to suppliers) for raw materials will increase by £5,000. Finally, we assume no other outstanding liabilities exist at 31 December 19X1. The cash budget for the year is shown in Table 16.11.

16.7 Budgeted income statement and balance sheet

We are now in a position to prepare a budgeted income statement and balance sheet for Windsor plc. Because we have reached the stage in the budgeting process where the attention of management will be directed towards the way in which the expected results of the forthcoming year will be shown in the company's external accounting reports, we shall present the income statement and balance sheet in a form suitable for publication. Details are given in Table 16.12. The budgeted income statement and balance sheet represent the summarised plans for the whole organisation for the forthcoming period.

Certain decisions and inferences might be made by top management on the basis of the projected figures. For example, management might calculate certain key ratios to determine whether the position revealed by the budgeted statements is satisfactory. *Profitability* ratios would examine the relationships between net income and turnover, and net income and capital employed. Focus on Windsor plc's *liquidity* situation would question whether the projected cash balance is adequate, whether the debtors are likely to pay on time, whether the stocks of finished goods and work in

Table 16.12 Windsor plc: budgeted income statement and balance sheet

	From Table	£	£
Budgeted income statement for the year to 31 December 19X1			
Sales	16.2		600,000
Less Cost of goods sold	16.8		420,000
Gross profit			180,000
Less Selling expenses	16.3	95,000	
General and administrative expenses	16.10	65,000	160,000
Budgeted net income			20,000
Budgeted balance sheet as at 31 December 19X1			
Fixed assets (net)*			285,000
Current assets:			
Stocks: Finished goods	16.8	15,000	
Work in progress		8,000	
Raw materials	16.5	7,000	
		30,000	
Debtors (£24,000 + £6,000)		30,000	
Cash	16.11	7,000	
		67,000	
Less Creditors (£12,000 + £5,000)		17,000	
Net current assets			50,000
Total net assets			335,000
Represented by:			
Issued share capital	16.1		240,000
Retained income at 1 January 19X1	16.1		75,000
Budgeted net income for the year			20,000
Total long-term funds			335,000

* The fixed asset balance is computed as follows:

	£
Balance as at 1 January (as per Table 16.1)	260,000
Capital additions (as per Table 16.10)	35,000
	295,000
Less Depreciation (as per Table 16.7)	10,000
Balance as per closing balance sheet	285,000

progress are likely to prove saleable, whether the relationship between the totals of fixed assets and current assets is satisfactory, and whether the current assets/current liabilities ratio is optimal. Attention to the funds employed by the business might query the rationale of *financing* operations without any debt capital.

The two budgeted statements as we have presented them are static, deterministic budgets. They show the projected results of operating only at a single expected level of activity. They should be interpreted with caution as it is unlikely that the firm will operate at exactly the level of activity embodied in the budgets. For control purposes it is imperative, as explained in the previous chapter, that the management supports the fixed master budget with a series of flexible budgets showing the expected results of operating at different levels of activity, and perhaps also with budgets showing, for example, the effects of changes in input and output prices.

In addition the conventions used to prepare the budgeted accounts are those commonly applied to the preparation of accounts for publication. For example, cost of goods sold includes allocated fixed costs and a charge for using fixed assets (a depreciation charge) based on an allocation of the original cost of assets. Hence, as we explained in Chapter 5 and subsequently, the figure for cost of goods sold may be a poor approximation to the expected relevant, opportunity cost of the goods to be sold. As an indication of what Windsor plc's published accounts will look like if actual performance for the year accords with budgeted performance, the budgeted income statement and balance sheet are satisfactory. However, insofar as they are used as a basis for authorising more detailed operating budgets, care must be taken to ensure that proper attention is paid to the sort of decision rules we have discussed in previous chapters.

16.8 Cash budgeting

We should not leave the subject of budgeting without a further, more detailed look at cash budgeting. Short-term cash budgeting focuses attention directly on the most critical aspect of short-term financial management – the day-to-day handling of cash resources. It entails making detailed estimates of when cash will be received from cash and credit sales, and when cash will be paid to the various suppliers of materials, capital, overheads and labour. Indeed the cash budget indicates the effect of the budgeted activities of all the functional areas of business on the flow of the firm's liquid resources, which represent the lifeblood of the organisation. Thus cash budgets are invariably prepared and revised at intervals not exceeding one month.

Why is cash budgeting so important? An organisation needs cash to facilitate its daily transactions, but it naturally wishes to avoid the accumulation of idle cash balances which represent a non-productive (wasteful) use of resources. For example, cash can be used to earn interest for the organisation by investment in short-term loans and bank deposits. The cash budget assists the financial manager in pointing out whether there is likely to be sufficient cash available for the (profitable) budgeted levels of activity. Equally the cash budget helps to indicate the periods, if any, in which cash resources are likely to be inadequate, thus allowing the manager to arrange additional finance as soon as possible to meet the cash bottleneck. The following example shows how a detailed cash budget might be prepared so as to reveal likely periodic surpluses and deficits.

The information below relates to Kenilworth plc for the six-month period to 30 June 19X1.

1. On 1 January cash on hand and at the bank is expected to total £5,000.

2. Debtors normally pay one-half of the amount due at the end of the month following sale, and one-half at the end of the second month after sale, whereas Kenilworth plc pays its creditors at the end of the month after purchase of the goods.

3. Budgeted sales and purchases are as follows:

	Sales (£)	Purchases (£)
November 19X0	20,000	10,000
December	25,000	12,000
January 19X1	25,000	22,000
February	27,000	19,000
March	30,000	18,000
April	30,000	18,000
May	30,000	18,000
June	30,000	18,000

4. General expenses of £5,000 will be paid at the end of each month.

5. A machine costing £18,000 is to be acquired and paid for at the end of March.

We can now prepare the cash budget as detailed in Table 16.13. The layout of the cash budget is of great importance, and should highlight the expected cash position month by month. Total monthly receipts and total monthly payments are itemised separately, and a balance representing either a cash surplus (as in January, April, May and June) or a cash deficit (as in February and March) is struck at the end of each month. This surplus (deficit) is added to (deducted from) the opening balance

Table 16.13 Kenilworth plc: cash budget January–June 19X1

	January (£)	February (£)	March (£)	April (£)	May (£)	June (£)
Cash receipts						
(A) Sales (debtors)	22,500	25,000.	26,000	28,500	30,000	30,000
Cash payments:						
Purchases (creditors)	12,000	22,000	19,000	18,000	18,000	18,000
Expenses	5,000	5,000	5,000	5,000	5,000	5,000
Cost of machine	–	–	18,000	–	–	–
(B)	17,000	27,000	42,000	23,000	23,000	23,000
Net cash receipts for the month (A − B)	5,500	(2,000)	(16,000)	5,500	7,000	7,000
Cash balance at start of month	5,000	10,500	8,500	(7,500)	(2,000)	5,000
Cash balance at end of month	10,500	8,500	(7,500)	(2,000)	5,000	12,000

for the month, to form the month's closing balance. Cash receipts represent half the sales of the preceding month, and half the sales of the pre-preceding month (e.g. the receipt of £22,500 in January is made up of £10,000 from November sales and £12,500 from sales in December). Cash payments to creditors are lagged by one month (e.g. the payment of £12,000 in January relates to the purchases made in December).

The example clearly reveals that cash shortages will occur during the six-month period, and that additional finance will be required during March and April to ensure the continuance of trading. As the shortage is apparently short-term, arising because the machinery payment is to be made during March, it may be possible to finance it by a variety of means. For instance, Kenilworth plc might negotiate with its bank for temporary overdraft facilities during the relevant period, it might attempt to negotiate stricter terms for debtor payments, or it might try to delay payments to creditors for an extra month. Alternatively it might, depending upon the level of stocks it holds, consider some short-term reduction in stock levels. It is one of the biggest advantages of a monthly cash budgeting system that it draws attention not only to cash surpluses and deficits, but also to the whole notion of optimal working capital management. It raises questions, as in the example of Kenilworth plc, concerning the period of credit allowed to debtors, the level of stocks held by the organisation, and the payment period allowed by creditors.

CHAPTER SUMMARY

This chapter has presented the steps involved in preparing a master budget for an organisation: that is, a set of operating and financial statements representing plans for a budget period. It is important to choose the appropriate starting point for the budgeting exercise by identifying the critical variable from which the nature and scale of operating activities will follow. In many cases the estimated level of sales is used as the primary determinant of activities. In estimating the amounts to be included in individual operating budgets, however, care must be taken to ensure that the correct variables, or drivers, are used to determine plans and expectations, and, in this sense, budgeting involves modelling the organisation.

The different budget statements should articulate with one another and ultimately lead to the budgeted income statement and balance sheet, which summarise the financial consequences of the planned operating activities. The cash budget summarises the effects of operations on the firm's liquid resources and allows management to plan for the financing of the activities embodied in the operating budgets.

REVIEW QUESTIONS

1. Describe and analyse the main functions of the organisation's master budget.

2. Explain the differences and relationships between a sales forecast and a sales budget.

3. You are the production director of a large organisation. Discuss the various interrelationships between your yearly budgets and the budgets of other functions within the organisation.

4. You are the sales director of a large organisation. Discuss the various interrelationships between your yearly budgets and the budgets of other functions within the organisation.

5. 'The success or failure of a business depends on its ability to manage cash. Thus the cash budget is of the utmost importance.' Discuss.

EXERCISES

16.1 The balance sheet of Mendelssohn Ltd at 1 January 19X0 is expected to be as follows:

Capital and liabilities	(£)	(£)	Assets	(£)	(£)
Ownership interest:			Fixed assets, at cost		870,000
Share capital		500,000	Less Accumulated		
			depreciation		210,000
Reserves		135,000			660,000
		635,000			
8% loan stock		200,000	Current assets:		
			Stock	150,000	
			Trade debtors	70,000	
			Cash	55,000	275,000
Current liabilities:					
Dividend due	40,000				
Trade creditors	60,000	100,000			
		935,000			935,000

The following is a summary of the transactions expected by the company during the year ending 31 December 19X0.

1. Sales are expected to amount to £800,000. All sales are on credit and Mendelssohn Ltd expects that 12% of the annual sales will not have been paid for at 31 December 19X0.

2. All purchases of stock are on credit and are expected to amount to £650,000. The company expects to owe its suppliers £65,000 at 31 December 19X0. It expects to have stocks on hand at that date of £250,000 at cost price.

3. New fixed assets are expected to be purchased for cash during the year, costing £150,000. No fixed assets will be sold. Depreciation is to be provided on all fixed assets (including those bought during the year) at the rate of 10% on cost.

4. Interest on the loan stock is payable annually in arrears on 31 December.

5. Operating expenses for the year (other than those mentioned above) are expected to amount to £65,000, payable as they are incurred.

6. The dividend due at 1 January 19X0 will be paid during the year, and the company intends to provide for a dividend of a similar amount at 31 December 19X0.

    (a) Prepare a budgeted income statement for the year ending 31 December 19X0, and a budgeted balance sheet as at that date.

    (b) Comment on the figures revealed by your budgets. (Solution at end of text.)

16.2 Paderewski plc has the following (summarised) balance sheet as at 30 April 19X2:

	£000	£000
Share capital		1,000
Revenue reserve (undistributed profit)		754
		1,754
4% debenture stock (long-term loan)		300
Current liabilities:		
Trade creditors	1,200	
Inland revenue (for tax)	30	
Bank overdraft	300	1,530
		3,584
Freehold land and buildings at cost		320
Manufacturing equipment, tools, dies, etc.		560
		880
Current assets:		
Stock of raw materials, work in progress and		
finished goods at cost or under		1,300
Trade debtors		1,404
		3,584

Estimates prepared in the accounting department for the following three months are as follows:

	£000
Sales on credit, spread equally over the three months (sales are on deferred terms: the debtors will pay in 12 equal instalments, the first falling in the month in which the debt is incurred)	576
Purchase of raw materials, spread equally over the three months (purchases will all be for cash, as suppliers will not give any more credit)	114
Manufacturing wages (payable in cash weekly): total for three months	228
Other expenses (non-manufacturing wages and salaries, insurance, heating and lighting, rates, etc.) (These will be payable in cash and arise evenly over the three months.)	237
It is estimated that it will be possible to collect in each month about $\frac{1}{6}$ of the debts due to the company at 30 April	
It is expected that $\frac{1}{3}$ of the trade creditors at 30 April will have to be paid in each of the three months	
The tax is payable immediately	
The expected sales will absorb finished goods at a book value (based on manufacturing labour and materials only) of	342
The bank overdraft limit (i.e. the maximum advance allowed) is	600
One quarter's interest on the debenture stock must be paid in July	

(a) Prepare a clear statement for the directors of the company showing, month by month, the estimated cash receipts and payments of the company for the next three months.

(b) Prepare an estimated income statement for the period and an end-period balance sheet. (Write £14,000 off equipment for depreciation.)

(c) Comment on the situation revealed by these statements. (Solution at end of text.)

16.3 You have been appointed management accountant to a company which has been operating at a low profit level over the last few years. The company does not operate a budgetary planning system, but based on present performance plus allowances for price and other cost increases, a preliminary profit forecast for the next 12 months shows the following:

Estimated sales   £3,750,000
Estimated net income   £5,000

The managing director is most perturbed and comments as follows:

It looks as if we are finished. At least £50,000 is needed to replace our old equipment. We have been putting this off for years and can now delay no longer. We are already overdrawn at the bank, and there is nothing to use as security. The directors, who between them own all of the shares in the company, are unable to provide the extra finance required and even if they could it wouldn't be worthwhile investing for the income we look like making.

(a) Comment on the managing director's statement.

(b) Suggest areas of investigation which might disclose possible sources of finance within the company and the matters which would have to be considered in respect of these.

16.4 Respighi Plastics Ltd, a manufacturer of moulded plastic containers, determined in October 19X8 that it needed cash to continue operations. The company began negotiating for a one-month bank loan of £100,000 on 1 November at 12% interest. In considering the loan, the bank requested a projected profit statement and a cash budget for the month of November.

The following information is available:

1. Sales were budgeted at 120,000 units per month in October 19X8, December 19X8 and January 19X9, and at 90,000 units in November 19X8.

2. The selling price is £2 per unit. Sales are invoiced on the 15th and the last day of each month. Terms are 2% discount if payment is made within 10 days, otherwise the full amount is to be paid within 30 days. Past experience indicated sales are made evenly throughout the month. Fifty per cent of the customers pay the invoiced amount within the discount period. The remainder pay at the end of 30 days, except for bad debts, which average 0.5% of gross sales.

3. The stock of finished goods on 1 October was 24,000 units. The finished goods stock at the end of each month is to be maintained at 20% of sales anticipated for the following month. The production process is such that there is no work in progress.

4. The stock of raw materials on 1 October was 22,800 kg. At the end of each month the raw materials stocks are to be maintained at not less than 40% of production requirements for the following month. Materials are purchased locally. Minimum quantity is 25,000 kg per shipment. Raw material purchases of each month are paid in the next month. Terms are net 30 days.

5. All salaries and wages are paid on the 15th and last day of each month for the period ending on the date of payment.

6. All manufacturing overhead and selling and administrative expenses are paid on the 10th of the month following the month in which the expenses are incurred. Selling expenses are 10% of gross sales. Administrative expenses, which include depreciation of £500 per month on office furniture and fixtures, total £33,000 per month.

7. The standard cost of a moulded plastic container, based on normal production of 100,000 units per month, is:

	£	
Materials, $\frac{1}{2}$ kg	0.50	
Labour	0.40	
Variable overhead	0.20	
Fixed overhead	0.10	(total budgeted = £10,000)
Total	1.20	

8. Fixed overhead includes depreciation on factory equipment of £4,000 per month. Over- or under-absorbed overhead (i.e. difference between £10,000 and the amount applied to production) is included in cost of sales.

9. The cash balance on 1 November is expected to be £10,000.

Assuming the bank loan is granted:

(a) Prepare schedules calculating stock budgets by months for

(i) finished goods production in units for October, November and December;
(ii) raw materials purchases in kg for October and November.

(b) Prepare a projected income statement for the month of November.

(c) Prepare a cash forecast for November showing the opening balance, receipts (itemised by dates of collection), payments and the closing balance.

16.5 It is April 19X6. The Trade Union Co-ordinating Committee has just walked out of the room. There is going to be a strike starting on the first day of May 19X6. It is thought that the strike may last two months.

The company's budget for 19X6 is as follows:

	£000 Total	Jan.	Feb.	Mar.	Apr.	May	June	July	Aug.	Sep.	Oct.	Nov.	Dec.
Material consumed	320	22	23	29	32	26	28	30	32	34	24	20	20
Direct wages	179	14	14	15	16	17	17	16	16	15	13	13	13
Other factory variable expenses	20	1	2	2	2	2	2	2	2	2	1	1	1
Factory fixed expenses:													
Depreciation	40	3	3	4	3	3	4	3	3	4	3	3	4
General	150	12	13	12	13	12	13	12	13	12	13	12	13
Head office fixed expenses	170	14	14	14	14	14	14	14	14	15	14	14	15
Selling expenses:													
Commission	55	2	2	3	4	5	6	7	8	9	4	3	2
Fixed	60	5	5	5	5	5	5	5	5	5	5	5	5
	994	73	76	84	89	84	89	89	93	96	77	71	73
Profit (loss)	71	(3)	(1)	(4)	(4)	6	11	21	32	44	3	(11)	(23)
Sales	1,065	70	75	80	85	90	100	110	125	140	80	60	50
Stock of materials (end of month)		20	25	20	30	30	35	35	40	25	20	20	20

Assumptions

1. Payment is made to suppliers of material one month after delivery. No materials will be bought during the strike.

2. The lag in payment of wages is $\frac{1}{8}$ of a month.

3. Factory variable and general expenses, head office expenses and fixed selling expenses are paid during the month incurred.

4. Sales commission is paid one month in arrear.

5. Debtors take two months' credit.

6. Cash balance at 30 April 19X6 is estimated at £14,000.

7. There will be no production during the strike. Sales lost in the strike will not be recovered subsequently. If the strike ends on 30 June, it will not be possible in the succeeding months to produce more than originally budgeted and the costs and stock levels will be as budgeted.

8. There is no work in progress or finished stock as the product is delivered daily.

(a) Assuming the strike lasts two months, prepare a statement of cash flow (showing the opening and closing cash balances) for each of the four months May, June, July and August.

(b) Assuming the strike is not settled, prepare a statement of cash flow on a monthly basis showing in which month the bank account goes into overdraft.

(c) Assuming that the strike lasts two months, prepare a statement showing the effect on budgeted profit for the year to 31 December 19X6.

Note

1. But see Chapter 9 for a more comprehensive discussion of selling price–demand relationships.

Variance analysis and standard costing

AIMS AND OBJECTIVES

☐ To discuss the role of standard costing.
☐ To explain and illustrate the calculation of variances between budgeted and actual performance.
☐ To interpret and explain the usefulness of variances for control.
☐ To underline the importance of keeping standards up to date.

In the previous two chapters we have examined the initial stage of the budgetary control process – its budgeting aspect. We now turn our attention to the subsequent stages of the process: namely, the measurement of actual performance and the comparison of this performance with budget expectations. Comparison between budget and actual provides control information through the method of *variance analysis*. Our approach will focus on the calculation of variances in one of the accountant's most frequently used systems of control, standard costing, to which we have referred in a number of previous chapters. In this chapter we review the principles of standard costing before going on to explain how variances might be calculated and to consider their interpretation and usefulness. We also discuss the particular problem of ensuring that standards are set at appropriate levels in order that variance analysis will generate useful control information.

17.1 The purposes of standard costing

When discussing the measurement of product costs in Chapter 7, we outlined how preset standards may be used for cost estimation. With this approach to cost measurement it is necessary periodically to compare actual results with the costs accounted for on the basis of the standard amounts. A standard costing system thus employs the concepts of budgeting whereby expectations (represented by the predetermined standards) are compared with actual results for the purposes of control.

Typically, standard costing systems possess the following significant elements:

- procedures for setting up and updating standards;

- a recording system, which may be separate from the firm's 'financial accounting' records, which gathers both standard and actual cost (and revenue) information, and computes differences, known as variances;

- the determination of the unit costs of the firm's products, divided into their raw material, labour, variable and fixed overhead elements;

- the use of a budgeting period (e.g. one year), subdivided into smaller (e.g. four-weekly) time periods which are used as the vehicle for comparing standard and actual costs;

- procedures for investigating material variances, and apportioning such variances to responsibility centres.

The primary purposes of a standard costing system are threefold:

1. To provide the management with a yardstick for the evaluation of performance.

2. To give information on those aspects of business operations which are not proceeding according to plan. This purpose recognises the importance of controlling both actual results and planning procedures.

3. To generate information which may be useful for future planning (e.g. for the setting of future standards). This purpose is especially important in a changing environment: for example, in times of rapid technological change or high inflation.

There are other less obvious purposes of a standard costing system. For example, because the proper setting and revision of standards requires a knowledge of all the functional areas of the business and their contribution to overall success, standard costing may encourage managers to understand more fully the nature of their business. By concentrating attention only on significant deviations from plan, as detailed by regular variance reports, managers do not waste valuable time on those areas of activity which are proceeding normally, or engage in random testing of different areas covered by the control system.

To best meet its purposes, a standard costing system should embody realistic standards. Hence most systems employ currently attainable standards rather than ideal standards as the yardstick for assessment and evaluation (see Chapter 15, pp. 329, for a discussion of currently attainable and ideal budgets). Currently attainable standards reflect the cost expected to be incurred under normally efficient working conditions.

We argue later in this chapter that if conditions change significantly during the period, then the attainable standards may no longer be current and should be changed, otherwise the system will fail to produce useful variances.

Figure 17.1 shows the breakdown of the profit variance (the difference between the expected and actual profit for the year) into its component cost and revenue variances. The main purpose of this chapter is to suggest how these variances might be calculated and what meaning might be ascribed to the resultant calculations. However, at this stage, a few preliminary views on the possible causes of variances are necessary, in order to give some background to the later analysis. It is important to try to identify the *causes* of particular variances, as different variances may call for different remedies. Bromwich has identified *five* major causes of variances, as follows:[1]

1. Inefficiency in operation: for example, failure to obtain a reasonable standard in the prevailing circumstances, through inability in one form or another, or through lack of motivation.

2. Incorrect original plans and standards, or originally correct plans and standards that have been invalidated by environmental changes (here, the reporting of variances may result in the revision of plans, and the process of variance analysis for planning can be described as being educational).

3. Poor communication of standards and budgetary goals.

4. Random fluctuations around standards and goals which are likely to be average targets.

5. If in budgeting (and in decision making) the interdependence of departments has not been taken into account, then action taken by one department may cause variances elsewhere within the firm (the suboptimisation problem).

Our primary concern in this chapter is with the identification of the first two causes, and the recognition of the potential importance of the fifth cause. To best achieve these purposes, we conduct our analysis in two stages. First, we identify any variances due to changes in *volume* during the period. Because this necessitates a revision or flexing of the budget to the actual volume attained, we term this volume difference a *budget revision* variance. Second, we analyse the differences between the revised budget and the actual figures. We term these differences *control* variances (this distinction between budget revision and control variances was introduced in Chapter 15, pp. 324–6). Control variances should indicate whether managers have achieved the best possible performance in the light of the (revised) budget, as only then will variances be based on a comparison of like with like. In addition, they should exclude as far as possible any factors not within the control of the person to be held responsible for the variance. A main reason for the split between budget revision and control variances is that their causes will probably be different, and will reflect the responsibility of different managers. For example, budget revision variances may reflect the forecasting and planning abilities of managers, whereas control variances are more likely to be caused by operating efficiencies and inefficiencies.

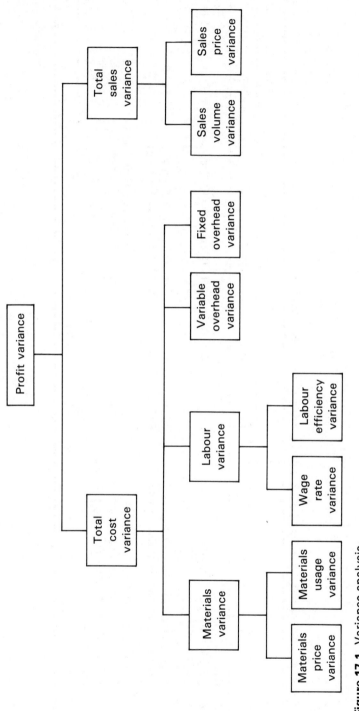

Figure 17.1 Variance analysis.

Table 17.1 Victoria plc: budgeted and actual results for the year to 31 December 19X0

| | Budget | | | Actual | |
	(£)	(£)		(£)	(£)
Total revenues					
Sales (15,000 units at £17 per unit)		255,000	(14,000 units at £17.85 per unit)		249,900
Less Total costs:					
Raw materials:					
Material P (15,000 kg at £2.20 per kg)	33,000		(14,500 kg at £2.20 per kg)	31,900	
Material Q (30,000 kg at £3.20 per kg)	96,000		(28,000 kg at £3.40 per kg)	95,200	
Labour:					
Unskilled (7,500 hours at £7.50 per hour)	56,250		(6,875 hours at £8.25 per hour)	56,719	
Skilled (1,500 hours at £12 per hour)	18,000		(1,400 hours at £12 per hour)	16,800	
Variable overhead (15,000 units at 75p per unit)	11,250			10,314	
Fixed overhead	21,600	236,100		22,500	233,433
Net profit		18,900			16,467

$\boxed{17.2}$ The mechanics of variance analysis

We shall use an example to illustrate our approach to the calculation and interpretation of variances. Victoria plc is a manufacturing company which produces and sells motor car components. It employs a standard costing system for planning and control. Table 17.1 shows the budgeted and actual results for the year to 31 December 19X0.

The following information is also relevant. Usage of both material P and material Q was expected to vary directly with each unit of output, as were the number of unskilled and skilled labour hours, and the element of variable overhead. Victoria plc followed its normal practice during the year to 31 December 19X0 of maintaining stocks at a constant level.

Our method of analysis of the difference between expected profit (£18,900) and actual profit (£16,467) rests on an understanding of the role of flexible budgeting. Flexible budgeting plays a vital role in generating useful control variances because, for control purposes, it is essential that actual costs and revenues incurred are compared to budgeted costs *at the actual level of activity*. Control and responsibility should go hand in hand in the standard costing system. Individual managers should be held responsible only for variances under their control.

It is therefore necessary first to flex the original budget of 15,000 units to the revised budget of 14,000 units. This eliminates any differences due to changes in volume, and allows us to compare actual performance with expected performance at a level of 14,000 units. Table 17.2 shows how we might achieve this.

The difference between columns 1 and 2 of £2,700 is the difference in profit (and contribution) due to the shortfall in sales volume: it is the difference generated by flexing the budget to the revised volume of 14,000 units. It thus represents the decline in volume of 1,000 units multiplied by the standard contribution per unit of 2.70. The standard contribution per unit is calculated as follows:

	£	£
Selling price		17.00
Less P (1 kg at £2.20)	2.20	
Q (2 kg at £3.20)	6.40	
Unskilled labour		
($\frac{1}{2}$ hour × £7.50)	3.75	
Skilled labour		
($\frac{1}{10}$ hour × £12.00)	1.20	
Variable overhead		
(1 unit at 75p)	0.75	14.30
Standard contribution per unit		2.70

Note that the expected level of fixed overhead, which does not enter the standard contribution per unit calculation, is unchanged for both volume levels. We shall suggest some possible causes for the loss of contribution of £2,700 in section 17.3.

We are now in a position to undertake the second stage of the analysis of variances – the comparison at the revised volume level of 14,000 units of the

Table 17.2   First estimation of variances

	Budgeted volume Standard prices (1)	Actual volume Standard prices (2)	Actual volume Actual prices (3)	Remaining variances (2)–(3) (4)
Volume (units)	15,000	14,000	14,000	
Sales	(£17) (£) 255,000	(£17) (£) 238,000	(£17.85) (£) 249,900	(£) 11,900 (F)
Materials:				
P	(£2.20) 33,000	(£2.20) 30,800	31,900	1,100 (U)
Q	(£6.40) 96,000	(£6.40) 89,600	95,200	5,600 (U)
Labour:				
Unskilled	(£3.75) 56,250	(£3.75) 52,500	56,719	4,219 (U)
Skilled	(£1.20) 18,000	(£1.20) 16,800	16,800	–
Variable overhead	(75p) 11,250	(75p) 10,500	10,314	186 (F)
	214,500	200,200	210,933	10,733 (U)
Contribution	40,500	37,800	38,967	1,167 (F)
Fixed overhead	21,600	21,600	22,500	900 (U)
Profit	18,900	16,200	16,467	267 (F)

expected profit of £16,200 with the actual profit of £16,467. This favourable difference of £267 is broken down into its constituent parts in column 4 of Table 17.2. We now deal with each of the constituent parts in turn.

Sales variance – £11,900 (F)

Column 4 shows a favourable sales variance of £11,900: that is, the actual revenue generated from the sale of 14,000 units was greater by £11,900 than the expected revenue at that volume. It can be readily seen that this variance is due to the increase in price of 85p multiplied by the 14,000 units sold. We can express this sales price variance (SPV) by means of the following formula:

$$SPV = AQ \times (AP - SP)$$

where AQ = actual quantity sold, SP = standard price, AP = actual price.
Thus, in our example we have:

$$SPV = 14,000 \times (17.85 - 17.00)$$
$$= £11,900 (F)$$

Note that we do not need to calculate a separate variance due to the change in sales volume, as we have already implicitly calculated the sales volume variance in arriving at the revised profit figure in column 2. Whether the sales price variance and the volume variance are useful for planning and control and whether they should be viewed independently, we shall discuss in the following section.

Raw material and labour variances

Raw material and labour variances are often referred to as direct cost variances. They are based on both monetary and non-monetary measures. For example, the use of raw materials will probably be measured first in terms of tons or kg used. Similarly, the efficiency with which the labour force performs its task might be expressed initially in a time dimension, in terms of hours or minutes.

Managers could exercise control by focusing solely on the quantity of materials used, or the time taken to perform the job, and comparing these non-monetary totals with the budget figures for material quantity and labour time. But how much information would this provide? Remember that one purpose of the control exercise is to monitor the effect of the firm's operations on the budgeted profit for the period. As profit is expressed in money terms, it is necessary to translate the non-additive hours, tons, litres, etc. into money values. Thus at the very root of direct cost variance analysis is a recognition of the effects of changes due to price and changes due to quantity, both of which must be expressed in cash terms.

Price variances (or *rate variances*) measure the difference between the amount the firm expected to pay for the actual quantity bought and the amount it did pay.

Usage variances (or *efficiency variances*) measure the difference between the quantity of a resource the firm expected to use for the actual activity level and the quantity it did use. This difference in quantity is usually expressed as a money amount by multiplying it by the standard price per unit. The total of the price and usage variances (or the rate and efficiency variances) is equal to the difference between the actual cost of a resource and the cost expected for the actual output level.

Price variances are not concerned with differences between the standard and actual purchase quantities of a resource, but rather with the differences between the standard and actual purchase price per unit of the quantity bought. They should be calculated at the time of purchase rather than at the time of use, in order to provide the quickest possible feedback for control purposes. The price variance (PV) is defined as the difference in price (standard price (SP) less actual price (AP)) multiplied by the actual quantity bought (AQ). It may be expressed by a formula similar to the one used to calculate the sales price variance:

$$PV = AQ \times (SP - AP)$$

The quantity variance (QV) is not concerned with price changes. It represents the difference between the standard quantity for the actual output (SQ) and the actual quantity used (AQ), multiplied by the standard cost price (SP). It may be expressed as:

$$QV = SP \times (SQ - AQ)$$

We can now use these definitions of price and quantity variance to analyse the differences arising in respect of raw materials and labour for Victoria plc.

1. *Material P – £1,100 (U)*. The price paid for P was £2.20 per unit. As this was the expected price, no price variance arises. However, as Table 17.1 shows, 14,500 kg of P were used to produce 14,000 units – 500 kg more than expected. Thus a material quantity or usage variance arises. We can calculate the effect of this by using the formula for quantity variances given above. This gives:

$$\begin{aligned}
QV \text{ (Material usage variance)} &= SP \times (SQ - AQ) \\
&= £2.20 \times (14,000 - 14,500) \\
&= £1,100 \text{ (U)}
\end{aligned}$$

2. *Material Q – £5,600 (U)*. The price paid for Q was £3.40 per kg. This is greater than the standard price of £3.20 per kg. Thus a price variance arises, calculated according to the price variance formula:

$$\begin{aligned}
PV \text{ (Material price variance)} &= AQ \times (SP - AP) \\
&= 28,000 \times (£3.20 - £3.40) \\
&= £5,600 \text{ (U)}
\end{aligned}$$

Note that no usage variance arises for Q. At an output level of 14,000 units, Victoria plc expected to use 28,000 kg of Q, which in fact represented the actual usage. The usefulness of these price and usage variances will be considered in the next section.

3. *Unskilled labour – £4,219 (U)*. Victoria plc expected to pay unskilled labour a standard rate per hour of £7.50. The actual rate paid was £8.25 per hour, and thus an unfavourable price (or rate) variance arises. Using the price variance formula, and substituting actual hours worked (AHW = 6,875 from Table 17.1) for actual quantities, we can calculate the cash effect of this variance as follows:

$$PV \text{ (Labour rate variance)} = AHW \times (SP - AP)$$
$$= 6,875 \times (£7.50 - £8.25)$$
$$= £5,156 \text{ (U)}$$

Elimination of the price variance leaves a further favourable difference of (£5,156 – £4,219) = £937. This further difference is explicable in terms of the usage (or efficiency) of labour. On the basis of an output of 14,000 units, unskilled labour was expected to work for 14,000/2 = 7,000 hours. However, only 6,875 hours were needed to produce the 14,000 units, and thus labour 'saved' 125 hours. We can calculate the effect of this extra efficiency by using the quantity variance formula, and by substituting the standard hours (SH) and the actual hours worked (AHW) for the standard and actual quantities. Thus we have:

$$QV \text{ (Labour efficiency variance)} = SP \times (SH - AHW)$$
$$= £7.50 \times (7,000 - 6,875)$$
$$= £937 \text{ (F)}$$

Note that no price or quantity variances arise in respect of skilled labour. The rate paid of £12 per hour is the standard rate for skilled labour, and the production of 14,000 units in 1,400 hours, the actual time taken, represents the expected level of efficiency.

Variable overhead – £186 (F)

Variable overhead for Victoria plc is expected to be incurred at a rate of 75p for each unit produced. Thus any variances between the variable overhead expected to be incurred at the actual level of output and the actual overhead incurred are due to favourable or unfavourable expenditure differences. The formula for calculating variable overhead expenditure variances is as follows:

$$VO \text{ (Expenditure variance)} = \text{Budgeted variable overhead at actual output level}$$
$$- \text{Actual variable overhead}$$
$$= (14,000 \text{ units} \times 75p) - £10,314$$
$$= £10,500 - £10,314$$
$$= £186 \text{ (F)}$$

Table 17.3 Victoria plc: standard costing statement for the year to 31 December 19X0

	F (£)	U (£)	(£)
Budgeted contribution at budgeted volume			
(15,000 components at £2.70)			40,500
Less Contribution lost due to reduction in volume			
(1,000 units at £2.70)			2,700
Budgeted contribution at actual volume			37,800
Remaining variances:			
Sales price	11,900		
Unskilled labour efficiency	937		
Variable overhead expenditure	186		
P-usage		1,100	
Q-price		5,600	
Unskilled labour rate		5,156	
	13,023	11,856	1,167 (F)
Actual contribution (14,000 components)			38,967
Less Budgeted fixed costs		21,600	
Fixed costs expenditure variance (U)		900	22,500
Actual profit (as per Table 17.1)			16,467

Fixed overhead – £900 (U)

As fixed overheads do not change with the level of output, it is not helpful (and indeed it may be misleading) to allocate them to individual units of production. The only meaningful variance for control purposes is the difference between the total amount expected to be spent on fixed overheads during the period and the actual amount spent. In the case of Victoria plc, this variance of £900 is the difference between £21,600 (budgeted fixed overheads) and £22,500 (actual fixed overheads).

We can now prepare a final control statement for Victoria plc, reconciling budgeted and actual contribution, and showing the actual profit figure as in Table 17.3.

17.3 The interpretation and usefulness of variances

Having explained the two-stage calculation of variances in the previous section, we are now in a position to interpret their meaning and discuss their usefulness. Each variance shown in Table 17.3 will be discussed in turn *in the context of the purposes of the standard costing system* as outlined at the start of this chapter.

Sales variances

Table 17.3 shows a favourable sales price variance of £11,900. Is the sales manager to be congratulated on this achievement? To begin to answer this question we should look at the other side of the sales coin – the number of units sold. Victoria plc expected to sell 15,000 units, but in fact sold only 14,000 units: that is, the price increase was accompanied by a fall in volume, as the workings of a competitive market would suggest.[2] Should we then equally blame the sales manager for failure to achieve the budgeted volume? If the shortfall of 1,000 units on sales was due entirely to the price increase, the benefit from the additional selling price per unit should be abated to some extent by the contribution lost on the shortfall: by £2,700. In other words, the net benefit from increasing selling price would be £9,200 (£11,900 minus £2,700).

Further consideration should convince us that we need more information about the state of the marketplace before we can say how well the sales force performed in the circumstances. For example, if demand in the marketplace has declined rapidly since standards were set, then the sales department may have done very well to sell 14,000 units at the increased price of £17.85. Thus the favourable net sales variance of £9,200 may be an inadequate reflection of managerial performance. The sales managers of Victoria plc may have taken advantage of their opportunities as well as possible, and indeed, have performed better than sales managers elsewhere. In this situation the loss of volume of 1,000 units may have been totally uncontrollable, in which case it may be inappropriate to reduce the favourable sales price variance of £11,900 by the lost contribution of £2,700. Indeed, as we explain later in this section, the loss of volume (and hence contribution) may be attributable to other factors for which *non-sales* managers *within the firm* are responsible.

If, however, demand for Victoria plc's goods has been particularly buoyant, then the loss of sales of 1,000 units may represent a controllable loss due to the inefficiency of the sales force. Or the price charged of £17.85 may have been too *low* at a volume level of 14,000 units. In this case sales managers may have failed to take advantage of the market situation. The real loss due to the fall in sales volume depends upon whether Victoria plc can recoup the sales in future periods. If sales are lost for ever, the real cost to the firm is the lost contribution from these sales; if sales are likely to be recouped in the future, the only cost is one of *time*. Persistently favourable or unfavourable volume variances might offer indications to top management as to the direction it should take: for example, a regularly favourable volume variance might indicate that the firm should increase its production capacity to take advantage of profitable market opportunities.

How should the sales price variance be evaluated? This depends largely upon whether the firm can influence the prevailing market price. If the firm has no control over the price, and hence the sales price variance is largely uncontrollable, there is little advantage to be gained in holding the sales force responsible for the difference, favourable or otherwise. In this case the only useful information to be derived from the sales price variance is as an aid to future planning. If the sales price variance is controllable, it should be used *in conjunction with* the volume variance (based on contribution lost or gained) in evaluating management. This underlines the important point that individual variances should not be viewed independently of their effects elsewhere in the organisation.

Raw materials variances

Table 17.3 shows two variances for raw materials – an unfavourable usage variance of £1,100 for P, and an unfavourable price variance of £5,600 for Q. Does this mean that the *buying* manager should be criticised for failure to secure the standard price for Q, and that the *production* manager should be penalised for inefficient use of P? Before we can answer these questions, we need to explore a little further the possible interpretations of these two variances.

Material price variance

A primary aim of top management is to evaluate the success of the materials buying manager in obtaining a favourable price. Comparison of the actual price paid with the budgeted price may reflect an insufficient amount of time spent on evaluating the 'quality' of suppliers, slowness in taking advantage of discount, and changes in material quality. But such comparisons may not be the best way of evaluating success if there have been substantial changes in the price of raw materials between the date at which the budget is set and the date of purchase. If the price change is due to market factors, as is most likely, then such a change will be outside the control of the buying manager, and so to say that he had done well or badly in generating a price variance may convey little useful information as to his buying skills. Thus to show how well the buying manager has competed in the market, the appropriate comparison should rest between the price paid for raw materials and *the best estimate of the market price at the date of purchase*. This comparison attempts to remove any uncontrollable factors from the evaluation. The unfavourable price variance for Victoria plc may therefore be outside the control of the buying manager, and may reflect poor budgeting. If this proves to be the case, it should be charged to the planners rather than the buying manager. In Chapter 15, we discussed the issue of participation in budget setting. It may be that, in practice, the dichotomy between budget setters and budget achievers is not clear cut. If the person responsible for implementing a budget has also played a substantial role in setting it, then variances should be interpreted with particular care. It may, for example, be unwise in these circumstances to reward the achievement of a favourable price variance without, at the same time, investigating carefully whether the budget price was reasonable in the circumstances which existed at the time the budget was set.

The trend in material price variances may give useful information for future planning. For example, a regularly favourable variance might suggest that the firm's planners are consistently pessimistic about future material prices, which may result in incorrect output level and selling price decisions (see, for example, Chapters 9–11). The price variance should not, however, be viewed in isolation from costs elsewhere in the firm. Consider the possible effects of (bulk) buying a large quantity of raw materials. A larger quantity demanded will often lead to a discount being offered by the supplier: that is, a favourable price variance. This decision in turn may lead directly to the incurrence of interest costs in relation to the additional finance required for the purchase and warehouse (and supervision) costs for the material's storage. These extra costs are due to the particular action of the buying manager, and all variances, wherever located in the organisation, due to this action should be attributable to the buying manager and not to other managers. Nor should material price variances be viewed in isolation from usage variances. For example, purchases of non-standard material at cheaper (or more expensive) prices may result in unfavourable (or favourable) usage variances. These interdependent variances, as far as they can be identified, should be attributable to the material buyer. In practice, the determination of such interdependences may be very difficult.

Material usage variance

The usage variance of £1,100 for P seems at first glance to be more controllable than the price variance for Q. After all, users of raw material are not as directly at the mercy of the market as are buyers. Thus inefficient use may be attributable to the production manager and may be due to such factors as changes in material quality, the efficiency of machine operators, changes in the material mix and non-standard production scheduling. But the usage variance may also hide some interdependences. We discussed in the previous paragraph how off-standard material, bought at off-standard prices, can make for usage problems. We must look also at *who* is using the material. For example, if the firm is employing unskilled instead of skilled labour, one consequence of this decision may be greater waste, resulting in an unfavourable material usage variance, which may be the fault not of the production manager, but rather of the personnel department.

The joint variance

One area of difficulty in the evaluation of raw material variances concerns the combined or joint variance. Figure 17.2 gives a diagrammatic example of this variance. (This diagram is unrelated to the example of Victoria plc.) The solid rectangle represents the standard cost of raw materials (9,000 kg at £5 per kg), and the larger dashed rectangle represents the actual cost (9,500 kg at £5.50 per kg). The shaded area between the two rectangles reflects the total variances. Clearly there is an unfavourable usage variance of 500 kg at £5 per kg = £2,500; and clearly there is an unfavourable price variance of 9,000 kg at 50p per kg = £4,500. But how do we evaluate the joint variance of £250 (the extra use of 500 kg at the additional price of 50p per kg), denoted by the top right-hand corner of Figure 17.2? Who is responsible for this joint variance? In our analysis in the previous section, we followed conventional practice and included the joint variance in the price variance: that is, we based the price variance on the actual quantity used. In this example, that practice would give an unfavourable price variance of $9,500 \times (£5.50 - £5.00)$, which equals £4,750. But should the buying manager be blamed for the increase in prices, or should the production manager be blamed instead for excessive use of materials? Each manager might argue that the variance is due to the action of the other. Thus fair apportionment of responsibility for the joint variance may be impossible, and it may be more meaningful to divide the total price variance of £4,750 into a 'pure' variance of £4,500 and a joint variance of £250. Whether this refinement is necessary in practice depends upon how the variances are to be used by management and how significant are these joint variances in the context of total variances.

Labour variances

Table 17.3 reveals two types of variance for unskilled labour – an unfavourable rate variance of £5,156 and a favourable efficiency variance of £937. What interpretation can be placed on these figures?

Labour rate variance

As in the case of raw materials price variances, labour rate variances may be due entirely to external, uncontrollable factors, such as national and local wage awards for individual grades and skills. In these cases the personnel department cannot be held responsible for rate changes. Certain rate changes, however, may be within the firm's responsibility: for example, changes in incentive schemes and changes in the class of labour used may be controllable, and, if so, should be charged to the responsible production manager. Regular variances in labour rate might give useful information for planning, and in particular might suggest some possible changes in the production process via the substitution of capital for labour or vice versa.

Labour efficiency variance

This arises because the labour force completed its task in more or less than the allotted time, and may be due, *inter alia*, to lack of supervision, poor training, changes in material quality and changes in working methods. The setting of standards for labour efficiency or productivity can be a complex and time-consuming task in itself – the notion of the correct 'time for the job' is one on which managers and workers may have very different views. Responsibility for these

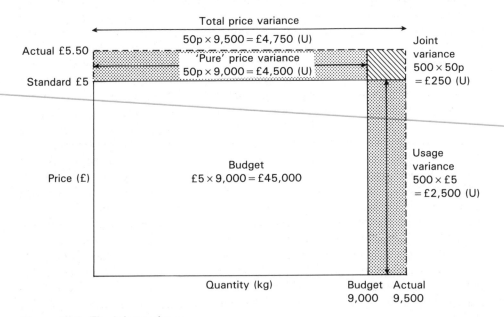

Figure 17.2 The joint variance.

variances depends partly upon conditions prevailing in the labour market. If, for example, less skilled labour has to be used because skilled labour cannot be obtained, then the standard time for the job may have to be lengthened to permit meaningful evaluations. If the standard time for the job is representative of the actual conditions pertaining during the period, then the labour efficiency variance may be fairly attributed to the production manager.

Our calculation in Table 17.3 showed the labour efficiency variance to be the product of the difference in hours expected and achieved for actual output and the standard rate per hour. But will this calculation always measure adequately the cost of labour inefficiency (or the benefit from labour efficiency)? The real cost of labour inefficiency may in fact be greater than the conventional computation allows. If, for example, the result of labour inefficiency is a loss of production which, because the firm is working at full capacity, will never be recovered, then the real cost of inefficiency is the wage rate *plus* the lost contribution on the (unsold) production. Only if the firm has spare capacity will the conventional variance appropriately measure the cost of inefficiency, as only then may production be recovered in future periods. (Note that, if the supply of materials or any other resource is limited, similar arguments to these apply in measuring the cost of inefficient usage or the benefit of efficient usage.)

Overhead variances

Table 17.3 shows two *expenditure* variances – a favourable variable overhead variance of £196, and an unfavourable fixed overhead variance of £900. These represent the only meaningful overhead variances for planning and control. They indicate whether the appropriate managers have kept their spending within the revised budget. It is inappropriate to compute any other overhead variances, of whatever form, for managerial decision-making purposes.[3]

Budget revision (sales volume) variances

Table 17.3 shows a lost contribution of £2,700 arising from the failure to attain the budgeted level of sales of 15,000 units. We have not yet attempted to explore directly the cause of this fall in volume, which we have termed a budget revision or volume variance. No information is given as to why it occurred. Several possible explanations might be offered, each of which might point to a different cause, and thus attract a different responsibility. Perhaps the sales manager had specified incorrectly the firm's demand–price relationship, and thus the original target figure of 15,000 units was unrealistic, even at the budget selling price of £17.00 per unit. Or perhaps the increase in selling price from £17.00 to £17.85 resulted in a decrease in the quantity demanded. The variance may thus be a planning error, to be charged to the sales planning manager, or a consequence of increasing selling price, to be set against the favourable sales price variance. Alternatively the volume change may be due to the failure of the sales force to meet a realistic target. In this case the variance arises from operating inefficiency and should be charged to the sales force. Other explanations might suggest that the loss of contribution was caused not by incorrect sales predictions or by the performance of the sales department, but rather by a restriction on the quantity available for sale resulting, for example, from labour inefficiency, production breakdowns, strikes or indeed a variety of less significant factors combining together to the detriment of the firm, each of which should be investigated to determine appropriate responsibility.

17.4 The investigation of variances

It is an art of good management to know when to investigate a variance. The need to investigate is not always self-evident. The important point to bear in mind when considering the investigation of variances is the cost involved relative to any benefits likely to be achieved. But this cost–benefit criterion for investigation poses a major practical problem. Although it may be possible to quantify with reasonable accuracy the costs of investigation, it is far less easy to put a value on the benefits. Thus it frequently happens that investigation is conducted on a subjective basis, in which educated guesswork is substituted for a more scientific or formal analysis.

The importance of investigating only material or significant variances is frequently stressed, and we may agree intuitively that the expenditure of time and money on the examination of immaterial or insignificant variances is a pointless task. But the terms 'materiality' and 'significance' present large measurement problems. What is a significant variance? Some variances will be small in amount, others will be large. As we have seen, some variances arise because actual costs are different from planned costs at the predicted level of activity; some arise because errors are made in the identification and measurement of actual costs; some arise because the level of activity actually attained is different from the plan; and others occur because the plan has proved to be unrealistic in the light of changed circumstances. Given all these varying circumstances and varying amounts, how is management to determine which variances are significant and thus worthy of investigation? We might offer at least two pieces of advice in deciding whether or not to investigate. First, managers should not necessarily be concerned with the absolute amount of any variance, but rather with the relationship of the variance to the costs of production if the particular variance is a cost variance, and the relationship of the variance to total sales revenue if the particular variance is a sales variance. Viewed in this light, a labour rate variance of £1,000 might be considered insignificant and not worthy of investigation if the total labour costs are £200,000, whereas a labour rate variance of £1,000 in relation to total labour costs of £20,000 (a variance of 5%) would normally be considered significant.

Second, managers should be aware of the potential usefulness of certain statistical techniques in measuring materiality or significance. For example, techniques of statistical quality control are often used to lay down, on the basis of the mean and standard deviation of particular variables, certain limits for randomness. This helps management to know whether individual variances are likely to be uncontrollable chance factors, or whether variances fall outside the limits for random deviation and therefore require a more detailed scrutiny.

17.5 Keeping standards up to date

Throughout our exposition of standard costing and variance analysis, we have referred only in passing to situations in which managers might need to review and update standards *during* the budget period. This exposition may be valid if no significant changes in the expected costs of input factors occur, and if expected sales prices do not change during the budget period: that is, if managers have properly anticipated price changes in setting standards. If, however, costs or sales prices do change, through the existence of such factors as *unanticipated* inflation, the pursuit of a new pricing policy or other environmental changes, it becomes a matter of great importance for management to ensure that budgets and standards remain at a realistic level.

The reason it is important to keep standards up to date relates to one of the basic purposes of the control exercise – the assessment of managerial effectiveness. To measure effectiveness in a meaningful way, we must compare like with like; thus to measure managerial effectiveness, we must compare actual costs and revenues with realistic standards existing at the time of incurring the costs and revenues. If this is not done, individual managers may be unfairly advantaged or disadvantaged by being assessed on the basis of obsolete standards.

Thus it becomes a major management decision to determine the frequency with which standards should be revised to reflect the impact of changes in prices and other factors. In revising standards, management should aim to strike a balance between the use of realistic standards for performance evaluation and a desire not to confuse the implementation of the control system by excessively frequent changes. With this balance in mind, firms may review and, if necessary, change standards half-yearly or quarterly or maybe monthly. With computerised information processing, some firms now operate systems where standards are recalculated immediately there is a change in input prices.

With periodic revisions of budgets and standards, the effects of inflation may be incorporated using either specific or general price indices. The use of specific indices for labour, material and overheads is preferable, and this information can often be obtained if there exist nationally agreed wage rates, and if long-term contracts for materials and services have been secured. If managers feel the inflated wage rate is to some extent negotiable, they must then decide whether to use an expected rate or a maximum rate in the budget. The chosen rate may well depend upon their own negotiating ability. There is a variety of published indices which offer indicators of specific inflation rates, but their usefulness for control purposes depends upon their applicability to future (changing) circumstances, and even where such indices exist, they may be applicable only to very loosely defined categories of expense. It may well be the case that managers will need more detailed forecasts of specific prices, which may be obtainable from discussions with suppliers.

Where information on specific indices is either unobtainable or too expensive, managers may be driven to use such general indices as the Retail Price Index. If such an index is used, managers will need to be aware of those situations in which the prices of the firm's particular inputs have changed at a rate different from the chosen index. If both specific and general indices are available, managers may be provided with indicators of the efficiency of input mixes, and the ability of those responsible to 'beat' inflation.

Thus, in conditions of changing prices, additional problems are presented to the management accountant. For example, at the *planning* stage of the standard costing exercise it may be that, as the budget passes through its various stages of preparation, individual managers add on to the budget a certain percentage to allow, in a rough and ready way, for the impact of inflation. In consequence, there is a danger of double-counting the effect of inflation. To avoid this it is necessary to spell out clearly the price change assumptions built into the budget. At the *control* stage it is important to analyse separately anticipated and unanticipated price changes, and to distinguish those that are controllable from those that are not. This type of analysis may provide information on price changes of the firm's own input and output factors, which can be used to improve future planning procedures.

CHAPTER SUMMARY

The effectiveness of management control of operations in pursuit of the organisation's objectives depends in part on the quality of information available as a basis for evaluating performance. In this chapter we have described how the methods of variance analysis can help provide control information to management, and illustrated variance calculations within a standard costing system.

The basic principle underlying variance analysis is the comparison between the expectations and targets established in the budget and the actual results experienced by the firm. Variance analysis involves breaking down this comparison into constituent parts, in order that management may be better able to judge where control actions are required. We have concentrated our discussion in this chapter on variances due to changes in the level of activity (*budget revision variance*), and the separate effects of variations in *price* and *efficiency* (or *usage*) on different areas of cost and revenue.

The value of variance analysis critically depends on the quality of the original budget and, under a standard costing system, the individual standards. As the budget amounts are used as benchmarks for evaluating actual outcomes, it is clear that the variances calculated will contain useful information only if the budget and standards are valid. A poorly constructed budget, using unrealistic assumptions, will give a poor basis for calculating variances and identifying areas for investigation. It is also important that standards are kept up to date, to ensure variances are calculated against realistic targets.

Variance analysis can contribute to the process of managerial control, but it will be only one part of the total information set managers will need to make control decisions. Variances provide a starting point for investigating operations, and raise questions rather than provide answers. By highlighting significant discrepancies between experience and expectations, variances direct management attention to areas of operation that require further investigation. Additional information will be needed to identify the underlying reasons, such as poor supply, inefficiency, bad planning or ineffective communication, *why* actual performance has varied from the budget plan, and to determine the appropriate control action.

REVIEW QUESTIONS

1. 'The technique of variance analysis is only useful if all variances associated with a particular decision can be identified.' Discuss.

2. 'Control and responsibility go hand in hand. No standard costing system should divorce the two.' Discuss.

3. 'Price and quantity variances are at the heart of any managerial control system.' Do you agree with this? Can you cite any other types of variance which may generate useful information?

4. Can you suggest any forms of business in which standard costing systems may be of little use? What characteristics would these businesses possess?

5. Discuss the difficulties in identifying material (i.e. significant) variances which should be subject to investigation.

EXERCISES

17.1 Scriabin Ltd, a company with two divisions, has recently installed a budgetary control system which is intended to help appraise managerial efficiency. The budget performance report for last month is:

		Division A	*Division B*
Sales in units:	Actual	7,500	5,000
	Budget	6,000	7,000
Price per unit (£):	Actual	15	30
	Budget	20	35
Total variable costs (£)*:			
Material (£):	Actual	40,000	25,000
	Budget	24,000	28,000
Labour (£):	Actual	22,500	30,000
	Budget	16,000	28,000
Total contribution to fixed overheads and			
profits (£):	Actual	50,000	95,000
	Budget	80,000	189,000

* Budget figures are based on budgeted sales.

Additional information, covering all the factors which affected performance during the month, is given:

1. The firm produces to order and keeps no stocks. The demand conditions assumed in the budget for division A did in fact apply during the month. It was, however, expected that the sales of division B would be 2,500 units under the original budget at the budget price because of a temporary decline in the market. This shortfall in volume is expected to be recouped at the budgeted price in the next month by working exceptional overtime at a cost of £10,000. The sales manager of division B was able partially to offset the temporary decline in sales by cutting the price to below the budget figure.

2. Both divisions use the same raw material, but each employs its own purchasing officer. Because of conditions in the world market, the price of the material rose at the beginning of the month by 50% over the budgeted price. The buyer in division B persuaded suppliers to pass on only half of this increase.

3. The production manager of division A has been able to cut material wastage by employing more skilled labour, costing £2,500 more than expected. A new factory has recently been built near division B, and by offering higher wage rates has attracted most of B's best workers. Scriabin Ltd has, as yet, not increased its wage rate, and the personnel manager of B has been forced to employ workers who can achieve only 50% of the budgeted output per hour.

Prepare a statement explaining the difference between budgeted and actual performance during the month, in the way you think will best enable management to trace and eliminate inefficiency. As far as possible, try to include information which will enable management to appraise the performance of each of the executives mentioned. Such information may alternatively be given as a brief commentary to your statement. (Solution at end of text.)

17.2 Morales Ltd manufactures rugby balls. As each ball is completed, it is booked out to a subsidiary company, Suk Ltd. Morales's budget for the seventh four-weekly control period of its financial year was as follows:

	£	£
Sales (6,000 units @ £24 each)		144,000
Variable costs:		
Bladders (6,000 @ £1.50 each)	9,000	
Leather (200 ten hide bales @ £228 each)	45,600	
Sundry and packaging materials	3,900	
Direct labour (1,000 hours @ £13.50 per hour)	13,500	
	72,000	
Fixed costs:		
Administrative and establishment expenses	12,717	
Staff and directors' salaries	24,783	109,500
Budgeted net profit		34,500

Due to water shortages during the summer drought, Morales was only able to manufacture during 60% of the budgeted production hours and was unable to sanction any overtime. Despite this the direct labour force was paid in full for the budgeted hours. Various other differences from budget occurred and the following are the actual figures for the period:

	£	£
Sales (4,000 units @ £27 each)		108,000
Variable costs:		
Bladders (4,000 @ £2.10 each)	8,400	
Leather (100 ten hide bales @ £400 each)	40,000	
Sundry and packaging materials	2,600	
Direct labour (1,000 hours @ £15 per hour)	15,000	
	66,000	
Fixed costs:		
Administrative and establishment expenses	13,155	
Staff and directors' salaries	24,945	104,100
Actual net profit		3,900

(a) Prepare a statement reconciling the budgeted contribution with the actual contribution, stating the variances in the way which you think will be most helpful to management. Present your calculations as schedules with references to the main statement.

(b) Comment briefly on any apparent interrelationships between the variances. (Solution at end of text.)

17.3 Birtwhistle Ltd manufactures soft drinks which are sold to retailers in cases of 144 bottles. The company installed a standard costing system in February 19X4. Exhibit 1 gives the standard cost and revenue data applicable to that month.

Exhibit 1
Standard cost and revenue data, February 19X4

	Per case	
	£	£
Standard selling price		10.00
Materials: 10 lb at 20p	2.00	
Labour: 0.4 hours at £7.50	3.00	
Overheads: Standard recovery rate	4.00	9.00
Standard profit		1.00

The overheads are all fixed and consist of administrative costs of £4,000, advertising of £10,000 and factory overheads of £26,000. The budgeted volume for February 19X4 is 10,000 units, which represents the maximum possible production given the small staff which is retained in the winter months.

During March the actual results for February became available, and from them the management accountant calculated the following variances:

Exhibit 2
Standard cost variances, February 19X4

	Favourable £	Adverse £
Sales volume variance		10,000
Materials price variance		360
Labour efficiency variances		1,518
Fixed overhead variances:		
Expenditure		2,000
Volume		4,000

No other variances occurred.

The management accountant had pressed for the introduction of standard costing, claiming that it would be instrumental in increasing the company's performance. When Exhibits 1 and 2 were presented to the management meeting, the report was not received with much enthusiasm. The following observations were made by managers present at the meeting:

Managing director:
'What's the point of a fixed overhead volume variance? The overheads are fixed aren't they? By the way, what were the actual results?'

Purchasing manager:
'The materials price variance is the result of a tax increase of 5%. I managed to prevent our supplying company passing on the whole of the increase by pointing out that we are its best customer. Anyway, it's only a 2% variance, so that doesn't matter. If you want my opinion, the standard is too tight and I don't think I should be judged against it.'

Sales manager:
'February had particularly bad weather with lots of snow, and that's the cause of the sales variance. In fact, the trade association have calculated that total market sales were 12% down on what was predicted. In January our sales fell by only 10%, which must have been better than the other companies we compete with. And don't forget, I could have sold 500 more cases if the factory could have provided them. And don't forget another thing, without that extra £1,000 worth of advertising, sales would have been lower still.'

(a) Reconstruct the actual results for February 19X4 to satisfy the managing director's request.

(b) Explain for the managing director how the fixed overhead volume variance is calculated and how it may be interpreted.

(c) Prepare a report on the company's performance for February 19X4. Give particular attention to the performance of the sales and purchasing managers, in the light of the additional information which they have provided and anything else which you consider relevant.

17.4 Nelson plc has operated a standard costing system for some time. It produces only one product, the portobello valve, and the standard costs for the valve for the current period are reproduced below:

	£ (per unit)
Direct labour: 1 hour at £9 per hour	9.00
Direct material: 4 lb at £7.5 per lb	30.00
Variable overhead: 2 hours at £1.5 per hour	3.00
Fixed overheads: 2 hours at £3	6.00
	48.00

The budgeted fixed overheads for the period were £30,000, based upon a budgeted level of production for the period of 5,000 units. The standard selling price for the valve was £75.

Recently the actual results for the period became available, and they are shown below:

		£
Sales (4,700 units)		361,900
Direct labour: 4,875 hours	46,310	
Direct material: 24,000 lb	174,000	
Variable overhead	16,550	
Fixed overhead	33,000	269,860
Profit		92,040

The production process for the valve is semi-automated and the flanging machine which is used is regularly inspected by the maintenance staff of Nelson.

The inspection is merely a visual check together with a discussion with the operatives working the machine. If all appears to be running well, no maintenance work is ordered. Nelson's maintenance staff do not maintain the flanging machine themselves, but call in the manufacturer's fitters. The manufacturer makes a fixed charge of £500 for a visit whether or not any maintenance work is needed. In the past when maintenance has been needed, the cost of repair (including all parts and labour from the manufacturer) has averaged £5,000. Normally, a repair requires the flanging machine to be stopped for 16 hours. If no repair is needed, the stoppage time for the machine is negligible. The contribution generated per hour by the flanging machine is £30. Over the last ten years the manufacturer's fitters have been called out on average once a month and on only 12 occasions did they find anything which needed repair. Nelson's production manager has estimated that the likely saving from repairing a faulty flanging machine would be £12,000 in present value terms.

There is some dissatisfaction with the way the flanging machine's maintenance is conducted. Nelson's maintenance manager has been criticised for not calling in the fitters often enough, but replies: 'It costs a fortune to stop production, and anyway, the operatives always say that the machine gobbles up material, but the manufacturers keep checking it and nothing is wrong. Why should I call in the manufacturers?'

(a) Calculate cost and sales variances for Nelson for the period in question.

(b) Prepare calculations to show whether the manufacturer's fitters should be called in to examine the flanging machine. Comment briefly upon the maintenance policy of Nelson.

In addition to the information given in the question, you are told that the maintenance department of Nelson is a cost centre and the manager's salary is related to the level of costs achieved in the year (the lower the costs, the more the manager is paid).

(c) Discuss and illustrate the effects of the cost centre policy on other departments in the firm and on the environment of the firm.

(d) Comment on the desirability of making the maintenance department a cost centre. What alternative policy could you suggest? Explain why your policy would be an improvement.

17.5 Wiley Ltd is a firm of sportswear manufacturers specialising in padded gloves and other protectors for a variety of sports. One of the major lines are cricketers' batting pads, and a great deal of effort is put into monitoring the costs of this item. The standard cost card for the production of a pair of batting pads is shown below:

	£
Materials: Cloth (10 ft^2 @ £0.20/ft^2)	2.00
Stuffing (2 kg @ £0.50/kg)	1.00
Buckles and straps (one set)	2.00
Labour	4.00
Variable overhead	6.00
Contribution	10.00
Selling price	25.00

Wiley has always exercised firm control over labour and overhead costs, but has felt somewhat 'in the lap of the gods' when it comes to materials costs. Over the first four months of the year, when much of the production takes place, 22,000 pairs of pads were produced at the following cost of materials:

	£
Cloth 245,000 ft²	48,000
Stuffing 45,000 kg	24,000
Buckles and straps 22,490 sets	47,229
	119,229

On reviewing the materials cost variances, it was pointed out that:

1. Though stocks of buckles and straps transferred to and used by the batting pads department had been recorded as 22,490, 200 in fact were transferred to the wicketkeepers' pads' department. It has also long been held that, as an easily concealed and useful item, an allowance of approximately 1% of standard usage should be made for theft – even though such an allowance is undesirable.

2. Management was surprised to see the standard cost card showing 10 ft² of cloth per pair of pads. It was always felt that an extra square foot should be allowed for trim loss, though after some recent modifications the average amount of trim loss per pair of pads was nearer 0.50 ft². With the benefit of hindsight a more realistic purchase price would have been £0.19 per ft², 20p being a somewhat pessimistic estimate.

3. At the start of each year, a decision has to be made over the type of stuffing to use. The three alternatives are referred to as S1, S2 and S3; they are of comparable price and quality, but require very different handling techniques, and so once the decision over the material is made it is difficult to change the decision. Material S3 was chosen although, as the following figures show, S1 would – with hindsight – have been better.

	Original estimate of price (£/kg)	Revised estimate of price (£/kg)
S1	0.55	0.54
S2	0.52	0.60
S3	0.50	0.55

(a) Calculate traditional price and usage variances for each of the three types of material used.

(b) Explain the limitations of traditional variance analysis.

(c) Produce a revised analysis in the light of the three notes given for:

    (i) buckles and straps;

  (ii) cloth;

  (iii) stuffing.

(d) Determine whether it is worth Wiley spending £750 on a simple financial modelling package designed to improve the chances of correctly estimating the price of stuffing. The cost of making the wrong decision over materials is assumed to be equal to the amount of the possibly avoidable planning variance. From past experience, without the package Wiley has selected the right material six times out of ten. They feel that with the package they will be able to improve this to eight times out of ten. The firm uses a ten-year time horizon and a discount rate of 10% for analysing such investments (the appropriate discount factor being 6.14).

(e) Set out the factors to be taken into account when deciding whether to investigate a variance.

Notes

1. See M. Bromwich, 'Standard costing for planning and control', in J. Arnold, B. Carsberg and R. Scapens (eds.), *Topics in Management Accounting*, Philip Allan, 1980.
2. See Chapter 9 for a more detailed discussion of sales demand–price relationships.
3. Many managerial accounting texts devote considerable space to the calculation of overhead 'efficiency', 'capacity' and 'idle time' variances. As we believe that the cost of such factors is (for purposes of planning and control) more appropriately measured by lost contribution, we do not include a discussion of such overhead variances here.

Divisional performance

AIMS AND OBJECTIVES

☐ To explain the nature of divisionalisation in large companies.

☐ To discuss different measures of divisional profitability.

☐ To explain and evaluate return on investment as a measure of divisional performance.

☐ To discuss how internal transfers of goods and services between divisions should be priced.

☐ To explain other problems in the application of the return on investment measure.

Issues in managerial accounting have so far been discussed without attempting to draw any distinction between the character, size and internal structure of individual organisations. We have, in effect, presumed a common interest by all organisations in the issues we have raised. That such a common interest may not necessarily exist is perhaps obvious when we remember that firms can be controlled by a single owner-manager, by a board of directors responsible to thousands of shareholders or by a variety of intermediate structures; that firms can produce a single product or a vast array of very different goods and services which are sold all over the world; that firms operate in monopolistic, highly competitive or other forms of market. All these factors, and more besides, tend to generate their own individual problems requiring their own individual solutions.

In this chapter we pay particular attention to the distinctive character of the (often large) divisionalised company and to some of the problems presented by such an organisation for managerial planning, decision making and control. Most of the issues have been raised, either explicitly or implicitly, in previous chapters: for example, a major problem in accounting for divisions is how to measure their performance. One frequently used measurement method is return on investment (ROI). This measure bears a strong similarity to the accounting rate of return explained in Chapter 14. Similarly, the sort of relevant costing issues discussed in Chapters 9, 10, 11, 12 and elsewhere are also relevant to a study of divisionalised companies.

18.1 Divisional structures

Large companies such as ICI, Hanson, Unilever and BAT Industries produce and sell a wide variety of different products, often in many different countries and continents. Because of the sheer complexity of operations in companies of this size, and the difficulty of a head office exercising direct control of operations, their decision making is decentralised and their operations are usually divisionalised. There is in practice no single, universally accepted definition of a division. In some organisations, 'divisions' and 'departments' are used interchangeably, but as a general rule, divisions are responsible for the profit earned from producing and selling a group of products. Thus companies are typically split into different divisions either in accordance with the products made, which is the more usual (e.g. division A might produce clothes, division B might produce toys, and so on), or on the basis of geography (e.g. division A, which produces clothes, toys and books, might be located in the United Kingdom; division B, which also produces clothes, toys and books, might be located in France, and so on). For example, the 1993 annual report and accounts for the media group Pearson includes 'business reports' for newspaper publishing, book publishing, television and visitor attractions (such as Madame Tussaud's), while the Community Hospitals Group plc 1994 report recognises a hospital division and a continuing care division. For very large companies, whose operations encompass totally different aspects of trade, divisionalisation might even be organised on an industry basis. For example, Daimler Benz, the major German industrial conglomerate, has a corporate structure involving four 'corporate units' with a number of divisions within each unit. The Mercedes-Benz unit has divisions for passenger cars and commercial vehicles; the AEG unit has divisions covering rail systems, microelectronics, diesel engines, automation and energy systems; the Deutsche Aerospace unit has five divisions, including aircraft and space systems; and the Debis unit has seven divisions, including financial services and real estate management.

The heart of divisionalisation is the delegation of decision making and authority to divisional managers and the retention of overall control by head office. The degree of head office involvement in divisional decision making depends on the structure as well as the strategic objectives of the organisation. Some large UK companies, such as Cadbury Schweppes plc and United Biscuits plc, are very closely involved with the planning and control activities of their various divisions, whose targets are likely to be phrased in terms of meeting long-term objectives: for example, improving their market share over a five-year period. Other companies, of whom GEC plc, Hanson plc and BTR plc would be examples, give their different divisions greater autonomy in decision making, but require them to meet strategic shorter-term financial goals. These organisations manage their divisions more by emphasising the importance of financial numbers than by adopting a patient approach to the achievement of longer-term strategic goals. The majority of UK companies follow a strategy which falls between these two approaches: that is, they attempt to give their divisions a longer-term orientation in pursuing particular objectives, while at the same time demanding more immediate financial returns.

Available evidence suggests that in these cases the more short-term 'numerical' emphasis will predominate.

Divisions usually represent individual responsibility centres within the total organisation – and responsibility usually extends to the return earned on assets employed by the division.

There are many advantages claimed for divisionalisation in large companies with a wide range of activities, including the following:

1. Because of the greater degree of authority granted to divisional managers, they may be motivated to achieving a better level of performance, both for their own divisions and for the firm as a whole.

2. As communication channels are narrowed, potential communication problems are cut down if divisional managers need not continually report their actions to head office.

3. Because divisional managers have a more intimate knowledge of their own divisions, they are more likely to understand, and be capable of dealing with, the problems peculiar to their divisions.

4. Perhaps most importantly, because divisional managers handle their own problems, top management is given more time and opportunity to focus its attention on the strategic decisions which necessarily affect the entire company: for example, decisions about which general areas of the company's activities should be expanded and which should be contracted in the long term. Decisions such as these require an overview of all the company's activities and, by their nature, cannot usually be delegated to divisional managers. As we have noted, most divisionalised companies undertake a diversified range of operations. Such diversification provides the company with a portfolio of activities, which results in a reduction in the company's overall level of risk, as we explained in Chapter 4. The maintenance of a well-balanced portfolio of activities must ultimately be the responsibility of top management.

It should not be thought that divisionalisation is without its problems. Consider the continuing situation facing the top management of ICI plc, one of the largest divisionalised UK companies, and a major multinational business. In 1994 ICI employed worldwide 67,500 people, generated total sales of £9,189 million, invested over £1 million every day in new plant, and at the end of the year showed a historical cost pre-tax profit of £408 million. This profit was generated from the operations of five individual divisions (or business sectors): paints, explosives, chemical-related materials (acrylics, coatings, etc.), industrial chemicals and regional businesses. Production facilities are located in the United Kingdom, Germany, Holland, France, Canada, USA, Brazil, Argentina, Australia, Japan, India and Pakistan, and during 1994 a new manufacturing plant was opened in the Republic of China.

How do the top managers of a company like ICI, located at the company's head office in London, plan, control and, above all, co-ordinate the activities of the various divisions in the very varied social, economic and political environments in which the company operates? Head office may, for example, lay down broad policies for the whole group in relation to the objectives and goals of the company; it may well develop specific long-term plans to achieve these goals, and perhaps set out targets to be met in the form of market shares, sales revenues and profits; and it may well take overall responsibility for the raising of corporate capital. It will certainly take responsibility for the co-ordination of the company's total activities. These are primarily general management issues. But how do the company's top managers ensure that individual divisional managers are pursuing goals which are best for the company as a whole, rather than for their own personal gain or satisfaction? How do they ensure that there is no conflict of goals between individual managers? For example, there may be a general loss of profitability within the company if autonomous divisions attempt to maximise their own profitability while, at the same time, decreasing the net profit of the total company. This is the problem of suboptimisation, to which we have referred in earlier chapters and to which we return later in this chapter. In the remainder of this chapter we shall look at areas of concern which are peculiar to divisionalised companies. We begin by examining different methods of assessing a division's financial performance.

18.2 Divisional profit measures

Profit, determined by a variety of different accounting measurements, is the measure most widely used to assess an organisation's performance. All listed companies in the United Kingdom must, for example, publish the earnings (or profits) attributable to each individual share in the company, and this earnings per share statistic is widely used by financial analysts and other external users as a leading measure of the company's success. Most organisations also require their divisions to achieve certain profit targets – thus ensuring that the company, and the divisions (or business units) which make it up, are evaluated by similar criteria. These decentralised units are, unsurprisingly, known as *profit centres*. For our purposes we shall define a profit centre as a business unit which has responsibility for both its revenues and its controllable costs: that is, it sells most of its output to external customers and makes its own purchasing and production decisions.

Many organisations take further the concept of profit responsibility by requiring their managers to be responsible not simply for an absolute level of profit, but also for an amount of profit which is related to the investment (controllable by the manager) in the business unit. Under this evaluation method, managers must seek to achieve an adequate return on investment (ROI). We will deal with ROI measures in the following section of this chapter. (We should note here that other forms of business unit exist in practice. Thus managers of *cost centres* will be held responsible only for the incurring of costs under their control, and will be rewarded accordingly if they succeed in minimizing those costs; and managers of *revenue centres* will have control only over the amount of revenue generated.)

The trickiest issue in applying the profit centre concept is in the choice of an appropriate profit measure. The choice of measure is very important because it may influence the decisions taken by the manager (e.g. if the manager has to cover the controllable fixed costs before striking a profit, he or she will, *ceteris paribus*, be more concerned with the absolute level of the division's fixed costs than will a manager who is asked to maximize a division's contribution margin). Table 18.1 shows a simple profit statement for a division from which we might extract at least four possible performance measures in the form of different profit figures.

Let us consider the possible usefulness of each of the four performance measures in turn:

1. *Contribution margin – £40,000.* This figure is useful in showing how much contribution the divisional manager has made to the fixed costs within that manager's control. However, it suffers as a performance evaluation measure for the very reason that, if managers are able to influence their cost structures by adjusting the balance of fixed and variable costs, they can adjust the contribution margin to their own advantage. Thus, at the very least, managers should be evaluated by a profit figure struck after charging controllable fixed costs.

2. *Controllable profit – £35,000.* This figure indicates the success of managers in using all the resources under their authority, and thus is perhaps the best single measure of managerial performance. It excludes the fixed costs over which a manager has no control, and thereby supposes that it is possible to determine clearly which fixed costs are controllable and which are not. In practice this split may be difficult to determine. Expenses such as depreciation and employees' wages may be classified as non-controllable only if divisional managers cannot influence the purchase and sale of fixed assets, and the levels of employment within the division. But in many organisations these decisions may be largely discretionary.

3. *Divisional profit before head office allocations – £25,000.* This figure represents the success of the division in generating profits towards meeting head office costs,

Table 18.1 Divisional profit statement

		£
	Sales revenue	150,000
	Less Variable cost	110,000
Performance measure (1)	Contribution margin	40,000
	Less Controllable fixed costs	5,000
Performance measure (2)	Controllable profit	35,000
	Less Non-controllable fixed costs	10,000
Performance measure (3)	Divisional profit before head office allocations	25,000
	Less Allocated head office costs	5,000
Performance measure (4)	Divisional pre-tax profits	20,000

and, as such, is probably a better evaluator of the *division* than of the *manager*. This is a most important point. It would be unfair to evaluate divisional managers on the results of decisions over which they have no control, but equally it is necessary to evaluate divisions' long-term contribution to head office costs after charging all expenses relating to each division, irrespective of the instigator and the time of the decision. If the divisional profit before head office allocations is insufficient to meet its share of allocations, questions concerning the long-term future of the division may be asked.

4. *Divisional pre-tax profits – £20,000.* This amount shows the 'bottom-line' profit of the division after all costs, identifiable and allocated, have been charged to it. We might query the purpose of allocating head office costs to divisions in order to arrive at a proper basis for evaluation. What do such allocations tell us? It is, of course, a truism that the total of all divisional profits must be greater than head office costs – otherwise the business will fail – but whether such allocations give useful information for evaluation is debatable. The root of the problem is the arbitrariness of the allocations. If divisional activities do not directly *cause* central costs, how are we to agree upon a defensible allocation mechanism for their *effect*? (And if divisional activities do cause central costs, how are we to quantify the costs attributable to the particular divisions?) It can be argued that if divisions bear a 'fair share' of central overheads, they will press to contain the growth in such central support activities. But the problems attendant on quantifying how fair the share should be seem to outweigh this consciousness raising. Divisional managers should be evaluated only on the activities, the effects of which they can control, and thus performance measurement – divisional profit before central allocations – seems a more appropriate basis for evaluating divisional profit performance.

Having examined the validity of different measures of profit centre performance, we now turn our attention to the measurement of the performance of *investment centres* (i.e. situations in which a division's responsibility extends beyond absolute profits, to the relative relationship between its profits and its investment base). Investment centres can be defined as divisions for which managers have the authority to determine both the nature of short-term operating decisions and also the amount and type of long-term investment decisions.

18.3 Return on investment

Return on investment (ROI) is probably the most widely used accounting technique for evaluating the performance of divisions within a firm. In principle, it is very similar to the accounting rate of return measure discussed in Chapter 14. The ROI statistic attempts to draw together in a single percentage figure those quantitative aspects of a division's performance which are relevant for planning and control purposes. 'Profitability' indices as expressed through ROI are then used as common measuring units to compare the performance of different divisions within the same firm – even though divisions may operate in very different environments and produce and sell very different ranges of products. A word of caution should be inserted immediately. Although a single ROI would normally encompass the overall results of the business, it is important to realise that individual activities may be achieving returns different from the average. If this is the case, then, ideally, both the selection and monitoring of investments should be based on a range of rates.

It should also be stressed that ROI is not an absolute measure of profit, but rather a relative one. For example, a division which makes a profit of £2 million does not necessarily contribute more to the overall success of the firm than a division making a profit of £1 million. The difference in profit between divisions may be explicable simply in terms of differences in size. Thus division X, showing a profit of £2 million with resources of £10 million, is generating an ROI of 20%, whereas division Y, which shows a profit of £1 million with resources of £4 million, is generating a higher ROI of 25%. As we shall see, the determination of both aspects of the ROI statistic, profit and investment, presents both conceptual and practical measurement problems to even the most alert management accountant.

At its most basic level, divisional return on investment can be presented simply as net profit for the division, divided by investment in divisional assets:

$$\text{ROI} = \frac{\text{Net profit}}{\text{Investment in net assets}}$$

The ROI formula can be broken down further into two measures of divisional performance: the margin achieved on the division's sales (profit margin) and the turnover of assets or investment turnover (sales divided by investment). This decomposition gives:

$$\text{ROI} = \frac{\text{Sales}}{\text{Investment in net assets}} \times \frac{\text{Net profit}}{\text{Sales}}$$

The profit margin on sales does not, of itself, produce success for a division, although the ability to reduce costs and thus increase margins is an important determinant of success. Profit must be related to the amount of resources used in its generation, and therefore the more sales that can be generated from a given amount of resources (i.e. a given investment in net assets), the more opportunity the division will have to generate its profit margins. Alternatively we might say that the fewer the assets needed by a division, the more assets will be made available for profitable use elsewhere in the firm. The ratio of sales to net assets is an important factor in divisional success.

A simple illustration should help to clarify the contribution of both parts of the ROI equation to the measurement of a division's performance. Suppose a firm has two divisions, division X and division Y, which produce and sell two different products. Division X deals in soap power, division Y in colour TV sets. Division X generates a net profit margin on sales of 5%, whereas division Y has a margin of 25%; thus in terms of profit margins on sales, division Y is certainly more successful. But we have assumed that companies will wish to maximise the return they generate on cash invested, not the return on sales. We need to know how effectively the investment base of each division has been used in generating these margins. Suppose we are told that X, the low-margin division, turns over its assets three times each year (i.e. has a ratio of sales to net assets of three), whereas Y turns over its assets three times every five years, or 0.6 times each year. We now have information to allow us to build up a more complete picture of the relative performance of each division. In ROI terms we have:

$$\text{Division X ROI} = \text{Asset turnover} \times \text{Profit margin}$$
$$= 3 \times 5\%$$
$$= 15\%$$

$$\text{Division Y ROI} = \text{Asset turnover} \times \text{Profit margin}$$
$$= 0.6 \times 25\%$$
$$= 15\%$$

This type of analysis shows how it is possible, by using the ROI statistic, to compare the efficiency with which different divisions, dealing in different products, use their net assets. In this case each division is earning the same 15% for the firm. Whether or not such a book return is satisfactory or even meaningful depends upon other issues: for instance, if top management has specified a target return of 20% to be achieved by each division, then, clearly, 15% is inadequate. If this is the case, thought should be given to possible alternative uses of divisional assets. Target ROIs should try to reflect the different risks attaching to the different operations of divisions. It is by no means obvious that all divisions within the same company should be judged on their ability to meet the same target percentage figure. Furthermore, as explained in Chapter 12 and discussed subsequently in this chapter, rates of return based on conventional accounting measures may be deficient and misleading indicators of performance. Indeed maximising ROI may lead managers to disregard the interests of the company in selecting projects which will simply increase their own divisions' ROI.

We might, at this preliminary stage, best sum up the debate on the usefulness of ROI as follows. As a measurement of performance, ROI has the following advantages:

1. It provides a relative measure which takes proper account of all the assets invested in the division.

2. The data necessary for its computation are compatible with those contained in conventional financial reports, and this aids the interpretation of the ratios by managers.

3. Because the ROI ratio can be subdivided into a series of explanatory ratios, it is a useful analytical device for examining various aspects of performance.

In summary, ROI is a defensible and practical approach to the evaluation of divisional performance as long as it is used in a manner which reflects an awareness of its limitations. Ideally, it would be used as one of a range of measures in order to review performance in the widest possible perspective. We will look at one possible alternative to ROI later in this chapter.

18.4 Some problems with return on investment measures

Simple and widely used as the ROI statistic is, there are nevertheless many problems in its computation and interpretation which must be addressed by management. These problems fall roughly into three categories, which are by no means mutually exclusive:

1. The problem in measuring revenues when some sales are made from one division to another within the firm. This is more commonly known as the *transfer pricing* problem.

2. The problem in determining and measuring appropriate expenses in arriving at divisional net profit. This problem is obviously compounded by the transfer pricing problem.

3. The problem in determining and measuring the asset base to be used to signify divisional investment.

In effect, the first two problem areas relate to the return element of the ROI statistic, whereas the third relates to the investment element of the statistic. We shall look at each of the three in turn.

18.5 Transfer pricing

The transfer pricing problem arises when some of a division's output is sold to another division, or if some of its services (e.g. computer services) are provided to another division. (For example, trading transfers between divisions of ICI were valued at £415 million in the 1994 accounts.) In such cases, certain very specific problems emerge as to how these interdivisional sales or transfers of goods and services should be priced.

The problem affects both the selling and the buying division: the pricing of transfers represents sales revenue to the selling division, and variable cost to the buying division. For example, suppose division G manufactures a component part which is subsequently assembled in division H as part of a finished product. Suppose for illustrative purposes that the entire output of G is 'sold' to H. The income statements of the two divisions can be represented in notational form as follows:

	Manufacturing Division G	Assembly Division H
Sales revenue	$P_G \times Q$	$P_H \times Q$
Less Variable costs	$-VC_G \times Q$	$-[(P_G \times Q) + (VC_H \times Q)]$
Fixed costs	$-FC_G$	$-FC_H$
Net profit	π_G	π_H

where P_G is the selling price (transfer price) per unit of G's goods; P_H is the selling price per unit of H's goods; Q is the quantity sold; VC_G is the variable cost per unit of producing and selling G's goods; VC_H is the variable cost per unit of producing and selling H's goods, additional to the cost of the component from G; FC_G is the fixed costs of G; FC_H is the fixed costs of H; π_G is the net profit of G, and π_H is the net profit of H.

Note that the price of the transferred good P_G influences the profit figures of both divisions – as a selling price in G and as part of the variable cost in H. Note also that these transactions may be represented purely by book-keeping entries. In some cases involving transfer prices, cash does not change hands directly between divisions. The establishment of an agreed transfer pricing system is critical, as transfer prices are used directly in the evaluation of the profitability of both G and H. Other reasons why the setting up of efficient transfer pricing systems are important are as follows:

1. As transfer price multiplied by volume equals revenue to the selling division, it is possible for even small differences in the transfer price to lead to (relatively) large changes in divisional profit if the division makes many interdivisional sales.

2. Different divisional profit figures may lead to different degrees of motivation of divisional management, which in turn could result in an underachievement of targets, and even in a loss of the advantages of divisionalisation.

3. Different transfer prices may deceive top management into believing, and acting on its belief, that individual divisions are more or less profitable than is actually the case.

By now the nature of the transfer pricing issue should be clearer. The issue is one of developing a system which both allows a performance measure to reflect the divisions' use of resources and, at the same time, ensures that there is an optimal allocation of the firm's resources. Suppose the following situation. Division B sells a product to outside customers at £9 per unit. It buys a major component for this product from division A for £7 per unit and incurs additional finishing costs of £3 per unit. Division B therefore loses £1 per unit and would decide to discontinue or seek an alternative source of supply. If the transfer price charged by A were reached as shown below, this might not be a wise decision from the company's viewpoint, and the transfer price should therefore be changed to encourage B to produce.

		£
Transfer price:	Variable costs	4
	Allocated fixed costs	1
	Profit	2
	Transfer price	7

The effect on the company's profit for every unit of the product sold to outside customers is an increase of £2, comprising the ultimate selling price received by B (£9), less the variable costs incurred by A (£4) and B (£3). B must be encouraged to produce. The transfer price must be lowered. Any figure below £6 would encourage B to accept the component; any figure above £4 would motivate A to supply that component. The conflict between head office and divisional objectives shows the need to attain goal congruence within the divisionalised structure. There are dangers that the performance of the whole company may be suboptimal.

The transfer pricing issue is a difficult one to resolve. If there is no external market for the goods or services involved, there is no obvious method of pricing transfers which consistently serves the twin functions of preserving divisional autonomy and ensuring firm-wide optimisation. There are in fact many possible alternatives available for the pricing of transfers. The price may, for example, represent the revenue which the selling division could receive if the good or service were sold on the open market, if such a market is available. This is the system employed by ICI (whose 1994 report notes that 'the Group's policy is to transfer products internally at external market prices'). Or the price could be based in some measure on the costs of producing the goods. If so, should only marginal costs be considered, or should prices be set equal to the 'full' costs of production plus some margin for the selling division's profit? Or the price might represent a 'halfway house' arrangement based upon negotiation between divisions and top management. We now turn to a consideration and illustration of each of these approaches to transfer pricing.

Market-based prices

Management's task in designing an appropriate transfer pricing system may be eased if there is an active, competitive outside market in the transferred goods. If this situation prevails, the use of market prices will provide a good basis for pricing transfers insofar as prices will at least be objective and verifiable and, perhaps most importantly, will provide a measure of opportunity cost: that is, if the selling division transfers goods to the buying division, the best alternative it forgoes is the revenue it could have received through sale on the open market. Equally the market price represents the best alternative the buying division foregoes if it does not purchase on the open market.

In order that the market-based system can work efficiently, it is imperative that individual divisions have the freedom to act independently – that selling divisions may sell either internally or externally as they wish, and buying divisions may have the same choice in their purchase decisions. This freedom helps to ensure that divisional profits are, as far as possible, not generated artificially. It may, however, involve the incurring of additional transaction costs which might detract from the advantages of the market-based system. For this reason some firms which use market prices for transferred goods deduct a small amount for 'normal' transaction costs.

How likely in practice is the existence of an active competitive market in similar products? It is the nature of the market which determines whether a unique market price exists. Very few markets are perfectly competitive and very few products are perfect substitutes for each other. If product specifications differ, it cannot really be said that the conditions for using market prices hold. Perhaps the biggest drawback to the use of market-based prices concerns the potential to create unused capacity in the selling division. For example, if division B decides suddenly to buy externally because the outside price is lower than the cost of purchase from division A, the selling division may be left with unsold stock and with capacity which may be unused in the future.

Cost-based prices

The optimal transfer price for the firm as a whole is represented by the opportunity cost of the transferred good or service to the selling division. We have seen that opportunity cost is measured by market price if a competitive intermediate market exists. If no competitive intermediate market exists, opportunity costs are measured not by market prices, but rather by the marginal or incremental cost to the selling division. If resources are not freely available within the firm, opportunity cost will be measured by the incremental cash flow of the selling division (the additional cash flows up to the point of transfer) plus any imputed cost for the scarce resources used by the selling division. This imputed cost (internal opportunity cost – see Chapter 12) ensures that the transferred good is priced at the best level relative to all alternative uses, and relative to all constraints on the company's optimisation. If the transfer price is set below total opportunity cost, the selling division will maximise its ROI, to the probable detriment of the firm's overall position, by producing no units of the good or service to be transferred, because it will be making an apparently negative contribution on each unit. If the transfer price is set above total opportunity cost, the buying division's marginal costs will be higher than the incremental cost to the firm as a whole of producing the transferred good or service, which will probably result in a higher than optimal selling price and a lower than optimal output level in the buying division. (See Chapters 8 and 9 for an explanation of the relationships among costs, selling prices and output levels.)

There is, however, a substantial practical problem with the use of opportunity cost-based transfer prices. By using only incremental costs to price his or her goods, the manager of the selling division is prevented from covering his or her fixed costs and from generating a profit. The selling division incurs a 'loss' equivalent to the fixed costs if all its output is sold to the buying division. This means that in effect the selling division ceases to be a profit centre and becomes instead a cost centre, with the attendant motivational loss which may result from removal of 'profit-maximising' status.

A possible solution to this problem is effectively to ignore strict economic analysis in pricing transfers, and to charge a price which is based, in some measure, on recovering fixed costs and allowing a 'fair' margin for profit. But here again controversial issues abound. How, for instance, is 'fairness' to be defined? Should it be taken to mean a fair margin on costs? Or a fair return on capital? And what method of (arbitrary) allocation is to be used to assign total fixed costs to individual products? Indeed many of the benefits of cost control in divisions may be lost if selling divisions are allowed to pass on their operating inefficiencies via the inclusion in the transfer price of a substantial overhead element.

One possible way out of the dilemma posed by the lack of a competitive market in the transferred good is to co-ordinate the output of the selling division with the purchase requirements of the buying division. Such co-ordination would seek to prevent any wastage of production capacity in the selling division, and would involve the buying division in a two-tier cost, and the selling division in a two-tier price. First, the buying division would contract for a proportion of the selling division's capacity, and would incur a *fixed* rent for using the facility; second, it would incur a cost equal to the selling division's variable cost of production for each unit purchased.

The following example illustrates some of the problems associated with the various forms of market-based and cost-based transfer pricing. Hillsborough plc has a producing division (1) that supplies several component parts to another producing division (2), which produces the company's main product. These component parts are listed below with relevant cost information:

Component	Variable cost per unit (£)	Quantity produced
A	4	20,000
B	6	20,000
C	10	30,000
D	1	10,000

The fixed costs of division 1, which would be avoided if the division were closed, amount to £160,000. These costs consist of the salary of the division managers, indirect labour costs, the costs of using machinery, etc. In calculating unit costs, the total fixed cost of £160,000 is allocated between the 80,000 units to be produced to arrive at a full cost per unit. The calculations are:

Component	Variable cost per unit (£)	Fixed cost per unit (£)	Full cost per unit (£)
A	4	2	6
B	6	2	8
C	10	2	12
D	1	2	3

In establishing transfer prices, full cost is used. In division 2, which uses the four components, the manager has authority to buy inside the company or to buy from an outside supplier. The outside prices are expected to remain constant over the future. At the present time, the outside prices are as follows:

Component	Outside price (£)
A	6.00
B	8.50
C	12.50
D	2.90

The manager of division 2 notices that the outside purchase price per unit for component D is 10p lower than the transfer price and places an order with an outside supplier. Division 1 stops producing component D, reallocates the fixed costs to the remaining units, and adjusts the full cost transfer prices.

   If there is little communication between the two divisions, we can begin to see the actions which the manager of division 2, acting in the interest of her own division, is likely to take. By recomputing the transfer prices of the remaining three components on the basis of an allocation of the £160,000 fixed costs among 70,000 components (A, B and C), we now have:

Component	Variable cost per unit (£)	Reallocated fixed cost per unit (£160,000 ÷ 70,000) (£)	Full cost per unit (£)
A	4	2.29	6.29
B	6	2.29	8.29
C	10	2.29	12.29

On the basis of these figures the manager of division 2 will place an outside order for component A, as the outside buying price of £6 is lower than the readjusted full cost transfer price of £6.29. Suppose she does this, and division 1 then ceases production of A. The recomputed transfer prices for B and C on the basis of an allocation of the fixed costs of £160,000 among 50,000 (B and C) are then:

Component	Variable cost per unit (£)	Reallocated fixed cost per unit (£160,000 ÷ 50,000) (£)	Full cost per unit (£)
B	6	3.20	9.20
C	10	3.20	13.20

The situation now is such that the adjusted transfer prices of B and C are higher than the outside prices. The manager of division 2 is now likely to order these two components from outside, and division 1 will have no production (or at least no sales!).

The principle underlying this simple and simplistic situation is an important one. By including allocated fixed costs in the transfer price, the buying division may tend to use outside suppliers, thus creating unused capacity in the selling division. The question may be raised as to whether division 1 should be eliminated altogether. The calculations in Tables 18.2 and 18.3 show that it is better to keep the division (resulting in a saving of total costs of £24,000), even if the fixed costs of division 1 could be avoided if the division were closed.

The full cost transfer price system does not encourage behaviour which is in the best interests of the company as a whole. Unless production is shut down completely, the marginal cost to the company of producing one unit of a component is its variable cost only, and provided that the manager of division 1 can charge the manager of division 2 a price in excess of the variable cost, the manager of division 1 is making a positive contribution towards the fixed costs of £160,000.

However, as the fixed costs of division 1 are avoidable on closure of the division, the division must charge a transfer price which generates a contribution each period of at least £160,000 (the level of avoidable fixed costs). If division 1 fails to do this, Hillsborough plc may consider it to be in the interests of the firm to close the division.

Table 18.2 Cost of operating division 1 if all components are manufactured

Component	Quantity	Variable cost (£)	Total (£)
A	20,000	4	80,000
B	20,000	6	120,000
C	30,000	10	300,000
D	10,000	1	10,000
			510,000
		Add Fixed cost	160,000
		Total cost	670,000

Table 18.3 Cost of buying parts outside

Component	Quantity	Price (£)	Total (£)
A	20,000	6.00	120,000
B	20,000	8.50	170,000
C	30,000	12.50	375,000
D	10,000	2.90	29,000
Total cost			694,000

Division 1 might best achieve this aim by adopting a two-tier price structure as explained previously: that is, it might charge division 2 each period with a flat-rate proportion of its fixed costs, depending upon the extent of division 2's demands on its capacity, plus a rate per unit sold to division 2, based on division 1's variable costs.

It should be remembered that, even if the financial analysis of divisions 1 and 2 does suggest that division 1 should be closed down and that division 2 should buy components from an outside supplier, there may be other non-quantitative factors which need to be considered. A decision to switch supply sources is often difficult and costly to reverse. It should not be made without consideration of future requirements and possible price changes. In addition, external purchase may result in division 2 losing a degree of control over the supply of vital components. But more important may be the social and indeed legal factors associated with such a decision. For example, the decision to cease taking components from division 1 may result in redundancies (and redundancy costs). Large companies have responsibilities to employees which cannot, and in our view should not, be ignored when policy decisions, such as the possible switch of suppliers, are considered.

Negotiated prices

Because of the problems associated with both market-based and cost-based prices, and in particular because of the rigid centralisation of policy associated with the latter, top management is frequently asked to act as an arbiter in fixing interdivisional prices. This arbitration leads to the generation of negotiated and flexible transfer prices. However, negotiated prices are artificial in the same way that full cost prices are artificial, and indeed suffer the further disadvantage that their use can make divisional performance more difficult to measure realistically and independently. The use of negotiated prices removes the discipline imposed by adhering to transfer prices that are based on measures determined in the marketplace, and which, as we have seen, provide an appropriate basis for interdivisional transactions.

18.6 Transfer pricing in practice

In recent years, surveys have been carried out regarding transfer pricing in industry. The following brief comments highlight several practical points which are useful in gaining a broad perspective on the transfer pricing problem. The development of transfer pricing policies is seen as a means of both motivating divisional managers and facilitating local decision making, as well as offering tax planning advantages if divisions are located in the 'right' country or region.

The surveys have also uncovered certain drawbacks. Transfer pricing policies can encourage divisions to increase their own profits artificially at the expense of corporate profits, and can take up much managerial time through lengthy disagreements on prices. Nor do prices set to optimise corporate profitability necessarily motivate divisional managers. In general, the surveys have consistently shown that transfer prices lag behind actual costs, and that divisional managers get too involved in earning income from other divisions instead of from external customers.

18.7 The determination of divisional expenses

Concern with transfer pricing is not the only important issue in determining a division's expenses for the purposes of calculating its ROI. Two further, interrelated questions arise: should divisions be charged for their use of central head office resources; and should divisions be charged, by way of an imputed interest cost, for the capital employed by the division? Each of these issues is now dealt with in turn.

Charge for central costs in ROI calculations

Most large organisations incur a block of costs, usually located at a head office, which directly or indirectly are intended to benefit all divisions within the organisation. These costs may be of two kinds: they may relate to the services provided to divisions, in the form of computing facilities, training programmes, legal advice, etc.; or they may relate to the costs of the central *administration*, such as the salary of the managing director, the costs of heating the administration's offices, and the rent of head office premises. These costs have the distinguishing feature that, generally speaking, their level is seldom controllable by divisional managers. It is difficult to envisage the sorts of decision which divisional managers are likely to take which could directly influence the amount of time which the firm's managing director devotes to particular divisions or indeed to particular aspects of overall policy.

The question then arises as to whether these central costs should be allocated to individual divisions. The answer, as always, depends upon the use to which divisional income figures are to be put. As we argued earlier in this chapter, the evaluation of the performance of the divisional manager should be undertaken on the basis of the division's controllable profit (sales revenue less all controllable costs), as this measures the manager's success in generating a profit (and thus an ROI) in terms of the resources under his or her control. Whether the ROI is sufficient depends upon the standard expected from the division. The divisional manager should not be assessed on the basis of divisional profit after allocating central costs.

While recognising the importance of covering central service and administration costs, we believe that this can best be achieved if head office encourages divisional managers to maximise controllable ROI.

Charge for using capital

The use of ROI as a means of evaluating divisional performance has not been universally accepted. Academic accountants in particular have challenged its usefulness, and have advocated in its stead an alternative evaluation method known as the *net residual income* (NRI) method.[1] The NRI method was developed in America by the General Electric Co. in the 1960s to assess the performance of its divisional managers, and to prevent suboptimisation within the company, the argument being that managers who maximise controllable residual income will be more likely to behave consistently with a corporate objective of maximising cash flows, than those who maximise ROI. The net residual income of a division represents the excess of its controllable operating income over its cost of capital (or minimum desired rate of return) multiplied by its capital employed.

The cost of capital is determined by top management and ideally should reflect the different risks of the divisions. A numerical example may help to clarify the issues involved.

Suppose that division A has net assets of £2,000,000 and generates a controllable annual profit of £300,000, thus producing an ROI of £300,000/£2,000,000 × 100% = 15% p.a. The company's overall target return is 12% p.a. On the basis of ROI, division A may be unwilling to invest in a project producing a return less than 15% p.a. as this would result in a reduction in its ROI, whereas under the NRI concept any project would be acceptable provided a positive income figure remains when the imputed interest charge is deducted from the division's profit, as follows:

Division A income statement (summary)

	£
Controllable profit	300,000
Less Imputed interest charge	
(12% × £2,000,000)	240,000
Net residual income	60,000

In this case, as the net residual income is positive after charging interest on the division's assets of £2,000,000 at the rate of 12% fixed by the company, the division should expand its operations, provided that it earns a return of at least 12%

p.a. on the incremental investment, even though the rate earned on the investment may be lower than the division's present ROI of 15% p.a. It must, however, be borne in mind that, in addition to all the problems of determining appropriate transfer prices, divisional expenses and divisional assets associated with the measurement of ROI, the net residual income concept involves the further task of determining an agreed imputed interest charge for each division. However, the concept of charging divisions for their use of capital is likely to make managers more aware of the costs of finance, with the attendant benefits to the company of such awareness.

The use of imputed interest charges in the evaluation of divisional performance has been the subject of much debate, and a discussion of the issues involved is outside the scope of an introductory text.[2] We might sum up the general conclusions of the debate by saying that the NRI method is needed only if divisional managers have control over the size of new investments. If top management determines the level of divisional investment in assets (e.g. if the investment in net assets in our example of £2,000,000 was fixed by head office), then no interest charge should be made for assessing the performance either of the division or of its manager. The manager of division A should simply attempt to maximise the controllable operating income, or, put another way, to maximise the return on the *fixed* divisional investment of £2,000,000.

As we noted earlier, some parallels exist between ROI and NRI and the different methods of investment appraisal discussed in Chapters 13 and 14:

1. Net residual income uses a similar approach to net present value as an appraisal method. The aim is to accept all projects showing a positive return (cash surplus) when discounted at the (division's) cost of capital.

2. ROI is similar to the internal rate of return method of investment appraisal. The decision rule using ROI is to accept all projects showing a percentage return greater than the division's minimum required rate.

18.8 The determination of the asset base

The choice of assets to be included in the base for evaluating divisional performance should be consistent with the choice of profit measure. Thus controllability should be the determining factor. Controllability relates to decisions. If divisional managers can take investment decisions which influence the size of the division's asset base, then such assets are controllable and should enter the division's ROI calculation. We will examine three particular problems which arise when choosing an appropriate investment base.

Definition of investment

Investment in a division can be measured by using various combinations of assets and liabilities (both fixed and current, short-term and long-term). For example, investment can be defined as the division's total assets (fixed plus current assets), net assets (total assets less total liabilities), fixed assets plus net current assets, or a number of other variants. In general, most companies, based on the argument that the primary purpose of ROI measurement is to evaluate the effectiveness of a division's operating management in using the assets entrusted to it, define divisional investment as total assets. This argument is supported by the observation that the appropriate amount of long-term indebtedness is an issue which is almost always handled at the company headquarters level. Alternatively, if liabilities are traceable back to a particular division, they should be accounted for by that division.

Valuation of assets

Most fixed asset valuation measures have both strengths and weaknesses, and the main alternatives for inclusion in ROI calculations are as follows:

1. *Net book value.* The major problem in using a depreciation-adjusted denominator is that this method will produce a continuously increasing ROI even if divisional profits remain constant over time. This problem is greatly compounded when assets, as is usually the case, are valued at historic cost. The net book value method could therefore encourage divisional managers to retain assets beyond their economic life in order to achieve higher ROI results.

2. *Gross book value.* This base still fails to overcome the problem of using a historic valuation, although the use of the higher value would prevent the rising return problem resulting from a depreciated asset base. In a very crude sense, the use of gross values could be viewed as incorporating an inflation adjustment, but there is no valid reason why original cost should have such a link to current values over time.

3. *Current value.* This would produce the most meaningful asset valuation, although the cost of obtaining the information could be high. Nevertheless ratios based on current, or opportunity, values should provide the best comparative statistics on the performance of different segments within the organisation, and of one company with another.

Allocation of joint assets

These problems arise because the assets directly traceable to the divisions of the business, when aggregated, do not equal the whole capital invested in the business. Therefore a decision has to be made as to whether or not to allocate joint (or corporate-held) assets to divisions. It is generally agreed that allocation of the cost of the physical assets used by head office is inappropriate, but that allocation of centrally held cash and debtors is feasible. Cash may be allocated if a basis for reflecting different demands can be determined; debtors on the basis of their origin.

CHAPTER SUMMARY

The problems of achieving managerial control over operations are likely to increase as the size of the organisation grows. Large companies are generally organised into divisions reflecting the spread of the firm's business activities, as a means of decentralising decision making and control. Divisionalisation is intended to give greater autonomy to divisional managers, and to reduce communication problems. Top management is released from day-to-day operational considerations to concentrate on strategic decisions. With a divisional structure, however, top management will still need to review the performance of the individual divisions and their managers, and in this chapter we have looked at some of the methods and problems of assessing divisional financial performance.

An important principle in control is that the lines of performance evaluation should be consistent with the responsibility structure in the firm. Under different structures, divisional managers may be responsible for costs, revenues, profit and investment, and different performance measures will be appropriate in each case. As a means of assessing performance relative to the size of the operations within a division, return on investment is commonly used as a measure of periodic results which takes account of the division's asset base as well as the level of profit achieved.

Measures of profit and return from divisions are obviously affected by the underlying data on performance, and will be sensitive to the measurement approaches used in respect of such matters as the pricing of transfers between divisions, the allocation of central charges and capital costs from head office to divisions, and the determination of divisional assets and their valuation.

REVIEW QUESTIONS

1. Explain the advantages and disadvantages of divisionalisation from the viewpoint of any large multinational company.

2. Discuss some of the accounting measurement problems inherent in the use of the ROI statistic.

3. Do you believe that all divisions within the same organisation should seek to attain the same ROI? Explain your arguments with reference to a hypothetical (or actual) company with many different divisions dealing in quite dissimilar activities.

4. 'The determination of appropriate transfer prices is the single most important motivational tool in encouraging divisional performance, where divisions of the same company deal actively with each other.' Discuss.

5. Explain some of the problems associated with the allocation of non-controllable fixed costs and head office expenses to individual divisions.

EXERCISES

18.1 A company has two divisions. Eastern division manufactures a unique timing device. It is never sold outside the company and it cannot be obtained from any other source. Western division incorporates this device in a finished product which it sells. One device is used for each unit of product. Most of eastern division's costs are fixed and for any output up to 1,000 units its total costs are £6,000. Thereafter total costs increase at the rate of £1,000 for every additional 1,000 units made. In the hope of optimising the division's results, eastern division's manager has set a transfer price of £5 per unit.

Western division's costs in assembling the timing device in the finished product and selling it are, in addition to the transfer price of the timing device, £12,000 for any output up to 1,000 units and £2,000 for every 1,000 units thereafter. Western division finds that it can increase its sales only by spending more on promotion or reducing selling prices. Western division's sales forecast is:

Sales in units	Net sales revenue per thousand units (£)
1,000	19,000
2,000	17,000
3,000	15,000
4,000	12,500
5,000	9,600
6,000	7,700

All costs, output rates and sales are per working day.

(a) Prepare a schedule of western division's costs (including purchases from eastern division). sales revenue and net income at the indicated sales levels.

(b) State what level of sales maximises western division's net income, and calculate eastern division's net income and the net income of the company at that level.

(c) Assume that the company's divisional structure and transfer pricing is abandoned and prepare a further schedule of costs, sales and net income for the company as a whole, at the indicated sales levels.

(d) State what level of sales maximises the company's net income, and explain why it differs from that calculated under a divisional organisation.

(e) State what transfer pricing policy will maximise the company's net income under the divisional organisation. (Solution at end of text.)

18.2 Willoughby plc, manufacturer of tractors and other heavy farm equipment, is organised along decentralised lines, with each manufacturing division operating as a separate profit centre. Each division head has been delegated full authority on all decisions involving the sale of the division's output, both to outsiders and to other divisions of Willoughby plc. Division C has in the past always purchased its requirement of a particular tractor-engine component from division A. However, when informed that division A was increasing its price to £150, division C's management decided to purchase the engine component from outside suppliers.

The component can be purchased by C for £135 on the open market. Division A insists that, owing to the recent installation of some highly specialised equipment and the resulting high depreciation charges, it would not be able to make an adequate profit on its investment unless it raised its price. A's management appealed to the top management of Willoughby plc for support in its dispute with C and supplied the following operating data:

C's annual purchases of tractor-engine component (units)	1,000
A's variable costs per unit of tractor-engine component (£)	120
A's fixed costs per unit of tractor-engine component (£)	20

(a) Assume that there are no alternative uses for internal facilities. Determine whether the company as a whole will benefit if C purchases the component from outside suppliers for £135 per unit.

(b) Assume that internal facilities of A would not otherwise be idle. By not producing the 1,000 units for C, A's equipment and other facilities would be assigned to other production operations, and would result in annual cash operating savings of £18,000. Should C purchase from outsiders?

(c) Assume that there are no alternative uses for A's internal facilities, and that the price of outsiders drops by £20. Should C purchase from outsiders?

(d) Assume that A could sell the 1,000 units to other customers at £155 per unit with variable selling costs of £5 per unit. Should C purchase the 1,000 components from outsiders at £135 per unit? (Solution at end of text.)

18.3 Wilks Ltd has two divisions. Division 1 is responsible for slaughtering and cutting unprocessed meat. Division 2 processes meat such as hams, bacon, etc. Division 2 can buy meat from division 1 or from outside suppliers.

Division 1 can sell at the market price all the unprocessed meat that it can produce. The 19X0 income statement for the company is given in the table below:

Wilks Ltd: income statement for the year ended 31 December 19X0

	£000	£000	£000
Total sales			1,800
Cost of goods sold:			
Opening stocks		0	
Manufacturing costs:			
Raw materials, division 1	500		
Labour, division 1	300		
Overhead, division 1	200		
Processing supplies, division 2	150		
Labour, division 2	200		
Overhead, division 2	100	1,450	
Cost of goods available for sale		1,450	
Less Closing stocks at cost:			
Division 1		0	
Division 2		100	1,350
Gross margin			450
Operating expenses:			
Sales and administrative, division 1	110		
Sales and administrative, division 2	120		
Head office overhead	140		
			370
Net profit before tax			80

Closing stocks of £100,000 are valued at the cost of production incurred in division 1. These stocks are as yet unprocessed. The market value unprocessed is £120,000. The sales for the year can be broken down as follows:

	£000
Division 1	400
Division 2	1,400
	1,800

The market value of the unprocessed meat actually transferred from division 1 to division 2 (exclusive of the closing stock) was £1,000,000.

(a) Prepare division income statements that might be used to evaluate the performance of the two division managers.

(b) Explain the transfer pricing policy you have used in preparing the statements, and state whether it is suitable for decision-making purposes.

18.4 Vaughan Ltd comprises three divisions. Divisions A and B manufacture components which they sell externally and transfer to division C. Raw materials are purchased for a central store from which they are issued to the operating divisions. The company operates a system of decentralised decision taking. It wishes to set transfer prices for components and materials such that divisional managers are motivated to take decisions likely to increase the wealth of shareholders. The following information is available on current divisional activities:

1. *Division A*: Manufactures component A, requiring per unit: 8 labour hours, 6 lb of material A and 4 lb of material B. The division can sell an indefinitely large quantity externally at the going price of £700 per unit.

2. *Division B*: Manufactures component B, requiring per unit: 6 labour hours, 4 lb of material A and 6 lb of material B. The division can sell up to 20,000 units p.a. at the selected price of £800 per unit.

3. *Division C*: Manufactures three products:

	Product X	Product Y	Product Z
Required per unit:			
Material B (lb)	8	4	6
Component A (units)	4	6	2
Component B (units)	2	6	4
Labour hours	20	12	16
Selling price per unit (£)	3,500	5,600	2,500
Maximum annual demand (units)	10,000	6,000	8,000

Resources available per annum are:
Labour: Division A   200,000 hr at £10 per hr
        Division B   160,000 hr at £10 per hr
        Division C   120,000 hr at £5 per hr
Material A – 200,000 lb at £20 per lb
Material B – as much as required at £50 per lb.

(a) Formulate the decision problem for the whole firm as a linear programming problem. Do *not* give a numerical solution.

(b) Explain how the desired transfer prices might be set. What can you say about their level without making calculations?

18.5 Eichner Ltd manufactures and distributes golf balls under the brand name Superjacks. The company has adopted a divisionalised structure with a manufacturing division which produces the balls and supplies them in bulk to a distribution division, which is responsible for packaging and marketing. Both divisions have considerable autonomy and both are evaluated as profit centres.

The manufacturing division has fixed costs of £25,000. The average variable cost is £1.50 + 0.0001q per dozen balls. The distribution division has fixed costs of £10,000 and constant variable costs of £2 per dozen balls. Eichner Ltd has recently commissioned a market research project which has revealed that the demand for Superjacks is such that a 25p reduction in the price of a carton of one dozen balls will result in demand increasing by 500 units. The existing price is £5 per dozen and the company is selling 20,000 cartons per year. The management of Eichner has not previously considered increasing the price because of competition from other manufacturers. However, they believe that a 25p increase in price would produce similar, though reversed, results to those resulting from a price reduction.

(a) Determine the price and output levels that would result in Eichner maximising its profits.

(b) Suggest a transfer price such that the divisional managements, acting independently, would arrive at the conclusions indicated in (a) above, and show how total corporate profit would be allocated between the divisions.

Now suppose that the chief executive of the manufacturing division has found a chain store that is prepared to purchase the unpacked balls in bulk at a price of £5 per dozen direct from the manufacturing division.

(c) Determine the transfer price that will ensure optimal decisions, from the corporate viewpoint, are taken by the individual divisional executives.

(d) Calculate the new corporate profit and show how it is divided between the divisions.

Notes

1. See, for example, D. Solomons, *Divisional Performance: Measurement and Control*, Irwin, 1965.
2. See, for example, C. R. Emmanuel and D. T. Otley, 'The usefulness of residual income', *Journal of Business Finance and Accounting*, Winter 1976; and R. W. Scapens, 'Profit measurement in divisionalised companies', *Journal of Business Finance and Accounting*, Autumn 1979.

Summary and review

AIMS AND OBJECTIVES

☐ To review the main objectives of the book.
☐ To summarise the main principles developed.
☐ To review the major problem areas identified.
☐ To review the current and likely future state of management accounting.

Our main concern in this book has been to identify and discuss the sort of accounting information which should be provided for managers of business organisations. This emphasis reflects the view that the purpose of *all* accounting is to provide information that assists its users to make good decisions. This does not imply that accounting is a purely technical, functional and objective activity. Throughout the book we have drawn attention to the interaction between accounting numbers and human behaviour, which affects the implementation and use of accounting systems in practice. However, it is a working assumption in the design of those systems within individual organisations that their purpose is to provide information which will assist with the decisions that need to be taken as the organisation pursues its objectives. If this is not the case, then accounting is likely to be sterile and of little social or economic value, and decision makers may well develop other, perhaps more informal, sources of useful information.

In Part 1 we discussed topics central to this view of accounting and, in particular, of management accounting. Although such an extensive coverage of basic principles is not found in all books on management accounting, we believe that it is essential to an understanding of the role of management accounting as part of an enterprise's total information system. In Part 2 we described how a firm's operations may be understood in terms of the behaviour of the costs associated with activities, and looked at how costs may be measured. In Part 3 we applied the principles from Part 1 and the understanding of the measurement of a firm's operations from Part 2 to a number of problems typically faced by managers, for which they require information from the firm's accounting system. We have not attempted to cover all the problem areas confronting managers: had we done so, the book would have been excessively long. Nevertheless we feel that the choice of areas covered in Part 3 is sufficiently comprehensive to illustrate the application to management problems of the basic principles of accounting information systems developed in Parts 1 and 2.

In this final chapter we review both the main objectives of the book and the principles suggested for the preparation of management accounting information. We also summarise the pertinent problems involved in the provision of management information as we have identified them. We conclude with a discussion of the current state of management accounting and with some suggestions about the directions in which it might develop.

19.1 Review of the objectives of the book

We outlined our main objectives in Chapter 1. They are as follows:

1. To provide a framework for the analysis of accounting problems: that is, problems of identifying the appropriate information which aids users' decisions.

2. To use the framework to identify principles which specify the particular information that should be made available to decision makers.

3. To apply these principles to a variety of managerial problems, and to suggest methods for solving those problems.

4. To describe accounting procedures that are used by practising management accountants, and to compare them with the procedures implied by our analysis.

We attempted to achieve the first and second objectives in Parts 1 and 2 and the third and fourth in Part 3. In so doing, we identified three main interdependent areas of management activity: decision making, planning and control. Each of these areas is reviewed briefly in the next section.

19.2 The main principles

In order to review the key principles in the identification of good management accounting information, it is helpful to consider separately the three areas of management activity mentioned above. For management *decision making*, our central theme has been to argue in favour of opportunity cost or relevant cost as the most appropriate measure of the economic costs and consequences of decisions. By opportunity cost or relevant cost is meant the incremental or differential effect on a firm's cash flows of pursuing a particular course of action. We considered the application of the opportunity cost concept to a number of decisions, including accept/reject decisions, output level decisions, pricing policy, the optimal use of scarce resources and decision making in divisions of organisations. We discussed the application of the concept to both short- and long-term decisions, the latter involving the determination and incorporation into the analysis of an interest rate, or cost of capital, to take account of the time value of money. Underlying our entire analysis is an objective of wealth maximisation or, more precisely, the maximisation of the discounted present value of an organisation's future net cash inflows.

Management *planning* is important because it provides the link between making decisions and controlling their implementation. Decisions which appear optimal may be of little benefit to a firm if they are not properly implemented. Plans, or budgets, embody the expected outcomes of particular decisions, and should be prepared in a form which is consistent with the achievement of the desired outcomes. They should also be prepared in a way that facilitates management control.

Simply stated, *control* comprises the frequent comparison of actual results with planned performance, and the subsequent investigation of variances. Because control implies comparison, it is important that like be compared with like if the analysis is to be meaningful. Thus control systems should be in a form consistent with the models used for planning. As we explained in Chapters 15 and 17, there are many different purposes of control systems. Two of these bear repeating here. The first is to motivate those responsible for implementing an organisation's plans. The second is to provide an organisation with information that will enable it to improve the quality of its performance in the future. A good control system will include frequent consideration and, if necessary, revision of organisational plans.

In this context it should be clear that decision making, planning and control are all parts of a dynamic, iterative process. A good management accounting system should reflect the interdependences between the three areas. To decide upon an optimal plan is merely the first step in a procedure that will continue and involve regular changes as long as the firm exists.

19.3 Some problems reviewed

Throughout the book we have attempted to direct attention to problems which are likely to arise in the development and implementation of management accounting systems. Some of the more important of these problems are reviewed below.

The first problem, which affects all decisions, is the existence of *risk and uncertainty* (discussed in some detail in Chapter 4 and subsequently referred to on numerous occasions). All decisions are concerned with choices between future courses of action, and the future is never certain. Thus all decisions are based on data that, to some degree, are uncertain. Although it is possible to specify the uncertainty involved in estimates and to adopt strategies which reduce the impact of uncertainty – for example, by using portfolio analysis – it should be remembered that uncertainty can usually be decreased only at the cost of a lower expected return and can never be eliminated. In consequence, all decisions involve a possible trade-off between risk and return. Such a choice depends upon individual preferences and cannot be determined by an inanimate decision model.

A second difficulty in the development of management accounting systems is the existence of *factors which cannot readily be expressed in financial terms*. This is a particular problem for organisations in the public sector, where social costs and benefits are often more important than in the private sector. For example, it is difficult to justify the existence of a police force, a motorway or even an urban transport system purely on the grounds of readily identifiable financial costs and benefits. The directly identifiable financial costs of such services normally outweigh their directly identifiable financial benefits. Yet the fact that they are provided suggests the existence of other, less easily measured benefits. The same difficulties arise, although to a lesser degree, in private sector organisations. The decision to provide a 'subsidised' works canteen may, in fact, be a sound long-term financial investment for a firm. It may result in lower wages having to be paid, in a reduction in the rate at which employees leave and a consequent reduction in re-employment and retraining costs, and in a decrease in the number of working days lost through ill health, resulting from an inadequate diet. Such benefits are difficult to quantify, however, and their incorporation in a decision analysis may, in some situations, occupy a substantial amount of management time. We return to this issue in more detail at the close of this chapter.

A further problem relates to the *relationship between a firm's management accounts and its external accounting reports*: that is, the reports it issues to its shareholders and to other groups outside the enterprise who have an interest in its performance (we took up this issue initially in Chapter 14). In some situations, the adoption of courses of action which seem desirable according to the decision models which we have advocated in this book may result in a deterioration in an enterprise's performance as measured in its external reports, particularly in the short term. Suppose, for example, that a firm is considering whether to invest £200,000 in a substantial advertising campaign. The advertising cost would be incurred in the coming year and would result in additional net cash inflows of £50,000 in the year after the campaign and in each subsequent year indefinitely. The firm's cost of capital is 10% p.a. In investment appraisal terms the project is very attractive: it has a net present value of £300,000 (£50,000/0.1 − £200,000) and an internal rate of return of 25% (£50,000/£200,000 × 100). However, in the firm's external reports, adoption of the project will probably lead to a decrease in reported income in the coming year, when some or all of the costs of the advertising campaign are recognised. It is true that the reported income of subsequent years will be higher than would have been the case without advertising, but some investors may decide to sell their shares at the end of the coming year on the basis of that year's reported results. The crux of the problem is this. If managerial decision making (which is based on future expectations) results in a course of action which, although worthwhile in the long run, reflects adversely on a firm's performance in the short run measured in its external reports, then users of the reports may make decisions which are not in their best long-run interests. Furthermore, since external reports are based on past performance and generally cover periods no longer than one year, they may not articulate well with managerial decision-making processes which emphasise the future and often involve a consideration of periods considerably longer than one year. This means that managers should bear in mind the impact of their decisions on externally reported performance and, in some cases, may decide to modify the decisions accordingly.

19.4 The current and future state of management accounting

In this book we have attempted to explain at an introductory level the current state of management accounting as it is reflected in the literature of the subject. Much of the current literature on management accounting is influenced substantially by work on applied economics and applied operations research which was undertaken largely in the two or three decades up to the early 1970s, and by studies on the design of information systems which have been undertaken primarily since then.

A major problem facing researchers and writers in the management accounting area is that surprisingly little reliable empirical evidence exists concerning the use of management accounting systems in practice. Until more evidence is available, it will be difficult for management accounting writers to ascertain which of their recommendations are useful to managers and which are not. An example of the difficulty is in the area of fixed overhead allocation. For many years, virtually all management accounting writers argued that allocating costs which are fixed is arbitrary and may be misleading, and yet the limited available empirical evidence suggested that many firms operate cost accounting systems that involve simplistic allocations of fixed costs to products, decisions and so on. More recently the ideas of activity-based costing have challenged the traditional bases for making cost allocations. Some firms have adopted these ideas, while others have retained existing costing systems. Much more research evidence is needed to understand why managements have chosen particular practices, and how the resulting information is used in making particular decisions, before it will be possible to evaluate the usefulness of different approaches to allocation for decisions in the real world.

Closer liaison is clearly required between those who practise management accounting and those who make recommendations about management accounting systems. Ultimately recommendations about 'best' management accounting systems, however plausible they may appear, are of little importance if they are not adopted in practice. However, we do know that there are major changes taking place in the world of business, and in particular in the nature of manufacturing technology. Perhaps the biggest challenge which faces management accounting is its ability to adapt to changes in the firm's operating environment. Accounting systems, such as those which we have discussed throughout this book, have been developed during periods when the primary aim of the firm's production managers has been to maximise the length of production runs of the same (standard) product, and so to minimise unit costs. Thus the management accountant has developed reporting tools, such as standard costing, which reflect a production setting of long runs with standard elements. The emphasis of standard costing is on rewarding the lowest *unit* costs of production: for example, via the generating of favourable labour efficiency variances and favourable material use variances. This environment has demanded purely financial information from the management accountant – information which records actual and budgeted costs and revenues from particular decisions. It has not concerned itself greatly with the more qualitative issues of product quality, number of defective units, amounts of warranty expense, customer loyalty, speed of processing orders, etc. As a consequence the accountant has not been called upon to develop recording and measurement techniques which address these qualitative issues.

The world of the 1990s and beyond is, however, not so simple. No longer do most firms engage in long production runs of standard products, irrespective of the saleability of the output. In the 1990s the consumer is king and, as Japanese manufacturers have shown for the last two decades, the production setting has to change to reflect this. In effect the aim of production is to meet, and to anticipate, changes in consumer taste and demand. Consumers require more new production lines, a greater variety of products within each line, and more design features within each individual product. To meet those constantly changing consumer requirements, firms are having to change their design and production technology to allow them to bring products quickly to market and then to produce at lower volumes in a cost-effective way. Flexibility and speed of change of machine use are the order of the day, and, indeed, many organisations are currently investing heavily in flexible manufacturing systems, in CADCAM systems, and in fully automated, computer-integrated plants. All of these technologies allow the firm, in varying degrees, to adapt speedily and cheaply to changes in market preferences. As the emphasis has moved away from long standard production runs and become one of *minimising* stock levels and *minimising* the total (rather than the unit) cost of production, the management accountant is having to reflect these changes in his or her measurement systems. This may not be easy. The change required in the mind-set is quite substantial.

New concepts and terms have entered the management accounting vocabulary. The emphasis of accounting systems is shifting away from purely the recording of costs to the supply of information related to the factors which are important for organisational profitability (sometimes called *critical success factors*). Management methods are increasingly becoming focused on *creating value*, *quality* and *customers*. For example, the ideas of *total quality management* (or TQM) emphasise the need to meet customer requirements. Operations may be analysed as a *value chain*: that is, as a sequence of activities which create product or service attributes that are of value to customers. Accounting information systems designed for the management of activities, seeking to make value-enhancing activities more efficient and to reduce or eliminate non-value-adding activities, are very different from traditional cost-based accounting systems.

The new production setting dictated by external factors requires measures of cost, quality, flexibility, service and innovation. These will, more and more, become the bases on which firms compete. At the moment, the training and practice of most accountants is rooted in the first of these bases – that of cost. The challenge over the next ten years will certainly be one of refining and specifying appropriate cost measurements (opportunity costing will be as important in the future as in the past), but will entail a closer knowledge on the part of the accountant of just where the firm's competitive advantage lies (Is it known as a quality firm? Does it compete on cost alone?), so that relevant measurements can be developed. It is likely that many of these measures will be non-financial. Thus we envisage that management accountants will concern themselves with measures of quality (changes in design, percentage of defects, percentage of items reworked), with measures of productivity (value added per employee, total factor productivity), with measures of innovation (number of high-performance products introduced, delivery times from inception to customer), with better use of inventory (elimination of set-up times, less use of floor space, introduction of just-in-time theories), with measures of workforce satisfaction (training levels, measures of absenteeism, employee suggestions for continuous improvement) and with measures of customer loyalty (number of customers retained over a specified period, number of new customers gained). These, and other allied issues, are not obviously paramount within the current domain of accounting measurement, but they are likely to be an indispensable condition of successful business in future years.

In this book we have attempted to provide a set of principles which will enable the management accountant of the future to respond to the new needs of the users of accounting information. The detailed application of the principles will evolve and change as the environment of economic activity changes. If management accountants do not get to grips with these issues, their role as primary providers of useful information for business decisions may be usurped by others.

REVIEW QUESTIONS

1. Discuss the main principles involved in developing information for management decision making, planning and control.

2. Outline the problems created by the existence of risk and uncertainty in decision making.

3. 'Enterprise reports to external users focus on the past. Information for managerial decision making focuses on the future. Thus consistency between information for external users and information for managers is unlikely.' Explain this statement and discuss its implications.

4. Discuss the difficulties which management accountants may experience in developing non-financial performance measures.

5. Do you believe it is the accountant's role to depart from his or her traditional responsibility of providing cost-based information?

Compounding and discounting tables

Year n	Future value $(1 + i)^n$	Present value $V_{\overline{n}}$	Sinking fund		Annuity	
			Future value $S_{\overline{n}}$	Annual amount $S_{\overline{n}}^{-1}$	Present value $A_{\overline{n}}$	Annual amount $A_{\overline{n}}^{-1}$
Interest rate 3.0%						
1	1.0300	0.970874	1.0000	1.000000	0.9709	1.030000
2	1.0609	0.942596	2.0300	0.492611	1.9135	0.522611
3	1.0927	0.915142	3.0909	0.323530	2.8286	0.353530
4	1.1255	0.888487	4.1836	0.239027	3.7171	0.269027
5	1.1593	0.862609	5.3091	0.188355	4.5797	0.218355
6	1.1941	0.837484	6.4684	0.154598	5.4172	0.184598
7	1.2299	0.813092	7.6625	0.130506	6.2303	0.160506
8	1.2668	0.789409	8.8923	0.112456	7.0197	0.142456
9	1.3048	0.766417	10.1591	0.098434	7.7861	0.128434
10	1.3439	0.744094	11.4639	0.087231	8.5302	0.117231
11	1.3842	0.722421	12.8078	0.078077	9.2526	0.108077
12	1.4258	0.701380	14.1920	0.070462	9.9540	0.100462
13	1.4685	0.680951	15.6178	0.064030	10.6350	0.094030
14	1.5126	0.661118	17.0863	0.058526	11.2961	0.088526
15	1.5580	0.641862	18.5989	0.053767	11.9379	0.083767
16	1.6047	0.623167	20.1569	0.049611	12.5611	0.079611
17	1.6528	0.605016	21.7616	0.045953	13.1661	0.075953
18	1.7024	0.587395	23.4144	0.042709	13.7535	0.072709
19	1.7535	0.570286	25.1169	0.039814	14.3238	0.069814
20	1.8061	0.553676	26.8704	0.037216	14.8775	0.067216
21	1.8603	0.537549	28.6765	0.034872	15.4150	0.064872
22	1.9161	0.521893	30.5368	0.032747	15.9369	0.062747
23	1.9736	0.506692	32.4529	0.030814	16.4436	0.060814
24	2.0328	0.491934	34.4265	0.029047	16.9355	0.059047
25	2.0938	0.477606	36.4593	0.027428	17.4131	0.057428
26	2.1566	0.463695	38.5530	0.025938	17.8768	0.055938
27	2.2213	0.450189	40.7096	0.024564	18.3270	0.054564
28	2.2879	0.437077	42.9309	0.023293	18.7641	0.053293
29	2.3566	0.424346	45.2189	0.022115	19.1885	0.052115
30	2.4273	0.411987	47.5754	0.021019	19.6004	0.051019

Year n	Future value $(1 + i)^n$	Present value $V_{\overline{n}|}$	Sinking fund Future value $S_{\overline{n}|}$	Sinking fund Annual amount $S_{\overline{n}|}^{-1}$	Annuity Present value $A_{\overline{n}|}$	Annuity Annual amount $A_{\overline{n}|}^{-1}$
Interest rate 4.0%						
1	1.0400	0.961538	1.0000	1.000000	0.9615	1.040000
2	1.0816	0.924556	2.0400	0.490196	1.8861	0.530196
3	1.1249	0.888996	3.1216	0.320349	2.7751	0.360349
4	1.1699	0.854804	4.2465	0.235490	3.6299	0.275490
5	1.2167	0.821927	5.4163	0.184627	4.4518	0.224627
6	1.2653	0.790315	6.6330	0.150762	5.2421	0.190762
7	1.3159	0.759918	7.8983	0.126610	6.0021	0.166610
8	1.3686	0.730690	9.2142	0.108528	6.7327	0.148528
9	1.4233	0.702587	10.5828	0.094493	7.4353	0.134493
10	1.4802	0.675564	12.0061	0.083291	8.1109	0.123291
11	1.5395	0.649581	13.4864	0.074149	8.7605	0.114149
12	1.6010	0.624597	15.0258	0.066552	9.3851	0.106552
13	1.6651	0.600574	16.6268	0.060144	9.9856	0.100144
14	1.7317	0.577475	18.2919	0.054669	10.5631	0.094669
15	1.8009	0.555265	20.0236	0.049941	11.1184	0.089941
16	1.8730	0.533908	21.8245	0.045820	11.6523	0.085820
17	1.9479	0.513373	23.6975	0.042199	12.1657	0.082199
18	2.0258	0.493628	25.6454	0.038993	12.6593	0.078993
19	2.1068	0.474642	27.6712	0.036139	13.1339	0.076139
20	2.1911	0.456387	29.7781	0.033582	13.5903	0.073582
21	2.2788	0.438834	31.9692	0.031280	14.0292	0.071280
22	2.3699	0.421955	34.2480	0.029199	14.4511	0.069199
23	2.4647	0.405726	36.6179	0.027309	14.8568	0.067309
24	2.5633	0.390121	39.0826	0.025587	15.2470	0.065587
25	2.6658	0.375117	41.6459	0.024012	15.6221	0.064012
26	2.7725	0.360689	44.3117	0.022567	15.9828	0.062567
27	2.8834	0.346817	47.0842	0.021239	16.3296	0.061239
28	2.9987	0.333477	49.9676	0.020013	16.6631	0.060013
29	3.1187	0.320651	52.9663	0.018880	16.9837	0.058880
30	3.2434	0.308319	56.0849	0.017830	17.2920	0.057830

Year n	Future value $(1 + i)^n$	Present value $V_{\overline{n}}$	Sinking fund		Annuity	
			Future value $S_{\overline{n}}$	Annual amount $S_{\overline{n}}^{-1}$	Present value $A_{\overline{n}}$	Annual amount $A_{\overline{n}}^{-1}$
Interest rate 5.0%						
1	1.0500	0.952381	1.0000	1.000000	0.9524	1.050000
2	1.1025	0.907029	2.0500	0.487805	1.8594	0.537805
3	1.1576	0.863838	3.1525	0.317209	2.7232	0.367209
4	1.2155	0.822702	4.3101	0.232012	3.5460	0.282012
5	1.2763	0.783526	5.5256	0.180975	4.3295	0.230975
6	1.3401	0.746215	6.8019	0.147017	5.0757	0.197017
7	1.4071	0.710681	8.1420	0.122820	5.7864	0.172820
8	1.4775	0.676839	9.5491	0.104722	6.4632	0.154722
9	1.5513	0.644609	11.0266	0.090690	7.1078	0.140690
10	1.6289	0.613913	12.5779	0.079505	7.7217	0.129505
11	1.7103	0.584679	14.2068	0.070389	8.3064	0.120389
12	1.7959	0.556837	15.9171	0.062825	8.8633	0.112825
13	1.8856	0.530321	17.7130	0.056456	9.3936	0.106456
14	1.9799	0.505068	19.5986	0.051024	9.8986	0.101024
15	2.0789	0.481017	21.5786	0.046342	10.3797	0.096342
16	2.1829	0.458112	23.6575	0.042270	10.8378	0.092270
17	2.2920	0.436297	25.8404	0.038699	11.2741	0.088699
18	2.4066	0.415521	28.1324	0.035546	11.6896	0.085546
19	2.5270	0.395734	30.5390	0.032745	12.0853	0.082745
20	2.6533	0.376889	33.0660	0.030243	12.4622	0.080243
21	2.7860	0.358942	35.7193	0.027996	12.8212	0.077996
22	2.9253	0.341850	38.5052	0.025971	13.1630	0.075971
23	3.0715	0.325571	41.4305	0.024137	13.4886	0.074137
24	3.2251	0.310068	44.5020	0.022471	13.7986	0.072471
25	3.3864	0.295303	47.7271	0.020952	14.0939	0.070952
26	3.5557	0.281241	51.1135	0.019564	14.3752	0.069564
27	3.7335	0.267848	54.6691	0.018292	14.6430	0.068292
28	3.9201	0.255094	58.4026	0.017123	14.8981	0.067123
29	4.1161	0.242946	62.3227	0.016046	15.1411	0.066046
30	4.3219	0.231377	66.4388	0.015051	15.3725	0.065051

| | | | Sinking fund | | Annuity | |
Year n	Future value $(1+i)^n$	Present value $V_{\overline{n}|}$	Future value $S_{\overline{n}|}$	Annual amount $S_{\overline{n}|}^{-1}$	Present value $A_{\overline{n}|}$	Annual amount $A_{\overline{n}|}^{-1}$
Interest rate 6%						
1	1.0600	0.943396	1.0000	1.000000	0.9434	1.060000
2	1.1236	0.889996	2.0600	0.485437	1.8334	0.545437
3	1.1910	0.839619	3.1836	0.314110	2.6730	0.374110
4	1.2625	0.792094	4.3746	0.228591	3.4651	0.288591
5	1.3382	0.747258	5.6371	0.177396	4.2124	0.237396
6	1.4185	0.704961	6.9753	0.143363	4.9173	0.203363
7	1.5036	0.665057	8.3938	0.119135	5.5824	0.179135
8	1.5938	0.627412	9.8975	0.101036	6.2098	0.161036
9	1.6895	0.591898	11.4913	0.087022	6.8017	0.147022
10	1.7908	0.558395	13.1808	0.075868	7.3601	0.135868
11	1.8983	0.526788	14.9716	0.066793	7.8869	0.126793
12	2.0122	0.496969	16.8699	0.059277	8.3838	0.119277
13	2.1329	0.468839	18.8821	0.052960	8.8527	0.112960
14	2.2609	0.442301	21.0151	0.047585	9.2950	0.107585
15	2.3966	0.417265	23.2760	0.042963	9.7122	0.102963
16	2.5404	0.393646	25.6725	0.038952	10.1059	0.098952
17	2.6928	0.371364	28.2129	0.035445	10.4773	0.095445
18	2.8543	0.350344	30.9057	0.032357	10.8276	0.092357
19	3.0256	0.330513	33.7600	0.029621	11.1581	0.089621
20	3.2071	0.311805	36.7856	0.027185	11.4699	0.087185
21	3.3996	0.294155	39.9927	0.025005	11.7641	0.085005
22	3.6035	0.277505	43.3923	0.023046	12.0416	0.083046
23	3.8197	0.261797	46.9958	0.021278	12.3034	0.081278
24	4.0489	0.246979	50.8156	0.019679	12.5504	0.079679
25	4.2919	0.232999	54.8645	0.018227	12.7834	0.078227
26	4.5494	0.219810	59.1564	0.016904	13.0032	0.076904
27	4.8223	0.207368	63.7058	0.015697	13.2105	0.075697
28	5.1117	0.195630	68.5281	0.014593	13.4062	0.074593
29	5.4184	0.184557	73.6398	0.013580	13.5907	0.073580
30	5.7435	0.174110	79.0582	0.012649	13.7648	0.072649

Year n	Future value $(1+i)^n$	Present value $V_{\overline{n}\rvert}$	Sinking fund Future value $S_{\overline{n}\rvert}$	Sinking fund Annual amount $S_{\overline{n}\rvert}^{-1}$	Annuity Present value $A_{\overline{n}\rvert}$	Annuity Annual amount $A_{\overline{n}\rvert}^{-1}$

Interest rate 7.0%

Year n	Future value $(1+i)^n$	Present value $V_{\overline{n}\rvert}$	Future value $S_{\overline{n}\rvert}$	Annual amount $S_{\overline{n}\rvert}^{-1}$	Present value $A_{\overline{n}\rvert}$	Annual amount $A_{\overline{n}\rvert}^{-1}$
1	1.0700	0.934579	1.0000	1.000000	0.9346	1.070000
2	1.1449	0.873439	2.0700	0.483092	1.8080	0.553092
3	1.2250	0.816298	3.2149	0.311052	2.6243	0.381052
4	1.3108	0.762895	4.4399	0.225228	3.3872	0.295228
5	1.4026	0.712986	5.7507	0.173891	4.1002	0.243891
6	1.5007	0.666342	7.1533	0.139796	4.7665	0.209796
7	1.6058	0.622750	8.6540	0.115553	5.3893	0.185553
8	1.7182	0.582009	10.2598	0.097468	5.9713	0.167468
9	1.8385	0.543934	11.9780	0.083486	6.5152	0.153486
10	1.9672	0.508349	13.8164	0.072378	7.0236	0.142378
11	2.1049	0.475093	15.7836	0.063357	7.4987	0.133357
12	2.2522	0.444012	17.8885	0.055902	7.9427	0.125902
13	2.4098	0.414964	20.1406	0.049651	8.3577	0.119651
14	2.5785	0.387817	22.5505	0.044345	8.7455	0.114345
15	2.7590	0.362446	25.1290	0.039795	9.1079	0.109795
16	2.9522	0.338735	27.8881	0.035858	9.4466	0.105858
17	3.1588	0.316574	30.8402	0.032425	9.7632	0.102425
18	3.3799	0.295864	33.9990	0.029413	10.0591	0.099413
19	3.6165	0.276508	37.3790	0.026753	10.3356	0.096753
20	3.8697	0.258419	40.9955	0.024393	10.5940	0.094393
21	4.1406	0.241513	44.8652	0.022289	10.8355	0.092289
22	4.4304	0.225713	49.0057	0.020406	11.0612	0.090406
23	4.7405	0.210947	53.4361	0.018714	11.2722	0.088714
24	5.0724	0.197147	58.1767	0.017189	11.4693	0.087189
25	5.4274	0.184249	63.2490	0.015811	11.6536	0.085811
26	5.8074	0.172195	68.6765	0.014561	11.8258	0.084561
27	6.2139	0.160930	74.4838	0.013426	11.9867	0.083426
28	6.6488	0.150402	80.6977	0.012392	12.1371	0.082392
29	7.1143	0.140563	87.3465	0.011449	12.2777	0.081449
30	7.6123	0.131367	94.4608	0.010586	12.4090	0.080586

Year n	Future value $(1+i)^n$	Present value $V_{\overline{n}\rceil}$	Sinking fund		Annuity	
			Future value $S_{\overline{n}\rceil}$	Annual amount $S_{\overline{n}\rceil}^{-1}$	Present value $A_{\overline{n}\rceil}$	Annual amount $A_{\overline{n}\rceil}^{-1}$
Interest rate 8.0%						
1	1.0800	0.925926	1.0000	1.000000	0.9259	1.080000
2	1.1664	0.857339	2.0800	0.480769	1.7833	0.560769
3	1.2597	0.793832	3.2464	0.308034	2.5771	0.388034
4	1.3605	0.735030	4.5061	0.221921	3.3121	0.301921
5	1.4693	0.680583	5.8666	0.170456	3.9927	0.250456
6	1.5869	0.630170	7.3359	0.136315	4.6229	0.216315
7	1.7138	0.583490	8.9228	0.112072	5.2064	0.192072
8	1.8509	0.540269	10.6366	0.094015	5.7466	0.174015
9	1.9990	0.500249	12.4876	0.080080	6.2469	0.160080
10	2.1589	0.463193	14.4866	0.069029	6.7101	0.149029
11	2.3316	0.428883	16.6455	0.060076	7.1390	0.140076
12	2.5182	0.397114	18.9771	0.052695	7.5361	0.132695
13	2.7196	0.367698	21.4953	0.046522	7.9038	0.126522
14	2.9372	0.340461	24.2149	0.041297	8.2442	0.121297
15	3.1722	0.315242	27.1521	0.036830	8.5595	0.116830
16	3.4259	0.291890	30.3243	0.032977	8.8514	0.112977
17	3.7000	0.270269	33.7502	0.029629	9.1216	0.109629
18	3.9960	0.250249	37.4502	0.026702	9.3719	0.106702
19	4.3157	0.231712	41.4463	0.024128	9.6036	0.104128
20	4.6610	0.214548	45.7620	0.021852	9.8181	0.101852
21	5.0338	0.198656	50.4229	0.019832	10.0168	0.099832
22	5.4365	0.183941	55.4568	0.018032	10.2007	0.098032
23	5.8715	0.170315	60.8933	0.016422	10.3711	0.096422
24	6.3412	0.157699	66.7648	0.014978	10.5288	0.094978
25	6.8485	0.146018	73.1059	0.013679	10.6748	0.093679
26	7.3964	0.135202	79.9544	0.012507	10.8100	0.092507
27	7.9881	0.125187	87.3508	0.011448	10.9352	0.091448
28	8.6271	0.115914	95.3388	0.010489	11.0511	0.090489
29	9.3173	0.107328	103.9659	0.009619	11.1584	0.089619
30	10.0627	0.099377	113.2832	0.008827	11.2578	0.088827

Year n	Future value $(1 + i)^n$	Present value $V_{\overline{n}|}$	Sinking fund Future value $S_{\overline{n}|}$	Sinking fund Annual amount $S_{\overline{n}|}^{-1}$	Annuity Present value $A_{\overline{n}|}$	Annuity Annual amount $A_{\overline{n}|}^{-1}$
Interest rate 9.0%						
1	1.0900	0.917431	1.0000	1.000000	0.9174	1.090000
2	1.1881	0.841680	2.0900	0.478469	1.7591	0.568469
3	1.2950	0.772183	3.2781	0.305055	2.5313	0.395055
4	1.4116	0.708425	4.5731	0.218669	3.2397	0.308669
5	1.5386	0.649931	5.9847	0.167092	3.8897	0.257092
6	1.6771	0.596267	7.5233	0.132920	4.4859	0.222920
7	1.8280	0.547034	9.2004	0.108691	5.0330	0.198691
8	1.9926	0.501866	11.0285	0.090674	5.5348	0.180674
9	2.1719	0.460428	13.0210	0.076799	5.9952	0.166799
10	2.3674	0.422411	15.1929	0.065820	6.4177	0.155820
11	2.5804	0.387533	17.5603	0.056947	6.8052	0.146947
12	2.8127	0.355535	20.1407	0.049651	7.1607	0.139651
13	3.0658	0.326179	22.9534	0.043567	7.4869	0.133567
14	3.3417	0.299246	26.0192	0.038433	7.7862	0.128433
15	3.6425	0.274538	29.3609	0.034059	8.0607	0.124059
16	3.9703	0.251870	33.0034	0.030300	8.3126	0.120300
17	4.3276	0.231073	36.9737	0.027046	8.5436	0.117046
18	4.7171	0.211994	41.3013	0.024212	8.7556	0.114212
19	5.1417	0.194490	46.0185	0.021730	8.9501	0.111730
20	5.6044	0.178431	51.1601	0.019546	9.1285	0.109546
21	6.1088	0.163698	56.7645	0.017617	9.2922	0.107617
22	6.6586	0.150182	62.8733	0.015905	9.4424	0.105905
23	7.2579	0.137781	69.5319	0.014382	9.5802	0.104382
24	7.9111	0.126405	76.7898	0.013023	9.7066	0.103023
25	8.6231	0.115968	84.7009	0.011806	9.8226	0.101806
26	9.3992	0.106393	93.3240	0.010715	9.9290	0.100715
27	10.2451	0.097608	102.7231	0.009735	10.0266	0.099735
28	11.1671	0.089548	112.9682	0.008852	10.1161	0.098852
29	12.1722	0.082155	124.1354	0.008056	10.1983	0.098056
30	13.2677	0.075371	136.3075	0.007336	10.2737	0.097336

Year n	Future value $(1 + i)^n$	Present value $V_{\overline{n}}$	Sinking fund		Annuity	
			Future value $S_{\overline{n}}$	Annual amount $S_{\overline{n}}^{-1}$	Present value $A_{\overline{n}}$	Annual amount $A_{\overline{n}}^{-1}$
Interest rate 10.0%						
1	1.1000	0.909091	1.0000	1.000000	0.9091	1.100000
2	1.2100	0.826446	2.1000	0.476190	1.7355	0.576190
3	1.3310	0.751315	3.3100	0.302115	2.4869	0.402115
4	1.4641	0.683013	4.6410	0.215471	3.1699	0.315471
5	1.6105	0.620921	6.1051	0.163797	3.7908	0.263797
6	1.7716	0.564474	7.7156	0.129607	4.3553	0.229607
7	1.9487	0.513158	9.4872	0.105405	4.8684	0.205405
8	2.1436	0.466507	11.4359	0.087444	5.3349	0.187444
9	2.3579	0.424098	13.5795	0.073641	5.7590	0.173641
10	2.5937	0.385543	15.9374	0.062745	6.1446	0.162745
11	2.8531	0.350494	18.5312	0.053963	6.4951	0.153963
12	3.1384	0.318631	21.3843	0.046763	6.8137	0.146763
13	3.4523	0.289664	24.5227	0.040779	7.1034	0.140779
14	3.7975	0.263331	27.9750	0.035746	7.3667	0.135746
15	4.1772	0.239392	31.7725	0.031474	7.6061	0.131474
16	4.5950	0.217629	35.9497	0.027817	7.8237	0.127817
17	5.0545	0.197845	40.5447	0.024664	8.0216	0.124664
18	5.5599	0.179859	45.5992	0.021930	8.2014	0.121930
19	6.1159	0.163508	51.1591	0.019547	8.3649	0.119547
20	6.7275	0.148644	57.2750	0.017460	8.5136	0.117460
21	7.4002	0.135131	64.0025	0.015624	8.6487	0.115624
22	8.1403	0.122846	71.4027	0.014005	8.7715	0.114005
23	8.9543	0.111678	79.5430	0.012572	8.8832	0.112572
24	9.8497	0.101526	88.4973	0.011300	8.9847	0.111300
25	10.8347	0.092296	98.3471	0.010168	9.0770	0.110168
26	11.9182	0.083905	109.1818	0.009159	9.1609	0.109159
27	13.1100	0.076278	121.0999	0.008258	9.2372	0.108258
28	14.4210	0.069343	134.2099	0.007451	9.3066	0.107451
29	15.8631	0.063039	148.6309	0.006728	9.3696	0.106728
30	17.4494	0.057309	164.4940	0.006079	9.4269	0.106079

			Sinking fund		Annuity	
Year n	Future value $(1+i)^n$	Present value $V_{\overline{n}|}$	Future value $S_{\overline{n}|}$	Annual amount $S_{\overline{n}|}^{-1}$	Present value $A_{\overline{n}|}$	Annual amount $A_{\overline{n}|}^{-1}$
Interest rate 15.0%						
1	1.1500	0.869565	1.0000	1.000000	0.8696	1.150000
2	1.3225	0.756144	2.1500	0.465116	1.6257	0.615116
3	1.5209	0.657516	3.4725	0.287977	2.2832	0.437977
4	1.7490	0.571753	4.9934	0.200265	2.8550	0.350265
5	2.0114	0.497177	6.7424	0.148316	3.3522	0.298316
6	2.3131	0.432328	8.7537	0.114237	3.7845	0.264237
7	2.6600	0.375937	11.0668	0.090360	4.1604	0.240360
8	3.0590	0.326902	13.7268	0.072850	4.4873	0.222850
9	3.5179	0.284262	16.7858	0.059574	4.7716	0.209574
10	4.0456	0.247185	20.3037	0.049252	5.0188	0.199252
11	4.6524	0.214943	24.3493	0.041069	5.2337	0.191069
12	5.3503	0.186907	29.0017	0.034481	5.4206	0.184481
13	6.1528	0.162528	34.3519	0.029110	5.5831	0.179110
14	7.0757	0.141329	40.5047	0.024688	5.7245	0.174688
15	8.1371	0.122894	47.5804	0.021017	5.8474	0.171017
16	9.3576	0.106865	55.7175	0.017948	5.9542	0.167948
17	10.7613	0.092926	65.0751	0.015367	6.0472	0.165367
18	12.3755	0.080805	75.8364	0.013186	6.1280	0.163186
19	14.2318	0.070265	88.2118	0.011336	6.1982	0.161336
20	16.3665	0.061100	102.4436	0.009761	6.2593	0.159761
21	18.8215	0.G53131	118.8101	0.008417	6.3125	0.158417
22	21.6447	0.046201	137.6316	0.007266	6.3587	0.157266
23	24.8915	0.040174	159.2764	0.006278	6.3988	0.156278
24	28.6252	0.034934	184.1678	0.005430	6.4338	0.155430
25	32.9190	0.030378	212.7930	0.004699	6.4641	0.154699
26	37.8568	0.026415	245.7120	0.004070	6.4906	0.154070
27	43.5353	0.022970	283.5688	0.003526	6.5135	0.153526
28	50.0656	0.019974	327.1041	0.003057	6.5335	0.153057
29	57.5755	0.017369	377.1697	0.002651	6.5509	0.152651
30	66.2118	0.015103	434.7451	0.002300	6.5660	0.152300

			Sinking fund		Annuity	
Year n	Future value $(1+i)^n$	Present value $V_{\overline{n}\rvert}$	Future value $S_{\overline{n}\rvert}$	Annual amount $S_{\overline{n}\rvert}^{-1}$	Present value $A_{\overline{n}\rvert}$	Annual amount $A_{\overline{n}\rvert}^{-1}$
Interest rate 20.0%						
1	1.2000	0.833333	1.0000	1.000000	0.8333	1.200000
2	1.4400	0.694444	2.2000	0.454545	1.5278	0.654545
3	1.7280	0.578704	3.6400	0.274725	2.1065	0.474725
4	2.0736	0.482253	5.3680	0.186289	2.5887	0.386289
5	2.4883	0.401878	7.4416	0.134380	2.9906	0.334380
6	2.9860	0.334898	9.9299	0.100706	3.3255	0.300706
7	3.5832	0.279082	12.9159	0.077424	3.6046	0.277424
8	4.2998	0.232568	16.4991	0.060609	3.8372	0.260609
9	5.1598	0.193807	20.7989	0.048079	4.0310	0.248079
10	6.1917	0.161506	25.9587	0.038523	4.1925	0.238523
11	7.4301	0.134588	32.1504	0.031104	4.3271	0.231104
12	8.9161	0.112157	39.5805	0.025265	4.4392	0.225265
13	10.6993	0.093464	48.4966	0.020620	4.5327	0.220620
14	12.8392	0.077887	59.1959	0.016893	4.6106	0.216893
15	15.4070	0.064905	72.0351	0.013882	4.6755	0.213882
16	18.4884	0.054088	87.4421	0.011436	4.7296	0.211436
17	22.1861	0.045073	105.9306	0.009440	4.7746	0.209440
18	26.6233	0.037561	128.1167	0.007805	4.8122	0.207805
19	31.9480	0.031301	154.7400	0.006462	4.8435	0.206462
20	38.3376	0.026084	186.6880	0.005357	4.8696	0.205357
21	46.0051	0.021737	225.0256	0.004444	4.8913	0.204444
22	55.2061	0.018114	271.0307	0.003690	4.9094	0.203690
23	66.2474	0.015095	326.2369	0.003065	4.9245	0.203065
24	79.4968	0.012579	392.4842	0.002548	4.9371	0.202548
25	95.3962	0.010483	471.9811	0.002119	4.9476	0.202119
26	114.4755	0.008735	567.3773	0.001762	4.9563	0.201762
27	137.3706	0.007280	681.8528	0.001467	4.9636	0.201467
28	164.8447	0.006066	819.2233	0.001221	4.9697	0.201221
29	197.8136	0.005055	984.0680	0.001016	4.9747	0.201016
30	237.3763	0.004213	1181.8816	0.000846	4.9789	0.200846

Year n	Future value $(1+i)^n$	Present value $V_{\overline{n}|}$	Sinking fund Future value $S_{\overline{n}|}$	Annual amount $S_{\overline{n}|}^{-1}$	Annuity Present value $A_{\overline{n}|}$	Annual amount $A_{\overline{n}|}^{-1}$
Interest rate 25.0%						
1	1.2500	0.800000	1.0000	1.000000	0.8000	1.250000
2	1.5625	0.640000	2.2500	0.444444	1.4400	0.694444
3	1.9531	0.512000	3.8125	0.262295	1.9520	0.512295
4	2.4414	0.409600	5.7656	0.173442	2.3616	0.423442
5	3.0518	0.327680	8.2070	0.121847	2.6893	0.371847
6	3.8147	0.262144	11.2588	0.088819	2.9514	0.338819
7	4.7684	0.209715	15.0735	0.066342	3.1611	0.316342
8	5.9605	0.167772	19.8419	0.050399	3.3289	0.300399
9	7.4506	0.134218	25.8023	0.038756	3.4631	0.288756
10	9.3132	0.107374	33.2529	0.030073	3.5705	0.280073
11	11.6415	0.085899	42.5661	0.023493	3.6564	0.273493
12	14.5519	0.068719	54.2077	0.018448	3.7251	0.268448
13	18.1899	0.054976	68.7596	0.014543	3.7801	0.264543
14	22.7374	0.043980	86.9495	0.011501	3.8241	0.261501
15	28.4217	0.035184	109.6868	0.009117	3.8593	0.259117
16	35.5271	0.028147	138.1085	0.007241	3.8874	0.257241
17	44.4089	0.022518	173.6357	0.005759	3.9099	0.255759
18	55.5112	0.018014	218.0446	0.004586	3.9279	0.254586
19	69.3889	0.014412	273.5558	0.003656	3.9424	0.253656
20	86.7362	0.011529	342.9447	0.002916	3.9539	0.252916
21	108.4202	0.009223	429.6809	0.002327	3.9631	0.252327
22	135.5253	0.007379	538.1011	0.001858	3.9705	0.251858
23	169.4066	0.005903	673.6264	0.001485	3.9764	0.251485
24	211.7582	0.004722	843.0329	0.001186	3.9811	0.251186
25	264.6978	0.003778	1054.7912	0.000948	3.9849	0.250948
26	330.8722	0.003022	1319.4890	0.000758	3.9879	0.250758
27	413.5903	0.002418	1650.3612	0.000606	3.9903	0.250606
28	516.9879	0.001934	2063.9515	0.000485	3.9923	0.250485
29	646.2349	0.001547	2580.9394	0.000387	3.9938	0.250387
30	807.7936	0.001238	3227.1743	0.000310	3.9950	0.250310

Year n	Future value $(1 + i)^n$	Present value $V_{\overline{n}\rceil}$	Sinking fund Future value $S_{\overline{n}\rceil}$	Sinking fund Annual amount $S_{\overline{n}\rceil}^{-1}$	Annuity Present value $A_{\overline{n}\rceil}$	Annuity Annual amount $A_{\overline{n}\rceil}^{-1}$
Interest rate 30.0%						
1	1.3000	0.769231	1.0000	1.000000	0.7692	1.300000
2	1.6900	0.591716	2.3000	0.434783	1.3609	0.734783
3	2.1970	0.455166	3.9900	0.250627	1.8161	0.550627
4	2.8561	0.350128	6.1870	0.161629	2.1662	0.461629
5	3.7129	0.269329	9.0431	0.110582	2.4356	0.410582
6	4.8268	0.207176	12.7560	0.078394	2.6427	0.378394
7	6.2749	0.159366	17.5828	0.056874	2.8021	0.356874
8	8.1573	0.122589	23.8577	0.041915	2.9247	0.341915
9	10.6045	0.094300	32.0150	0.031235	3.0190	0.331235
10	13.7858	0.072538	42.6195	0.023463	3.0915	0.323463
11	17.9216	0.055799	56.4053	0.017729	3.1473	0.317729
12	23.2981	0.042922	74.3270	0.013454	3.1903	0.313454
13	30.2875	0.033017	97.6250	0.010243	3.2233	0.310243
14	39.3738	0.025398	127.9125	0.007818	3.2487	0.307818
15	51.1859	0.019537	167.2863	0.005978	3.2682	0.305978
16	66.5417	0.015028	218.4722	0.004577	3.2832	0.304577
17	86.5042	0.011560	285.0139	0.003509	3.2948	0.303509
18	112.4554	0.00889	2371.5180	0.002692	3.3037	0.302692
19	146.1920	0.006840	483.9734	0.002066	3.3105	0.302066
20	190.0496	0.005262	630.1655	0.001587	3.3158	0.301587
21	247.0645	0.004048	820.2151	0.001219	3.3198	0.301219
22	321.1839	0.003113	1067.2796	0.000937	3.3230	0.300937
23	417.5391	0.002395	1388.4635	0.000720	3.3254	0.300720
24	542.8008	0.001842	1806.0026	0.000554	3.3272	0.300554
25	705.6410	0.001417	2348.8033	0.000426	3.3286	0.300426
26	917.3333	0.001090	3054.4443	0.000327	3.3297	0.300327
27	1192.5333	0.000839	3971.7776	0.000252	3.3305	0.300252
28	1550.2933	0.000645	5164.3109	0.000194	3.3312	0.300194
29	2015.3813	0.000496	6714.6042	0.000149	3.3317	0.300149
30	2619.9956	0.000382	8729.9855	0.000115	3.3321	0.300115

Further reading

Part 1 Basic framework

Background concepts, organisations and the role of management accounting

Benston, G., 'Cost accounting and managerial decisions (an introduction)', in G. Benston (ed.), *Contemporary Cost Accounting and Control*, 2nd edition, Dickenson, 1979.

Cooper, D. J., 'A social and organisational view of management accounting', in M. Bromwich and A. G. Hopwood (eds.), *Essays in British Accounting Research*, Pitman, 1981.

Cyert, R. M. and J. G. March, *A Behavioral Theory of the Firm*, Prentice Hall, 1969.

Demski, J. S., *Information Analysis*, 2nd edition, Addison Wesley, 1989.

Emmanuel, C. R., D. T. Otley and K. Merchant, *Accounting for Management Control*, Chapman and Hall, 1991.

Kaplan, R. S., 'The evolution of management accounting', *Accounting Review*, July 1984.

Kaplan, R. S., 'Management accounting (1894–1994): development of new practices and theory', *Management Accounting Research*, September/December 1994.

Lee, T., 'The information needs of management', in *Making Corporate Reports Valuable: The Literature Survey*, Institute of Chartered Accountants of Scotland, Edinburgh.

Otley, D., 'Management control in contemporary organisations: towards a wider framework', *Management Accounting Research*, September/December 1994.

Pendlebury, M. W., 'Management accounting in local government', *Financial Accounting and Management*, May 1994.

Puxty, A. G., *The Social and Organizational Context of Management Accounting*, Academic Press, 1993.

Risk and uncertainty

Ball, R. and P. Brown, 'Portfolio theory and accounting', *Journal of Accounting Research*, Autumn 1969.

Brealey, R. A and S. C. Myers, *Principles of Corporate Finance*, 4th edition, Chapters 7–9, McGraw-Hill, 1991.

Hertz, D. B., 'Risk analysis in capital investment', *Harvard Business Review*, January/February 1964.

Modigliani, F. and G. A. Pogue, 'An introduction to risk and return', *Financial Analysts' Journal*, March/April 1974.

Sharpe, W. F., *Investments*, Prentice Hall, 1985.

Wealth, discounting and present values

See 'Capital investment appraisal methods' below.

Relevant cost

See 'Pricing, output and other operating decisions' below.

Part 2   Cost information

Ahmed, M. N. and R. W. Scapens, 'Cost allocation theory and practice: the continuing debate', in D. Ashton, T. Hopper and R. W. Scapens (eds.), *Issues in Management Accounting*, Prentice Hall, 1991.

Benston, G. J., 'Multiple regression analysis of cost behaviour', *Accounting Review*, October 1966.

Bhimani, A. and D. Pigott, 'Implementing ABC: a case study of organisational and behavioural consequences', *Management Accounting Research*, June 1992.

Bright, J., R. E. Davies, C. A. Downes and R. C. Sweeting, 'The deployment of costing techniques and practices: a UK study', *Management Accounting Research*, September 1992.

Brignall, T. J., L. Fitzgerald, R. Johnston and R. Silvestro, 'Product costing in service organisations', *Management Accounting Research*, December 1991.

Brunton, N. M., 'Evaluation of overhead allocations', *Management Accounting* (US), July 1988.

Christensen, J. and J. S. Demski, 'The classical foundations of modern costing', *Management Accounting Research*, March 1995.

Cooper, R., 'ABC: a need not an option', *Accountancy*, September 1990.

Cooper, R. 'Five steps to ABC systems design', *Accountancy*, November 1990.

Cooper, R. and R. S. Kaplan, 'How cost accounting distorts product costs', *Management Accounting* (US), April 1988.

Cooper, R. and R. S. Kaplan, 'Measure costs right: make the right decisions', *Harvard Business Review*, September/October 1988.

Drury, C., 'Activity-based costing', *Management Accounting* (UK), September 1989.

Howes, J., 'Costing for contracting', *Management Accounting* (UK), November 1994.

Innes, J. and F. Mitchell, *Activity-Based Costing: A review with cases*, Chartered Institute of Management Accountants, 1990.

Keegan, D. P. and R. G. Eiler, 'Let's reengineer cost accounting', *Management Accounting* (US), August 1994.

Liao, S. S., 'The learning curve: Wright's model v. Crawford's model', *Issues in Accounting Education*, Fall 1988.

Mitchell, F., 'A commentary on the applications of ABC', *Management Accounting Research*, September/December 1994.

Pogue, G. A., 'Process costing', *Students' Newsletter*, Chartered Association of Certified Accountants, November 1985.

Skinner, R. C., 'Process costing', *Abacus*, December 1980.

Wells, M. C., 'Some influences on the development of cost accounting', *Accounting Historians Journal*, Fall 1977.

Zimmerman, I., 'The cost and benefits of cost allocations', *Accounting Review*, July 1979.

Part 3   Applications

Pricing, output and other operating decisions

Ajinkya, B., R. Atiase and L. S. Bamber, 'Absorption versus direct costing; income reconciliation and cost–volume–profit analysis', *Issues in Accounting Education*, fall 1986.

Arnold, J. A. and R. W. Scapens, 'The British contribution to opportunity cost theory', in M. Bromwich and A. Hopwood (eds.), *Essays in British Accounting Research*, Pitman, 1981.

Banker, R. D. and J. S. Hughes, 'Product costing and pricing', *Accounting Review*, July 1994.

Dillon, R. D. and J. T. Nash, 'The true relevance of relevant costs', *Accounting Review*, January 1978.

Dudiek, T. S., 'Pricing strategies for manufacturers', *Management Accounting* (US), November 1989.

Geitzman, M., 'Make or buy revisited: some lessons from Japan', *Management Accounting* (UK), November 1994.

Jenkins, D. O., 'Cost–volume–profit analysis', *Management Services*, March/April 1970.

Koehler, R. and C. A. Neyhart, 'Difficulties in flexible budgeting', *Management Planning*, May/June 1972.

Leininger, W., 'Opportunity costs: some definitions and examples', *Accounting Review*, January 1977.

Lere, J. C., 'Product pricing based on accounting costs', *Accounting Review*, April 1986.

Schneider, A., 'Joint product cost-plus pricing', *Journal of Business Finance and Accounting*, Summer 1986.

Shim, E. and E. Sudit, 'How manufacturers price products', *Management Accounting* (US), February 1995.

Tishlias, D. P. and P. Chalos, 'Product pricing behaviour under different costing systems', *Accounting and Business Research*, Summer 1988.

Vickers, D., 'On the economics of break-even', *Accounting Review*, July 1960.

Limited resources and dual prices

Dev, S., 'Linear programming dual prices in management accounting and their interpretation', *Accounting and Business Research*, Winter 1978.

Dev, S., 'Linear programming and production planning', in J. Arnold, B. Carsberg and R. W. Scapens (eds.), *Topics in Management Accounting*, 1980.

Salkin, G. and J. Kornbluth, 'Linear programming in financial planning', *Accountancy Age*, 1973.

Samuels, J. H., 'Opportunity costing: an application of mathematical programming', *Journal of Accounting Research*, Autumn 1965.

Capital investment appraisal methods

Brealey, R. A and S. C. Myers, *Principles of Corporate Finance*, 4th edition, chapters 2, 3, 5 and 6, McGraw-Hill, 1991.

Bromwich, M. and A. Bhimani, 'Strategic investment appraisal', *Management Accounting* (UK), March 1991.

Collier, P. and G. Gregory, 'Investment appraisal in service industries: a field study analysis of the UK hotels sector', *Management Accounting Research*, March 1995.

Colwyn Jones, T. and D. Dugdale, 'Academic and practitioner rationality: the case of investment appraisal', *British Accounting Review*, March 1994.

Ho, S. S. M. and R. H. Pike, 'Risk analysis in capital budgeting contexts: simple or sophisticated?', *Accounting and Business Research*, Summer 1991.

Kee, R. and B. Bublitz, 'The role of payback in the investment process', *Accounting and Business Research*, Spring 1988.

Lapsley, I., 'Investment appraisal in UK non-trading organizations', *Financial Accountability and Management*, Summer 1986.

Luckett, P. F., 'ARR vs IRR: a review and an analysis', *Journal of Business Finance and Accounting*, Summer 1984.

Nothcott, D., *Capital Investment Decision Making*, Academic Press, 1992.

Pike, R. H., 'An empirical study of the adoption of sophisticated capital budgeting practices and decision-making effectiveness', *Accounting and Business Research*, Autumn 1988.

Pike, R. H. and M. B. Wolfe, *Capital Budgeting in the 1990s*, Chartered Institute of Management Accountants, 1988.

Romano, P., 'The capital investment decision: how to make it', *Financial Executive*, July/August 1991.

Budgeting and variance analysis for control

Archer, S. and D. Otley, 'Strategy, structure, planning and control systems and performance evaluation: Rumenco Ltd', *Management Accounting Research*, December 1991.

Barnes, P., 'Which variances are worth investigating?', *Accountancy*, December 1979.

Bromwich, M., 'Standard costing for planning and control', in J. A. Arnold, B. V. Carsberg and R. W. Scapens (eds.), *Topics in Management Accounting*, Philip Allan, 1980.

Brownell, P. and M. McInnes, 'Budgetary participation, motivation, and managerial performance', *Accounting Review*, October 1986.

Choudhury, N., 'Responsibility accounting and controllability', *Accounting and Business Research*, Summer 1986.

Collins, F., 'The budgeting games people play', *Accounting Review*, January 1987.

Hofstede, G. H., *The Game of Budget Control*, Tavistock, 1968.

Hopwood, A. G., *Accounting and Human Behaviour*, Prentice Hall, 1976.

Jacobs, K., 'Budgets: a medium of organizational transformation', *Management Accounting Research*, March 1995.

Lyne, S. R., 'The role of the budget in medium and large UK companies and the relationship with budget pressure and participation', *Accounting and Business Research*, Summer 1988.

Otley, D. T., *Accounting Control and Organizational Behaviour*, Heinemann, 1987.

Puxty, A. G. and D. Lyall, *Cost Control into the 1990s: A Survey of Standard Costing and Budgeting Practices in the UK*, Chartered Institute of Management Accountants, 1989; see also *Management Accounting* (UK), February 1990.

Skousen, C. R., 'Budgeting practices in local government in England and Wales', *Financial Accountability and Management*, Autumn 1990.

Divisional performance

Abdel-Khalik, A. R. and E. J. Lusk, 'Transfer pricing: a synthesis', *Accounting Review*, January 1974.

Bhimani, A., 'Performance measures in UK manufacturing companies: the state of play', *Management Accounting* (UK), December 1993.

Charles, I., 'The economics approach to transfer price', *Accountancy*, June 1985.

Charles, I., 'Transfer price solution where market exists', *Accountancy*, July 1985.

Coates, J., E. Davis, C. Emmanuel, S. Longden and R. Stacy, 'Multinational companies performance measurement systems: international perspectives', *Management Accounting Research*, June 1992.

Dearden, J., 'Measuring profit centre managers', *Harvard Business Review*, September/October 1987.

Emmanuel, C. R and K. P. Gee, 'Transfer pricing: a fair and neutral procedure', *Accounting and Business Research*, Autumn 1982.

Gregory, A., 'A review of divisional manager performance evaluation', *Management Accounting* (UK), January 1988.

Pass, C., 'Transfer pricing in multinational companies', *Management Accounting* (UK), September 1994.

Scapens, R. W. and T. J. Sale, 'An international study of accounting practices in divisionalised companies and their association with organizational variables', *Accounting Review*, April 1985.

Wright, M. and S. Thompson, 'Divestment and the control of divisionalised firms', *Accounting and Business Research*, Summer 1987.

General reviews

Ashton, D., T. Hopper and R. Scapens (eds.), *Issues in Management Accounting*, 2nd edition, Prentice Hall, 1995.

Boer, G., 'Five modern management accounting myths', *Management Accounting* (US), January 1994 and *Accountancy*, June 1994.

Bromwich, M. and A. Bhimani, *Management Accounting: Evolution not Revolution*, Chartered Institute of Management Accountants, 1989.

Choudhury, N., 'In search of relevance in management accounting research', *Accounting and Business Research*, Winter 1986.

Drury, C., S. Braund, P. Osborne and M. Tayles, *A Survey of Management Accounting Practices in UK Manufacturing Companies*, Chartered Association of Certified Accountants, 1992.

Hart, H., 'A review of some recent major developments in the management accounting field', *Accounting and Business Research*, Spring 1981.

Johnson, H. and R. S. Kaplan, *Relevance Lost: The Rise and Fall of Management Accounting*, Harvard Business School Press, 1987.

Kaplan, R. S., 'Measuring manufacturing performance: a new challenge for managerial accounting research', *Accounting Review*, October 1983.

Otley, D., 'Developments in management accounting research', *British Accounting Review*, Autumn 1985.

Scapens, R. W., *Management Accounting: A Review of Contemporary Developments*, Macmillan, 1985.

Spicer, B. H., 'The resurgence of cost and management accounting: a review of some recent developments in practice, theories and case research methods', *Management Accounting Research*, March 1992.

Solutions to selected end of chapter exercises

3.1 Mr Bizet's present wealth

$$= 20{,}000 + \frac{80{,}000}{(1.15)} + \frac{30{,}000}{(1.15)^2} + \cdots + \frac{30{,}000}{(1.15)^{21}}$$

$$= 20{,}000 + 80{,}000 V_{\overline{1}|}\ 15\% + 30{,}000(a_{\overline{21}|}\ 15\% - a_{\overline{1}|}\ 15\%)$$
$$= 20{,}000 + 80{,}000(0.8696) + 30{,}000(6.3125 - 0.8696)$$
$$= £252{,}860$$

Alternative calculation

$$= 20{,}000 + 80{,}000 V_{\overline{1}|}\ 15\% + 30{,}000(a_{\overline{20}|}\ 15\% \times V_{\overline{1}|}\ 15\%)$$
$$= 20{,}000 + 80{,}000(0.8696) + 30{,}000(6.2593 \times 0.8696)$$
$$= £252{,}860$$

3.2 (a) Value of Dvorak (£000s)

$$= \frac{500}{(1.2)} + \frac{550}{(1.2)^2} + \frac{600}{(1.2)^3} + \frac{700}{(1.2)^4} + \frac{700}{(1.2)^5} + \cdots$$

$$= 500\ V_{\overline{1}|}\ 20\% + 550\ V_{\overline{2}|}\ 20\% + 600\ V_{\overline{3}|}\ 20\% + \frac{700}{0.2} \times V_{\overline{3}|}\ 20\%$$

$$= 500(0.8333) + 550(0.6944) + 600(0.5787) + \frac{700}{0.2}(0.5787)$$

$$= £3{,}171{,}300$$

(b) Other factors include the risk of the company's expected dividend payments and non-financial factors such as the prestige of the company and the political and moral beliefs of the owners.

4.1   (a) *Machine A*

NPV for 2,000 units $= -40,000 + 2,000(30 - 10)\ a_{\overline{3}|}\ 6\%$
$= -40,000 + 2,000(30 - 10)(2.6730) = +£66,920$
NPV for 3,000 units $= -40,000 + 3,000(30 - 10)(2.6730) = +£120,380$
NPV for 5,000 units $= -40,000 + 5,000(30 - 10)(2.6730) = +£227,300$

Machine B

NPV for 2,000 units $= -100,000 + 2,000(30 - 5)(2.6730) = +£33,650$
NPV for 3,000 units $= -100,000 + 3,000(30 - 5)(2.6730) = +£100,470$
NPV for 5,000 units $= -100,000 + 5,000(30 - 5)(2.6730) = +£234,130$

(b) Expected NPVs:

$A = 66,920(0.2) + 120,380(0.6) + 227,300(0.2) = +£131,070$
$B = 33,650(0.2) + 100,470(0.6) + 234,130(0.2) = +£113,840$

Recommend machine A, subject to the comments in (c) below.

(c) The expected net present value (ENPV) is strictly valid as an accept/reject signal only if one of the following conditions applies:

(i) The project will be undertaken a large number of times under independent conditions (e.g. insurance).

(ii) The decision maker/risk taker has a neutral attitude to risk (i.e. is neither risk avoiding nor risk seeking).

(iii) The project is very small relative to the organisation's total set of projects.

If none of these conditions applies, it is necessary to take account of the attitudes to risk of those taking or affected by the decision, and to consider the relationship between the returns expected from the project under consideration and the returns expected from other projects or from investments in other companies.

4.2   (a) *Expected annual sales (units)*

Year 1		*Year 2*		*Year 3*	
$0.2 \times 5,000$	$= 1,000$	$0.2 \times 2,500 =$	500	$0.2 \times 1,000 =$	200
$0.2 \times 10,000$	$= 2,000$	$0.3 \times 5,000 = 1,500$		$0.2 \times 2,500 =$	500
$0.4 \times 20,000$	$= 8,000$	$0.3 \times 7,500 = 2,250$		$0.3 \times 5,000 = 1,500$	
$0.1 \times 25,000$	$= 2,500$	$0.1 \times 10,000 = 1,000$		$0.3 \times 7,500 = 2,250$	
$0.1 \times 30,000$	$= 3,000$	$0.1 \times 20,000 = 2,000$		–	–	–
Expected value $= \underline{16,500}$		$\underline{7,250}$		$\underline{4,450}$	

Contribution to fixed costs and profits per toy = £10

£

Present value of contribution at 5% = £165,000 × 0.9524 = 157,150
£72,500 × 0.9070 = 65,760
£44,500 × 0.8638 = 38,440

261,350

Less	£	
Present value of costs – Purchase price	200,000	
Forgone sale of design	25,000	225,000
Expected net present value		36,350

(b) The use of simple probabilistic models of the expected monetary value type has to be approached with caution. Specifically, EMV ignores:

(i) Attitudes to risk. To spin a coin for a 50:50 chance of winning or losing 5p, and to spin a coin for a 50:50 chance of winning or losing £10,000, both have an EMV of zero. Yet few people would be indifferent as between two such gambles. EMV ignores attitudes to risk (or, more strictly, implies risk neutrality).

(ii) The relationship between a project and other projects already undertaken by or being considered by the company. It also ignores the relationship between a project's returns and the returns available from investments in the shares of other companies. The study of these interrelationships is dealt with in the literature on portfolio analysis, and is relevant for project appraisal decisions.

For these reasons it is more likely that the project will be accepted by a very large company undertaking many similar projects than by a small one. The consequences of a few failures out of a wide portfolio are less catastrophic than the failure of an enterprise's sole project.

5.1 (a) Redrafted statement

		£	£
Materials:	A (see note 1)	16,250	
	B (see note 2)	11,250	27,500
Labour:	Other than foreman (see note 3)	62,500	
	Replacement for foreman (see note 4)	19,500	82,000
Machinery:	Replacement for leased machine (see note 5)	75,400	
	Already owned (see note 6)	32,500	107,900
Total cost			217,400
Contract price offered			300,000
Contribution to fixed overheads and profit			82,600

Notes:

1. The original cost of material A is the result of a previous decision and cannot be altered by any decision made now. It is therefore irrelevant. The opportunity cost of using A on this contract is its value in its best alternative use, i.e. the higher of £12,500 (for which it could be sold) and £16,250 (its value as a substitute for another material less the cost of adaptation). Consider whether there are any holding costs involved in keeping material A and using it as a substitute.

2. The original contract price and the subsequently agreed discount for material B are the consequences of past decisions and hence irrelevant. The only alternative to using B on the contract is to sell it for £11,250 and this is its opportunity cost.

3. It is assumed that labour is freely available at this rate.

4. The foreman's wages of £25,000 will be payable whether or not the contract is accepted and may therefore be ignored. However, if the contract is accepted, the company will incur an incremental cost of £375 per week for 52 weeks (the cost of a replacement for the foreman) and this incremental cash outflow of £19,500 is a cost of accepting the contract.

5. The cost of the machine presently leased at £1,250 per week will be the same whether or not the contract is accepted (assuming that there are no costs involved in moving it from the other department) and need not be included. However, the cost of replacing it (a total of £1,450 per week) is an incremental cost of the contract and must be included (£1,450 × 52 = £75,400).

6. The depreciation figure charged by the cost accountant in respect of the machine already owned is an apportionment of historical cost and hence irrelevant. The real cost of using the machine in this case is the fall in its resale value during the period of the contract, i.e. £32,500.

7. As we are concerned with incremental costs and revenues, the arbitrary 'recovery' of overheads is meaningless. We are told that overhead expenses are fixed, i.e. are the same whether or not the contract is accepted, and they may therefore be ignored.

8. The timing of the cash flows of the contract has been ignored. This may be acceptable where a relatively short period of time is being considered, e.g. under one year.

(b) The redrafted statement seems to suggest that the contract should be accepted as it provides a positive contribution to fixed overheads and profit. But we must consider the effects of delaying construction of the new canteen for one year (e.g. possibility of strikes). This will probably have to be the subject of a value judgement by management. If management decide to reject the contract, we may say, on the basis of the redrafted statement, that they are valuing the cost of delaying construction of the canteen at £82,600 at least.

5.2 Cost of strike

	£	£
Contribution lost:		
Sales revenue (1,000 cars)		15,000,000
Less Materials (see note 1)	3,000,000	
Production labour (see note 2)	1,500,000	
Fall in machine value (see note 3)	4,500,000	
Variable overheads (see note 4)	300,000	9,300,000
Loss of contribution		5,700,000
Less Saving on overhaul (see note 5)	270,000	
Increased contribution next month		
(see note 6)	2,475,000	2,745,000
Cost of strike		2,955,000

Notes:

1. It is assumed that materials are freely available at a market price of £3,000 per car.

2. It is assumed that no payment is made to production labour during the strike.

3. Depreciation based on book value is not relevant as it merely represents an arbitrary writing off of historical cost. Assuming that the machinery is not sold at the beginning of the strike, the fall in value of £600,000 per week will occur whether or not production continues. It is therefore not relevant in assessing the cost of the strike. However, the fall in value due to use (sometimes called the user cost) is avoided and must be included as a saving, i.e. $10 \times £450,000 = £4,500,000$.

4. Those overheads which are fixed regardless of the level of production may be ignored as they are payable with or without the strike. The overheads which are avoided as a result of the strike must be included in the statement as a saving, i.e. $10 \times £30,000 = £300,000$.

5. By utilising the maintenance staff to carry out the major overhaul, the company pays only for materials (£30,000). An outside contractor would have charged £300,000. A saving of £270,000 is effected which would not have been possible without the strike.

6. The sales manager feels that about one-half of the lost production could be made up and sold next month. The contribution from these sales will reduce the cost of the strike to the company, i.e.

	£	£
Sales revenue (500 cars)		7,500,000
Less Materials	1,500,000	
Production labour (at time and a half)	1,125,000	
Fall in machine value	2,250,000	
Variable overheads	150,000	5,025,000
Contribution		2,475,000

7. A number of other points should be considered. For example:

(a) Was the overhaul really necessary?

(b) Is machine capacity adequate to make up one-half of the lost production next month?

(c) Will the market buy the extra production and the normal monthly production next month at the price assumed?

(d) What interest costs are involved in delaying some production for one month?

6.1 (a) (i) B

(ii) F

(iii) C

(iv) H

(v) E

(vi) K

(vii) G

(viii) D

(b) Graph A could represent the cost of a photocopy machine. The cost of each copy is 5p, but with a minimum rental charge of £300 per month. The minimum rental will only be exceeded when more than 6,000 copies are required.

Graph J could represent the cost of a service similar to (vi) in (a):

10p per unit for the first 2,000 units
12p per unit for the next 2,000 units
15p per unit for all subsequent units

(c)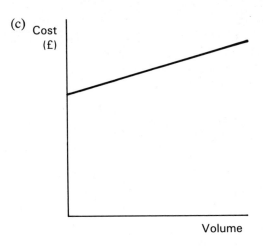

This represents the cost of using a telephone.

The basic rental is a fixed cost per quarter.

The cost of calls made varies with use.

6.2 (a) *Break-even point*

$$BEP = \frac{Fixed\ costs}{Contribution\ per\ unit} = \frac{50,000 + 11,500}{10 - (5 + 0.9)}$$

$$= \frac{61,500}{4.10}$$

$$= 15,000\ units\ or\ £150,000\ sales$$

(b) *Expected profit*

Sales of £200,000 represent 20,000 units
∴ Contribution from 20,000 units @ £4.10 = 82,000
  Less Fixed costs   61,500
  Profit   £20,500

(c) *Revised profit*
   (i) New price £10 less 5% = £9.50
   (ii) New volume   = 24,000 units
      Effect of price cut   = 20,000 units × 15% = 3,000 units
      Effect of advertising   = 20,000 units × 5% = 1,000 units
                                                      4,000 units

   (iii) Contribution 21,000 units × (9.50 − 5.90) = 75,600
                        3,000 units × (9.50 − 6.00) = 10,500
                                                       86,100

      Less Fixed costs as before   61,500
             Advertising   7,500   69,000
      Revised profit   £17,100

(d) *Alternative revised profit*

(i) 1% rebate represents 10p per unit (£10 × 0.01 = 10p)
The new contribution is therefore
£4.10 – 10p = £4 on 21,000 units
and £3.90 on remaining 3,000 units

		£	£
∴ Contribution	21,000 units × £4		84,000
	3,000 units × £3.90		11,700
			95,700
Less Fixed costs as before		61,500	
Advertising		20,000	81,500
Revised profit			£14,200

∴ This alternative is not as good as the original proposal, as it *reduces* profit by £2,900.

7.1 (a)

Overheads allocated to jobs	£	Total costs	£
2XC45			
Manufacture: 1,000 hours × 10 =	10,000		
On-site: 500 hours × 7.5 =	3,750		
	13,750	Overheads	13,750
		Labour	8,500
		Materials	22,700
			44,950
2FR56			
Manufacture: 2,250 hours × 10 =	22,500		
On-site: 1,100 hours × 7.5 =	8,250		
	30,750	Overheads	30,750
		Labour	18,900
		Materials	48,100
			97,750
3DR67			
Manufacture: 500 hours × 10 =	5,000		
On-site: 300 hours × 7.5 =	2,250		
	7,250	Overheads	7,250
		Labour	3,700
		Materials	8,100
			19,050

(b) Manufacturing

Total overheads allocated at £10/hour (£)	Actual overheads (£)
10,000 + 22,500 + 5,000 = 37,500	41,500

On-site

Total overheads allocated at £7.50/hour (£)	Actual overheads (£)
3,750 + 8,250 + 2,250 = 14,250	12,200

7.2 (a) *Allocation of all overheads on the basis of processing hours*

		GTD4 (£)		XTD7 (£)
Cost of material inputs		16,000		14,000
Labour cost		12,000		9,000
Overhead cost (600 × 12.50*)		7,500	(480 × 12.50)	6,000
		35,500		29,000
Unit cost	÷ 3,000	£11.83	÷ 2,500	£11.60

*Total overhead costs £250,000 ÷ Total processing hours 20,000 = £12.50

(b) *Allocation of overheads on the basis of cost drivers*

Rates for each cost driver

		£
Handling materials	£30,000 ÷ 500 times machines filled	= 60/time
Set-up	£80,000 ÷ 2,000 hours set-up	= 40/hour
Inspection	£90,000 ÷ 600 inspections	= 150/inspn
Maintenance	£50,000 ÷ 20,000 hours processing	= 2.50/hour

		GTD4 (£)		XTD7 (£)
Cost of material inputs		16,000		14,000
Labour cost		12,000		9,000
Overhead costs				
Handling materials	(30 × 60)	1,800	(5 × 60)	300
Set-up	(100 × 40)	4,000	(20 × 40)	800
Inspection	(30 × 150)	4,500	(10 × 150)	1,500
Maintenance	(600 × 2.50)	1,500	(480 × 2.50)	1,200
		39,800		26,800
Unit cost	÷ 3,000	£13.27	÷ 2,500	£10.72

(c) The analysis using cost drivers has had a significant effect on the estimation of costs for GTD4. Using processing hours to allocate all overheads produces a unit cost of £11.83, while cost-driver-based allocations give £13.27/unit. Processing hours is therefore inaccurate as an allocation base for this product for this period. It cannot be assumed that the two measurement bases would produce similar figures in future months, however. There is also evidence from the analysis of costs for the XTD7 product that the general allocation using processing hours is producing overestimates of costs for at least some products. Management should consider whether January is a representative month for the type of production that will normally be undertaken, whether anything unusual has affected the cost estimates for January, the costs of maintaining the more detailed system required for the cost-driver-based system, and the benefits of the more accurate information from that system.

8.1   (a) *Calculation of new selling price*

	Existing costs (£)		Revised costs (£)
Materials	$30.00 + 7\frac{1}{2}\%$	$=$	32.25
Labour	$7.50 + 10\%$	$=$	8.25
Variable expenses	$3.00 + 5\%$	$=$	3.15
	40.50		43.65

Contribution at present is 40% of sales. Thus, to maintain current contribution ratio, the new marginal cost must equal 60% of selling price.
The new selling price must be:

$$£43.65 \times \frac{100}{60} = £72.75$$

(b) *Alternative sales volume required*

$$\text{Sales volume in current year} = \frac{\text{Sales value}}{\text{Sales price}} = \frac{£1,012,500}{£67.50}$$

$$= 15,000 \text{ units}$$

	£
Contribution is $15,000 \times £27 =$	405,000
Less Fixed overhead	105,000
$\therefore$ Current profit	£300,000

	£
In the forthcoming year profit required is	300,000
and fixed overheads are	108,150
$\therefore$ Contribution required	£408,150

The new contribution per unit will be £67.60 − £43.65 = £23.85

$$\text{The sales volume required is } \frac{£408,150}{£23.85} = 17,113 \text{ units}$$

8.2   (a) First categorise costs as fixed or variable for 19X2:

	19X2	Adjustment	19X3	Fixed (a)	Variable p.u. (b)
Sales (and output)	100,000	+30%	130,000		
Selling price	£10		?		
Materials ($\frac{3}{6}$ × £600,000 ÷ 100,000)	£3	+20%	£3.60		£3.60
Direct labour ($\frac{2}{6}$ × £600,000 ÷ 100,000)	£2	+15%	£2.30		£2.30
Indirect production overhead ($\frac{1}{6}$ × £600,000)					
Fixed	£40,000	+5%	£42,000	£42,000	
Variable (balance ÷ 100,000)	£0.6	+10%	£0.66		£0.66
Selling expenses					
Variable $\left(\dfrac{8\% \times £150,000}{30,000}\right)$	£0.4	No change	£0.40		£0.40
Fixed (£150,000 − £0.4 [100,000])	£110,000	No change	£110,000	£110,000	
Administrative expenses					
Fixed	£100,000	+6%	£106,000	£106,000	
				£258,000	£6.96

For profit = £200,000

$$\pi = Px - (a + bx)$$

where $x = 130,000$ ∴ $200,000 = P(130,000)$
$$- (258,000 + 130,000 \times 6.96)$$
∴ $P.130,000 = 200,000 + 1,162,800$
∴ $P = £10.483$ Unit sales price = £10.483

(b) If $P = £10$, for $\pi = £200,000$

$$\text{rearranging } x = \frac{a + \pi}{P - b} = \frac{258,000 + 200,000}{10 - 6.96}$$

∴ $x = 150,658$ ∴   150,658 units must be sold at the old price.

(c) If $P = £10.483$, $x = 110,000$

$$\pi = 10.483\ (110,000) - (258,000 + 6.96 \times 110,000)$$

$$\pi = £129,530$$

$\therefore$ Average profit will be £129,530.

9.1 First calculate sales revenue at 'cost-plus' prices:

	£
Paper	22,000
Consumables $\left(\dfrac{3,000}{24,000} = 12\frac{1}{2}\% \text{ of paper cost}\right)$	2,750
Labour (85% of capacity £120,000)	102,000
Fixed overheads $\left(\dfrac{96,000}{120,000} = 80\% \text{ of labour}\right)$	81,600
'Total cost'	208,350
'Profit' (10% of total cost)	20,835
Sales revenue	229,185

Income statement for current year

	£	£
Sales revenue		229,185
Less Paper (given in question)	22,000	
Consumables (given in question)	2,250	
Wages (per last year)	120,000	
Fixed costs (per last year)	96,000	240,250
Loss for year		11,065

The loss has arisen because labour has been paid while 'idle' and because fixed overheads have not been fully 'recovered'.

Mr Sisley's pricing system may be criticised because:

1. No account is taken of demand conditions.

2. Percentage relationships are set using historical rather than expected relationships.

3. Fixed costs are charged on an arbitrary basis to jobs.

4. Paper is charged out at historical, rather than current, costs.

5. No account is taken of the existence of spare capacity. Additional jobs could possibly have been obtained at a price below 'full cost' but above incremental cost.

9.2   (a) *Report to the managers of Schein Ltd*

The calculations in the appendix show that hiring specialist machinery would be the most economical way of providing the required machine capacity.

It may be possible to reduce the length of the period of hire, and therefore the cost, by one of the following methods:

1. Working overtime, and so completing the contract in three weeks instead of four, resulting in a saving of £900 in the hire costs. This will require payment of an overtime premium of, say, £1.50 per hour, or £240 over the total period of 160 hours. The net saving would be £660.

2. Introducing a second shift in order to produce the output in two weeks instead of four. In this case, the hire charge would be £2,400 (160 hours at £15 per hour). The cost of the shift premium would be, say, £1.50–£3.00 per hour, costing an additional £240–£480. The net saving would therefore be £960–£720.

The price to be charged will depend on whether the units to be modified could otherwise have been sold at the regular selling price of £108, or whether they are additional units which would not otherwise have been manufactured. Possible prices under both assumptions are:

	Units would not otherwise have been manufactured (£)	Units could otherwise have been sold (£)
Variable cost of standard product (400 × £60)	24,000	
Selling price forgone on standard product (400 × £108)		43,200
Hire costs for machinery	3,600	3,600
Additional labour (160 hours @ £9 per hour)	1,440	1,440
Minimum price	29,040	48,240
Allocated fixed costs (400 × £30)	12,000	
Mark-up (20% on total cost)	8,208	8,208
Target price	49,248	56,448

The 'target price' would allow for a 'normal profit'. However, it may be that a higher price would be more appropriate to compensate for the disruption to normal production. On the other hand, as Schmitt is a good customer, a lower price may be quoted for a special job in order to retain the company's goodwill. The possibility of a regular order for the modification should be considered, along with the idea of putting the modification on general sale.

Appendix: Alternative sources of specialist machinery
The following information relates to the costs of the alternative methods of obtaining specialist machinery to enable you to modify your existing product to Schmitt's specification. In the presentation of this information, labour costs have been omitted from the initial analysis as they are common to all alternatives.

(1) *Adapting existing machinery*

	£
Cost of adapting	4,500
Cost of reinstalment	5,400
Maintenance (160 hours at £4.50 per hour)	720
Insurance (2% of £13,500)	270
	£10,890

Note: Insurance has been calculated assuming that the value of the machine is increased by the cost of adaptation.

(2) *Hiring specialist machinery*

Hire charge – 4 weeks at £900 per week   £3,600

Note: The variable charge of £15 per hour for 40 hours per week (£600 per week) does not meet the minimum of £900 per week.

(3) *Purchasing specialist machinery*

	£
Loss in value from operation (400 units at £6 per unit)	2,400
Extra cost to cover transaction expenses – 10% of (£15,000 – £2,400)	1,260
Maintenance (160 hours at £4.50 per hour)	720
Insurance (2% of £15,000)	300
	£4,680

(b) If Schmitt is likely to place a continuing order for the modified product, the costs of the three alternatives should be reappraised.

The cost of adapting existing machinery would be reduced by the £5,400 reinstalment cost. However, after three months it would be necessary to acquire an additional machine, which would probably cost about £9,000. Insurance costs would still be for a year, but would cover the whole period of a year.

To hire the machine would cost a minimum of £900 per week and is not likely to be the most economical form of production.

The cost of purchasing specialist machinery will be proportionally the same, as the machine loses value at the rate of £6 per unit. The life of the machine should be considered in relation to the life of the project. The insurance costs per unit would be much lower, as the operating time is likely to be for a year.

10.1 (a) Minimum price for special order = that which is sufficient to cover variable costs

$$= 60 \times 200 = £12,000$$

Anything over £12,000 generates a positive contribution to profit.

(b) If B is terminated, only direct costs will be saved. It will save £81,000 but will lose £112,000 revenue, so loss will increase without B. As B is making a positive contribution, it should be retained.

(c) *A and B purchase rather than manufacture*

		£
Manufacture: Net revenues		32,750
Purchase: Revenue from sales		287,000
Costs A	140,000	
B	88,000	228,000
		59,000
Distribution costs, etc.		43,050
		15,950
Rent received		30,000
		45,950

Purchase for resale would give a higher return than current manufacture, but other factors such as ability to rent, closure costs, continuity of supply and purchase price are important to the decision.

10.2 (a) *Alternative annual budgets*

	Keep toy department (£)	Extend clothing department (£)	Use for storage (£)
Benefits: Gross profit	26,500	22,500	–
Rent saved	–	–	4,000
General administrative costs saved	–	–	500
	26,500	22,500	4,500
Costs:			
Sales assistant's wage (Cost of replacements – existing assistants will be employed in any case)	7,000	7,000	0
Supervisor (Salary payable in any case so irrelevant. But value of general administrative duties are cost of keeping toy department – assume zero)	0	0	0
Establishment costs	3,000	2,000	1,500
Rent (Unaffected by decision)	0	0	0
	10,000	9,000	1,500
Surplus	£16,500	£13,500	£3,000

Keeping the toy department open produces £3,000 more surplus than the next best alternative (extending the clothing department). However, if the value of the supervisor as a general administrator is more than £3,000 per annum, it may be better to close the toy department and to use the space to extend the clothing department. The directors should also consider possible interdependences between the demands for different products: for example, are customers who enter the store to buy toys more likely also to buy clothes or other products?

Net income per £ of sales is only a partial measure of performance. Most organisations wish to maximise the income earned on each £ of capital invested, not on each £ of sales. So a department which earns an income of 10p per £ of sales and produces only £1 of sales each year per £ of capital employed is doing less well than a department which earns an income of 5p per £ of sales, but which makes £5 of sales each year per £ of capital employed.

11.1 (a) There are two faults with the accountant's statement:

(i) It includes allocated fixed costs and thus fails to show the incremental effect of each product on Spohr's total cash flows.

(ii) It does not show how efficiently each product uses labour, the one scarce resource.

To calculate an optimal plan, it is necessary to rank products according to the contribution they produce per unit of (scarce) labour required.

	Product					
	A	B	C	D	E	F
Selling price	£135	£177	£123	£129	£153	£135
Less Variable costs (materials, labour and variable overheads)	75	99	75	87	108	96
Contribution per unit	£60	£78	£48	£42	£45	£39
Labour hours per unit	6	7.5	5	4	3	2.5
Contribution per labour hour	£10.00	£10.40	£9.60	£10.50	£15.00	£15.60
Ranking	5	4	6	3	2	1

Optimal plan

Product	Output (maximum demanded up to labour limit)	Labour hours required	Contribution (£)
F	600	1,500	23,400
E	400	1,200	18,000
D	1,000	4,000	42,000
B $\left(\dfrac{4,300}{7.5}\right)$	573.3	4,300	44,720
		11,000	£128,120

Reservations about the optimality of the plan include:

(i) Estimates are uncertain.

(ii) Costs and revenues may be non-linear.

(iii) Product demands may be interdependent.

(b) The historical cost of stocks is not relevant for current decisions, regardless of whether prices have fallen or risen since acquisition. The relevant cost of using stock depends on the alternatives currently available for it, and will usually be equal to its replacement cost (where the stock is in regular use) or to its realisable value or value in use elsewhere within an organisation.

11.2 (a) Fixed costs should be ignored in determining the optimal production plan, as they are unaffected by levels of production. The objective is to maximise total contribution. Expected contributions per unit of each product are:

	Hi	Fi
Selling price	£130	£160
Variable cost	£90	£100
	£40	£60

Let x_1 = quantity of Hi produced and sold
x_2 = quantity of Fi produced and sold

Formulation is:

Maximise	$40x_1 + 60x_2$	(objective function)
subject to	$7x_1 + 14x_2 \leqslant 28{,}000$	(labour constraint)
	$33x_1 + 22x_2 \leqslant 66{,}000$	(machine constraint)
	$x_1, \quad x_2 \geqslant 0$	(non-negativity constraints)

(b)

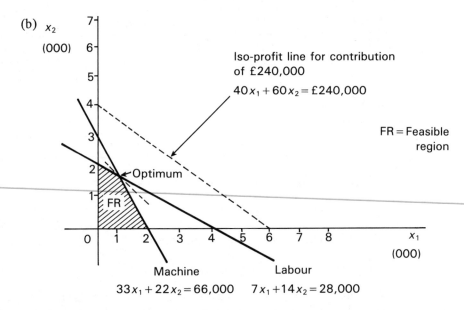

The optimal point is where highest 'iso-profit' line touches the boundary of the feasible region. From the graph, optimum is where labour and machine constraint lines intersect.
  Optimal production levels:

By observation $x_1 = 1{,}000$ $x_2 = 1{,}500$

For more precision, optimal production levels may be found by solving the two *effective* constraint lines as simultaneous equations:

$$7x_1 + 14x_2 = 28,000$$
$$33x_1 + 22x_2 = 66,000$$
$$x_1 = 1,000 \qquad x_2 = 1,500$$

Optimal production plan: Hi = 1,000 units
Fi = 1,500 units

Expected profits

	£
Contribution: Hi (1,000 × £40)	40,000
Fi (1,500 × £60)	90,000
	130,000
Fixed costs	95,000
Profit	35,000

(c) The limitations of linear programming in solving problems such as this depend on how well the conditions implied by the linear programming formulation simulate real world conditions. The main limitations are:

(i) Selling price per unit is assumed constant for all outputs (up to any demand constraint which is included in the formulation).

(ii) Variable cost per unit is assumed constant for all outputs, implying a constant price per unit of each input factor and constant productivity.

(iii) Fractional output levels are assumed to be possible. (This is not a problem at present for Mussorgsky Ltd.)

(iv) Non-financial costs and benefits are not included.

(v) Interdependences between the demands for products, or between the supplies of inputs, are ignored.

(vi) Costs may be calculated (incorrectly) on a historical cost, rather than an opportunity cost basis.

(vii) No explicit account is taken of uncertainty.

(viii) The constraints are assumed to be completely rigid.

12.1 Differential cash flows

	Complete (£)	Scrap (£)
Sales proceeds	+200,000	+20,000
Sales of plans and specifications		+35,000
Material X (700 lbs at £27 − value of best alternative use as substitute for material A)	−18,900	
Material Y − 2,000 lb in stock, *save* £8 − £6 if use	+4,000	
− 5,000 lb to buy at £12	−60,000	
Grade A labour (5,000 hours at £5)	−25,000	
Grade B labour (10,000 hours at £7 + £1)	−80,000	
Overheads	0	
	+20,100	+55,000

Past expenditure and compensation are irrelevant.

It is better to scrap the detectors by £34,900.

Other factors include:

(i) Prestige from producing blue noise detectors.

(ii) Value of learning experience of production for future activities.

(iii) Chance of securing future business in Ruritania.

(iv) Uncertainty of estimates.

12.2 (a)

		Siroe (£)		Ezio (£)
Selling price		540		660
Use of A10 (£90 per tonne)	(1)	(90)	(3)	(270)
Use of B11 (£70 per tonne)	(3)	(210)	(1.5)	(105)
Variable plant cost (80 − 20)		(60)		(60)
Contribution per tonne		180		225

Let S equal number of tonnes of siroe and E equal number of tonnes of ezio produced and sold each day.

$$
\begin{aligned}
\text{Maximise} \quad & 180S + 225E \\
\text{Subject to:} \quad & S + 3E \leq 25 && \text{(A10)} \\
& 3S + 1.5E \leq 37.5 && \text{(B11)} \\
& S + E \leq 13 && \text{(Plant hours)} \\
& S, \quad E \geq 0 && \text{(Non-negativity)}
\end{aligned}
$$

Plotting these on a graph shows that the highest contribution is obtained at the point where the plant hours and A10 constraints intersect, i.e. where:

$$S + E = 13$$
$$S + 3E = 25$$

Solving as simultaneous equations gives $S = 7$
$E = 6$

Susanna should produce 7 tonnes of siroe and 6 tonnes of ezio each day.

Contribution = $7(180) + 6(225) = £2,610$

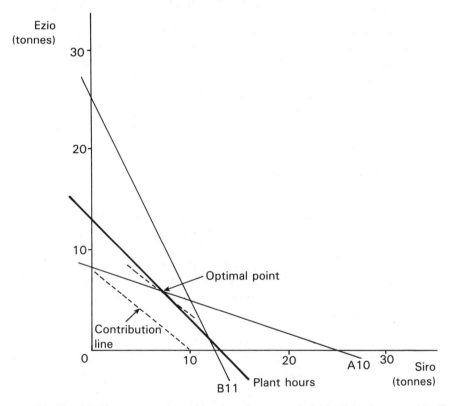

(b) The binding constraints are plant hours and A10. B11 is not a binding constraint and so its dual price is zero.

If available *plant hours* are increased by 1, the equation of the constraint line becomes:

$$S + E = 14$$
$$S + 3E = 25$$

Gives $S = 8.5$
$E = 5.5$

New contribution = $8.5(180) + 5.5(225) = £2,767.50$

Hence, dual price of plant hours is £2,767.50 – £2,610 = £157.50 per hour.

If available *A10* is increased by 1 tonne, the equation of the constraint line becomes:

$$S + 3E = 26$$
$$S + E = 13$$

Gives $\quad S = 6.5$
$$E = 6.5$$

New contribution = 6.5(180) + 6.5(225) = £2,632.50

Hence, dual price of A10 is £2,632.50 – £2,610 = £22.50 per tonne.

(c) In this example, linear programming provides a solution to the problem faced by the production manager – there is no other obvious way of solving it. Note that no account has been taken of uncertainty.

Dual prices are useful here because they allow the manager to decide how much extra it is worth paying in order to obtain an extra unit of each scarce resource. Susanna probably cannot change the availability of A10, but she might be able to increase the length of time for which the plant is used each day.

13.1 (a) Net present value to Mozart Limited:

$$NPV = -30,000 + 8,000V_1\,5\% + 10,000\ V_2\,5\% + 17,000\ V_3\,5\%$$
$$= -30,000 + 8,000(0.9524) + 10,000(0.9070) + 17,000(0.8638)$$
$$= -30,000 + 7,620 + 9,070 + 14,680 = +£1,370$$

(b) (i) Nielson is satisfied (as stated in question). Poulenc can borrow one half of the present value of the cash inflows from the project (i.e. he can borrow the present value of the dividends he expects to receive):

Poulenc can borrow ($\frac{1}{2} \times$ £31,370)	£15,685 at 5%
	(and go on cruise)
Interest year 1 at 5%	785
	16,470
Repay end year 1 ($\frac{1}{2} \times$ £8,000)	4,000
	12,470
Interest year 2 at 5%	624
	13,094
Repay end year 2 ($\frac{1}{2} \times$ £10,000)	5,000
	8,094
Interest year 3 at 5%	406
	8,500
Repay end year 3 ($\frac{1}{2} \times$ £17,000)	8,500

By borrowing, and using his dividends to repay the loan, Poulenc is £685 better off if the project is accepted than if it is rejected. So the company is acting in the best interests of both shareholders by accepting the project.

(ii) Nielson is still satisfied (as stated in question). Present value of Poulenc's dividends at 10% is:

$$4,000V_1\ 10\% + 5,000V_2\ 10\% + 8,500V_3\ 10\%$$
$$= 4,000(0.9091) + 5,000(0.8264) + 8,500(0.7513) = \underline{£14,154}$$

which is the maximum amount he could borrow and repay out of his share of the project dividends. He would be better off with an immediate dividend of £15,000. So the company is not acting in the best interests of both shareholders.

(c) The above analysis suggests that the net present value rule results in correct investment decisions provided that all shareholders have the same 'cost of capital' as the company, even if their consumption preferences vary. Any shareholder can adjust his or her dividend receipts to fit his or her desired consumption pattern by lending or borrowing. (b) (ii) suggests that the net present value rule needs to be applied cautiously where shareholders' costs of capital differ from the company's (e.g. where capital markets are imperfect). In this case it may not be possible for shareholders to adjust their consumption patterns by lending or borrowing without incurring an interest cost different from the company's.

13.2 (a) *Net present value of project*

	£	£
Investment outlay		150,000
Annual contribution: £(50 − 30) × 5,000 = 100,000		
Less Annual fixed costs	40,000	
	60,000	

Present value = 60,000 × $a_{\overline{4}|}$ 10% = (60,000 × 3.17) = 190,200

Net present value +40,200

(b) *Variable costs*

$$\text{Net annual receipts to break even} = \frac{150,000}{3.17}$$

$$= £47,319$$

$$\text{Variable costs can increase by } \frac{60,000 - 47,319}{5,000} \text{ p.u.} = \frac{12,681}{5,000}$$

$$= £2.54 \text{ p.u.}$$

∴ Sensitivity = [2.54/30 × 100]% = 8.47%

Annual volume
Annual contribution to break-even $= £(47,319 + 40,000) = £87,319$

i.e. volume can fall to $\dfrac{£87,319}{£20} = 4,366$ (i.e. by 634)

$\therefore$ Sensitivity $= [634/5,000 \times 100]\% = 12.68\%$

Annual fixed costs
Can rise by $(60,000 - 47,319)$ $\qquad\qquad = 12,681$
$\therefore$ Sensitivity $= [12,681/40,000 \times 100]\% = 31.7\%$

Purchase of machine
Can rise by £40,200
$\therefore$ Sensitivity $= [40,200/150,000 \times 100]\% = 26.8\%$

Product life
Net present value over 4 years $\qquad\qquad = +40,200$
Net present value over 3 years $\qquad\qquad = \quad -600$
$\therefore$ Break-even life is approximately 3 years
$\therefore$ Sensitivity $= (\frac{1}{4} \times 100)\%$ $\qquad\qquad = 25\%$

Cost of capital
NPV at $10\% = +40,200$
NPV at $15\% = -150,000 + 60,000 \; a_{\overline{4}|} \; 15\% = +21,000$
NPV at $20\% = -150,000 + 60,000 \; a_{\overline{4}|} \; 20\% = +5,400$

$$\text{IRR} = 20\% + \left(\dfrac{5,400}{21,000 - 5,400}\right) 5\% = 21.73\%$$

$\therefore$ Cost of capital can increase by 11.73%
$\therefore$ Sensitivity $= 117.3\%$

(c) The project seems profitable. It is not highly sensitive to any estimate, although variable costs and volume are most critical.
Note: Remember

   (i) Final decision depends on attitude to risk.

   (ii) Possible combination errors (interdependent components).

   (iii) 'Acceptable' margin may vary from component to component.

14.1 (a)

	Project 1		Project 2
(i) Accounting rate of return			
Average profit before			
depreciation	200,000		500,000
Depreciation $(556-56)/5$	100,000	$(1,616-301)/5$	263,000
Profit	£100,000		£237,000
Capital employed			
$(556+56)/2$	£306,000	$(1,616+301)/2$	£958,500
Rate	32.7%		24.7%
(ii) Net present value			
Annual cash flow			
$200a_{\overline{5}|}$ (3.352)	670,400	$500a_{\overline{5}|}$	1,676,000
Scrap value $56V_{\overline{5}|}$(0.497)	27,800	$301V_{\overline{5}|}$	149,600
Outlay	(556,000)		(1,616,000)
	+£142,200		+£209,600
(iii) Internal rate of return			
(use trial and error to			
obtain NPV of zero)			
	try 25%		try 20%
Annual cash flow			
$200a_{\overline{5}|}$ (2.689)	537,800	$500a_{\overline{5}|}$ (2.991)	1,495,500
Scrap value $56V_{\overline{5}|}$ (0.328)	18,400	$301V_{\overline{5}|}$ (0.402)	121,000
Outlay	(556,000)		(1,616,000)
	£200		£500
(iv) Payback period			
Outlay/annual flow	556/200=		1,616/500=
	2.8 years		3.2 years

(b) Accept project 2 according to the NPV criterion in spite of counter-implications of other methods. Net present value has the advantage of reflecting consumption potential with respect to timing.

The rate of return methods do not measure the absolute value of the consumption potential, but rather the return relative to the outlay (size distortion).

The accounting rate of return fails to concentrate on the timing of cash flows.

The payback fails to consider all cash flows and details of timing, although it may act as a screening device, and as a proxy measure for risk.

14.2   (a) The projects should be evaluated using the net present value (NPV) method of appraisal. NPVs are as follows:

$$A = -5,000 + 4,000V_1 10\% + 1,500V_2 10\% + 1,100V_3 10\%$$
$$= -5,000 + 4,000(0.9091) + 1,500(0.8264) + 1,100(0.7513)$$
$$= +£702$$
$$B = -10,000 + 1,000a_{\overline{2}|} 10\% + 13,900V_3 10\%$$
$$= -10,000 + 1,000(1.7355) + 13,900(0.7513)$$
$$= +£2,179$$
$$C = -6,000 + 2,200a_{\overline{3}|} 10\%$$
$$= -6,000 + 2,200(2.4869)$$
$$= -£529$$

Project B should be accepted rather than project A (as the former has a higher NPV). Project C should be rejected (as it has a negative NPV). The conflict with the accountant's advice in respect of projects A and B arises because the internal rate of return (IRR) is an unreliable means of choosing between mutually exclusive projects. As regards project C, the accountant has interpreted IRR incorrectly; the decision rule is to accept projects with IRRs greater than the company's cost of capital (10% here). Thus project C should be rejected according to both the NPV and IRR criteria.

    In general, where NPV and IRR give conflicting advice the former should be preferred because:

  (i) NPV is based on a valuation model and measures the present value of future consumption changes if a project is accepted.

  (ii) IRR ignores the size of a project's outlay and returns (project B here produces a lower average return than project A but on a higher average investment).

  (iii) IRR is an average, rather than a marginal measure.

  (iv) IRR suffers technical problems when project cash flows are unorthodox (e.g. multiple IRRs, no IRR).

  (b) IRR may be applied to mutually exclusive projects (A and B) in a way that gives the same advice as NPV. The application involves assessing whether it is worthwhile investing in project B rather than in project A (i.e. is the *incremental* investment in project B worthwhile?). In this application, the problem is reduced to an accept or reject decision, where IRR generally gives the same advice as NPV. The incremental cash flows associated with investment in B rather than A are as follows:

	t_0	t_1	t_2	t_3
B	−10,000	+1,000	+1,000	+13,900
A	−5,000	+4,000	+1,500	+1,100
B − A	−5,000	−3,000	−500	+12,800

The IRR of this incremental investment may be found by trial and error and linear interpolation:

NPV at 10%
$$= -5,000 - 3,000V_1 10\% - 500V_2 10\% + 12,800V_3 10\%$$
$$= -5,000 - 3,000(0.9091) - 500(0.8264) + 12,800(0.7513)$$
$$= +£1,476$$

NPV at 15%
$$= -5,000 - 3,000V_1 15\% - 500V_2 15\% + 12,800V_3 15\%$$
$$= -5,000 - 3,000(0.8696) - 500(0.7561) + 12,800(0.6575)$$
$$= +£429$$

NPV at 20%
$$= -5,000 - 3,000V_1 20\% - 500V_2 20\% + 12,800V_3 20\%$$
$$= -5,000 - 3,000(0.8333) - 500(0.6944) + 12,800(0.5787)$$
$$= -£440$$

$$\text{IRR(B-A)} = 15 + \frac{429}{(429 + 440)}(5) = 17.47\%$$

As the IRR of the incremental investment is greater than the company's cost of capital, it is worthwhile investing in B rather than A. This is the same advice as was obtained (much more easily) using the NPV method.

Note: If necessary the IRR of the incremental investment could be calculated more precisely by calculating NPVs at 17% and 18% before interpolation.

16.1   (a) Mendelssohn Ltd budgeted income statement for the year ending 31 December 19X0

	£000	£000
Sales		800
Less Cost of goods sold (150 + 650 − 250)		550
Gross profit		250
Less Depreciation (10% × [870 + 150])	102	
Loan interest	16	
Operating expenses	65	183
Income		67
Less Dividend		40
Add to reserves		27

Mendelssohn Ltd budgeted balance sheet at 31 December 19X0

	£000	£000
Fixed assets, at cost (870 + 150)	1,020	
Less Accumulated depreciation (210 + 102)	312	708
Current assets		
Stock	250	
Trade debtors (12% × 800)	96	346
		1,054
Less Current liabilities		
Dividend due	40	
Trade creditors	65	
Bank overdraft (see below)	87	192
		862
Represented by Share capital		500
Reserves (135 + 27)		162
8% loan stock		200
		862

Note:

Cash budget for 19X0

	£000	£000
Cash in hand at 1 January		55
Add Receipts from customers (70 + 800 − 96)		774
		829
Less Payments to suppliers (60 + 650 − 65)	645	
Purchase of fixed assets	150	
Loan interest paid	16	
Operating expenses paid	65	
Dividend paid	40	916
Cash deficit at 31 December		87

(b) The figures reveal that, although the company expects an income of £67,000 during 19X0 (more than enough to cover the proposed dividend), the cash balance of £55,000 will become a deficit of £87,000. This reduction in cash is due primarily to the purchase of fixed assets and the increased credit granted to customers. The company will need to make arrangements to acquire the required finance if it is to survive the year ahead. The figures provide the opportunity to discuss the relationship between accounting income and changes in cash balances.

16.2 (a) Paderewski plc cash budgets, May–July 19X2

	May £000	June £000	July £000	Total £000
Receipts				
Collections from old debtors				
($\frac{1}{6} \times 1{,}404$)	234	234	234	702
Collections from new debtors				
($\frac{1}{12} \times \frac{1}{3} \times 576$)	16			
($\frac{1}{12} \times \frac{1}{3} \times 576 \times 2$)		32		
($\frac{1}{12} \times \frac{1}{3} \times 576 \times 3$)			48	96
	250	266	282	798
Payments				
Suppliers for old debts ($\frac{1}{3} \times 1{,}200$)	400	400	400	1,200
Suppliers for new purchases ($\frac{1}{3} \times 114$)	38	38	38	114
Manufacturing wages ($\frac{1}{3} \times 228$)	76	76	76	228
Other expenses ($\frac{1}{3} \times 237$)	79	79	79	237
Inland revenue	30			30
Debenture interest ($\frac{1}{4} \times 4\% \times 300$)			3	3
	623	593	596	1,812
Surplus/(deficit) for the month	(373)	(327)	(314)	(1,014)
Balance at start of month	(300)	(673)	(1,000)	(300)
Surplus/(deficit) at end of month	(673)	(1,000)	(1,314)	(1,314)

(b) Paderewski plc budgeted income statement, May–July 19X2

	£000	£000
Sales		576
Less Manufacturing labour and materials	342	
Other expenses	237	
Debenture interest	3	
Depreciation	14	596
Loss for the period		20

Paderewski plc budgeted balance sheet at 31 July 19X2

	£000	£000
Share capital		1,000
Revenue reserve (754 – 20)		734
		1,734
4% debenture stock		300
Current liabilities:		
Trade creditors	0	
Bank overdraft (limit)	600	600
Additional finance required (1,314 – 600)		714
		£3,348
Freehold land and buildings, at cost		320
Manufacturing equipment, net of depreciation (560 – 14)		546
		866
Current assets:		
Stocks	1,300	
Trade debtors (1,404 + 576 – 798)	1,182	2,482
		£3,348

(c) The budgeted loss for the period is £20,000. However, the finance required increases from £300,000 to £1,314,000 due primarily to the harsh terms imposed by creditors and the generous terms allowed to customers. The main short-term problem is to find the £714,000 finance required over and above the current overdraft limit. In the longer term, the company should realise that, despite the extremely generous credit terms allowed to customers, a contribution sufficient to cover costs is not being earned (particularly when account is taken of the interest which will have to be paid on new finance).

17.1 Accounts for last month run as follows:

	Division A		Division B	
	Actual (£)	Budget (£)	Actual (£)	Budget (£)
Sales	7,500 @£15 112,500	6,000 @£20 120,000	5,000 @£30 150,000	7,000 @£35 245,000
Materials	40,000	24,000	25,000	28,000
Labour	22,500	16,000	30,000	28,000
	62,500	40,000	55,000	56,000
Contribution	50,000	80,000	95,000	189,000
Contribution per unit		£13⅓		£27

Results may helpfully be analysed as follows:

Division A			Responsibility of
Budgeted profit		£80,000	
Less Loss from selecting wrong point on demand curve $7,500(15 - 6\frac{2}{3}) -$ $6,000(20 - 6\frac{2}{3})$		£17,500	Executive who set price
		£62,500	
Materials price variance ($\frac{1}{3} \times$ £40,000)	£13,333(U)		Market conditions
Gain from economy of material			
$£24,000 \times \dfrac{7,500}{6,000} -$			
$£(40,000 - 13,333)$	£3,333		
Offset by extra labour cost	£2,500	£833(F) £12,500	Production manager
Actual Profit		£50,000	

Division B			Responsibility of
Budgeted profit		£189,000	
Less Loss from fall in market conditions $2,500(35 - 8)$		£67,500	Market conditions
		£121,500	Make up next period but for £10,000 of extra cost
Less Loss from selecting new point on demand curve $5,000(30 - 8) - 4,500(35 - 8)$		£11,500	Sales manager
		£110,000	
Materials price variance $5,000 \times £4 \times 50\%$	£10,000		Market conditions Buyer gets credit
Offset by special negotiation $\frac{1}{2} \times$ £10,000	£5,000		
	£5,000(U)		
Labour efficiency $(5,000 \times £4 - £30,000)$	£10,000(U)	£15,000	Whoever sets wage
Actual profit		£95,000	rates – not production manager

This example rests on two important principles of analysis:

1. Where a decision affects volume, the gain or loss should be measured in terms of changes in contribution.

2. It is important to separate uncontrollable variances due to external factors from those attributable to internal actions.

17.2 (a)

		Original budget		Flexed budget		Actual	Variances
Sales (units)		6,000		4,000		4,000	
		(£)		(£)		(£)	(£)
Sales revenue	(£24)	144,000	(£24)	96,000	(£27)	108,000	12,000(F)
Bladders	(£1.50)	9,000	(£1.50)	6,000	(£2.10)	8,400	2,400(U)
Leather	(200 × £228)	45,600		30,400	(100 × £400)	40,000	9,600(U)
Materials		3,900		2,600		2,600	–
Labour (1,000 hrs					(1,000 hrs		
@ £13.50)		13,500		9,000	@ £15.00)	15,000	6,000(U)
		72,000		48,000		66,000	
Administrative expenses		12.717		12,717		13,155	438(U)
Salaries		24,783		24,783		24,945	162(U)
		109,500		85,500		104,100	
Net profit		£34,500		£10,500		£3,900	£6,600(U)

£24,000(U)   £6,600(U)

Computation of variances

Sales volume variance	(2,000 units × contribution per unit £12)	
		= £24,000 (U)
Bladders Price variance	4,000 × (£2.10 – £1.50)	= £2,400 (U)
Leather Price variance	100 × (£400 – 228)	= £17,200 (U)
Use variance	33⅓ bales × £228	= £7,600 (F)
Labour Rate variance	1,000 hrs × (£15 – £13.50)	= £1,500 (U)
Idle time variance	(5,000 – 3,000) hrs × £2.70	= £5,400 (U)
Efficiency	(3,000 – 3,333⅓) hrs × £2.70	= £900 (F)
Fixed costs		= £600 (U)

Revised statement for four-week control period

			£
Budgeted contribution (6,000 units × £12)			72,000
Less Sales volume variance			24,000(U)
Budgeted contribution for actual volume			48,000
Operating variances			
	F	U	
	£	£	
Sales price	12,000		
Bladders Price		2,400	
Leather Price		17,200	
Use	7,600		
Labour Rate		1,500	
Idle time		5,400	
Efficiency	900		
	20,500	26,500	6,000(U)
Actual contribution			42,000
Actual fixed overheads budgeted		37,500	
Add Unfavourable variance		600	38,100
Actual net profit			£3,900

(b) Possible interrelationships may exist between unfavourable price variances for bladders and leathers, which perhaps reflect higher quality raw materials, and favourable use variances for both leather and, in particular, labour efficiency. It may be more efficient for the labour force to work with better raw materials and this may reflect in the above computations.

18.1 (a) Western division income statement

Sales units per day	1,000	2,000	3,000	4,000	5,000	6,000
	(£)	(£)	(£)	(£)	(£)	(£)
Net sales revenue	1,900	3,400	4,500	5,000	4,800	4,620
Costs:						
Eastern division transfer costs	500	1,000	1,500	2,000	2,500	3,000
Western division costs	1,200	1,400	1,600	1,800	2,000	2,200
	1,700	2,400	3,100	3,800	4,500	5,200
Net income (loss)	200	1,000	1,400	1,200	300	(580)

(b) A sales level of 3,000 units per day maximises Western division's net income at £1,400. At 3,000 units per day, Eastern division's net income will be:

	£	£
Transfer revenue from Western (at 50p per unit)		1,500
Fixed costs	600	
Additional costs (£100 per 1,000)	200	800
Net income		700
Company net income:		
Western division revenue		4,500
Western division costs	1,600	
Eastern division costs	800	2,400
Net income		2,100

(c) Company income statement

Sales units per day	1,000	2,000	3,000	4,000	5,000	6,000
	(£)	(£)	(£)	(£)	(£)	(£)
Net sales revenue	1,900	3,400	4,500	5,000	4,800	4,620
Costs:						
Fixed to 1,000 units	1,800	1,800	1,800	1,800	1,800	1,800
Additional variables						
(£300 per 1,000)	–	300	600	900	1,200	1,500
	1,800	2,100	2,400	2,700	3,000	3,300
Net income	100	1,300	2,100	2,300	1,800	1,320

(d) The company's net income is maximised at a sales level of 4,000 units per day. Under divisional organisation, a sales level of 3,000 units maximises Western division income because of the fact that sales revenue per unit falls as sales volume increases, whereas the transfer price per unit remains constant. Consequently, marginal sales revenue for the 1,000 units above 3,000 is £500, which does not cover transfer cost plus Western Division marginal cost £(500 + 200).

The sales level to maximise company income, however, will be the same whatever reporting structure is adopted. Any calculation should ignore intra-company profits so that the effect on company income may be assessed clearly. Thus, the marginal revenue of £500 more than covers company marginal costs £(200 + 100) for the 1,000 units between 3,000 and 4,000, and it is only when sales exceed 4,000 that company income is reduced.

(e) Transfer pricing is a mechanism for preserving autonomy of profit centres so that profit centre managers are motivated to improve their own performance and consequently company efficiency. In this company, an alteration to the transfer price would not alter company income, but merely the respective proportion of Western and Eastern divisions.

There is a danger, however, that the transfer pricing policy may cause divisional members to act against company interests. For example, on the basis of a transfer price of 50p per unit, Eastern division makes a profit of £400 for every additional 1,000 units; as a result, the manager may see his main objective to be to increase production, whereas in fact production in excess of 4,000 units will actually reduce company income.

It would appear that the most appropriate transfer price, from a company point of view, would be one which reflects the cost structure of Eastern division: that is, a basic price per unit up to 1,000 units per day, which reduces as volume increases until the normal capacity of Eastern division is reached, when the price would be increased. Based on a reasonable return on capital employed, the price would be set to maximise Eastern division's income at normal capacity, and optimum company sales level could be assessed clearly under a divisional organisation.

18.2 (a) The company as a whole will not benefit if division C buys on the outside:

	£
Purchase costs from outsider, 1,000 units @ £135	135,000
Less Savings in variable costs by reducing division A output, 1,000 units @ £120	120,000
Disadvantage to the company as a whole	£15,000

(b) The company will benefit if C purchases from the outsider:

	£
Purchase costs from outsider, 1,000 units @ £135	135,000
Less Savings in variable and fixed costs, 1,000 units @ £138 (£120 + £18)	138,000
Advantage to the company as a whole	£3,000

(c) The company will benefit if C purchases from the outside supplier:

	£
Purchase costs from outsider, 1,000 units @ £115	115,000
Less Savings in variable costs by reducing division A output, 1,000 units @ £120	120,000
Advantage to the company as a whole	£5,000

(d) The company as a whole would benefit in this situation if C purchased from outsiders, since the £15,000 disadvantage to the company as a whole by purchasing from the outside supplier would be more than covered by the £30,000 contribution margin of A's sale of the 1,000 units to other customers.

	£
Purchase costs from outsider, 1,000 units @ £135	135,000
Less Variable cost savings, 1,000 units @ £120	120,000
Disadvantage to the company as a whole	£15,000
A's sales to other customers, 1,000 units @ £155	155,000
Less Variable costs, 1,000 units @ £125	125,000
Contribution margin	£30,000

Index

volume
of sales and sensitivity margin 272
variance 325–6, 360
see also CVP

WACC (weighted average cost of capital)
268–90
wealth and wealth maximisation in decision-
making 15, 36–58
compound interest tables, using 48–54
meaning and importance 40–2

non-financial data 45–7
time value of money 40–2
see also present values
Weaver, W. 35
weighted average cost of capital 268–90
Wolf, M.B. 299, 311
working capital, impact of 261–2

Yizheng Chemical Fibre Company 257
Young, S.M. 158